SAGE was founded in 1965 by Sara Miller McCune to support the dissemination of usable knowledge by publishing innovative and high-quality research and teaching content. Today, we publish over 900 journals, including those of more than 400 learned societies, more than 800 new books per year, and a growing range of library products including archives, data, case studies, reports, and video. SAGE remains majority-owned by our founder, and after Sara's lifetime will become owned by a charitable trust that secures our continued independence.

Los Angeles | London | New Delhi | Singapore | Washington DC | Melbourne

Inclusive Finance India Report 2016

Inclusive Finance India Report 2016

M.S. Sriram

SAGE

Los Angeles | London | New Delhi
Singapore | Washington DC | Melbourne

First published in 2017 by

SAGE Publications India Pvt Ltd
B1/I-1 Mohan Cooperative Industrial Area
Mathura Road, New Delhi 110 044, India
www.sagepub.in

ACCESS Development Services
28, Hauz Khas Village
New Delhi 110 016
www.accessdev.org

SAGE Publications Inc
2455 Teller Road
Thousand Oaks, California 91320, USA

SAGE Publications Ltd
1 Oliver's Yard, 55 City Road
London EC1Y 1SP, United Kingdom

SAGE Publications Asia-Pacific Pte Ltd
3 Church Street
#10-04 Samsung Hub
Singapore 049483

Published by Vivek Mehra for SAGE Publications India Pvt Ltd, Phototypeset in 10/12 pt Minion Pro by Diligent Typesetter India Pvt Ltd, Delhi and printed at Sai Print-o-Pack, New Delhi.

Library of Congress Cataloging-in-Publication Data Available

ISBN: 978-93-860-6219-2 (PB)

SAGE Team: Rajesh Dey, Alekha Chandra Jena, Sobana Paul and Rajinder Kaur

Cover photograph courtesy: ACCESS.

Sponsors & Partners

WORLD BANK GROUP

MetLife Foundation

SIDBI

भारतीय लघु उद्योग विकास बैंक

SMALL INDUSTRIES DEVELOPMENT BANK OF INDIA

mastercard.

Supported under FIF Managed by NABARD

NABARD

Rabobank

Dia

Contents

List of Tables, Figures, Boxes, Appendices, and Abbreviations

Tables

Figures

Boxes

Appendices

Abbreviations

AEPS	Aadhar Enabled Payment Systems
AKRSPI	Aga Khan Rural Support Programme India
ANBC	Adjusted Net Bank Credit
APMAS	AP Mahila Abhivruddhi Society
APY	Atal Pension Yojana
ATM	Automated Teller Machines
B2B	Business-to-Business
B2C	Business-to-Consumers
BC	Business Correspondent
BCBS	Basel Committee on Banking Supervision
BM	Bank Mitr
BMGF	Bill and Melinda Gates Foundation
BPCL	Bharat Petroleum Corporation Limited
BRAC	Bangladesh Rural Action Committee
BSBDA	Basic Savings and Bank Deposit Accounts
CAGR	Compounded Annual Growth Rate
CASA	Current Accounts, Savings Accounts
CBS	Core Banking Solution
CBSG	Community-Based Savings Groups
CD	Credit Deposit
CDC	Commonwealth Development Corporation
CGT	Compulsory Group Trainings
CIC	Credit Information Companies

CRAR	Capital to Risk weighted Assets Ratio
CSR	Corporate Social Responsibility
DBT	Direct Benefit Transfer
DFS	Department of Financial Service
DPO	Departmental Post Office
DRI	Differential Rate of Interest
Ekyc	Electronic Know Your Customer
FIF	Financial Inclusion Fund
FITF	Financial Inclusion Technology Fund
FWWB	Friends of Women's World Banking
FY	Financial Year
G2P	Government-to-Person
GCC	General Credit Card
GDS	Grameen Dak Sewak
GLP	Gross Loan Portfolio
GNPA	Gross Non Performing Assets
GoI	Government of India
IBA	Indian Banks Association
ICT	Information and Communication Technology
IFC	International Financial Corporation
IGMSY	Indira Gandhi Matritva Sahyog Yojana
IMEF	India Microfinance Equity Fund
IMO	Instant Money Order
IMPS	Immediate Payment System
IPPB	India Post Payments Bank
IT	Information Technology
JAM	Jan-Dhan-Aadhar-Mobile
JLG	Joint Liability Groups
JPB	Jio Payments Bank
KBS	Krishna Bhima Samruddhi
KCC	Kisan Credit Card
KYC	Know Your Customer
LAB	Local Area Banks
LPG	Liquefied Petroleum Gas
MDR	Merchant Discount Rate
MFI	Microfinance Institutions
MFIN	Microfinance Institutions Network
MGNREGA	Mahatma Gandhi National Rural Employment Guarantee Act
MOF	Ministry of Finance
mPoS	Mobile Point of Sale
MSME	Micro, Small and Medium Enterprises
MUDRA	Micro Units Development and Refinance Agency (Bank)
NABARD	National Bank for Agriculture and Rural Development
NABFINS	NABARD Financial Services
NAFSCOB	National Federation of State Co-operative Banks
NBFC	Non-Banking Financial Company
NBFC-MFI	Non-Banking Financial Company–Microfinance Institution
NGO	Non-Governmental Organizations
NPA	Non-Performing Asset
NPCI	National Payments Corporation of India
NPS	National Pension Scheme
NRLM	National Rural Livelihoods Mission
NSAP	National Social Assistance Programme
NSS	National Savings Scheme

NULM	National Urban Livelihoods Mission
OD	Overdraft
P2P	Person-to-Person
PACS	Primary Agricultural Co-operative Society
PAN	Permanent Account Number
PAR	Portfolio at Risk
PB	Payments Bank
PDC	PACS Development Cells
PLI	Postal Life Insurance
PMJDY	Prime Minister's Jan Dhan Yojana
PMJJBY	Pradhan Mantri Jeevan Jyoti Bima Yojana
PMSBY	Pradhan Mantri Suraksha Bima Yojana
PoS	Point of Sale
POSB	Post Office Savings Bank
PPI	Prepaid Instruments
PSIG	Poorest State Inclusive Growth
PSL	Priority Sector Lending
PSLC	Priority Sector Lending Certificates
RBI	Reserve Bank of India
RICT	Rural Information Communication Technology
RIDF	Rural Infrastructure Development Fund
RPLI	Rural Postal Life Insurance
RRBs	Regional Rural Banks
SBA	Small Borrowal Account
SBI	State Bank of India
SCB	Scheduled Commercial Banks
StCB	State Co-operative Banks
SFB	Small Finance Banks
SGSY	Swarna Jayanti Gram Swarozgar Yojana
SJSRY	Swarna Jayanti Shahari Swarozgar Yojana
SHG	Self Help Group
SHGBLP	SHG Bank Linkage Programme
SIDBI	Small Industries Development Bank of India
SKDRDP	Sri Kshetra Dharmasthala Rural Development Programme
SME	Small and Medium Enterprises
SRO	Self-Regulatory Organizations
StCB	State Co-operative Banks
UBRB	Un-Banked Rural Branches
UCB	Urban Co-operative Bank
UIDAI	Unique Identification Authority of India
USB	Ultra-Small Branch
USO	Universal Service Obligation

Foreword

In August 2016, a big announcement was made through a short newspaper report. Ratan Tata, Chairman Emeritus of the Tata Group; Vijay Kelkar, the former Finance Secretary; and Nandan Nilekani, Cofounder of Infosys, have planned to start a microfinance institution (MFI). "Avanti," meaning modest, is the name of the proposed MFI.

In India, over the last decade and a half, MFIs have struggled to gain legitimacy as credible institutions, even though they have demonstrated their ability to deliver financial services to unbanked low-income households sustainably. Scathing doubts on their modus operandi, governance, high interest rates, transparency, client treatment, profitability, among others, continued to hound, as these MFIs struggled to grow and expand. It was only after the Andhra Pradesh crisis in 2010 when the Reserve Bank of India (RBI) stepped in and issued a series of regulatory guidelines that these debates on the MFI credibility abated. Over the last five years, the MFIs in India have been able to gain significant credibility. In fact, perhaps in recognition of the fact that MFIs can truly help in advancing financial inclusion, of the 10 small finance bank licenses, as many as 8 went to MFIs besides Bandhan, which was earlier awarded a universal bank license. Now, with the most credible names in the corporate sector such as Ratan Tata and Nandan Nilekani starting a FI, this channel's credibility will be significantly buttressed. To accomplish durable outcomes from financial inclusion efforts, eventually, there is a need to identify and create institutions that are designed and mandated to serve this specific client segment.

Meanwhile, the nation's flagship program like the Prime Minister's Jan Dhan Yojana (PMJDY), a juggernaut, has continued to roll and advance, reaching over 240 million persons with bank accounts, on the last count. Even though it has been two years since the program was launched, it still continues to be a priority of the NDA Government. For a very large complex program like the PMJDY, showing significant benefits trickling down in quick time is perhaps an inappropriate expectation; there is steady and incremental progress. Account opening has reached saturation levels. Percentage of dormant accounts is dwindling. About 190 million RuPay cards have been issued. And about 130 million accounts have been linked to Aadhaar, enabling greater direct benefit transfer (DBT), which in turn has helped in a greater level of transactions in PMJDY accounts. In addition to liquid petroleum gas (LPG) subsidy and Mahatma Gandhi National Rural Employment Guarantee Act (MGNREGA) wages, the government is considering more and more subsidies to be brought under DBT. Although the last-mile connectivity through business correspondents (BCs) is improving, the lack of infrastructure is not helping matters. Most PMJDY account holders continue to transact through the BCs, mostly cash in and cash out. Even now, about 25% of accounts have zero balance. The overdraft facility of INR 5,000 under the program has hardly taken off. Similarly, only a very few have been covered under the three social protection schemes, relating to insurance and pension, announced under the program last year. The new customers that the PMJDY seeks to include are largely unaware of the banking system, and unless a strong emphasis is made in developing their financial awareness and capabilities, they will not benefit from this significant national effort and investment, certainly not in the short run.

One other important initiative of the present government is "Digital India," under which there is a major effort to digitally connect the country. While this may not directly relate to financial inclusion, PMJDY is likely to get a huge boost from creation of significant digital infrastructure in the country. New phraseology such as "JAM Trinity," "India Stack," and "Whatsapp Moment" are doing the rounds as the game changers.

With Aadhaar seeding, greater penetration of smartphones (now being made affordable by the likes of Reliance Jio), several Fintech companies coming into play, payment wallets being introduced, and more emphasis on use of technology by the new generation banks that will roll out soon, emphasis by the government of bringing more subsidies under DBT and introduction of UPI will all revolutionize payments and accelerate the move towards a "cashless" economy, ushering a new era of digital finance in the country.

Outside of PMJDY, while last year, 10 licenses were issued for small finance banks and 11 for payments banks (PBs), two new categories of banks created by the RBI, these banks are ready to roll out any time soon. The covenants of these banks are structured such that even though there may be no statutory obligations, they necessarily, as fait accompli, will cater to small ticket size transactions and advance FI in India. Since 8 of the 10 small finance banks are erstwhile MFIs, they are quite familiar with the low-income household clientele. While the small finance banks, two of which have already started operations, seemed quite sorted on how they will go about their business, there seems to be some fuzziness among the PBs on their business strategies. Three of the 11 PB licensees have already opted out, and now there is some skepticism among the others on their business strategies. However, with these banks starting operations, there is expected to be significant new approaches, products, and technologies in reaching out to lower-end clients and in last-mile connectivity. Even new universal banks have developed niche strategies for this segment. While IDFC has conceptualized its Bharat Banking initiative, Bandhan continues to be faithful to its MFI clients of the past.

Self Help Group Bank Linkage Program (SHHBLP), an inventive initiative of NABARD, was perhaps the first serious, structured effort in financial inclusion. However, ironically, even though it had very large numbers under its fold, while on the one hand, it could never get integrated into the PMJDY strategy, on the other hand, it got largely "hijacked" by NRLM, bringing in heavy doses of subsidy. The pace at which the program has grown in the last few years has been rather slow and sluggish, with few new groups being formed. Self Help Promoting Institution NGOs are being eased out and state-level NRLM teams are forming and nurturing new SHGs. NPA levels continue to be high. Although per capita savings levels are growing, groups' getting new loans is going down. An important initiative of NABARD's is the "digitization" of the SHG data. This is an important initiative, and with transparent transaction records of SHGs available, hopefully the supply side will respond better, and perhaps provide bigger loans to well performing SHGs. A few private banks like ICICI Bank, have designed their own linkage programs with appropriate due diligence in place, enabling the bank to provide higher levels of loans. Using SHGs for providing livelihoods finance to its members could be a way of enhancing SHG loan sizes, and perhaps also reducing delinquencies. The model for this still needs refinement. SHG Bank Linkage is an important program, with about 8 million groups, and appropriately needs critical revitalization.

Once considered peripheral and perhaps discredited, MFIs, in the last few years, have increasingly been mainstreamed as an important stakeholder in the formal financial ecosystem as a credible channel and as credible institutions. The last two years has seen significant action within the MFI channel. All the big MFIs have become banks: one a universal bank and eight ready to roll out as small finance banks. Just Ujjivan and Equitas by themselves raised a capital of about ₹200 billion through their IPOs. Several other MFIs too attracted sizeable investments. Banks have once again begun to pour funding into MFIs for on-lending. Gram Vidiyal was acquired by IDFC, largely to meet its priority sector lending. Several other banks are also similarly acquiring stakes in MFIs for the same purpose. Many MFIs have begun operating as BCs, mostly private banks. In some manner, this is a positive trend.

However, there are worrisome trends as well. The sector, in the past few years, has been growing at a frenzied pace. While client outreach grew at about 45%, GLP grew by almost two times, by 85%. This growth is clearly heating up the sector and throwing up signals of high levels of overindebtedness. Out of over 500 districts in which all the MFIs are operating, about 50% of the total portfolio is concentrated in 80 districts. Based on a research commissioned by ACCESS, several clients had loans outstanding from over five sources. Some cases of suicides by clients are beginning to get reported, and industry watchers are expressing deep worry on the phenomenon. Indeed, the sector is showing signs of overheating, and many are predicting a 2010 like bubble building.

The *Inclusive Finance India Report 2010*, this year, has covered all channels, institutions, and policy pronouncements. The report covers far greater detail and insightful analysis of how financial inclusion in India has progressed over the last one year. Special thanks are due to Professor Sriram for the painstaking efforts put in by him to collect, comprehend, and collate all relevant information, data, and trends for the report.

Sriram took two very significant initiatives this year for strengthening the content and bringing in diverse perspectives into the report. Two closed door roundtables were organized for the new differentiated banks about to start operations; one for the small finance banks in partnership with IIM Udaipur; and the other in partnership with the College of Agriculture Banking for PBs. All licensees participated in these two roundtables, and we were fortunate to have Deputy Governor N. S. Vishwanathan, from the RBI with his team present in both roundtables, with whom the licensees shared their woes and worries, as well as their roll out plans.

The other important initiative by Sriram was to conduct detailed interviews with four former governors of the RBI. These interviews were very rich, and have helped in tracing the evolution of financial inclusion in the country. Perspectives from these interviews have been interestingly and inventively woven into relevant chapters. I am tempted to bring all these four interviews, along with the interview of Professor Raghuram Rajan from last year into a book form. While I thank Sriram for all these super efforts, hectic travelling, interactions with key stakeholders, and the research as well as putting together the report in time, now that Sriram has established a template for the report, it will be most appropriate for him to continue to author the 2017 Report.

Several stakeholders and industry experts each year support this incredibly complex task of bringing the *Inclusive Finance India Report* together. Without their support and generous time, this task would be hard to accomplish. At the outset, I would like to thank the four former RBI governors, namely, Dr C. Rangarajan, Dr Bimal Jalan, Dr D. Subbarao and Dr Y.V. Reddy for sparing their time for the detailed interviews. I would personally like to thank N.S. Vishwanathan, deputy governor, RBI, for sparing two full days for the two roundtables. I also take this opportunity to thank NABARD, particularly Chintala and Subrata; MFIN, Ratna and Sadhan, and particularly Satish, for sharing useful data and their perspectives for this report. I am very grateful to Pramod Panda, Principal, College of Agriculture Banking, and Janat Shah, Director, IIM Udaipur, for providing the venue and hospitality for the two roundtables. Importantly, I would like to thank Arindom Datta and Rabobank; Krishna and MetLife Foundation; Harish Dave and Subrata at NABARD; Rohan at MasterCard; Jennifer and Girish at IFC; Saneesh at Dia Vikas; and Ramakrishna and Prakash at SIDBI for their support and sponsorship of the report. Without their contribution, this elaborate effort could not have been accomplished. ACCESS feels privileged to receive, year after year, significant support from a diverse range of stakeholders.

Finally, I would like to thank my small team at ACCESS and ACCESS-ASSIST to have provided outstanding support to get the report out in time. I would like to thank Radhika, for the leadership she provided to the team in organizing the tasks. I'm proud of the great effort put in by Sivani in providing all the necessary support to the author. Importantly, I was very impressed by the superlative efforts made by Keerti in providing all support to the author—fixing meetings, transcribing interviews, downloading reports, collating data, and accompanying the author for meetings. As always, I'd like to thank Lalitha for making all the logistic arrangements for the author, effortlessly and with a smile.

ACCESS feels very proud to have continued to bring out the *Inclusive Finance India Report* for the 11th consecutive year. We keep receiving feedback on its usefulness as a credible comprehensive reference document for those tracking financial inclusion in India, both within and outside the country. Across the 13 chapters of the report, extensive coverage of the full ecosystem that supports financial inclusion in the country has been attempted, and I hope that as in the past, the 2016 Report too will be of value. The report, as traditionally happens, will be released at the Inclusive Finance India Summit in December in Delhi.

Vipin Sharma
Chief Executive Officer
ACCESS Development Services

Preface

The year 2016 has been interesting in many ways for inclusive finance. New institutions are in the making, more niche players like peer-to-peer lenders are being recognised, and the regulator is also talking of putting out a framework for interest-free banking. The government has been pushing the agenda of direct benefit transfers that makes the poor an integral part of the banking system and there have been several experiments in use of digital cash and technology to make banking universally accessible. Technology is also pushing towards settlement of transactions in a cashless format. With new small finance banks and payments banks ready to roll out their business, the space is getting to be more and more interesting.

This report tries to capture all these happenings, and excitement is a considered fashion, putting in data where it is available. Compared to last year's report, there is one additional chapter that has been added—that of rural co-operative system. It is well-known that this system has the best physical presence and has been generally ignored. It may have been ignored because of the difficulty of getting data and also because the growth rates and innovations are not exciting enough. However, it is important to ensure that we track the sector and that an important piece in the inclusion architecture does not fall by the wayside—first from discussions, then from policy engagement.

This report also has been able to place more recent data on both self-help groups and regional rural ranks and thanks are due to National Bank for Agriculture and Rural Development (NABARD) for bringing out these two data sets in a professional manner. Thanks are also due to Microfinance Institutions Network (MFIN) for bringing out detailed and regular data on Non-Banking Financial Company–Microfinance Institution (NBFC MFIs) and Sa-Dhan for bring out the data once a year on a broad brush of participants in the inclusive finance space, particularly data on NGOMFIs. These two resource books have been immensely helpful in shaping much of the microfinance chapter. The data made available by CRIF High Mark helped in having a better look at the granular data pertaining to microfinance institutions. Like last year, the gaps are in two important sectors of inclusion: microinsurance and micropensions. These are identified gaps which one may try to fill in future years.

On the broad format, I have tried to be consistent with the format of the previous year and also provided data on the same formats so that it becomes useful for people looking for longitudinal data. I have also provided two chapters on the emerging institutions and their plans—the small finance banks and the payments banks. I have tried to expand the chapter where frontier work is happening—the digital inclusion.

There are several people who work in the ecosystem who make a report of this size, magnitude, and diversity to work. It is extremely difficult for me to acknowledge each one of their contributions. However, I have tried to acknowledge the inputs I have received specifically in the respective chapters. Chapters of this report have been reviewed at the draft stage by experts who went out of their way to provide inputs at short notice. However, I would like to specially thank the following persons:

- Dr C. Rangarajan, Dr Bimal Jalan, Dr Y.V. Reddy, and Dr D. Subbarao, former governors of the Reserve Bank of India (RBI) who willingly gave multiple slots of time for interviews about financial inclusion. We have only carried excerpts of those interviews in this report but their patience and kindness is gratefully acknowledged.
- N.S. Vishwanathan, Deputy Governor, the RBI, who was very encouraging and was present in two important consultations we had about small finance banks and payments banks; Janat Shah of IIM Udaipur

for organising a consultation on small finance banks and P.K. Panda of College of Agricultural Banking Pune for organising a consultation on payments banks.

- Pallavi Chavan, Dr Alok Pande, Ajay Tankha, D. Krishna, Madhumita Das, Chinmay Tumbe, Girija Srinivasan, C.S. Reddy, N. Srinivasan, Ratna Vishwanathan, Brahma Subrahmanyam, and Y.C. Nanda for providing me feedback on the chapters.
- Hasna Ashraf, a student of IIT Madras who interned with me and provided significant inputs for three chapters.
- Anuradha Eshwaran and Srishti Pandey, erstwhile students of IIMB and NLSIU respectively who worked on payments banks.
- G.R. Chintala, U.S. Saha and Subrata Gupta of NABARD for spending time and making data available.
- M. Balachandran and A.P. Hota and their team at National Payments Corporation of India (NPCI) who explained with patience the exciting work they are doing.

I am also thankful to Access Assist for providing me with this opportunity to write the report and for their constant support. Anshu Singh who would work relentlessly and cheerfully, ably succeeded by Keerti Bhandary; Sivani Sankar who took so much of burden on the two important consultations and was always available in spite of multiple pressures; Lalitha Sridharan who cheerfully managed the logistics; Radhika Agashe for being with the project throughout; and of course Vipin Sharma for all his persuasive and organizational skills. It has been a pleasure working with this team.

I would also like to thank my wife Gowri and son Arjun who were very much a part of this team—who helped me to relax amidst the stress of doing such a time-bound project.

M.S. Sriram

Introduction

1

Chapter

OVERVIEW

The issue of financial inclusion has continued to occupy mainstream attention in several ways. During the initial part of the year 2016, two important events marked significant steps in the direction of a larger agenda of having more and more exchanges through the formal financial system. First, the committee set up by the Reserve Bank of India (RBI) to suggest a medium-term path on financial inclusion submitted its report with a wide range of recommendations. The passing of Aadhaar (targeted delivery of financial and other subsidies, services, and benefits bill of 2016) gave a legal framework for the ambitious Aadhaar project of the Unique Identification Authority of India (UIDAI).

In addition to the approval, the Basel Committee on Banking Supervision (BCBS) issued a guidance note on the regulation and supervision of institutions relevant to financial inclusion (see Box 1.1 for highlights). While the BCBS has been engaged in deliberations of supervisory framework for financial inclusion, the fact that this note came from a source that is concerned about global stability of the banking system is indicative of the importance that the agenda of financial inclusion has assumed.

Box 1.1 Guidance for Supervisors: Ten Principles

1. Legal, regulatory, and supervisory framework

To ensure that the appropriate laws and regulations that protect the customers are in place and, if not, to work toward providing a framework for protecting the customers.

2. Role of the oversight bodies

To ensure that the definition of the role of multiple supervisors (functional supervisors, operational supervisors, and so on) are clearly defined and a coordination mechanism is established so that the multiple supervisors work in tandem.

3. Equitable and fair treatment of customers
4. Disclosure and transparency

To ensure that the customers are aware of the product they are subscribing to with all its possibilities and limitations.

5. Financial education and awareness
6. Responsible business conduct of financial services providers and authorized agents
7. Protection of consumer assets against fraud and misuse
8. Protection of consumer data and privacy
9. Complaints handling and redress
10. Competition

To ensure that the competitive practices are not unfair, do not restrict choices, and are responsible.

Source: BIS (2015).

The G20 meet in China in July 2016 issued high-level principles of digital financial inclusion and discussed this issue in the meeting of the central bankers and finance ministers of the member nations.

The common theme underlying each of these initiatives is that there is a greater recognition that the issue of financial inclusion has to be addressed very urgently; the issue has to be addressed using multiple approaches—institutional, policy, programmatic, and regulatory. Therefore, while there were initiatives to open up the banking space for niche and specialized banks, there were also initiatives in the policy architecture to push and nudge the agenda of inclusion. However, the one basic theme across all these initiatives was about leveraging technology to the fullest.

While in the past the concern was significantly about establishing the identity of the customer to ensure that the institutions in the banking system were in compliance with the Know Your Customer (KYC) norms, the trends seem to indicate that the use of technology is moving toward making the inclusion agenda more focused and meaningful. The technology will be used in ensuring that there is deduplication; the borrower-level data would be used as credit history to build models on the behavioral patterns of borrowers which helps in determining the appropriate design of financial products; remittances happen seamlessly; payments of benefits from the government system could happen faster and on the basis of objectively verifiable trails; access points can be increased manifold; and access to the institution could be provided directly to the hands of the customer through platforms that use mobile phone technology. This is a period where fundamental changes are being introduced in the use of technology—largely, information technology toward reaching banking services to the poor.

INSTITUTIONAL INITIATIVES

During the year, three small finance banks (SFB) and one payments bank (PB) got the final license. Seven SFBs and seven PBs were well on their way to get a final license. The details of the initiatives taken last year and being implemented this year are discussed in greater detail in Chapters 11 and 12.

Three new organizational forms were discussed during the year. First was bringing peer to peer lending platforms on to a regulatory framework. The RBI during the year released the draft guidelines. In addition, the RBI indicated that the draft guidelines for offering interest-free products in the banking system (as recommended by the Mohanty Committee) would be examined. The same was the case with wholesale banks. In addition, the RBI also put out draft guidelines for providing on-tap licensing facilities for commercial banks.

Ecosystem

There were many discussions and initiatives on the overall ecosystem development. The Mohanty Committee set up by the RBI for looking at the medium-term path for financial inclusion provided several recommendations to improve the ecosystem. Some of these included a geographical information system mapping of all banking points so that the regulators could get a good understanding of the spatial spread and harmonization of credit reporting systems across all lenders, so that there would be common reporting standards and the data could be easily comparable.

While there was a good spread of automated teller machines (ATMs) both in the rural and urban areas, data indicated that the regional rural banks (RRBs) have been slow in opening the ATMs even on their premises. The Mohanty Committee suggested the use of the Financial Inclusion Fund (FIF) to increase the penetration of ATMs, to facilitate interoperability of Micro ATMs, and to spread the use of mobile technology that is interoperable. While the committee did not specifically mention RRBs, that probably should be the first priority in terms of expanding the digital-cum-physical footprint. In addition, the Mohanty Committee recommended setting up a universal service obligation fund and routing of corporate social responsibility (CSR) investments to address the concerns of viability in difficult areas to address the issue of physical access to services.

The committee made two other recommendations which are important:

- The improvement and digitization of land records and making available credit eligibility certificates on even to tenant farmers by making it Aadhaar linked.
- Removing the subvention for agricultural credit and diverting those resources for a crop insurance scheme for small and marginal farmers (RBI 2015).

Customer Protection

In February 2016,[1] the union cabinet gave approval for promoting payments through cards and digital means. This was a multi-pronged strategy to reduce the usage of cash through the use of short-term and medium-term measures. The measures included removal of charges and surcharges, and moderation of merchant discount rates to encourage people to move toward a less cash economy. On the other hand, there would also be measures that would prevent cash transactions beyond a certain limit, making it mandatory to adopt the digital means. This initiative on the one hand would create a transaction trail that helps in prevention of money laundering and illegal activities, and on the other would be inclusive for the poor as their transactions would be captured—making them eligible for services from the formal sector.

[1] http://pib.nic.in/newsite/PrintRelease.aspx?relid=136755, accessed September 20, 2016.

In a recent development, the interministerial group on deposit taking has submitted a draft bill for banning unregulated deposits (called the Banning Bill; Ministry of Finance, GOI 2016). The RBI followed up the initiative by launching a website, "Sachet," where the information on the entities that are licensed and authorized to accept deposits will be put up.[2] This website will also have provision for people to share information regarding institutions accepting illegal deposits, and for lodging complaints. While all institutions do not come under the purview of the RBI, the action against illegal deposits will be taken through the state-level coordination committees.

Regulatory

On the regulatory side, the most significant event during the year was the passing of the Aadhaar Bill. While Aadhaar did not have a legal backing and was seen as a project, with the passing of the bill as a money bill, it received a statutory status. While there is still no clarity whether Aadhaar should be made mandatory, there have been some recent notifications that address the issue. The entire process of enrolment and usage of Aadhaar number was questioned in the Supreme Court and the court had mandated that while Aadhaar could be used for certain purposes, such as provision of liquefied petroleum gas (LPG) subsidy, payment of Mahatma Gandhi National Rural Employment Guarantee Act (MGNREGA) wages, and public distribution system, the court had also directed that the enrolment should be voluntary and no person should be denied of any services because she/he does not have an Aadhaar enrolment. The main issue addressed here was exclusion on account of not having an Aadhaar enrolment. In addition, there were issues pertaining to the safeguards pertaining to privacy (including issues pertaining to data sharing).

The Mint reported:

> New regulations on Aadhaar notified on Wednesday put the onus on the central and state governments to ensure that people eligible for subsidies do not miss out on them for lack of the unique identity number. It is up to the governments to make sure that all eligible beneficiaries are enrolled in Aadhaar.[3]

The Supreme Court in its interim orders had ruled that no beneficiary should be denied benefit if s/he does not have an Aadhaar number. However, the news report seems to indicate that the agency providing the benefit should be responsible for the beneficiary to get an Aadhaar number in order to seek the benefits but does not have a provision for the benefits to go to the members without Aadhaar. Therefore, there still may be some regulatory clarity that would come in. However, there is much action happening on the basis of Aadhaar platform and many of the policy recommendations are based on the assumption that Aadhaar number could be seamlessly used in multiple applications.

For instance, the Mohanty Committee recommended the mapping of Aadhaar number with credit accounts to the credit bureau information to trace multiple borrowings and help overcome customer over-indebtedness. Even in case of microfinance institutions (MFIs), the Microfinance Institutions Network (MFIN) has been moving toward Aadhaar-based identity de-duplication for understanding the indebtedness. In one sense, it appears inevitable that Aadhaar would become the primary identity mover that will not only do the paperless identity verification at the first instance of customer on-boarding but will also be the platform for authentication at the transaction level. Going forward, there may be common Aadhaar-based identity verification standards for multiple verticals of financial inclusion across regulators (banking, telecom, insurance, mutual funds, and so on).

In that sense, the passage of the Aadhaar Bill should be seen as one of the most significant pillars in the inclusion architecture.

Policy

In addition to the issue of getting the poor and the vulnerable into the mainstream banking architecture, particular emphasis is being laid on digital financial inclusion. With the Government of India (GoI) giving a further fillip to the Jan Dhan-Aadhaar-Mobile (JAM) framework it is imperative that there is an intention to move most of the financial transactions on to the digital platform, particularly on to the mobile platform. This agenda is much larger than just the financial inclusion agenda, because the technology becomes an integrative part of the policy making.

These initiatives are to be seen as the future roadmap of financial inclusion, where a particular service—be it credit or remittance is seen as a starting point for providing a suite of financial services to the customers. The discourse, whether it is about

[2] http://sachet.rbi.org.in/, accessed October 1, 2016.

[3] http://www.livemint.com/Politics/oTad2gp1lMzi8t-2FI2MBoN/Centre-mollifies-Aadhaar-critics.html?utm_source=newsletter&utm_medium=email&utm_campaign=newsletter, accessed September 20, 2016.

targeted benefits using Aadhaar or the supervisory framework enunciated by BCBS, has the banking system at the core of its design. The organizations that offer narrower financial services, the institutions that have functional specialization are necessary institutions in the scheme of things (largely to integrate customers into the formal system) and these institutions have to be seen as necessary and different. As things unfold—particularly with the targeted delivery of benefits on the Aadhaar platform—it would be interesting to see how the role of the narrow banks such as PBs, the postal network, and the MFIs emerge in the coming years.

The fundamental distinction is between institutions that take deposits and the institutions that offer services other than savings and thrift. While the business logic looks at deposits as a source of inexpensive funding for the lending operation and a service to be offered to the customers, the supervisory architecture looks at these as resources of the poor and the uninformed parked in the institutions and, therefore, the overarching supervisory framework being that of protecting the depositor rather than significant business or profit-based principles. Therefore, solvency of the organization takes precedence over all other concerns. The players in this space have to recognize the dichotomy of the concerns of the supervisor which requires large amounts be stashed away as cash and liquidity reserves for meeting the unlikely liquidity needs of the depositors, and also ensuring solvency of the organization itself. But once we remove the deposit-taking function from the organization, the supervisory architecture moves from the solvency concerns to that of protecting the vulnerable customers. The BCBS architecture is thus divided into two significant parts—the regulatory and supervisory element for banks and other deposit taking institutions and the customer protection framework for non-deposit taking institutions.

The moment we talk about digital financial inclusion, the question of a customer protection framework for digital transaction assumes importance. While the conventional elements of the customer framework would certainly apply to this platform as well, there are additional safeguards to be imposed on the privacy, and the caveats that prevent profiling and the aggressive lending based on data mining needs to be considered.

PROGRESS: INTERMEDIA SURVEY

Unlike 2015, there were no major studies on the benchmarking of the Indian financial inclusion sector except the Intermedia Tracker. The Crisil Inclusix is done periodically and the latest inclusix numbers were captured in the previous year. The highlights of the intermedia study indicated a general progress in financial inclusion indicators. While the other numbers discussed in this report are based on numbers put out by the institutions themselves, the Intermedia study is based on the assessment of the demand side and gives a sense of the quality of inclusion. The highlights of the findings are given in Box 1.2.

Box 1.2 Financial Inclusion Insights from Intermedia

- As a measure of demand-side data of individuals, rather than households, the FII program found that bank account ownership increased from 52% in mid-2014 to 63% by mid-2015.
- FII data shows that 42% of adult Indians are active bank account holders.

While bank account registration and access grows, mobile money use and awareness remains low.

- Mobile money awareness is at 10% and use is at just 0.5%.

Financial inclusion is on the rise in India, driven in large part by the growth in bank account access and registration.

- Almost 7 in 10 (65%) Indian adults are now financially included, meaning they have accounts at financial institutions offering at least one of the following services: savings, insurance, investments, or money transfers.
- More adults are financially included now then were in 2014 (54%), largely due to the growth in bank and nonbank financial institution (NBFI) accounts.
- Individuals living below the poverty line and those living in rural localities saw substantial increases in financial inclusion, that is, 12% and 11% respectively. This signifies financial inclusion is growing for the most vulnerable adults in India.

The gender divide on financial inclusion has decreased.

- More women are financially included in 2015 than were in 2014, growing from 48% to 61%.
- Men experienced only 9% more financial inclusion than women did, growing from 60% to 69%.

Financial inclusion corresponds to greater financial planning for all and financial security for poorer segments.

- Financially excluded individuals living on less than $2.50 a day are more likely to have had to go without necessities, such as food, medicine, or cooking fuel, due to lack of money than their financially included counterparts.
- Financially included individuals are more likely to have a plan in place to help them cope with unexpected financial shocks, such as losing a job, than financially excluded Indians.

Banks continue to be the primary means of financial access in India.

- In 2013 and 2014, banks were the most widely used financial services among adults and the trend continued in 2015. In fact, with the advent of Prime Minister's Jan Dhan Yojana (PMJDY) accounts, banks have continued to maintain a stronghold on financial access.
- Mobile money registered account use has remained static across years.

NBFIs continue to be prominent tools for banking activities among women, rural, and poor populations.

- There was higher growth in registered NBFI accounts versus registered mobile money accounts, though not as high as the growth in bank accounts. Active NBFI account use also grew from 5% to 6%.
- Of the approximately 9% of adults with registered NBFI accounts (including those who use NBFI accounts exclusively and non-exclusively), 66% are women, 70% live in rural areas, and 75% live on less than $2.50 a day.
- The use of savings and lending groups and post office accounts is more common than the use of MFI accounts in India.

More account holders actively use their accounts.

- Active account holders for any financial service increased 14% between 2014 (31%) and 2015 (45%), primarily led by an increase in active bank account holders.
- The greatest growth in active account holders was seen with bank accounts which increased from 29 to 42%.

With the growth in bank accounts, activities reflect more basic use and are in line with a large number of new users.

- Advanced use of bank account services (i.e., bill pay and loans) by active account holders decreased from 38% in 2013 to 21% in 2015.
- Use of the services for basic activities and remittances saw a huge increase, rising from 59% in 2013 to 77% in 2015. These shifts are mostly attributable to the large increase in the number of new bank account holders using banks for the first time.

FINSCOPE STUDY

Finscope conducted a comprehensive study in four of the poorest states of India under the UK Aid-funded Poorest State Inclusive Growth (PSIG) program. While the study was not only about financial inclusion but also about savings and borrowings behavior, asset profiling, and understanding income and expenditure patterns, what the study found in the four poorest states—Madhya Pradesh, Bihar, Odisha, and Uttar Pradesh—is very interesting and indeed promising because even in what is termed as underdeveloped and poor areas, the access to formal financial system seems to be ubiquitous. Look at Figure 1.1. The figure shows that about 4.5% of the respondents had access to multiple institutional options, about 5.8% of the respondents were left out, and a mere 1.4% of the respondents were exclusively with the informal sector.

Figure 1.2 gives a more nuanced look at how people in the poorest states are accessing financial services. When we look at those numbers, it is only

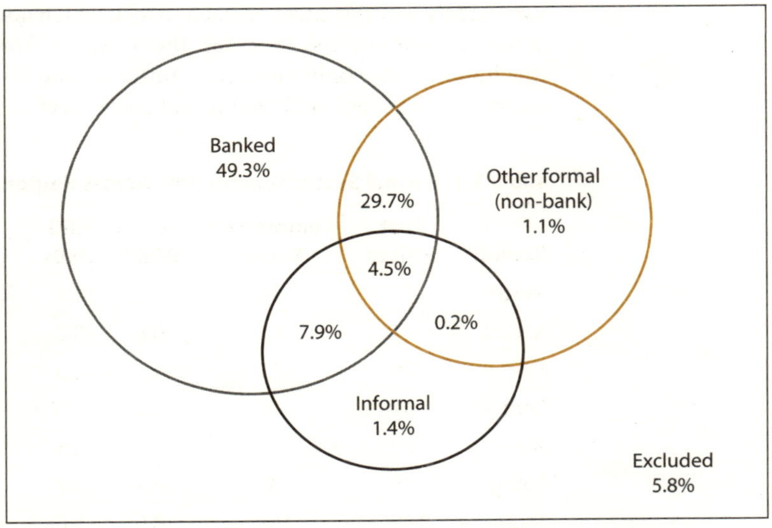

Figure 1.1 Household Overlaps in Uptake of Financial Products/Services

Source: Finscope Consumer Survey India (Under the PSIG Program) 2015.

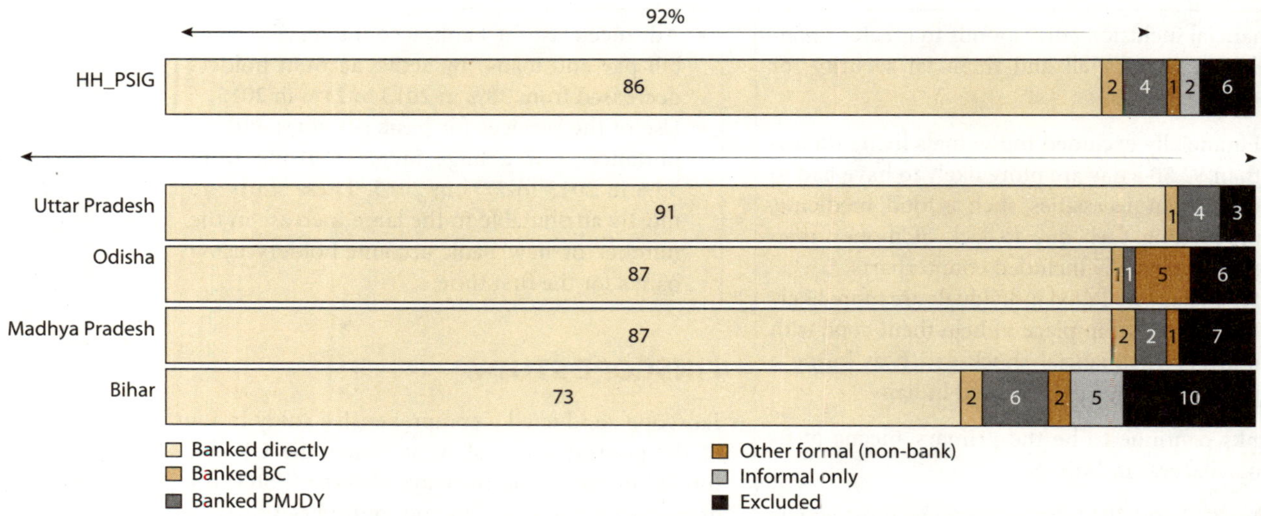

Figure 1.2 Household Financial Access Strand

Source: Finscope Consumer Survey India (Under the PSIG Program) 2015.

Bihar that stands out with a high degree of exclusion from the formal sector. The biggest band shows that most of the poor are already in the formal banking system largely by accessing the bank branch in their individual capacity.

A COMPREHENSIVE LOOK AT THE PROVIDERS

There has been progress in the physical outreach of touchpoints. Table 1.1 gives a comprehensive look at the touchpoints that are available across institutional forms. It is important to note that the quality and range of services of each of these verticals vary widely. For instance, postal network which accounts for slightly less than half the formal sector touchpoints offer only savings, remittance, and insurance services, but not banking and credit services. Similarly the MFIs offer only some types of loans and not comprehensive services. Most of the self-help groups (SHGs) do not offer scale. However, what is important is to understand the way the network is penetrated and how it could be leveraged for undertaking meaningful financial inclusion.

The story about the regional spread does not significantly change with the southern region having almost 44% of the formal sector touchpoints. A large part of the skew is because of SHGs where the southern region has almost 45% share, while the banking and postal network account for about a third of all the outlets. This brings back the question of a strategy on regional diversity of the formal sector presence. One of the recommendations to address the issue of regional disparity has been to look at the problem of access differently and pro-actively use technology. While there could be issues in setting up

Table 1.1 **Formal Sector Touchpoints Across Regions as of March 2016 (Numbers in '000s)**

Region	Post Offices	Commercial Banks	RRBs	RRB USBs	UCBs	MFIs	Viable PACS	Total Formal	SHGs	Total Touchpoints
North	22	20	3.0	1.4	0.4	0.6	9.1	57	390	447
N. East	7	3	0.8	0.2	0.1	0.2	1.8	13	430	443
East	29	17	4.5	0.3	0.2	2.0	14.0	67	1,700	1,767
Central	32	20	6.3	1.3	0.5	2.3	10.8	73	820	893
West	22	18	1.4	0.6	6.6	1.6	21.0	71	1,020	1,091
South	43	32	4.9	1.7	2.0	3.3	10.3	97	3,550	3,647
Total	155	109	20.9	5.6	9.7	10.0	67.0	377	7,910	8,287

Source: Author's computations.

Note: Post Office and PACS data is for March 2015.

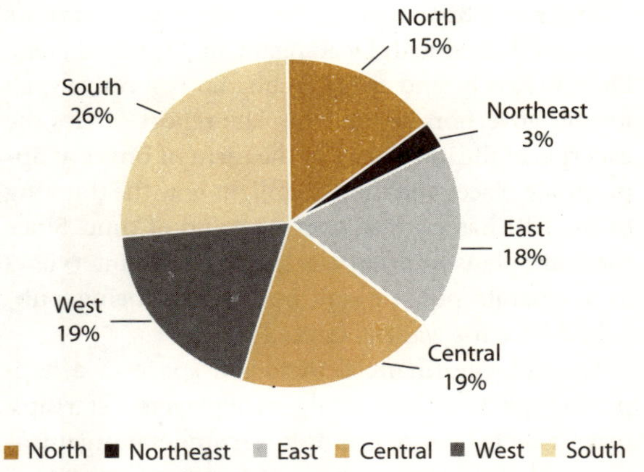

Figure 1.3 Regional Spread of Formal Sector Touchpoints

brick and mortar branches, the mobile technology based on the JAM trinity set-up could be used. There was a discussion on whether some areas are not only unviable to set up a physical branch, but also may be unviable for setting up telecom infrastructure—particularly where density of population is low. One of the suggestions to overcome this was to use non-commercial funding—either the CSR funds or the universal service obligation fund as a non-lapsable fund—to ensure that the financial divide and the digital divide is addressed in a dovetailed manner (RBI 2015).

While the new generation players like MFIs are marking their presence in the eastern and the northeastern regions, their impact is not significant in comparison to the residual exclusion. Figures 1.3 and 1.4 speak for themselves.

APPROACH AND ORGANIZATION OF THE REPORT

This report broadly continues the same pattern as the last year's report. The report covers all the institutional verticals—banks, RRBs, cooperatives, SHGs, MFIs, and India Post. A significant addition to this year's report is the chapters on the plans of SFBs and PBs as well as a chapter on Primary Agricultural Cooperative Societies (PACS). There is also

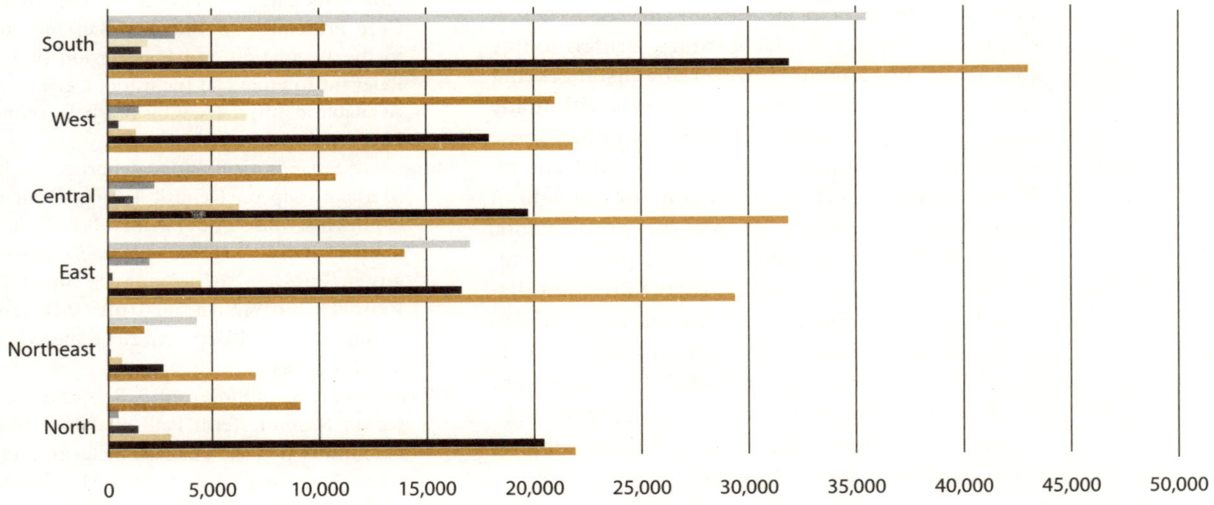

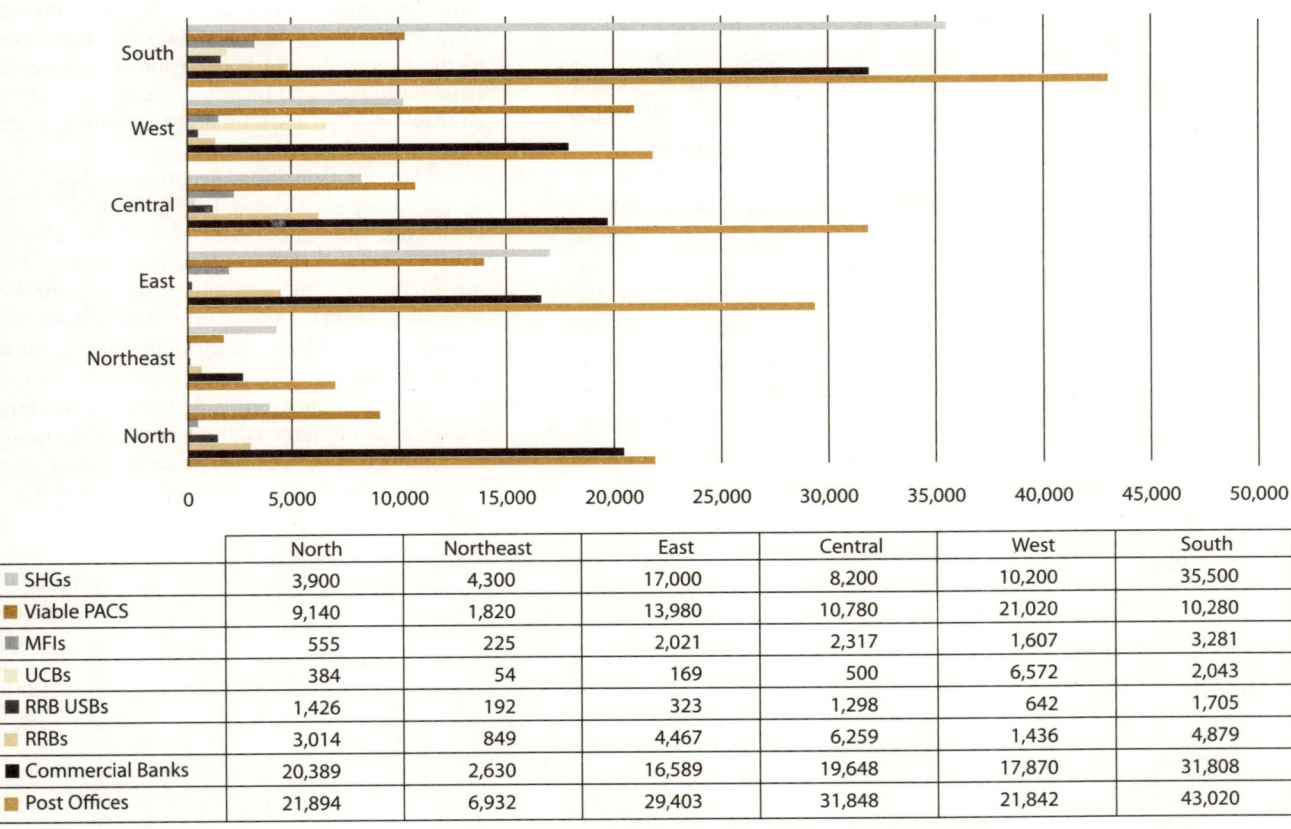

	North	Northeast	East	Central	West	South
SHGs	3,900	4,300	17,000	8,200	10,200	35,500
Viable PACS	9,140	1,820	13,980	10,780	21,020	10,280
MFIs	555	225	2,021	2,317	1,607	3,281
UCBs	384	54	169	500	6,572	2,043
RRB USBs	1,426	192	323	1,298	642	1,705
RRBs	3,014	849	4,467	6,259	1,436	4,879
Commercial Banks	20,389	2,630	16,589	19,648	17,870	31,808
Post Offices	21,894	6,932	29,403	31,848	21,842	43,020

SHGs Viable PACS MFIs UCBs RRB USBs RRBs Commercial Banks Post Offices

Figure 1.4 Spread of Touchpoints in Various Regions Ordered by Institution Type

Source: The data are from the respective institution's web sites.
Note: The data for Post Offices and PACS are for March 2015. The SHG Numbers are in '000s.

a chapter that reviews the PMJDY and a chapter is dedicated to the developments in the area of digital financial inclusion. An omission is the micro-insurance and the micropensions chapter, which could not be included due to various reasons.

This year, the updated data for SHGs and RRBs and the upper tier cooperatives was easily available from National Bank for Agriculture and Rural Development (NABARD) and, thus, on most of the verticals, the data for March 2016 has been provided.

The report intends to be a reference document for data and the significant happenings in the financial inclusion space. While there is much research happening which cuts across many years, care has been taken to look at the outputs that came out between October 2015 and September 2016—largely to keep the report current and also to avoid repetitions. Unlike one-off reports, an annual publication will have to take care to stick to a time period and the report earnestly tries to stick to this time period.

There are many impressions and subjective opinions that are prevalent in the inclusive finance sector. These impressions and stand-alone innovations have been incorporated in the report when there is a reference available from a written source in a formal document. However, the instances that have come out in personal interactions with many experts have not been incorporated unless these were backed by a formal mention in a document. However, the report does not contain the data of individual enterprises, or one-off experiments, except to illustrate or demonstrate a point. Therefore, it is quite likely that the report does not discuss large initiatives such as the ones carried out by Dhan Foundation, Sree Kshetra Dharmasthala Rural Development Programme (SKDRDP) or NABARD Financial Services. These data are subsumed in the larger SHG data and the same applies to microfinance institutions and other verticals.

In the run-up to writing the report, four interviews were conducted with Dr Rangarajan, Dr Bimal Jalan, Dr Y.V. Reddy, and Dr D. Subbarao respectively, all former governors of the RBI. The report carries the excerpts of the interviews in the form of boxes at appropriate places and these highlight how the thinking of the RBI has evolved over a period of time. Since there are plans to bring out the complete interviews as a separate publication, they are not being published here for want of space.

Overall, the financial inclusion space in a happening space, with an amalgam of players—startups, private sector entities, non-governmental organizations (NGO), cooperatives, government programs, private and public banks, and niche players—all of whom seem to be wanting to serve the excluded customer in their own unique way. These are possibly the most exciting times and the report is a small effort to document the journey of inclusive finance.

REFERENCES

BIS (Bank for International Settlements). 2015. Consultative Document: Guidance on the Application of Core Principles for Effective Banking Supervision to the Regulation and Supervision of Institutions Relevant to Financial Inclusion. Geneva: BIS, 3540. Available at: http://www.bis.org/bcbs/publ/d351.pdf (Accessed on March 16, 2016).

Ministry of Finance, GOI. 2016. Report of the Inter Ministerial Group on Deposit Taking. Draft report for comments, Ministry of Finance, New Delhi: Government of India. Available at: http://financialservices.gov.in/Public%20Comments%20on%20the%20Report%20of%20the%20Inter-Ministerial%20Group%20on%20Deposit%20Taking.pdf (Accessed on May 7, 2016).

RBI (Reserve Bank of India). 2015. Report of the Committee on Medium Term Path on Financial Inclusion. Committee Report, Financial Inclusion and Development Department (FIDD), RBI. Mumbai: RBI.

A Review of the Banking System[1]

2

Chapter

There has been a renewed focus on inclusive banking in the past few years, both with the initiative of the government with the encouragement of the RBI. With all the banks (including RRBs) getting on to the Core Banking Solution (CBS) platform, the technological base is laid. In past years, there was a significant change in the approach. First, on the definitional side, the RBI defined financial inclusion and articulated providing four basic services to the excluded, a significant shift from the credit-led inclusion and the account-opening drives. Second, in the spatial front, the RBI introduced the mandate that 25% of the incremental branches opened have to be located in unbanked locations. Third, as a part of the inclusion drive, the RBI identified locations that have population of more than 2,000 without a bank branch and mandated that the banking system has to cater to these locations and have a touchpoint. Fourth, the RBI advised the banks to submit board-approved financial inclusion plans, which were reviewed regularly. The RBI also constituted a high-level financial inclusion advisory committee to monitor the progress of inclusion.

On the other hand, the new government launched the new PMJDY scheme that put account opening on a mission mode, and used those accounts to map with Aadhaar for de-duplication and laid out a base for direct benefit transfer (DBT) monies to be channelized. As we discuss in Chapter 4 on PMJDY, there was both a push and a pull strategy to get people to the banks. This chapter reviews the progress of the banking system as a whole including the RRBs. However, Chapter 3 will look exclusively at the progress of the RRBs.

BRANCH NETWORK

On the banking side, the expansion of branches continued. From a total of 125,863 outlets that were reported in March 2015, the number increased to 132,587 by March 2016 and added another 1,427 branches in the next quarter. The latest numbers of branches are given in Table 2.1 and Appendix 2.1 has detailed numbers on the progress of banking indicators.

Due to the mandate of the RBI that 25% of the new branches have to be opened in rural locations, the branches in rural and semi-urban locations have kept with the pace of growth of the overall number of branches. The growth of outlets according to their location is given in Figure 2.1. It can be seen from the figure that the rural and semi-urban branch networks are growing faster than the other segments, even though the requirement is now to open only 25%

Table 2.1 Branches of Scheduled Commercial Banks

Branches of Scheduled Commercial Banks	March 2015	March 2016	June 2016
All scheduled commercial banks	148	149	149
of which, regional rural banks	56	56	56
No. of reporting offices			
Rural	48,033	49,902	50,421
Semi-urban	33,523	35,704	36,056
Urban	23,522	24,794	25,062
Metropolitan	20,785	22,187	22,475
Total	125,863	132,587	134,014

Source: Commercial Banks at a Glance. Reserve Bank of India. http://dbie.rbi.org.in/DBIE/dbie.rbi?site=publications, accessed September 1, 2016.

[1] The author is thankful to Pallavi Chavan for useful comments on an early draft of this chapter.

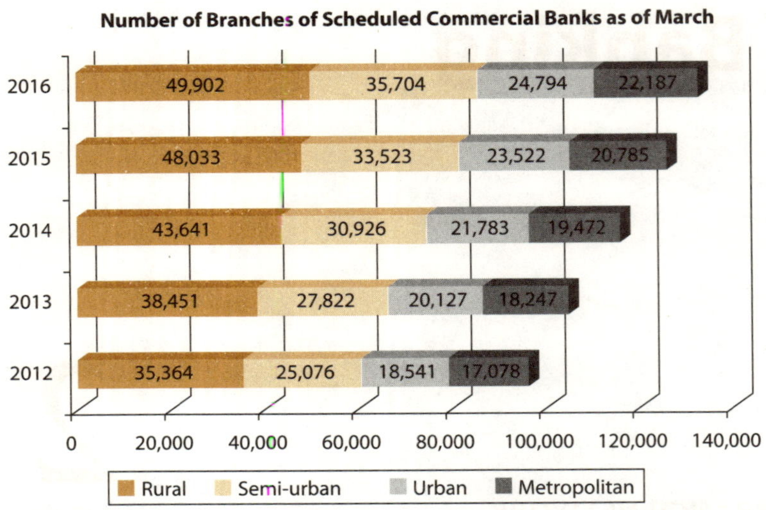

Figure 2.1 Bank Branch Network 2012–16

Source: http://dbie.rbi.org.in/DBIE/dbie.rbi?site=publications, accessed September 1, 2016.

of the incremental branches in unbanked locations. While the growth of branches in rural areas had fallen much below the rates of the urban and metropolitan branches in the early part of this decade, the growth of rural branches was faster in the last three years.

However, the raw data on the number of branches in rural and semi-urban areas might be misleading because there could be multiple bank branches in a single location, particularly if that location is adequately monetized with ample commercial activity. Therefore, it is important to look at total locations that are banked rather than just the rural branches. The data on unique banked locations in the rural and semi-urban locations are given in Table 2.2.

As can be seen in Figure 2.2, the growth of unique rural locations is lagging far behind the rate of growth of the rural branches per se. While the regulation requires the banks to have a footprint in rural (unbanked) locations and therefore it is evident that a

Table 2.2 **Number of Unique Rural and Semi-urban Locations That Are Served by Banks**

	Rural						Semi-urban					
Year	**2011**	**2012**	**2013**	**2014**	**2015**	**2016**	**2011**	**2012**	**2013**	**2014**	**2015**	**2016**
North	4,451	4,685	5,111	5,830	6,466	6,664	616	624	635	646	655	644
N. East	1,089	,099	1,127	1,197	1,270	1,312	146	146	150	154	154	151
East	6,814	6,983	7,186	7,671	8,190	8,369	930	940	956	989	1,067	1,085
Central	6,996	7,259	7,753	8,716	9,374	9,533	1,020	1,047	1,070	1,094	1,106	1,102
West	3,445	3,566	3,828	4,383	4,713	4,834	789	792	800	812	817	818
South	5,986	6,337	6,803	7,598	8,267	8,270	2,445	2,497	2,534	2,591	2,643	2,577
Total	28,781	29,929	31,808	35,395	38,280	38,982	5,946	6,046	6,145	6,286	6,442	6,377

Source: http://dbie.rbi.org.in/DBIE/dbie.rbi?site=publications, accessed September 1, 2016.

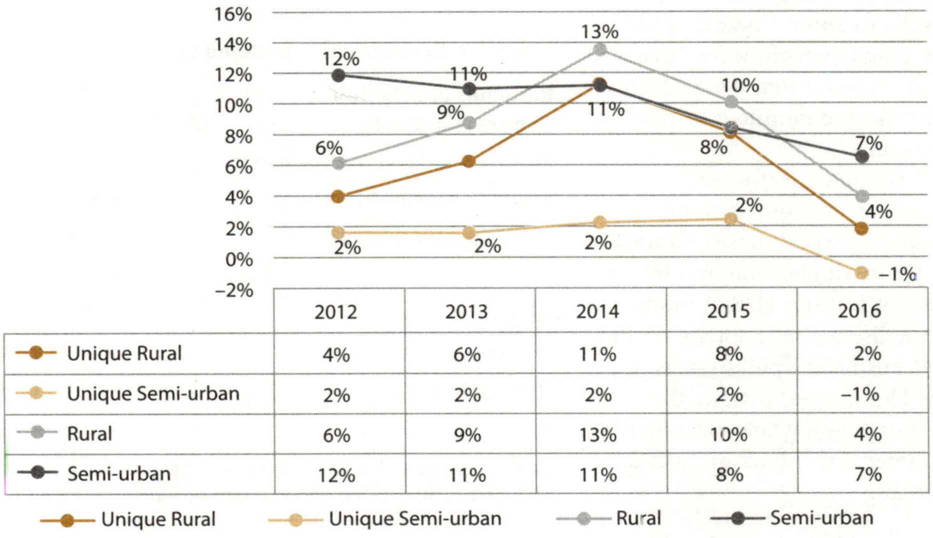

Figure 2.2 Growth Rate of Bank Branches in Rural and Semi-urban Areas

Source: http://dbie.rbi.org.in/DBIE/dbie.rbi?site=publications, accessed on September 1, 2016.

larger proportion of the rural branches are unique in their locations. As of March 2016, it can be seen that the rural branch presence is in about 38,000 villages as against a total number of 49,000 rural branches. The story of semi-urban branches is somewhat different. The 35,000-plus semi-urban branches were located in about 6,000-plus locations, indicating that these centers attracted banks even without a mandate from the RBI.

BEYOND THE BRANCH NETWORK

The roll out of technology—both in terms of digitization of the back end and the general development of digital mediums including the telecom network can now be fully leveraged to reach out to even remote locations. As can be seen from Table 2.3, the past few years have seen an exponential growth in the outreach models, thereby providing

Table 2.3 Financial Inclusion: Summary of Progress (Including RRBs)

Particulars	Year Ended March 2010	Year Ended March 2013	Year Ended March 2014	Year Ended March 2015	Year Ended March 2016
Banking outlets in villages—branches	33,378	40,837	46,126	49,571	51,830
Banking outlets in villages—branchless mode[a]	34,316	227,617	337,678	504,142	534,477
Banking outlets in villages—total	67,694	268,454	383,804	553,713	586,307
Urban locations covered through business correspondents (BCs)	447	27,143	60,730	96,847	102,552
BSBD A/c through branches (no. in million)	60	101	126	210	238
BSBD A/c through branches (amount in ₹ billion)	44	165	273	365	474
Basic savings bank deposit A/c through BCs (no. in million)	13	81	117	188	231
Basic savings bank deposit A/c through BCs (amtount in ₹ billion)	11	18	39	75	164
Total basic savings bank deposit A/c (no. in million)	74	182	243	398	469
Total basic savings bank deposit A/c (Amount in ₹ billion)	55	183	312	4,440	638
OD facility availed in BSBDAs (no. in million)	0.2	4	6	8	9
OD facility availed in BSBDAs (amount in ₹ billion)	0.1	2	16	20	29
KCCs (no. in million)	24	34	40	43	47
KCCs (amount in ₹ billion)	1,240	2,623	3,684	4,382	5,131
GCCs (no. in billion)	1	4	7	9	11
GCCs (amount in ₹ billion)	35	76	1,096	1,302	1,493
ICT A/cs BC transaction during the year (no. in million)	27	251	329	477	827
ICT A/cs BC transaction during the year (amount in ₹ billion)	7	234	524	860	1,687
On-site ATMs of banks (public, private, foreign banks)					101,950
Off-site ATMs of banks (public, private foreign banks)					97,149
ATMs of Cooperative Banks					4,664
ATMs of RRBs					1,024
White Label ATMs					14,169
BSBD: Basic savings bank deposit					

Source: Annual Report of 2014–2016 Reserve Bank of India. Mumbai: RBI; ATM statistics from NPCI.

Note: [a]The branchless mode outlets include business correspondents, ATMs, point of sale (PoS) points, ultra-small branches, mobile vans and any other mechanism that provides a touchpoint for the customer of the bank.

a banking touchpoint almost in the neighborhood of the customer. While the physical infrastructure and branchless touchpoints have followed a more aggressive growth path than the traditional channels, it can also be seen that the number of BSBD accounts have shown a great progress in the last two years, largely due to the PMJDY program. We can see a sixfold increase in the number of accounts in the past five years with a tenfold increase in the balance in these accounts. This achievement is largely seen in the last two years due to PMJDY. The numbers that have not shown exponential growth are the numbers pertaining to overdrafts (ODs), Kisan Credit Cards (KCC) and general credit cards (GCC). The next phase of the government's mission should be to get convergence between the PMJDY accounts and the KCC accounts that would cover a large number of small farmers and share croppers who would be poor and would greatly benefit from this convergence.

A look at Table 2.3 and an analysis of the numbers in Table 2.4 shows that the physical outreach of branches and business correspondents (BC) has led to a growth in the number of BSBD accounts. During the past year, the average number of accounts both at the branch and the BC levels grew significantly, but the average balance in the accounts is somewhat static. While the balance in the accounts maintained at the BC level has gone up, it is still a very small amount.

In addition to the bank branches, a network of 534,477 branchless outlets (including ATMs, point of sale [PoS] points, BCs, ultra-small branches, and customer service points) in rural areas and 102,552 urban outlets operated as business correspondents as of March 2016.

Apart from the physical presence of outlets with human interface, an impressive 199,000 ATMs have been deployed, of which 101,950 were on-site ATMs and were considered an integral part of the branch, while the other half were counted in the branchless touchpoints discussed previously. The distribution of ATM points across various types of locations is given in Figure 2.3.

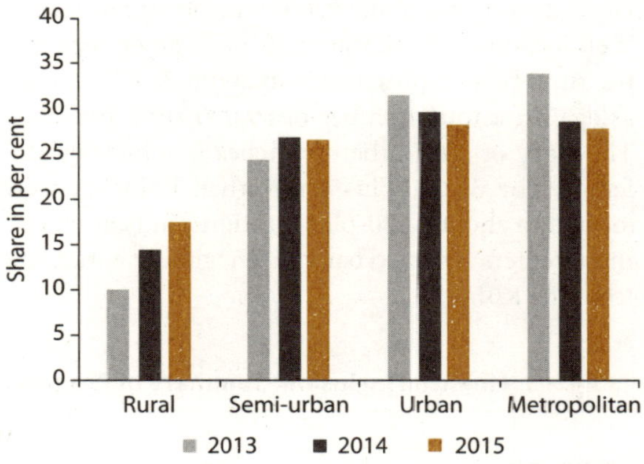

Figure 2.3 Geographical Distribution of ATMs

Source: RBI.

Credit and debit cards of the banks can be swiped for commercial transactions in 1.39 million PoS locations. In addition to these transactions, a total of 662 million debit cards and 24.5 million credit cards have been issued by the banks, thereby allowing the customers the choice of transacting at a time of their choice. A look at the transaction data indicates that both in terms of number of transactions as well as the amount transacted, the customers are overwhelmingly preferring transactions at the ATM to withdraw cash at the first instance than to use the PoS option in the case of debit cards, while the number of transactions on the PoS device seems to be higher in the case of credit cards. Obviously, the preference seems to be more bank driven than the ubiquitous use of technology. With prepaid wallets and the new PBs coming into the picture, the amount of transactions on the digital mode is expected to grow substantially.

Table 2.4 Financial Inclusion Progress—Numbers Unpeeled

Particulars	Year Ended March 2010	Year Ended March 2013	Year Ended March 2014	Year Ended March 2015	Year Ended March 2016
Number of BSBD A/cs per branch	1,803	2,468	2,731	4,236	4,592
Average balance per BSBD A/c (₹)	735	1,633	2,169	1,738	1,992
Number of BSBD A/cs per BC	387	357	346	370	432
Average balance per BSBD A/c (₹) (BC)	805	224	334	397	710
Percentage of BSBD A/cs availing OD	0.27%	2.20%	2.43%	1.90%	2%
Average OD balance in BSBD A/cs	500	400	2,711	2,618	3,222

Source: Computations by the Author based on Table 2.3.

Box 2.1 Former Governor Dr Bimal Jalan on Approach to Financial Inclusion

MSS: If you are looking at it as a central banker's perspective, one is to encourage institutional innovation, new banks, small finance banks, payments banks, and so on which are coming together. The second is the policy push, say, I'll give you one license in metropolitan area you have to open four elsewhere. And third is to mandate, like priority sector a portion of your portfolio will go to agriculture … so these are a combination of things that one needs to do or is there a preferred….

Dr Jalan: No. In our situation, we have adopted all these canons, namely, that access to government finances or network banking should not be dominated only by the better off sections, but it must have an outreach. But the other part to it is that the outreach cannot be at the cost of depositors who are also relatively less well off.

MSS: Yes, of course it is not an either-or situation. But, if we look back at the regional spread, we have seen that the south and west have been more banked than the central, eastern and northeastern sectors. Is there a way in which an institution like RBI can try and achieve some sort of a regional balance?

Dr Jalan: RBI is trying to do that by encouraging setting up of banks in the northeastern sector and giving certain amount of support and opening their own offices, but we must remember that ultimately we are dealing with other people's money.

MSS: Right, you are indicating that the aggressive measures should not be at the cost of safety.

Dr Jalan: Yes, safety becomes very important, and the process has to be such that these institutions are viable over the long term and are there to serve the cause.

MSS: You are indicating that access should be coupled with safety and viability.

Dr Jalan: Yes, these have to be balanced and one can't be impatient with that part. Where you need to transfer funds, then the state has to step in and transfer funds like subsidies and this has already happened, with PMJDY.

MSS: If you look at it historically the state has looked at this entire inclusion with a credit perspective: how do you make non-usurious credit available to the poorer sections of the society? Whether it's IRDP or all other old government schemes, all driven more toward access to credit, including agriculture. It's only the self-help group movement, the Swabhimaan scheme as well as Jan DhanYojana, which turned it around to focus on an account where people could save and transact.

Dr Jalan: As you are aware, both the RBI and the government have already undertaken some important initiatives last year which should contribute substantially to expand financial inclusion in India. The most important financial inclusion initiative by the present government is, of course, the launch of PMJDY which was launched in August 2014. Within a short period since its launch, this new initiative has already played an enormous role in expanding financial inclusion. I understand that under PMJDY 20 crore bank accounts have already been opened and people have deposited nearly ₹30,000 crores in these accounts. The trend of "zero" balance accounts share in the total number of accounts is also declining, thereby implying that the rural population has already started doing transactions through the banking system. The share of rural accounts in total is as high as 70%. This is most welcome.

In the current year's budget, a further initiative has been taken to launch Jan Suraksha initiative which provides several social security measures and particularly insurance and pension penetration in the country.

With all these initiatives, what we are trying is to make the transfer of subsidies to the poor easier. Then the other most important thing is the reduction in administrative costs, which makes it possible to deliver what you are actually spending. In the PDS system, for every rupee that we transfer, we spend ₹2.65 in administrative costs. I am talking about findings of a study in 2002. But you see the DBT technology has changed that completely. But it'll take time for this to expand. And that we should be prepared to accept, because we want not only the means of transfer but also means of safe transfer.

MSS: I am a bit curious. In the pre-liberalization era, the rhetoric of inclusion was dominated by making credit accessible and providing physical outreach. But if you go back and look at the Credit Deposit ratios of rural branches, you would find that these branches are deposit dominated. Now we are focusing on savings accounts which is also deposit oriented. So is the access to credit getting pushed aside?

Dr Jalan: No it'll take time. Earlier, it was mainly cash kept at home. Now, you have a branch, if you have a cooperative society you deposit whatever cash you have, whatever money you have for the monthly expenses, whatever it is, and you get a small interest. The credit system requires little more paperwork, the assessment of credit worthiness, and so on and so forth. Depositing your own money is easier. If you want to deposit your money, nobody is asking for credit appraisal. But with credit, there has to be an appraisal or you will be financing debt. Therefore, you need to see deposits as the first step in inclusion and wait for credit growth to naturally happen.

SMALL BORROWAL ACCOUNTS: AN ANALYSIS

The opening of PMJDY or BSBD accounts give a limited view of inclusion—they represent the people who are outside of the banking system being brought into the banking system. However, if one were to look at those who are within the banking system and if they are getting access to credit, it may be useful to look at how the small borrowal accounts (SBAs) are performing. A SBA is defined as an account where the sanction is less than ₹200,000. Earlier the definition of a SBA was limited to ₹25,000 and was revised in 1999 to the current figure. However, the data is available in both the categories.

To get a perspective, it is important to note that loans less than ₹25,000 form 20.7% of the total accounts but yield only less than half a percent of the portfolio. On the other end of the spectrum, more than 70% of the portfolio of banks again comes from less than half a percent of accounts. Clearly, the data is stacked against the poorer customers, because this is going to be transaction intensive. That is the reason we find that the number of accounts even under the SBA (new) category of ₹200,000 skewed more toward the ₹25,000–200,000 range.

If that data is examined, it is clear that all the efforts of financial inclusion happening over the years has not affected the off-take of small credit directly from the banks. It is clear from Table 2.5 that the absolute number of accounts that had a sanction limit of less than ₹25,000 has actually fallen from 45 million accounts in 2010 to around 30 million in 2015. The amount sanctioned has also fallen both in absolute terms.

However, in the other bucket of amounts above ₹25,000 but less than ₹200,000, the accounts and amounts have been growing and the number of accounts have remained in the same proportion to the total number of accounts of the banking system. This means that the overall number of customers in

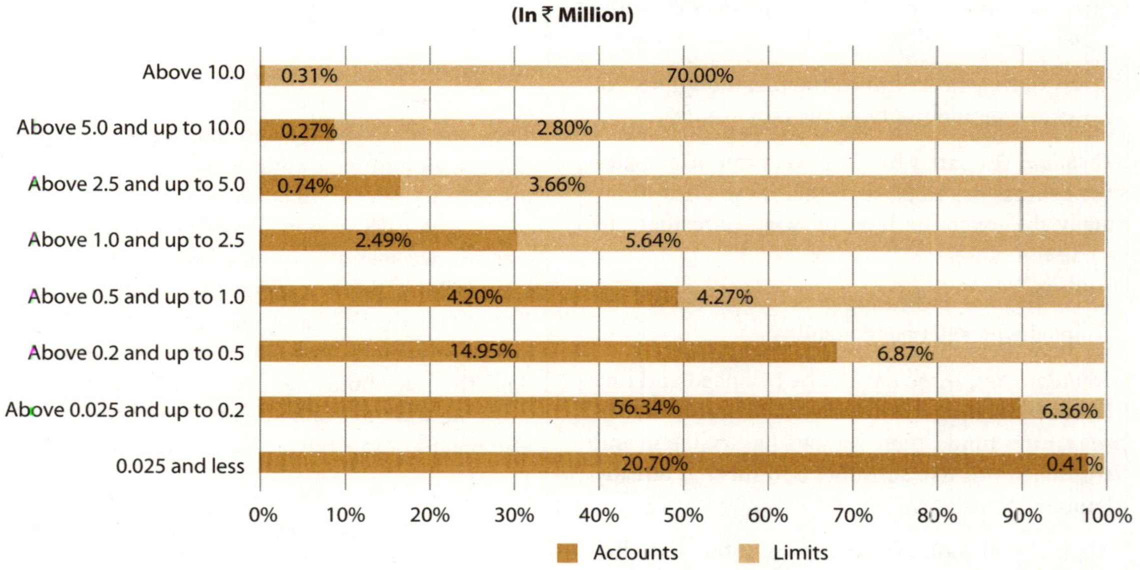

Figure 2.4 Outstanding Credit According to Size of Loan

Source: Data from Basic Statistical Returns of Scheduled Commercial Banks in India, Vol. 44, March 2015.

Table 2.5 Details of Credit to Small Borrowal Accounts over the Years

Year Ending March 31 →	2011	2012	2013	2014	2015	2016
Loan amount less than ₹25,000						
Number of accounts (million)	43.32	44.05	30.88	32.57	29.86	29.24
Percentage to total accounts	36%	34%	24.1%	23.50%	20.70%	21.33%
Limit sanctioned (million)	566,710	701,440	428,593	436,318	429,595	416,304
Percentage to total amounts	0.73%	0.91%	0.5%	0.50%	0.4%	0.38%
Amount outstanding (million)	473,990	762,160	736,827	436,318	359,945	349,011
Percentage to total outstanding	1.16%	1.59%	1.3%	0.60%	0.5%	0.48%
Loan amount ₹25,000 to ₹200,000						
Number of accounts (million)	58.83	65.06	71.43	76.66	81.27	74.95
Percentage to total accounts	49%	50%	56%	55.20%	56.30%	53.92%
Limit sanctioned (million)	4,574,070	5,056,960	5,734,745	6,170,673	6,645,862	6,143,433
Percentage to total amounts	5.93%	6.58%	6.90%	6.50%	6.40%	5.62%
Amount outstanding (million)	3,364,890	3,804,050	4,411,501	4,895,252	5,315,041	4,716,281
Percentage to total outstanding	8.26%	7.92%	8.00%	7.80%	7.70%	6.45%
Total up to ₹200,000						
Number of accounts (million)	102.15	109.11	102.31	109.23	111.13	104.19
Percentage to total accounts	85%	83%	80%	79%	77.0%	75.25%
Limit sanctioned (million)	5,140,780	5,758,400	6,163,337	6,606,991	7,075,457	6,559,737
Percentage to total amounts	6.66%	7.49%	7.40%	7.00%	6.80%	5.60%
Amount outstanding (million)	3,838,880	4,566,210	5,148,328	5,331,569	5,674,536	5,065,292
Percentage to total outstanding	9.42%	9.51%	9.30%	8.40%	7.75%	6.93%

Source: Banking Statistical Returns for the years 2012, 2013, 2014, 2015 and 2016. Mumbai: RBI. Data for 2016 is from the Quarterly BSR1 Outstanding Credit of Scheduled Commercial Banks, http://dbie.rbi.org.in/DBIE/dbie.rbi?site=publications#!9, accessed October 3, 2016.

Note: The gender-wise break-up of the accounts and the amounts indicate that 75.4% of the loan accounts and 75.1% of the loan amounts have been made to men. The data for 2016 relates only to commercial banks and does not include data of RRBs.

this segment have kept pace (and grown marginally faster) with the growth of the customer base of the banks. However, while the absolute amount to this segment has gone up, the proportionality has marginally come down.

These accounts do not strictly represent the accounts of the "poor," because the data has been classified according to the size of the account. But still they represent the lower segment of the customers. If the data is sliced further, it is evident that about 83% of the accounts and 87% of the amounts would have gone to individuals. A large part of this portfolio (about 54% of the total number of SBA and 73% of amounts) represent direct lending to agriculture (see Table 2.6).

However, given that the banks are aggressively getting customers to the bank and the definition of financial inclusion not only includes a deposit account but also a loan account, this segment—particularly smaller loans of less than ₹25,000—should have shown an increase. It might still take time before the new customers are provided with all the four services envisaged by the RBI in its definition of financial inclusion. All the exuberance on the outreach, the increased accounts, and the roll out of technology does not seem to have resulted in tangible business for the banks in a meaningful manner.

A recent study by Chavan (2016) has some interesting and nuanced findings about SBAs. She argues that there was a fall in the focus on SBAs between 1991—when the policy moved toward liberalization and there were no branch opening requirements, and financial inclusion targets were passively subsumed under the priority sector lending targets—and 2005—a year in which the focus on financial inclusion was laid and the thrust continues. During the

Table 2.6 Purpose-wise Breakup of Small Borrowal Accounts as of March 31, 2015

	Accounts (Million)	% of Total	Sanction (₹ Trillion)	% of Total	Outstanding (₹ Trillion)	% of Total
Agriculture	63.62	57%	3,626.50	76%	3,884.33	58%
Direct	60.24	54%	3,459.70	73%	3,698.58	56%
Indirect	3.39	3%	166.80	4%	185.75	3%
Industry	1.62	1%	58.93	1%	79.20	1%
Transport operators	1.04	1%	29.44	1%	76.83	1%
Professional and other service	2.61	2%	80.02	2%	124.08	2%
Personal loans	32.75	29%	680.45	14%	2,144.85	32%
Housing	1.87	2%	92.66	2%	141.45	2%
Consumer durables	0.57	1%	24.95	1%	34.62	1%
Other personal loans	30.30	27%	562.84	12%	1,968.77	30%
Trade	4.78	4%	188.77	4%	232.97	3%
Wholesale trade	0.28	0%	9.94	0%	13.28	0%
Retail trade	4.50	4%	178.83	4%	219.69	3%
Finance	0.29	0%	17.45	0%	17.24	0%
All others	4.42	4%	64.34	1%	98.78	1%
Total	111.13	100%	4,745.91	100%	6,658.28	100%

Source: Banking Statistical Returns 2015. Mumbai: RBI (2016).

period, she argues, not only did the actual amounts of credit go down, but the number of accounts also went down. However, post-2005, she argues, the situation has vastly improved, particularly if one were to consider the real numbers than the nominal numbers. However, one significant point that Chavan (2016) makes is that with the opening of newer branches and the thrust on lending, the rural customers seem to be fairly well served in comparison to the urban poor who are further marginalized. Similarly, small customers in well-banked regions seem to be marginalized as against the customers in regions that are low on penetration statistics.

This is an interesting and important insight that tells us that as the overall activity moves toward the larger customers, or to areas where it is possible to find larger customers (urban areas and well-developed regions), the business imperative will ignore the smaller customers. It is important that the state thinks of an alternate strategy for ensuring meaningful inclusion of the excluded in well-banked and urban regions.

The discussion includes both the commercial banks and the RRBs, and the contribution of RRBs to this agenda would be significant considering that by design they are serving the smaller customers and have a higher requirement of priority sector advances. The RRBs by design have greater proportion of rural branches. The exclusive details of RRBs will be discussed in Chapter 3.

In examining the performance of the banks in the agenda of inclusion, it is important to recognize that there are not only the traditional institutions like cooperatives (both rural and urban) that have been serving the inclusive customers in the formal space. The statistics of the cooperative structure does not feature in this chapter. Similarly, there is a significant amount of participation by the Non-Banking Finance Company–Microfinance Institution (NBFC-MFI) and SHGs, which together have a credit outstanding more than a trillion rupees. The limits set for MFI loans is up to a maximum of ₹100,000 as per the NBFC-MFI master circular (RBI, 2014). It is clear that the microfinance sector has started significantly contributing to the overall agenda of inclusion on the credit side. In addition to this, there are also micro enterprise loans under the Prime Ministers' Mudra Yojana (PMMY) re defined as loans under ₹50,000. These loans are captured under the micro, medium and small enterprises (MSME) segment in the priority sector list. These will also be counted in the SBAs discussed previously. So the achievements of the banks should be seen in a larger perspective of the banking sector financing the MFI sector and creating additional outreach.

Table 2.7 "Small" (<₹25,000) Term Deposits from Customers over the Years

Year Ending March 31 →	2010	2011	2012	2013	2014	2015
Number of accounts (million)	53.28	52.62	53.85	55.70	66.80	
% of total number of accounts	37.10%	35.80%	32.80%	30.90%	33.30%	32.0%
Growth		−1.27%	2.30%	3.32%	16.61%	
Amount (₹ billion)	1,405.21	1,691.67	1,375.19	1,387.30	1,130.10	
% of total deposits collected	5.10%	5.20%	3.60%	3.10%	2.20%	1.4%
Growth		16.93%	−23.01%	0.87%	−22.76%	

Source: Banking Statistical Returns, 2011, 2012, 2013, 2014 and 2015. Mumbai: RBI.

While there is enough data at the granular level on the borrowings, the data on the deposit/savings side is a bit sketchy. The cut on deposit size is not available in the current statistics. The performance on the small deposits is not significantly better than the progress on loans. While the RBI does not define "small deposit accounts" for the purpose of analysis, term deposits less than ₹25,000 have been considered. If Table 2.7 is examined, it is evident that while the number of accounts has grown marginally in the earlier years, but significantly in 2013–14, the amount of deposits collected has indeed fallen. Therefore, it can be safely said that the entire activity of financial inclusion of account opening and providing for outlets is not necessarily getting reflected in the main activity of the bank of collecting deposits and providing loans. The details of deposits are available in Appendix 2.2 and those of credit are in Appendices 2.3, 2.4, 2.5, and 2.6.

PRIORITY SECTOR LENDING

While SBA might be one way of looking at inclusivity, another way is to look at the achievements in the targets given for priority sector lending. During the past year, the norms for the priority sector were made a bit more stringent. Apart from the target that was kept for weaker sections, there were additional sub-targets given for lending to small and marginal farmers as well as micro-enterprises. While this was tightened, the RBI also notified and opened up a platform for trading of priority sector achievements through priority sector lending certificates (PSLCs). A look at the achievement under the priority sector lending (PSL) norms in Table 2.8 shows that on the whole both the banks have almost achieved the targets on an overall basis. However, we also see a shortfall in direct agriculture and in weaker section lending targets by private sector banks, where those banks preferred indirect agriculture to direct agriculture. The private banks and foreign banks were quite active in the MSME sector.

Table 2.8 Achievement Under Priority Sector Advances by Categories of Banks (March 2015)

₹ in Billion

	Public Sector	Private Sector	Foreign Banks	Total
ANBC	45,850	12,284	3,007	61,141
Off balance sheet exposure	5,423	3,554	1,733	10,710
Direct agriculture	13%	10%	0%	12%
Indirect agriculture	4%	8%	1%	5%
Total agriculture	17%	18%	1%	17%
Weaker sections	11%	6%	1%	9%
MSME	14%	18%	8%	15%
Housing	5%	6%	1%	5%
Educational	1%	0%	0%	1%
Total priority sector	38%	43%	32%	39%

Source: Statistical Tables Relating to Banks in India STRBI: Table No. 17, http://dbie.rbi.org.in/DBIE/dbie.rbi?site=publications#!3, accessed September 4, 2016.
Note: ANBC: Adjusted net bank credit.
MSME: Micro Small and Medium Enterprises.

But the nonachievement of loans in the weaker section segment is indicating that while sectoral clients could be dealt with, dealing with small and scattered clients who are poor remains a problem.

As we go forward, there will be more and more people chasing the priority sector targets. The MFIs that have now been awarded banking license will have to find ways and means of not only lending to agriculture, but also achieving the steep number of 75% of adjusted net bank credit (ANBC) under the priority sector. As of now, the MFIs which have been issued bank licenses can consider themselves as having achieved the targets because most of their portfolio not only qualifies for priority sector but also for weaker section loans. However, they would be under pressure to build an agriculture book. While SFBs are prohibited from buying PSLCs (except for sub-targets when the overall targets are achieved) they will be net sellers of PSLCs. So the new architecture is a bit of good news that the banks can trade these certificates (or swap them) for a nominal fee and still specialize, but the bad news is that the sub-targets have become sharper and more stringent. The details of how the RBI administers the PSLC are given in Box 2.2.

Box 2.2 Details of PSLC Trading Guidelines

A scheme of PSLCs was introduced in April 2016. The RBI provided a platform to enable trading in the certificates through its CBS portal (e-Kuber). All scheduled commercial banks (including RRBs), urban cooperative banks, small finance banks (when they become operational), and local area banks (LABs) are eligible to participate in trading. Some of the main features of the scheme are:

- Four kinds of PSLCs: Agriculture, small and marginal farmers (SF/MF), microenterprises, and general can be bought and sold via the platform.
- The certificates will have a standard lot size of ₹2.5 million and its multiples.
- There will be no transfer of credit risk on underlying assets as there is no transfer of tangible assets or related cash flows.
- Banks will be permitted to issue PSLCs up to 50% of the previous year's priority sector lending achievement without having the underlying assets in their books. Banks should meet priority sector targets through direct lending and net PSLCs.
- Banks may be required to invest in the Rural Infrastructure Development Fund (RIDF)/ other funds to the extent of the shortfall.
- A bank with a shortfall in achieving any sub-target (for example, SF/MF, microenterprises) will have to buy specific PSLCs to achieve the target. However, if a bank has a shortfall only with respect to the overall target, it could buy any PSLC.
- PSLCs will not be valid beyond the reporting date (March 31), irrespective of the date of first sale.
- A bank's priority sector lending achievement will be computed as the sum of outstanding priority sector loans and the net nominal value of the PSLCs issued and purchased. Such computation will be done separately where sub-targets are prescribed as on the reporting date.

Source: Annual Report of RBI. Mumbai: RBI. 2016.

CREDIT TO WEAKER SECTIONS AND WOMEN

The definition of weaker sections (see Box 2.3) is broad based and has two elements in it. The first element is where weaker sections could be reached through organized structures. For instance, the beneficiaries under National Rural Livelihoods Mission (NRLM), National Urbal Livelihoods Mission (NULM), and SHGs in general have institutional structures and more than ₹500 billion was given as loans to these sections. However, small farmers, artisans, manual scavengers, and members of the minority communities are somewhat difficult to reach. The

Box 2.3 Definition of Weaker Sections Under the Priority Sector Lending Norms

Category

(a) Small and marginal farmers;
(b) Artisans, village, and cottage industries where individual credit limits do not exceed ₹50,000;
(c) Beneficiaries of Swarnjayanti Gram Swarozgar Yojana (SGSY), now NRLM;
(d) Scheduled castes and Scheduled tribes;
(e) Beneficiaries of differential rate of interest (DRI) scheme;
(f) Beneficiaries under Swarna Jayanti Shahari Rozgar Yojana (SJSRY), now NULM;
(g) Beneficiaries under the scheme for rehabilitation of manual scavengers;
(h) Loans to SHGs;
(i) Loans to distressed farmers indebted to non-institutional lenders;
(j) Loans to distressed persons other than farmers not exceeding ₹50,000 per borrower to prepay their debt to non-institutional lenders;
(k) Loans to individual women beneficiaries up to ₹50,000 per borrower;
(l) Loans sanctioned under (a) to (k) to persons from minority communities as may be notified by GoI from time to time. In states where one of the minority communities notified is, in fact, in majority, item (l) will cover only the other notified minorities. These states/union territories are Jammu and Kashmir, Punjab, Meghalaya, Mizoram, Nagaland, and Lakshadweep.

Source: Report of the Internal Working Group to Revisit Existing Priority Sector Lending Guidelines. Mumbai: RBI. March 2015.

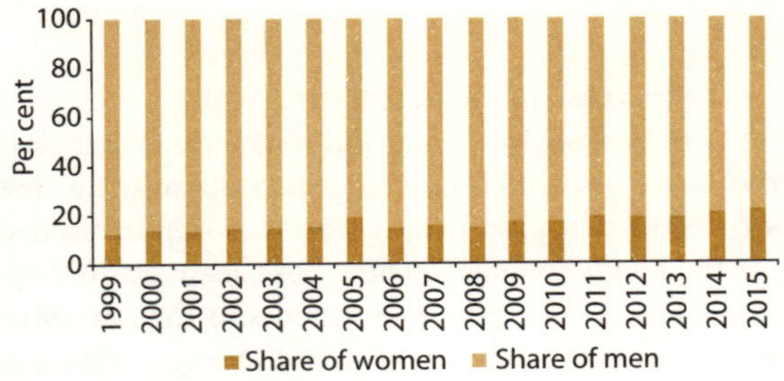

Figure 2.5 Share of Bank Credit Under SBAs by Gender

Source: Chavan (2016).

difference in the achievement of the private sector versus the state-owned banks may also be partly explained by the overall exposure that the public sector banks have toward these organized set of borrowers.

Similarly, Chavan (2016) argues that the relative share of women in the SBA has been going up steadily and this largely represents the rural areas. Even this growth could be attributed to the growth of SHGs and their linkage to the banking system.

NONPERFORMING ASSETS IN PSL

One of the important aspects up for discussion during the year was the issue of nonperforming assets (NPAs). If the portfolio of PSL advances were to be reviewed for the past three years, it is evident that they have improved relatively, though on the whole the proportion of NPAs is slightly higher than the proportion of advances to the PSLs (Table 2.9). What is important to note is that the private sector banks seem to be doing very well on managing NPAs in the priority sector portfolio. The fact that the achievement of private sector banks on the PSL targets is marginally higher than public sector banks is to be considered. However, data in Table 2.8 shows that the private sector banks are achieving targets through lending to MSME, housing, and indirect agriculture segments—which carry relatively larger ticket sizes and fall short on the sub-segments of agriculture direct and weaker section loans. The public sector banks are looking at achieving these tougher targets, even though they

Table 2.9 Relative Share of Advances and NPA over the Years

	Priority Sector		Non Priority Sector	
Bank Group	**Share of Advances**	**Share of NPAs**	**Share of Advances**	**Share of NPAs**
Public sector banks				
2013	32%	43%	68%	57%
2014	33%	37%	67%	63%
2015	34%	36%	66%	64%
Nationalized banks				
2013	32%	42%	68%	58%
2014	34%	38%	66%	62%
2015	35%	36%	65%	64%
SBI group				
2013	31%	44%	69%	56%
2014	32%	34%	68%	66%
2015	30%	36%	70%	64%
Private sector banks				
2013	30%	26%	70%	74%
2014	32%	27%	68%	73%
2015	31%	23%	69%	77%
All SCBs (excluding foreign banks)				
2013	31%	41%	69%	59%
2014	33%	36%	67%	64%
2015	33%	35%	67%	65%

Source: Statistical Tables Relating to Banks in India (Table 18), http://dbie.rbi.org.in/DBIE/dbie.rbi?site=publications#!9, accessed on September 5, 2016.

may not be as lucrative and may result in a greater NPA. The dilemma of the profit versus inclusion seems to be addressed more easily in state-controlled banks.

CONCLUDING NOTES

Overall, the year had some mixed results to report. Post-2005, ever since the banks adapted the financial inclusion planning and reintroduced quotas for opening of branches in unbanked locations, it can be seen that there is a renewed vigor in opening branches. While a large part of the rural branches are in locations where there is a unique branch, what is more interesting is the growth of branches in semi-urban locations where the banks have spread their branches in locations where other bank branches are operating. This shows that the banks would go to locations, if the locations promised business.

While the mission mode of PMJDY has resulted in opening of accounts, this should only be seen as an effort to create an ecosystem for a more meaningful inclusion program. This has not resulted in credit accounts at ₹25,000 level take off in a big way (as against the exponential growth shown by this segment by the MFIs discussed in Chapter 10).

The data granularity on deposits does not help us to do much analysis and if reporting on deposits gets more detailed there could be enough research to provide policy inputs to both the government and the RBI.

The increase in the penetration with weaker sections and expansion of portfolio to increase the relative share of women has happened possibly due to structures that provided aggregation opportunities for the banks to engage with these segments of the population. Therefore, investments in the community ecosystem of formation and strengthening of SHGs and similar such efforts should continue. It would be much smarter to make public investments in creating the ecosystem for the vulnerable to engage with the banking system rather than to provide transactional subventions.

As data seem to indicate, and as argued by Chavan (2016), just allowing the markets to evolve does not seem to naturally help the cause of inclusion. However, smart policies that mandate lending to vulnerable sections seems to produce results. In this context, there might be much more to cheer in the coming years with two initiatives. First, the policy initiative that mandates sub-targets for dealing with micro enterprises and marginal and small farmers will pressure the banks to find innovative ways of dealing with these customers. Second, the ecosystem initiative of setting up Mudra and opening of SFBs and PBs will drive institutional innovation. Going by the history of how mandates and ecosystem innovations have panned out, this could only be a positive news.

APPENDIX 2.1
Progress of Commercial Banking at a Glance

Important Indicators	June 1969	March 2011	March 2012	March 2013	March 2014	March 2015
No. of commercial banks	89	169	173	155	151	152
Scheduled commercial banks	73	165	169	151	146	148
Of which: Regional rural banks	–	82	82	64	57	56
Nonscheduled commercial banks	16	4	4	4	5	4
Number of offices of SCBs in India^	8,262	90,263	98,330	105,437	117,280	125,672
(a) Rural	1,833	33,683	36,356	39,195	45,177	48,498
(b) Semi-urban	3,342	22,843	25,797	28,165	31,442	33,703
(c) Urban	1,584	17,490	18,781	19,902	21,448	22,997
(d) Metropolitan	1,503	16,247	17,396	18,175	19,213	20,474
Population per office (in thousands)	64	13	12	12	11	10
Deposits of SCBs in India (₹ billion)	46	52,080	59,091	69,343	79,134	88,989
Of which: (a) Demand	21	6,417	6,253	7,672	8,272	7,801
(b) Time	25	45,663	52,838	61,672	70,862	81,188
Credit of SCBs in India (₹ billion)	36	39,421	46,119	53,932	61,390	64,998
Deposits of SCBs per office (₹ million)	5.6	577	601	658	675	708

Important Indicators	June 1969	March 2011	March 2012	March 2013	March 2014	March 2015
Credit of SCBs per office (₹ million)	4.4	437	469	512	524	517
Per capita deposits of SCBs (₹)	88	43,034	48,732	55,445	62,252	68,576
Per capita credit of SCBs (₹)	68	32,574	38,033	43,123	48,294	50,089
Deposits of SCBs as percentage of national income (NNP at factor cost, at current prices)	16	82	81	84	86	80
SCBs' advances to priority sector (₹ billion)	5	13,373	14,909	18,180	21,549	23,782
Share of priority sector advances in total credit of SCBs (percent)	14	34	32	34	35	37
Share of priority sector advances in total non-food credit of SCBs (percent)	15	35	33	34	36	37
Credit deposit ratio	78	76	78	78	78	73
Investment deposit ratio	29	29	29	29	28	29
Cash deposit ratio	8	7	6	6	5	6

Source: Basic Statistical Returns of Commercial Banks in India, Vol. 44. Mumbai: RBI, 2015.
Note: ^ Excludes administrative offices.

APPENDIX 2.2
Distribution of Term Deposits of Scheduled Commercial Banks

Percentage Distribution of Term Deposits of Scheduled Commercial Banks According to the Size of Deposits and Broad Ownership Category March 2015 (%)

Size of Deposits (in ₹ Million)	Individuals		Others		Total	
	No. of Accounts	Amount	No. of Accounts	Amount	No. of Accounts	Amount
Less than 0.025	31.5	2.4	36.6	0.3	32.0	1.4
0.025 and above but less than 0.1	36.4	13.1	29.5	1.6	35.7	7.7
0.1 and above but less than 1.5	31.3	55.7	28.7	7.6	31.0	33.0
1.5 and above but less than 10.0	0.8	15.9	4.0	13.7	1.1	14.9
10.0 and above	0.0	12.9	1.2	76.8	0.1	43.0
Total	100.0	100.0	100.0	100.0	100.0	100.0

Source: Basic Statistical Returns of Commercial Banks in India, Vol. 44. Mumbai: RBI, 2016.

APPENDIX 2.3
Outstanding Credit to Small Borrowal Accounts According to Population Group

Numbers in Million; Amount in ₹ Billion

Population Group	Up to ₹ 0.025 Million			Between ₹ 0.025 and ₹ 0.2 Million			Above ₹ 0.2 Million		
	No. of Accounts	Credit Limit	Amount Outstanding	No. of Accounts	Credit Limit	Amount Outstanding	No. of Accounts	Credit Limit	Amount Outstanding
Rural	12	196	182	31.32	2,410	2,197	7,005	6,205	3,605
Semi-urban	7	114	106	24.41	2,026	1,845	8,863	7,305	5,64
Urban	4	49	42	9.72	857	724	7,204	15,609	10,273
Metropolitan	7	71	30	15.80	1,352	550	10,042	68,360	43,590
All India	30	430	360	81.27	6,646	5,315	33,114	97,479	63,110

Source: Basic Statistical Returns of Commercial Banks in India, Vol. 44. Mumbai: RBI, 2016.

APPENDIX 2.4
Outstanding Credit to Small Borrowal Accounts According to Category of Borrowers

Percentage Distribution of Outstanding Credit to Small Borrowal Accounts of Scheduled Commercial Banks According to Broad Category of Borrowers March 2015 (%)

	Individual							
	Male		Females		Other		Total	
Population Group	No. of Accounts	Amount Outstanding	No. of Accounts	Amount Outstanding	No. of Accounts	Amount Outstanding	No. of Accounts	Amount Outstanding
Rural	77.1	78.5	20.0	18.6	2.9	2.8	100.0	100.0
Semi-urban	70.9	72.3	25.8	24.6	3.3	3.1	100.0	100.0
Urban	70.7	70.0	25.3	24.2	4.0	5.8	100.0	100.0
Metropolitan	81.4	77.0	16.7	16.6	1.9	6.5	100.0	100.0
All-India	75.4	75.1	21.7	21.2	2.9	3.7	100.0	100.0

Source: Basic Statistical Returns of Commercial Banks in India, Vol. 44. Mumbai: RBI, 2016.

APPENDIX 2.5
Outstanding Credit to Small Borrowal Accounts According to Occupation

Population Group-wise Outstanding Credit of Small Borrowal Accounts of Scheduled Commercial Banks According to Occupation March 2015 (Amount in ₹ Million)

	Rural			Semi-urban		
Occupation	No. of Accounts	Credit Limit	Amount Outstanding	No. of Accounts	Credit Limit	Amount Outstanding
I. Agriculture	34,319,948	2,085,191	1,964,697	22,843,094	1,541,314	1,486,471
1. Direct finance	32,669,166	1,994,887	1,879,548	21,600,963	1,464,814	1,414,958
2. Indirect finance	1,650,782	90,304	85,149	1,242,131	76,500	71,513
II. Industry	668,549	33,173	26,039	438,515	25,762	19,809
III. Transport operators	109,263	12,153	8,778	164,952	17,287	13,947
IV. Professional and other services	769,857	42,370	34,171	654,674	37,649	29,872
V. Personal loans	3,972,382	278,918	221,552	5,200,054	401,533	309,053
1. Loans for housing	555,603	44,165	33,057	546,962	48,495	33,192
2. Loans for purchase of consumer durables	172,440	11,941	8249	155,678	13,006	9,213
3. Other personal loans	3,244,339	222,812	180,247	4,497,414	340,032	266,648
VI. Trade	1,984,635	104,249	83,409	1,406,739	84.523	66,287
1. Wholesale trade	95,141	5,265	4,395	90,469	4,675	3,801
2. Retail trade	1,889,494	98,984	79,014	1,316,270	79,849	62,486
VII. Finance	139,558	10,267	7,274	91,364	7,182	4,943
VIII. All others	958,187	39,598	32,234	807,567	24,743	20,204
Total bank credit	42,922,379	2,605,920	2,378,155	31,606,959	2,139,994	1,950,586

	Urban/Metropolitan			All India		
Occupation	No. of Accounts	Credit Limit	Amount Outstanding	No. of Accounts	Credit Limit	Amount Outstanding
I. Agriculture	6,461,809	433,164	401,041	63,624,851	3,626,505	3,884,332
1. Direct finance	5,968,672	404,071	375,189	60,238,801	3,459,701	3,698,577
2. Indirect finance	493,137	29,093	25,852	3,386,050	166,804	185,755

Occupation	Urban/Metropolitan No. of Accounts	Urban/Metropolitan Credit Limit	Urban/Metropolitan Amount Outstanding	All India No. of Accounts	All India Credit Limit	All India Amount Outstanding
II. Industry	510,837	33,356	38,898	1,617,901	58,935	79,204
III. Transport operators	761,742	54,103	36,237	1,035,957	29,440	76,829
IV. Professional and other services	1,186,636	60,038	49,471	2,611,167	80,019	124,081
V. Personal loans	23,575,682	1,614,240	716,237	32,748,118	680,451	2,144,845
1. Loans for housing	767,788	75,206	50,087	1,870,353	92,659	141,455
2. Loans for purchase of consumer durables	245,742	17,158	11,432	573,860	24,947	34,620
3. Other personal loans	22,562,152	1,521,876	654,718	30,303,905	562,844	1,968,771
VI. Trade	1,386,793	83,274	67,441	4,778,167	188,773	232,970
1. Wholesale trade	92,121	5,085	7,047	277,731	9,940	13,281
2. Retail trade	1,294,672	78,189	60,394	4,500,436	178,833	219,689
VII. Finance	55,388	5,021	4,229	286,310	17,449	17,238
VIII. All others	2,657,026	46,347	32,693	4,422,780	64,342	98,785
Total bank credit	36,595,913	2,329,543	1,346,246	111,125,251	4,745,913	6,658,284

Source: Basic Statistical Returns of Commercial Banks in India, Volume 44. Mumbai, RBI (2016).

APPENDIX 2.6
Bank Group-wise Credit According to Loan Size and as of March 2015

(Accounts in Million, Amounts in ₹ Billion)

Bank Group	Population Group	Less than ₹0.025 Million No. of Accounts	Less than ₹0.025 Million Credit Limit	Less than ₹0.025 Million Amount Outstanding	₹0.025 to 0.20 Million No. of Accounts	₹0.025 to 0.20 Million Credit Limit	₹0.025 to 0.20 Million Amount Outstanding	Above ₹0.20 Million No. of Accounts	Above ₹0.20 Million Credit Limit	Above ₹0.20 Million Amount Outstanding
SBI and Associates	Rural	1,289	23	21	5,897	478	432	1,717	2,968	972
	Semi-urban	1,223	21	19	7,104	626	553	3,169	2,167	1,682
	Urban	281	4	3	1,907	192	147	2,178	3,276	2,416
	Metro	96	1	1	557	59	38	1,512	12,009	8,525
	All India	2,888	49	45	15,464	1,354	1,169	8,576	20,420	13,595
Nationalized Banks	Rural	4,522	78	72	14,685	1,139	1,057	3,402	2,265	1,910
	Semi-urban	2,694	46	42	10,874	914	845	3,775	3,347	2,630
	Urban	1,142	17	15	4,475	405	354	3,006	7,658	5,350
	Metro	408	4	6	1,547	155	138	2,393	32,071	22,056
	All India	8,766	145	135	31,581	2,613	2,393	12,575	45,342	31,946
Foreign Banks	Rural	0	0	0	0	0	0	0	23	18
	Semi-urban	0	0	0	0	0	0	0	16	9
	Urban	3	0	0	11	1	1	21	276	83
	Metro	1,225	11	2	2,982	266	64	1,061	7,011	3,178
	All India	1,228	11	2	2,994	267	64	1,081	7,326	3,289

(Continued)

(Continued)

Bank Group	Population Group	Less than ₹0.025 Million			₹0.025 to 0.20 Million			Above ₹0.20 Million		
		No. of Accounts	**Credit Limit**	**Amount Outstanding**	**No. of Accounts**	**Credit Limit**	**Amount Outstanding**	**No. of Accounts**	**Credit Limit**	**Amount Outstanding**
Regional Rural Banks	Rural	4,843	81	78	9,757	716	639	1,467	627	453
	Semi-urban	1,301	22	21	3,279	249	230	578	265	212
	Urban	177	3	3	547	46	40	198	146	109
	Metro	10	0	0	40	4	3	32	28	23
	All India	6,331	106	102	13,623	1,015	913	2,275	1,066	797
Private Sector Banks	Rural	945	14	11	986	77	69	419	323	252
	Semi-urban	1,970	25	23	3,162	238	217	1,341	1,509	1,109
	Urban	2,624	25	21	2,783	213	183	1,802	4,253	2,315
	Metro	5,105	54	21	10,675	869	307	5,046	17,241	9,808
	All India	10,645	118	75	17,605	1,397	776	8,607	23,325	13,483
Total	Rural	11,598	196	182	31,324	2,410	2,197	7,005	6,205	3,605
	Semi-urban	7,188	114	106	24,419	2,026	1,845	8,863	7,305	5,641
	Urban	4,227	49	42	9,723	857	724	7,204	15,609	10,273
	Metro	6,845	71	30	15,801	1,352	550	10,042	68,360	43,590
	All India	29,858	430	360	81,267	6,646	5,315	33,114	97.479	63,110

Source: Basic Statistical Returns of Commercial Banks in India Volume 44. Mumbai: RBI, 2016.

REFERENCES

Chavan, P. 2016, September. "Bank Credit to Small Borrowers: An Analysis Based on Supply and Demand Side Indicators." Reserve Bank of India Occasional Papers, No. 35 (1 and 2). Mumbai: RBI.

RBI (Reserve Bank of India). 2014. *Master Circular Non Banking Finance Company -Microfinance Institutions" (NBFCMFIs) Directions*. Reserve Bank of India, Department of Non Banking Supervision. Mumbai: RBI. Available at: https://www.rbi.org.in/scripts/BS_ViewMasCirculardetails.aspx?id=9012#4 (Accessed on October 1, 2016).

Regional Rural Banks

3

Chapter

There have been changes in the inclusive finance architecture in the past year, and this has significant implications for the survival and performance of RRBs, as they look into the future. The RBI issued in-principle licenses for 10 SFBs, thereby potentially changing the landscape for inclusive finance in India. These licenses were given to existing MFIs, a LAB, and a Non-Banking Finance Company (NBFC). The 10 institutions together represent about ₹330 billion in portfolio as of March 2016 as against a portfolio of ₹2,067 billion of all the RRBs together. There were two new licensees who had a portfolio size similar to the top six RRBs and the rest of them had smaller portfolios. However, it is important to note that the SFBs would have greater degree of operational freedom in opening rural branches, operate in a more diversified geographical setting, and have access to recapitalization and flexibility in offering profitable products. However, the new banks also have the lending requirements of priority sector on par with RRBs at 75% of the adjusted net bank credit. Therefore, the RRBs need to be wary of the new SFBs taking away the best of the RRB customers in areas that have significant economic activity, while the RRBs operating in the backward and remote areas would be left with the task of developmental banking. As the space opens up, it would be very interesting to see the competition emerging. As of now, the extant business of the entities that have got licenses has limitations on accessing resources and offering loan products.

On the other hand, there was no effect of the amendment carried out to the RRB Act that opened up space for new investors to come in. The changes brought about (and reported in the previous report) potentially could get in a set of private sector investors, along with board positions subject to the proviso that the majority control would remain in the

Box 3.1 Dr Y.V. Reddy on the Question of Privatization of RRBs

MSS: So my next questions are on SFB and RRB.

Dr Reddy: RRB was conceptually right, but it failed.

MSS: But now with consolidation …

Dr Reddy: I don't know how the consolidation process is going, but when I was there the proposal was to have one RRB for one sponsor bank in one state.

MSS: More or less in that direction. There are 57 banks now.

Dr Reddy: My point originally also was, you are talking of privatizing nationalized banks etc., you can just as well privatize RRBs.

MSS: Actually first step toward that has happened last year, there was an RRB act that was amended, allowing the fourth investor to come in and the bill says the government and banks total will be 51%. But they have said that in recognition of this, you could have an independent director etc. So the concept of private participation has started creeping in.

Dr Reddy: That doesn't help. As long as RRB is under a separate statute, it cannot change. You have to convert these into banking companies, and then privatize.

MSS: That is to reduce government ownership below 50%.

Dr Reddy: No no, the percentage is irrelevant when an institution is under a statute, and not under Companies Act.

MSS: But Nayak committee suggested because that will less than 50% ownership, the public sector banks will be out of CVC, RTI, and other things and therefore....

Dr Reddy: No I am not sure if it is the case, again I may be wrong. Legally, when it is under a statute, it is under CVC. When it is under company law, the definition of a government company applies to it. All I am saying is that RRBs were established under the RRB Act, once you covert it to company, then company law will apply. Then the definition of a government company comes, and the share of the government becomes relevant.

government ecosystem. However, Tankha (2015) reports that at least one RRB is trying to get permissions for a public offering of shares. There would be some time before the investments come in, but if indeed the amendments pave way for investments, there is a possibility that the larger and the healthier RRBs would grow faster.

With one merger, the total number of RRBs came down from 57 to 56 in 2015 and remained at the same number by March 2016. It appears that this number will be a stable number as there has been no further action on consolidation of RRBs ever since. However, what is important is the growth of the RRB touch-points that have been going up. After remaining flat in terms of number of branches, there was a growth of about 10% by 2015 and a marginal growth in the branch spread in 2016. However, what is important is that the RRBs as a group added 5,586 ultra-small branches (USB) to their network, thereby increasing the footprint beyond the regular branches (see Table 3.1). More importantly, the ultra-small branches came up in large numbers in North, Central, and Western regions (in addition to South)—areas that were relatively underbanked.

Overall the RRBs continue to be significantly present in the rural and semi-urban areas. During the past five years, the RRB branch network grew by nearly 20%, but this was not in sync with the growth of the branch network of the banking system as a whole (see Table 3.2). That is the reason we find that the relative share of the RRBs in the total banking network is falling between 2011 and 2016. This is reflected in the relative share going down across all the four segments, but given the policy of asking banks to open 25% of their incremental branches in unbanked locations, there is a growth in the number of unique locations—particularly in the rural areas where commercial banks are present (see Chapter 2 on banking).

Table 3.1 RRB Branch Network over the Years (According to Region)

Region	1996	2011	2012	2013	2014	2015	2016	USBs 2016
North	1,980	2,171	2,312	2,469	2,618	2,849	3,014	1,426
Northeast	667	693	696	696	721	822	849	192
East	3,610	3,742	3,796	3,836	4,057	4,424	4,467	323
Central	4,670	4,912	5,127	5,440	5,821	6,146	6,259	1,298
West	1,022	1,052	1,142	1,192	1,294	1,378	1,436	642
South	2,723	3,328	3,556	3,849	4,028	4,644	4,879	1,705
Total	14,672	15,898	16,629	17,482	18,539	20,263	20,904	5,586

Source: Basic Statistical Returns of Scheduled commercial banks in India. Mumbai: RBI, various years; Regional Rural Banks Key Statistics. 2016. Mumbai: NABARD.

Table 3.2 RRB Branch Network over the Years (According to Location)

	Share of RRBs in the Banking Network							Share of RRBs in the Banking Network (2016)
Location	2011	(2011)	2012	2013	2014	2015	2016	
Rural	11,778	34.97%	12,263	12,850	13,609	14,644	15,606	31.27%
Semiurban	3,026	13.25%	3,192	3,362	3,569	4,011	3,846	10.77%
Urban	960	5.49%	1,009	1,080	1,153	1,345	1,282	5.17%
Metro	134	0.82%	165	190	208	260	170	0.77%
Total	15,898	17.61%	16,629	17,482	18,539	20,263	20,904	15.77%

Source: Basic Statistical Returns of Scheduled commercial banks in India. Mumbai: RBI, various years. Regional Rural Banks Key Statistics. 2016, Mumbai: NABARD.

Table 3.3 Recapitalization of RRBs: Various Phases

Phase	Number of RRBs Recapitalized	Amount of Recap (₹ Billion)
Till January 2000 (six phases)	187 (158 fully, 29 partially)	21.88
2007–08	27	17.96
2012	27 (16 fully capitalized, 11 partially capitalized)	10.00
2013*	10 (new, of which 8 fully capitalized and 2 partially) all the 11 that were partially capitalized were fully capitalized in 2013	12.00
2014	2 (completion of the capitalization process)	
2015–16	3 RRBs	0.15

Source: Trend and Progress of Banking in India, Various Years. Mumbai: RBI; NABARD Annual Report 2015–16.
Note: * Total 40 RRBs have been identified for recapitalization. Period for completion of the entire process has been extended up to March 2014 with a total outlay of ₹22 billion.

The last report highlighting the performance of RRBs for 2014 had indicated that there were no RRBs that had incurred losses during that year. However, that record was short-lived, with five RRBs slipping into a loss for years ending 2015 and 2016. Eight of the RRBs had accumulated losses (though three of them had current profits). Four of the RRBs had capital-to-risk weighted adjusted ratio (CRAR) of less than the stipulated 9%. The government provided share capital assistance to these RRBs (Table 3.3).

Box 3.2 Former Governor C. Rangarajan on Consolidation of RRBs

MSS: Let me come back to you regarding the RRB issue. Your report had suggested that there should be no further consolidation of the RRBs. Your report came out in 1992 but there has still been some consolidation and now we have stabilized it to 57. We don't know whether it will be further consolidated. There was this sense that there should be one RRB per state or two RRBs per state. By doing this are we looking at only the viability part of it.

Dr Rangarajan: What is the concept of RRBs? The concept of RRBs is essentially close to Local Area Banks (LAB). The region was not defined in terms of a state, the region was defined to be much smaller.

MSS: It was in fact closer to the village cooperatives.

Dr Rangarajan: Being bound with the region was an important dimension of the concept. And that will create local interest and local initiatives. So if we merge RRBs across districts and create one per state, I don't know whether the RRB will be different from a commercial bank.

MSS: The other thing that is happened with RRBs is an amendment to the Act, which allowed a fourth shareholder to come in. State government, central government, sponsor bank, and a private investor could be shareholders provided that the combined shareholding of the state and the central government does not go below 50%. And along with it there also came a provision that there will be an independent director which they will appoint, which might be outside the system. Is that a good direction to go? Will that get some dynamism in RRBs?

Dr Rangarajan: Basically, we are converting RRBs into ordinary commercial banks. After this change, will they remain committed to the original mandate? It is not very clear. Because inclusion of private sector by itself is not a bad idea; this we had done with the nationalized banks.

BEYOND THE BRANCH NETWORK

All the RRBs are completely computerized and interoperable and they have started setting up ATMs and started issuing debit cards. This enabled the banks to not only set up ATMs but also issue debit cards. The RRBs together had issued 28 million RuPay Debit cards as of August 2016. Compared to the skew that 3 of the 19 banks had 79% of the ATMs last year, this year two more banks, Andhra Pragati Grameen Bank and Karnataka Vikas Grameen Bank, started rolling out their ATMs (see Table 3.4). However, there is much progress to be achieved, even if one were to think of an on-site ATM at each of the branches. While it is possible for the customers of the RRBs to operate their cards in the merchant establishments and in the ATMs of other banks including the white label ATMs, the interchange

Table 3.4 ATM Network of Regional Rural Banks

Bank Name	Total
Allahabad UP Gramin Bank	153
Andhra Pradesh Grameena Vikas Bank	2
Andhra Pragathi Grameena Vikas Bank	59
Baroda Gujarat Gramin Bank	8
Baroda Rajasthan Kshetriya Gramin Bank	10
Baroda Uttar Prdaesh Gramin Bank	5
Chaitanya Godavari Grameena Bank	29
Deccan Gramina Bank	2
Dena Gujarat Gramin Bank	8
Karnataka Vikas Gramin Bank	83
Kashi Gomati Samyut Gramin Bank	43
Kaveri Grameena Bank	1
Kerala Gramin Bank	277
Maharashtra Gramin Bank	10
Malwa Gramin Bank	2
Odisha Gramya Bank	25
Pragathi Krishna Gramin Bank	250
Prathama Gramin Bank	42
Rajasthan Marudhara Gramin Bank	5
Sutlej Gramin Bank	10
Total	1,024

Source: National Payments Corporation of India.

charges would turn out to be very high—given that the customers would have small ticket transactions, it is important that the RRBs quickly roll out their own infrastructure in their area of operations.

BUSINESS

The performance of the RRBs marginally improved in terms of profitability from 2014 to 2015, but deteriorated to levels lower than 2014 in the year 2016. Also from all the banks making profits, five banks slipped to losses for two years running. These banks are operating in difficult areas—Jammu and Kashmir, Jharkhand, Manipur, Nagaland, and Rajasthan. A detailed analysis of the business potential of these banks needs to be done to see if they would be sustainable in the long run. In the meantime, with the intervention of NABARD, three of them were recapitalized by the government to attain a CRAR of 9%. While the consolidation has led to some vibrancy, the space needs to be watched carefully as the RRBs brace up for competition from the SFBs, which have a similar priority sector lending requirements and the pressure to open rural branches.

Table 3.5 shows that the general improvement in the overall financial performance of RRBs from the time the consolidation started to the current year.

A look at the numbers show two trends that are worrying—the share of current accounts and savings

Table 3.5 Performance of RRBs over the Years (Figures for March 31 of Each Year)

Details	2011	2012	2013	2014	2015	2016
No. of RRBs	82	82	64	57	56	56
No. of branches	16,024	16,914	17,867	19,082	20,024	20,924
Net profit (₹ billion)	17.85	18.86	22.73	26.94	27.45	24.35
Profit/loss making RRBs	75/7	79/3	63/1	57/0	51/5	51/5
Deposits (₹ billion)	1,662	1,863	2054	2333	2,731	3,151
Loans and advances (₹ billion)	947	1,130	1359	1589	1,810	2,073
Credit-deposit (CD) ratio (%)	59.51	63.3	64.82	66.56	66	66
Share of CASA in deposits (%)	60.35	58.51	57	56.88	52	51
Share of PSA (%)	83.5	80	86		84	87
Share of agri advances to total (%)	55.7	53	63		59.5	64.3
Share of advances to SF/MF (%)						42.31
Advances to weaker sections (%)						52.61
Gross NPA (%)	3.75	5.03	6.08	6.09	6.15	6.58
Net NPA %	2.05	2.98	3.59	3.52		3.94
Branch productivity					226 mn	249 mn
Staff productivity					53 mn	59 mn

Source: Trend and Progress of Banking India, Various Years. Mumbai: RBI; Financial Statements of RRBs. Mumbai: NABARD; Regional Rural Banks Key Statistics 2016, NABARD.

accounts (CASA) in RRBs has come down from about 60% to about 51%. CASA deposits are low-cost deposits which help in the profitability of the banks, and this number is significantly higher than the other commercial banks. However, as the RRBs are consolidating and moving toward bigger customers, the term deposit share may be going up. The reduction in CASA in itself is not a worry as long as the other parameters are in check. The other parameters—the credit deposit ratio which shows the break-up between cash invested in investment and held in balances versus cash given away as advances—has remained flat at around 66% and this figure needs to be significantly high for the banks to earn profits. The relative share of priority sector advances and within that a significant share of agricultural advances opens the bank to risk of default. It can be seen in the NPA figures that these have significantly gone up from the year in which consolidation started. Therefore, there is a need to now look at the business mix of the RRBs in depth and ensure that the advantages of the consolidation are not frittered away.

FINANCIAL INCLUSION

While RRBs by definition were all about financial inclusion, particularly in the spirit in which they were set up, there have been many pulls and pressures on them and the policy has also moved. They were initially conceived as specialized local institutions that would have the cost structure and the local feel of a co-operative and the professionalism of a bank. However, over the years, the cost structure, particularly on the human resources front, has moved on par with the public sector banking system. While they have lost the cost advantage, the other limitations of geographic concentration, asset concentration, and limited growth and diversification opportunities haunt the RRBs. In the past years, there have been attempts to unshackle the RRBs by way of consolidation, easing of priority sector norms and allowing them to do other businesses. While this has helped in pulling up the RRBs a bit, they still are shackled from many limitations that lead them toward unviability. Therefore, the performance of RRBs in financial inclusion should be seen in this perspective.

Credit

Table 3.6 has details of loans made by RRBs in the loan categories of less than ₹25,000 and in the category of ₹25,000–200,000 (defined as SBAs). The numbers show that both the absolute number of accounts and the amount disbursed under the category of amounts up to ₹25,000 has decreased. While this is the case with banks also, the movement away

Table 3.6 Details of Credit to Small Borrowal Accounts over the Years

Year Ending March 31 →	2011	2012	2013	2014	2015
Loan amount less than ₹25,000					
Number of accounts (million)	9.88	9.33	7.77	6.89	6.33
Percentage to total accounts	49.28%	44.99%	38.32%	32.07%	28.48%
Limit sanctioned (₹ billion)	164.20	167.43	115.31	115.24	105.71
Percentage to total amounts	13.85%	10.80%	5.27%	4.98%	4.84%
Amount outstanding (₹ billion)	151.26	162.22	142.52	108.92	102.07
Percentage to total outstanding	15.42%	13.94%	10.49%	6.86%	5.63
Loan amount ₹25,000 to ₹200,000					
Number of accounts (million)	9.34	10.29	10.95	12.60	13.62
Percentage to total accounts	46.55%	49.63%	53.98%	59%	61.29%
Limit sanctioned (billion)	662.80	720.90	794.58	915.14	1,014.79
Percentage to total amounts	55.91%	46.50%	36.30%	40%	46.42%
Amount outstanding (billion)	547.24	612.33	696.36	812.91	912.86
Percentage to total outstanding	55.77%	52.61%	51.26%	51%	50.37%
Total up to ₹200,000					
Number of accounts (million)	19.22	19.62	18.72	19.49	19.95
Percentage to total accounts with RRBs	95.82%	94.62%	92.30%	91%	89.77%

(Continued)

(Continued)

Year Ending March 31 →	2011	2012	2013	2014	2015
Limit sanctioned	827.01	888.33	909.89	1,030.37	1,120.50
Percentage to total amounts	69.76%	57.29%	41.56%	44.52%	51.25%
Amount outstanding (million)	698.50	774.56	838.89	921.84	1,014.93
Percentage to total outstanding with RRBs	71.19%	66.55%	61.75%	58.02%	56.00%

Source: Basic Statistical Returns of Scheduled Commercial Banks in India for the Years 2011–2015. Mumbai: RBI.
Note: The gender-wise break-up of the accounts and the amounts indicate that more than 75% of the loan accounts and amounts have been made to men.

from small accounts is a difficult contradiction that one may have to live with. Possibly the consolidation and profitability comes at a price, but what needs attention is the intermediary category of up to ₹200,000. There needs to be focused attention on this category of borrowers, to ensure that they do not get crowded out. While the proportions of RRBs are much better than commercial banks on the inclusion parameter, the directionality of the movement is not desirable.

Priority Sector

The targets for priority sector lending has been changing over the years. Initially, when RRBs were set up, they were expected to lend only to the target group comprising small and marginal farmers, landless laborers, rural artisans, and other weaker sections of society (RBI 2014). However, this was later changed and RRBs were permitted to lend 60% of their incremental lending to any sector, and later in 1997, their targets for priority sector were brought on par with commercial banks—in keeping with the overall thrust toward market-oriented liberalization policies. However, in 2002, based on a review, the targets for priority sector lending for RRBs were revised upwards to 60% of their ANBC. This target was retained, even when the definition of what constituted priority sector underwent some subtle changes. In December 2015, this target was again revised upwards to 75% of ANBC. This number is now on par with the target given to the SFBs. See Box 3.3 for details.

A closer examination of the purpose-wise breakup of the portfolio of the RRBs shows that a large portion of the portfolio goes to agriculture, and within that for direct finance to agriculture (Table 3.7). Unlike commercial banks, which are content at barely reaching the minimal requirements of the priority sector obligations (at 18% ANBC to agriculture, and to the extent possible through indirect, large credit), the RRBs continue to serve agriculture, and that too through direct loans. In 2015, 73% of

Box 3.3 New Guidelines for Priority Sector Lending to RRBs

The salient features of the new guidelines are:

- Targets: 75% of total outstanding to the sectors eligible for classification as priority sector lending and sub-sector targets as indicated in subsequent paragraphs.
- Categories of the Priority Sector: Medium enterprises, social infrastructure and renewable energy will form part of the priority sector, in addition to the existing categories, with a cap of 15% of total outstanding.
- Agriculture: 18% of total outstanding should be advanced to activities mentioned under agriculture.
- Small and Marginal Farmers: A target of 8% of total outstanding has been prescribed for small and marginal farmers within agriculture.*
- Micro-enterprises: A target of 7.5% of total outstanding has been prescribed for micro-enterprises.**
- Weaker Sectors: A target of 15% of total outstanding has been prescribed for weaker sections.
- Monitoring: Priority sector lending will be monitored on a quarterly as well as annual basis.

(* RRBs that have not achieved the 8% sub target may achieve the same in a phased manner, that is, 7% by March 2016 and 8% by March 2017.)

(** RRBs that have not achieved the 7.5% sub target may achieve the same in a phased manner, that is, 7% by March 2016 and 7.5% by March 2017.)

The revised guidelines will be operational with effect from January 1, 2016. The priority sector loans sanctioned under the guidelines issued prior to this date will continue to be classified under priority sector till repayment/maturity/renewal.

Source: Regional Rural Banks PSL Targets and Classification, circular available at https://www.rbi.org.in/scripts/NotificationUser.aspx?Id=10155&Mode=0, accessed on September 11, 2016.

Table 3.7 Purpose-wise Breakup of Credit Accounts of RRBs as of March 31, 2015

Purpose	No. of Accounts (Million)	Relative % to Total	Credit Limit (₹ Billion)	Relative % to Total	Amount Outstanding (₹ Billion)	Relative % to Total
I. Agriculture	16.27	73%	1,427.69	65%	1,220.15	67%
1. Direct finance	15.71	71%	1,387.31	63%	1,184.39	65%
2. Indirect finance	0.56	3%	40.38	2%	35.76	2%
IV. Professional and other services	0.52	2%	67.62	3%	53.46	3%
V. Personal loans	2.31	10%	347.01	16%	276.44	15%
1. Housing	0.50	2%	130.74	6%	107.21	6%
2. Consumer durables	0.12	1%	19.32	1%	14.51	1%
3. Vehicles	0.11	1%	24.52	1%	18.35	1%
4. Education	0.10	0%	23.36	1%	20.98	1%
6. Others	1.48	7%	149.07	7%	115.39	6%
Vi. Trade	1.33	6%	117.15	5%	94.95	5%
2. Retail trade	1.30	6%	112.53	5%	91.24	5%
VII. Finance	0.18	1%	35.65	2%	22.62	1%
VIII. All others	1.62	7%	191.02	9%	144.69	8%
Total bank credit	22.23	100%	2,186.15	100%	1,812.30	100%

Source: Basic Statistical Returns of SCBs in India, http://dbie.rbi.org.in/DBIE/dbie.rbi?site=publications#!3, accessed on September 10, 2016.

the loan accounts and 67% of the loan balances were for agriculture.

What is more important is the customer profile who received the agricultural loans from the RRBs. The data put out by NABARD on the ground level flow of credit to agriculture, across institutional forms, shows that RRBs reach out to small and marginal farmers in a higher proportion than even the cooperatives—both in number of accounts and credit purveyed. The only difference between data for 2007–08 to 2014–15 is that the average loan size for small and marginal farmers has significantly moved up. RRBs seem to have purveyed a higher loan ticket size, possibly while the cooperatives continue to be engaged with the smaller ticket loan sizes for these borrowers.

Share of SF/MF in Ground Level Credit Folw to Agriculture (2007–08 and 2014–15)

Agency	2007–08					2014–15				
	No. of accounts (lakh)		Loan disbursed (₹ crore)		Avg loan amt of SF/MF (₹)	No. of accounts (lakh)		Loan disbursed (₹ crore)		Avg loan amt of SF/MF (₹)
	Total	SF/MF	Total	SF/MF		Total	SF/MF	Total	SF/MF	
Commercial Banks	174.8	97.4 (55.8)	81,088	52,231 (28.8)	53,625	426.2	195.4 (45.9)	604,376	197,540 (32.7)	101,075
Cooperative banks	201.8	117.9 (58.4)	48,258	22,609 (46.9)	19,176	306.9	202.8 (66.1)	138,470	78,736 (56.9)	38,830
RRBs	62.7	42.2 (67.3)	25,312	15,019 (59.3)	35,590	120.5	87.8 (72.9)	102,483	70,390 (68.7)	80,153
Total	439.3	257.5 (58.6)	254,658	89,859 (35.3)	34,897	853.6	486.0 (56.9)	845,328	346,666 (41.0)	71,326

Figure 3.1 Share of Small and Marginal Farmers in Ground-level Credit Flow

Source: Corporate Planning Department, NABARD, Mumbai (compiled from reports collected from IBA, Cooperative banks and RRBs).
Note: Figures in parenthesis refer to share in total of that agency.

The break-up of the portfolio of the RRBs has some implications and some opportunities as we go forward. The change in the priority sector targets given by RBI is at best symbolic because historically RRBs have been achieving the 75% norm and a significant amount from agriculture and weaker sections, even when it was not obligatory. However, the new norm ensures that as they consolidate and grow, they will not deviate from the requirements of inclusion. In that sense, the move by the RBI, though symbolic, is welcome to ensure that the mission of the RRBs are ring-fenced. In his paper, Tankha (2015) expressed deep concern about the mission drift of the RRBs, given the consolidations and the amendments to the RRB Act. While that is to be given due consideration, the question of viability and long-term sustainability cannot be wished away. The move by the RBI to have more stringent priority sector lending norms while unshackling the RRBs from other aspects may be a good one.

Given that the new priority sector lending norms even for the banks are more stringent both for agriculture (small and marginal farmers) and for micro-enterprises—both areas where RRBs seem to be naturally getting their portfolio—and the fact that these targets have to be achieved on a quarterly basis, there would be scope for RRBs to actively trade on the PSLC obligations platform and earn some fee based income, even with the portfolio remaining on the balance sheet.

While the deployment of credit to agriculture should be seen with a great deal of satisfaction from a larger inclusion perspective, it is also important to note that this leads to a significant concentration risk in one activity, an activity subject to political processes of waivers. This is also a portfolio that continues to have interest-rate caps and, therefore, might not be lucrative. Going forward, the RRBs might want to focus on this sector because of their inherent strength, but quickly churn the portfolio through securitization deals and then look for opportunities beyond the current concentrated portfolio. Their size, and consequently their leadership that comes from a more senior level of bankers will afford such an opportunity.

Deposits

The data on the break-up of deposits by size was not available for RRBs separately. However, the break up was available according to the location of the branches (Table 3.8).

Even in case of commercial banks, it is known that the rural areas usually are net savers and contribute more to deposits than take credit. The story with RRBs is no different, leading to a low CD ratio which was discussed earlier. A significant chunk of deposits is coming from savings accounts, indicating that the account holders are invariably individuals. Businesses are not allowed to open savings accounts. Thus, it is also clear that these banks largely cater to smaller individuals. The ownership data of the accounts is available in Table 3.9 and the details are in Appendices 3.1 and 3.2.

However, it is important to notice that the fundamental change that is happening between 2014 and 2015 where the share of institutions both in terms of number of accounts and amounts deposited has significantly moved up. One the same note it is also important to note the relative share of women in the number of accounts and deposits are increasing. The increase in the share of institutions, however, needs a further investigation to understand the nature of change. The only two aspects that the RRBs need to consider are a greater deployment of credit (represented by a better CD ratio) and a lower level

Table 3.8 Deposits of RRBs Classified According to the Location of the Branches as of March 31, 2015

(Accounts in Million, Amounts in ₹ Billion)

Type of Deposits →		Current		Savings		Term		Total	
Population Group	No. of Offices	No. of Accounts	Amount	No. of Accounts	Amount	No. of Accounts	Amount	No. of Accounts	Amount
Rural	14,614	1,074	54	122,457	850	10,678	645	134,209	1,549
Semi-urban	3,856	620	29	33,325	320	3,919	323	37,864	672
Urban	1,285	166	22	6,669	119	1,734	254	8,568	395
Metro	250	22	6	989	18	230	39	1,241	62
All India	20,005	1,882	111	163,440	1,307	16,562	1,261	181,883	2,679

Source: RBI Datawarehouse, http://dbie.rbi.org.in/DBIE/dbie.rbi?site=publications#!9, accessed on September 19, 2016; Basic Statistical Returns of Scheduled Commercial Banks in India. Mumbai: RBI.

Table 3.9 Deposits of RRBs Classified According to Ownership of March 2014 and 2015

(Accounts in Million, Amounts in ₹ Billion)

	March 2014		March 2015		March 2014		March 2015	
Details	**Accounts**	**% of Total**	**Accounts**	**% of Total**	**Amount**	**% of Total**	**Amount**	**% of Total**
Male	99	66%	91	50%	1,469	63%	1,437	54%
Female	34	23%	49	27%	424	18%	510	19%
Institutions	17	12%	42	23%	440	19%	732	27%
Total	151	100%	182	100%	2,333	100%	2,679	100%

Source: RBI Datawarehouse, http://dbie.rbi.org.in/DBIE/dbie.rbi?site=publications#!9, accessed on September 9, 2016.

of NPAs that would keep the profitability on track. It would be interesting to see the progress of these institutions now that the next phase of consolidation is concluded.

LOCAL AREA BANKS

While the RRBs were consolidating, was this a year of sunset for LABs? The biggest LAB, Capital LAB, was converted into a SFB and was the first to start operations as an SFB. Of the others, Coastal LAB applied for a SFB license in a strategic tie-up with KBS LAB, but it failed to obtain a license, and Subhadra LAB continued to operate. The RBI annual report indicated, "Consultations with the central government on broad options for the future set-up of LABs were underway during the year" (RBI 2016). The report on trend and progress of banking suggested, "With the Capital Local Area Bank Ltd. getting the Reserve Bank's 'in-principle' approval for the license for Small Finance Bank (SFB), share of the LABs in the total banking assets will get further reduced" (RBI 2015). Both the statements clearly indicate that LABs as a category may eventually be shut down. In any case, after the last licensing, the approach of the RBI has been to discourage the setting of new LABs and this may be the formal indication of closure of one institutional experiment that was made in the banking sector. By March 2015, the assets of LABs had grown by 22% and the income had grown by 16%, but this number includes Capital LAB which in itself represented more than 70% of this sub-segment of banks. This possibly is indicative in the approach of the RBI on the inclusion of LABs in its periodic policy reviews. For instance, while the priority sector lending classification and targets have been revised from time to time (the last being December 2015) for RRBs, they have remained at a level that was prescribed for LABs when they were set up, on par with the commercial banks.

Coastal LAB[1]

After Capital LAB became a SFB, Coastal LAB was the largest LAB. It had a total business of ₹5.63 billion as of March 2016. While the bank remained profitable, most other details were not available in the public domain.

KBS LAB[2]

Krishna Bhima Samruddhi (KBS) LAB had a total business of ₹3.2 billion in 2015–16 and with a growth of 12.54% over the previous year. Its gross NPA was 2.09% and the net NPA was 0.63%. It had a comfortable CRAR of more than 20%, indicating that it could have leveraged better and accessed more deposits. It had a much better CD ratio than the RRBs at 76.84%. The priority sector advances of KBS LAB were to the extent of 82.7% far in excess of the 40% prescribed for LABs. However, most of the advances were classified as general purpose loans.

Subhadra LAB[3]

Subhadra was the smallest bank of the lot, just crossing a total business of ₹1 billion during the year 2014–15, operating with a mere 10 branches. During the year, it also had an NPA of 2.84%, a high CD ratio of more than 99%. Subhadra had a capital of ₹224 million and a net worth of ₹306 million by 2014–15. Not further data about Subhadra was available on the public domain.

[1] Data for this section sourced from the website of Coastal LAB at http://www.coastalareabank.com/, accessed on September 12, 2016.

[2] Data for this section sourced from the website of KBS LAB http://kbsbankindia.com/downloads/KBS-Annual-Report-15-16.pdf, accessed on September 12, 2016.

[3] Data for this section sourced from the website of Subhadra LAB at http://www.subhadrabank.com/, accessed on September 13, 2015.

CONCLUDING NOTES

From the performance of the RRBs, it is apparent that they are now in a zone where their consolidation process is almost over and they have stabilized at a new normal. There have been opinions on whether this consolidation was desirable from the larger objective of inclusion, but it is evident that in the 40 years of existence of RRBs the conundrum between outreach and sustainability has not been solved. With the SFBs coming in, the landscape for inclusive finance is going through a fundamental change and this space needs to be watched as to how RRBs will respond and cope. Clearly there are too many stakes involved and it is too early to speculate about the future course, but in areas where the business was difficult, strains have already shown up, even after consolidation.

APPENDIX 3.1
Deposits and Credit (Including Credit of Small Borrowal Accounts) of RRBs

March 2015 (Accounts in Million, Amounts in ₹ Billion)

		Deposits (Balance)		Total Credit (Outstanding)		Of Which: Credit to Small Borrowers (Outstanding)	
Region	**No. of Offices**	**No. of Accounts**	**Amount**	**No. of Accounts**	**Amount**	**No. of Accounts**	**Amount**
North	2,796	16.61	355.20	1.64	249.56	1.18	90.37
Haryana	609	3.64	89.88	0.38	63.22	0.27	22.63
Himachal Pradesh	189	0.99	29.72	0.09	10.27	0.07	3.49
Jammu and Kashmir	288	1.31	30.93	0.13	13.96	0.11	5.81
Punjab	374	1.91	51.61	0.20	44.66	0.11	8.78
Rajasthan	1,336	8.76	153.06	0.83	117.46	0.62	49.67
Northeast	783	10.72	151.43	0.94	72.34	0.83	33.40
Arunachal Pradesh	28	0.13	3.65	0.01	1.00	0.01	0.17
Assam	465	7.33	78.77	0.58	41.47	0.53	23.28
Manipur	21	0.28	1.82	0.01	0.70	0.01	0.35
Meghalaya	62	0.35	11.23	0.04	5.61	0.03	1.37
Mizoram	66	0.47	14.30	0.05	7.16	0.04	2.24
Nagaland	11	0.02	0.64	0.00	0.20	0.00	0.06
Tripura	130	2.14	41.02	0.25	16.20	0.21	5.93
East	4,389	38.92	533.97	5.03	281.06	4.76	179.39
Bihar	2,012	15.77	211.81	2.32	115.90	2.24	91.70
Jharkhand	434	2.78	45.89	0.46	18.58	0.44	12.47
Odisha	971	7.34	122.14	1.10	69.63	1.03	40.86
West Bengal	972	13.02	154.13	1.15	76.95	1.03	34.35
Central	6,066	65.55	813.13	5.77	455.46	5.10	259.22
Chhattisgarh	595	5.86	73.36	0.35	22.71	0.32	14.45
Madhya Pradesh	1,256	9.50	160.76	1.00	91.37	0.88	51.99
Uttar Pradesh	3,942	48.92	550.34	4.29	323.82	3.81	188.23
Uttarakhand	273	1.27	28.68	0.13	17.56	0.10	4.54
West	1,379	9.54	164.58	1.02	102.65	0.90	51.21
Gujarat	663	4.21	81.11	0.40	43.62	0.33	18.17
Maharashtra	716	5.33	83.46	0.63	59.03	0.57	33.04

Region	No. of Offices	Deposits (Balance)		Total Credit (Outstanding)		Of Which: Credit to Small Borrowers (Outstanding)	
		No. of Accounts	Amount	No. of Accounts	Amount	No. of Accounts	Amount
South	4,592	40.54	660.59	7.83	651.23	7.18	401.34
Andhra Pradesh	1,055	9.36	154.52	1.99	155.06	1.81	98.10
Karnataka	1,663	13.87	253.69	1.98	217.93	1.75	112.72
Kerala	579	5.08	85.81	1.37	104.66	1.29	71.75
Tamil Nadu	468	2.85	57.50	1.06	60.58	1.03	50.77
Puducherry	33	0.18	3.65	0.06	3.76	0.06	3.30
All India	794	9.20	105.41	1.37	109.23	1.24	64.70

Source: RBI Datawarehouse. Basic Statistical Returns of SCBs in India. http://dbie.rbi.org.in/DBIE/dbie.rbi?site=publications#!3, accessed on September 9, 2016.

APPENDIX 3.2
Deposits of RRBs as of March 31, 2015

(Accounts in Million, Amounts in ₹ Billion)

Region/State/ Union Territory	No. of Offices	Current		Savings		Term		Total	
		No. of Accounts	Amount	No. of Accounts	Amount	No. of Accounts	Amount	No. of Accounts	Amount
North	2,796	380	9	14,511	170	1,718	177	16,608	355
Haryana	609	66	2	3,369	48	206	39	3,641	90
Himachal	189	10	0.6	757	10	222	20	990	30
Jammu and Kashmir	288	27	2	1,049	15	235	14	1,310	31
Punjab	374	216	1	1,503	21	190	30	1,908	52
Rajasthan	1,336	62	3	7,832	77	865	74	8,759	153
Northeast	783	232	12	9,785	83	707	56	10,724	151
Arunachal	28	3	1	111	2	12	1	125	4
Assam	465	152	5	6,716	46	459	28	7,328	79
Manipur	21	7	0.2	266	1	8	1	280	2
Meghalaya	62	7	0.6	323	7	25	4	354	11
Mizoram	66	2	3	460	7	12	5	474	14
Nagaland	11	0.2	0.08	20	0.3	2	0.2	22	1
Tripura	130	62	3	1,890	21	189	17	2,141	41
East	4,389	239	21	34,316	286	4,366	226	38,921	534
Bihar	2,012	137	13	14,244	131	1,394	69	15,774	212
Jharkhand	434	5	1	2,449	26	330	19	2,784	46
Odisha	971	25	4	6,241	54	1,076	64	7,342	122
West Bengal	972	72	4	11,382	76	1,567	75	13,021	154
Central	6,066	470	40	60,733	484	4,347	289	65,550	813
Chhattisgarh	595	64	3	5,502	48	294	22	5,860	73
MP	1,256	105	19	8,429	68	965	74	9,499	161

(Continued)

(Continued)

Region/State/ Union Territory	No. of Offices	Current No. of Accounts	Current Amount	Savings No. of Accounts	Savings Amount	Term No. of Accounts	Term Amount	Total No. of Accounts	Total Amount
UP	3,942	292	18	45,748	353	2,878	179	48,917	550
Uttarakhand	273	10	0.7	1,054	14	210	14	1,273	29
West	1,379	83	3	8,593	76	860	85	9,536	165
Gujarat	663	42.	2	3,614	30	551	49	4,208	81
Maharashtra	716	40	2	4,979	45	309	36	5,328	83
South	4,592	478	25	35,501	207	4,564	428	40,543	661
AP	1,055	32	9	8,163	45	1,167	101	9,362	155
Karnataka	1,663	190	11	11,817	78	1,860	165	13,867	254
Kerala	579	189	3	4,433	31	457	52	5,079	86
Tamil Nadu	468	28	1	2,413	18	411	39	2,851	58
Puducherry	33	1	0.2	168	1	14	3	183	4
Telangana	794	38	1.5	8,508	34	656	70	9,202	105
All India	20,005	1,882	111	163,439	1,307	16,562	1,261	181,883	2,679

Source: RBI Datawarehouse, http://dbie.rbi.org.in/

REFERENCES

RBI (Reserve Bank of India). 2014. *RRBs: Master Circular on Priority Sector Lending*. Available at https://www.rbi.org.in/scripts/BS_ViewMasCirculardetails.aspx?id=9020, accessed on September 11, 2016.

———. 2015. *Report of the Trend and Progress of Banking in India 2014–15*. Mumbai: RBI.

———. 2016. *Reserve Bank of India Annual Report 2015–16*. Mumbai: RBI.

Tankha, A. 2015. *Regional Rural Banks and Financial Inclusion: Policy Imperatives*. Mumbai: PSIG, SIDBI.

A Review of PMJDY[1]

4
Chapter

INTRODUCTION

In the previous report, we had discussed the PMJDY and its launch in detail. While successive governments have recognized the need for financial inclusion and moved strategically, those initiatives were seen as supply-side strategies. While even the PMJDY was also a supply-side strategy—in encouraging people to open accounts as a first step before creating conditions of transacting in those accounts—it had a demand-side element to it. The demand-side element was in recognizing the fact that it was not sufficient to take the bank to the people—by establishing physical presence—but also equally important to get the people to the bank. The focus on accounts, rather than outlets, was a significant paradigm shift. During the year, there was much action on making this more meaningful by launching the direct benefit transfer (DBT) initiatives which pushed transaction volumes into the PMJDY accounts.

In the past year we reviewed the progress of PMJDY in achieving universal coverage by a two-pronged strategy of pushing the system on a mission mode enrolment and communication strategy of pulling the customers into the banks by offering incentives—direct incentives such as insurance coverage, RuPay cards, and OD, as well as indirect incentives of DBT. The progress of PMJDY after the first phase is reviewed in this chapter. A section of the chapter focusses on the progress of the DBT initiatives.

The PMJDY rested on six pillars and was to be rolled out in two phases. The six pillars were:

- Universal access to banking services
    - Each district to have a sub-service area covering 1,000 to 1,500 households
    - Banking service to be available within a reasonable distance of about 5 km radius
- Providing basic banking accounts, with OD facilities and a RuPay debit card
- Financial Literacy Programme
- Creation of a credit guarantee fund
- Providing micro-insurance
- Providing unorganized sector pension scheme

The first three pillars were to be covered in Phase I, ending August 2015, and the other pillars were to be covered by August 2018. The progress at the end of Phase 1 is given in Table 4.1.

PROGRESS

One of the criticisms of the PMJDY accounts was that, while the accounts were opened on a mission mode, the usage of the accounts were not taking off. From the month-on-month numbers, it is evident that the account opening might be reaching saturation levels. In the second phase, apart from adding products to the accounts, it is also essential to focus on transaction volumes. It is clear that the PMDJY increased the penetration of bank accounts. However, even now, about 24.55% of accounts do not have any balance in them.

[1] The author is extremely thankful to Ms Hasna Ashraf, student of MA in Development Studies, Indian Institute of Technology, Madras, who contributed significantly for the research and did the early draft of this chapter. The author is also thankful to Dr Alok Pande, Additional Director General, All India Radio (formerly with Department of Financial Services, Ministry of Finance, Government of India) and Shri Ajay Tankha for feedback on the early draft of this chapter.

Table 4.1 PMJDY Performance in Phase 1 (up to August 2015)

Bank Category	Rural (No. in Million)	Urban (No. in Million)	Total A/cs opened (Million)	No. of RuPay Cards (Million)	Balance (Amt ₹ Billion)	No. of A/cs with '0' Balance (Million)	Average Balance per Active A/c (₹)
Public sector banks	75.3	61.9	137.2	126.2	175.57	62.1	2,612
Percentage share	71%	89%	78%	81%	78%	77%	
RRBs	26.8	4.6	31.4	23.2	37.48	15.0	2,271
Percentage share	25%	7%	17%	15%	17%	19%	
Private banks	4.2	2.8	7.0	6.2	10.89	3.2	2,943
Percentage shares	4%	4%	4%	4%	5%	4%	
Grand total	106.3	69.3	175.7	155.6	223.94	80.4	2,349

Source: PMJDY Performance Report, Phase 1, http://pmjdy.gov.in/account-statistics-country.aspx, accessed on August 20, 2015.

Table 4.2 PMDJY Performance After Phase I (up to August 2016)

Bank Category	Rural (No. in Million)	Urban (No. in Million)	Total A/cs Opened (Million)	No. of RuPay Cards (Million)	Balance (Amt ₹ Billion)	No. of A/cs with '0' Balance (Million)	Average Balance per Active A/c (₹)
Public sector banks	98.7	77.7	176.4	147.15	317.87	43.63	2,394
Percentage share	71%	90%	78%	80%	79%	79%	
RRBs	34.3	5.6	39.9	27.9	69.75	8.43	2,216
Percentage share	25%	6%	18%	15%	17%	15%	
Private banks	5.1	3.2	7.0	7.8	15.09	3.08	3,849
Percentage shares	4%	4%	4%	5%	4%	6%	
Grand total	138.2	86.5	224.7	182.8	402.72	55.14	2,375

Source: http://pmjdy.gov.in/ArchiveFile/2016/7/13.07.2016.pdf, accessed on July 23, 2016.

A study conducted by MicroSave, in December 2015 (Sharma, Giri, and Chadha 2016) showed account dormancy stands at 28%. The dormancy was attributed to lack of information on operational procedures, product features, and account duplication. The MicroSave study also indicated that only 67% of the respondents indicated that the PMJDY account was their first account, indicating a high level of duplication, largely because of the "push" strategy (Sharma, Giri, and Chadha 2016). This is not surprising, given the fact that in the "push" strategy, particularly pertaining to the seeding of Aadhaar numbers with the bank accounts for DBT of LPG subsidy, the circular indicated that accounts under PMJDY be opened "even if the household already has a bank account".[2] This was to ensure that the benefit transfers happen to the account in whose name the LPG connection was, while the PMJDY account for the household could be opened in a different person's name in the household.

From the numbers in Tables 4.1 and 4.2, it is evident that the proportion of zero-balance accounts are falling, the number of accounts opened are going up, and the total amount of deposits in PMJDY accounts has increased. However, it is also important to note that the average balance in the active accounts is somewhat static, except for an increase in the balances of PMJDY accounts in private sector banks.

In an investigative by the *Indian Express* revealed in mid-September 2016, it was found through a series of Right to Information applications that many of the banks had reduced the zero-balance accounts with a token deposit of amounts ranging from ₹1 to ₹5. These deposits were done by staff, under pressure from the banks to reduce the zero-balance status. The report said,

> In the case of Punjab National Bank, which has opened 1.36 crore Jan Dhan accounts of which 39.57 lakh (almost 29%) are those with deposits of Re 1. Bank of Baroda has 1.4 crore Jan Dhan

[2] Government of India (2014). *Circular Number 6/38/2012-FI (C-66449),* dated December 29, 2014. Department of Financial Services, Ministry of Finance, Government of India. New Delhi.

Table 4.3 Select Statics of Individual Banks on PMJDY

Bank Name Public Sector Banks	PMJDY Accounts with RuPay Cards	Average Balance in Active PMDJY Accounts	Percentage of Zero-Balance Accounts	Accounts with Aadhaar Seeding
Oriental Bank of Commerce	96%	9,224	10%	48%
Central Bank of India	75%	1,410	10%	53%
Punjab National Bank	72%	1,517	9%	50%
Vijaya Bank	99%	1,057	2%	74%
Punjab and Sind Bank	99%	3,812	0%	67%
RRBs Sponsored By:				
Canara Bank	100%	2,490	12%	76%
Andhra Bank	88%	1,161	9%	83%
Central Bank of India	93%	2,463	9%	33%
Punjab National Bank	72%	2,149	2%	43%
Punjab and Sind Bank	70%	175	0%	100%

Source: Data from the PMDJY website, http://pmjdy.gov.in/ArchiveFile/2016/7/27.07.2016.pdf, accessed on August 8, 2016. Calculations by the author.

> accounts of which 12.97 lakh (9.26 per cent) have deposits of Re 1. There's also UCO Bank with 74.6 lakh Jan Dhan accounts of which 11.06 lakh (14.83 per cent) have deposits of Re 1.[3]

However, the report did not allude to any collusion from the management of banks. It merely stated that the staff was under pressure from the top management to reduce the number of zero-balance accounts, and the staff resorted to this practice. A report like this puts the static numbers of average balance of the accounts in a greater perspective.

It would be interesting to look at the nuances of how some of the banks are performing on the PMJDY (Table 4.3). The public sector banks are doing much more work in this area than the privatesector banks, both in terms of number of accounts opened and in keeping them active. Punjab and Sind Bank (and the RRBs sponsored by them) have nil or negligible zero-balance accounts, with good Aadhaar seeding. However, in terms of numbers, it is Punjab National Bank which seems to have aggressively opened PMJDY accounts—not only is it the second largest on number of accounts opened (after State Bank of India). It has one of the lowest number of zero-balance accounts. However, it lags behind in the number of accounts with Aadhaar seeding or in terms of average balance in active accounts. If PMJDY were to be successful across the banking system, there may be lessons to be learnt from individual banks which have taken this up at scale.

EFFECTIVENESS

Even as the overall thrust has moved away from the mission mode of both pushing the bankers to open accounts and pulling the customers through the saturation of the residual families that are still excluded, the opening of accounts continues under the scheme. One of the reasons for this increase might be because of the pull of DBT.

MicroSave (see Box 4.1) has been conducting dipstick surveys to evaluate the last-mile efficacy of how the PMJDY is rolling out. MicroSave has conducted three waves of surveys to understand the availability of the last-mile architecture in the form of Bank Mitrs (BMs) and the type of transactions that are being done in the PMJDY accounts. While we had discussed the findings of the first wave report during the last year, there are two more waves of the reports available now. Based on the numbers, it is now clear that the mission mode of opening accounts set-up a foundation for a long and detailed exercise of meaningful financial inclusion. The numbers indicated by the Wave 3 study of MicroSave show that while the numbers of people getting enrolled and linked to the banking system is showing a much flatter trend, the quality of the linkage is getting better.

The news on most of the parameters are good. It is not as euphoric as the numbers that were being

[3] http://indianexpress.com/article/business/banking-and-finance/how-banks-cut-their-zero-balance-jan-dhan-accounts-one-rupee-trick-3028190/ report of *Indian Express*, accessed on September 13, 2016.

Box 4.1 Findings of the MicroSave Dipstick Study on PMJDY: Wave 3

BM Outreach Indicators and Infrastructure Readiness

- There is a significant improvement in the availability of BMs. While availability stood at 89% and 84% in wave I and wave II respectively, availability is recorded at 97% in wave III.
- Transaction readiness of BMs, as a percentage of available BMs, also improved from 54% and 79% in wave I and wave II respectively, to 81% in wave III.
- BM dormancy has increased marginally from 7.9% in wave II to 11%. This is a very worrying trend.
- Presence of signage has improved and 85% of the outlets had a bank and/or BM logo.
- 73% of BM devices were Aadhaar-enabled. RuPay card-enabled devices were 50% in wave III.
- The average number of transactions per BM per month stands at 301, up by 44% from 209 in wave II. Enhanced transactions also resulted in 72% growth in monthly BM remuneration, recorded at ₹4,692 in wave III, from ₹2,724 in wave I.
- About 73% of the BMs interviewed were trained in financial literacy. Frequency of visit by bank staff to BM location improved. Only 9% BMs were never visited by a branch staff in wave III.

Customer Outreach Indicators

- About 80% of the customers interviewed rated BM as their first preference for conducting transactions, as against ATM and bank branch
- About 62% of customers interviewed felt that Aadhaar enrolment has helped make their financial transactions easier, for reasons such as "easy and quick transactions," "potential to receive DBT," and its usage as an identity proof.
- Duplication of customer accounts increased. About 67% of the customers indicated that PMJDY was their first account, in comparison to 86% in waves I and II. Incentive-based account opening and, channel remuneration seem to have resulted in multiple accounts being opened for customers.
- About 47% of customers have received RuPay cards (up from 43% in wave II). Aadhaar enrolment was at 77%. About 62% of the customers interviewed had linked their PMJDY accounts with Aadhaar.

Source: Sharma, Giri, and Chadha (2016).

put out in the last year, but tempered by reality in rolling out this complex scheme. The study also clearly indicates two significant aspects:

1. There needs to be an effective and meaningful linkage between the bank branch and the customer. This linkage was designed as the BC, but multiple rounds of studies have indicated problems with the way the BC model is rolled out and the banking system seems to be coming to grips with the issue now, and the model is getting stabilized.
2. There needs to be efforts to keep the account live, and this could happen through transaction throughput. The aggressive linking of DBT schemes is expected to drive transactions into the PMJDY accounts.

POLICY INITIATIVES

Recognizing the need to have a strong connect between the bank branch and the customer, the RBI made an announcement as a part of the monetary policy statement of April 2016. This statement indicated two initiatives that addressed the core issue at the last mile connectivity. Firstly, the RBI proposed that it would establish a framework for training and certification of BC, and would request the Indian Banks Association (IBA) to work with agencies to establish the system of training and certification. In addition, the RBI announced that it would create a registry of BCs.[4] In addition to the announcement, the RBI also indicated these two initiatives were identified for immediate implementation in its annual report (RBI 2016). Both these initiatives go a long way in adding more meaning to the function of BC, providing a growth path, and building in some stakes for the BCs to continue operating.

While the RBI was working on making the ecosystem ready for the bank accounts to be active, the government on the other hand, was ensuring that the throughput of transactions increased through its JAM strategy. The government, in order to indicate the strategic importance of the scheme, took multiple initiatives. The importance that the government has accorded to JAM is evident in the fact that an entire chapter in the economic survey was dedicated to this topic.

1. The PAHAL scheme which was the initial flagship program of providing direct cash transfers of

[4] Reserve Bank of India (2016). *First Bi-monthly Monetary Policy Statement 2016–17 by Raghuram G. Rajan, Governor*. Mumbai: RBI, April 5, 2016, https://www.rbi.org.in/Scripts/BS_PressReleaseDisplay.aspx?prid=36654, accessed on July 27, 2016.

subsidy to LPG subscribers, which was started in 54 districts was extended to all the districts of the country starting January 2015. With the elimination of beneficiaries earning more than ₹1 million per annum—through voluntary disclosure—the scheme is now focused more sharply on the relatively poorer segments of the society, and has provided a basis for a voluntary classification of beneficiaries rather than the earlier universal coverage. This could also form a basis for weeding out non-poor Jan-Dhan accounts in future.

2. There have been some initiatives that try to sharpen the definition of PMJDY accounts like enrolling new customers who are eligible for LPG subsidy. The government also instructed that if the beneficiaries have other accounts into which the subsidies and benefit transfers are flowing in, they should be designated as a PMJDY account, thereby bringing these accounts on a single platform. Conversion of these accounts to a PMJDY account will also accord the other benefits associated with the account—insurance cover, OD facility, and RuPay card. This might also reduce account duplication and dormancy.
3. In a series of circulars, the scope of DBT was extended to all the centrally sponsored schemes which involved transfer of cash subsidies and payments. These included the Mahatma Gandhi National Rural Employment Guarantee Act (MGNREGA) wages, old age pensions, scholarships, and so on. The prime minister's office also instructed all to ministries to actively identify schemes that could be brought under the DBT fold.
4. It also extended the scope of the JAM trinity to have Aadhaar-enabled payment systems (AEPS) authentication of beneficiaries, even when the benefit was in-kind like the public distribution scheme. While this does not extend the scope to banking, it has the potential to convert in-kind subsidies into cash subsidies at a future date.
5. It extended the scope of bank-account-based direct payment of wages of all people working for the schemes, the *anganwadi* workers, teachers in aided schools, and so on. This initiative creates an ecosystem where the people who are in touch with the beneficiaries of PMJDY also get an understanding of the touch and feel of banking, and provides the scope to make this initiative habit forming.
6. The DBT mission itself was shifted to the cabinet secretariat to be directly monitored by the prime minister's office signaling the strategic significance of the initiative.

While this chapter does not discuss the merit of cash transfers and the process of identification of the beneficiaries, the initiatives indicate that the ecosystem and the context for increased use of bank accounts is being effectively created by the government and the other agencies.

DIRECT BENEFIT TRANSFERS

These initiatives have started showing some results. The total number of beneficiaries under DBT schemes stood at 300.1 million in February out of which 187.5 million accounts have been Aadhaar-linked. A total of ₹47.06 billion of subsidies under various schemes have been directly transferred to the beneficiaries in the month of February 2016. While the Aadhaar linkage is with 62% of the accounts that have been enrolled for this purpose, only about 34% of the payments happened using the Aadhaar bridge.[5]

While DBT has a significant role to play in sustaining activity in accounts, its effectiveness is dependent on Aadhaar seeding for the purposes of weeding out the fake accounts and for ensuring that cash does not leak in the intermediate stages. A 100% linkage of bank accounts to Aadhaar is assumed for targeted disbursement of DBTs. Out of 290 million DBT beneficiaries, only 51.63% of them had Aadhaar-linked bank accounts as of September 2015.[6] It is evident that Aadhaar is not essential for either opening a bank account or for transfer of benefits to the beneficiaries. Till recently, Aadhaar did not have a legal backing as the act giving a legal legitimacy to Aadhaar was not passed. However, the importance of Aadhaar is being increasingly recognized for the purposes of de-duplication, better targeting of benefits, and building up a database and, therefore, Aadhaar has become an integral part of the discourse on inclusion. The breakthrough that Aadhaar would achieve in inclusion is highlighted by the former RBI Governor Dr Subbarao in Box 4.2.

The next big introduction to the DBT platform is kerosene. This is expected to affect the poorer segments of the society, and earlier during the year the government announced implementation of DBT in kerosene on pilot basis in 33 districts identified by 9 state governments (Chhattisgarh, Haryana, Himachal Pradesh, Jharkhand, Madhya Pradesh, Maharashtra, Punjab, Rajasthan, and Gujarat).[7] The

[5] DBT Report, http://cabsec.nic.in/dbt/dbtrfeb.html, accessed on May 23, 2016.

[6] DBT Report, http://cabsec.nic.in/dbt/dbtr4.html, accessed on May 23, 2016.

[7] Press Information Bureau (2016), *DBT Scheme for Kerosene* [Press Release] at http://pib.nic.in/newsite/PrintRelease.aspx?relid=137552, accessed on May 22, 2016.

Table 4.4 Framework for Spread of JAM Across the Country

		LPG	Kerosene	Food	Fertiliser	Within-govt JAM
First-mile	Eligibility	Household	Household	Household	Individual	Scheme
	Targeting	Universal	Targeted (BPL)	Targeted (BPL)	Targeted (farmers)	All central government scheme expenditure
	Beneficiary database	Digitised	Most digitised	Most digitised	None	Public Finance Management System
Middle-mile	Within-government coordination	Central Petroleum Ministry with OMCs	Central Petroleum & Food Ministries with all State PDS	Central Food Ministry with all State PDS	Central Fertilizer Ministry with fertilizer manufacturers	Expenditure Department with Central Ministries
	Supply chain interest groups	LPG distributors	Fair Price Shops	Fair Price Shops	Fertiliser retailers	N/A
Last-mile	Beneficiary vulnerability	3%	49%	51%	62%	N/A
	Beneficiary financial inclusion	33%	83%	78%	100%	N/A
Where to JAM?	Leakages	24%	46%	Wheat - 54%, Rice - 15%	40%	14%
	Central government control	High	Low	Low	High	Very high
What kind of JAM?	Recommended policy option	JAM	BAPU	BAPU	BAPU/JAM	JAM

Source: Government of India. Economic Survey 2015–16, 63, http://indiabudget.nic.in/es2015-16/echapvol1-03.pdf, accessed on July 31, 2016.

model it follows is similar to the LPG scheme, aiming at weeding out duplicates and transferring the subsidy amount directly into the account of the eligible citizens.

In terms of the amount distributed, the year 2015–16 saw the distribution of ₹610 billion to around 300 million. Out of this, ₹250 billion was distributed to beneficiaries of MGNREGA and ₹210 billion to beneficiaries of the PAHAL scheme,[8] both of which are the most important schemes where the DBT concept has been applied with vigor. This is a significant rise from ₹440.35 billion distributed to 296 million beneficiaries in 2014–15.[9] Table 4.4 gives a framework of how JAM framework will move in times to come and we can see that financial inclusion through PMJDY is an integral part of the strategy.

Box 4.2 Former Governor Subbarao on DBT

The technology breakthroughs of the last decade have made it possible to turn the FI program from supply-led to demand-led. Today the government is pushing DBT which makes poor people actively want to open a bank account. I believe the DBT initiative has given a great fillip to the FI program. Poor households enter the banking system for the purpose of accessing the DBT, and hopefully they will soon demand and get all other products and services that a bank can offer.

The present government deserves the credit for pushing DBT and JDY aggressively. But we must also recognize that they are building on the foundations laid by the previous government. Recall that it was the previous government which started two pilots for DBT in Chandigarh and Coimbatore. Today's DBT is building on those lessons of experience.

ASSOCIATED PMJDY PRODUCTS

RuPay Cards

While the reduction of zero-balance accounts calls for celebration, it is already clear that the average balances have not significantly gone up in the

[8] Press Information Bureau (2016), *PM Reviews Progress of Aadhar and Direct Benefit Transfer Programmes* [Press Release], http://pib.nic.in/newsite/PrintRelease.aspx?relid=145126, accessed on May 17, 2016.

[9] Government of India (2016). *Economic Survey 2015-16*, http://www.unionbudget.nic.in/es2015-16/echapter-vol1.pdf, accessed on May 19, 2016.

non-zero-balance accounts. It is also important to examine the level of transactions. Transactions are indicators to know the level of activity in accounts. While detailed transaction level data are not available for the PMJDY accounts, it is possible to look at the transactions on the RuPay cards. As of April 2016, 260 million RuPay cards were issued of which 177 million were associated with PMJDY accounts.[10] The RuPay cards issued on PMJDY accounts form 68% of the cards issued and it can be assumed that most of them were issued to first time users. While there is statistics available from the National Payments Corporation of India (NPCI) about the use of cards with a break up between debit and credit cards and where they were used including ATMs and PoS devices, the usage in the banks' own ATMs are not captured. Therefore, analyzing much of the data pertaining to the RuPay cards issues under the PMJDY may not lead to deep insights. But circumstantially, one could say that the PMJDY account holders—who are most likely to be the inclusive finance customers—would be exclusively debit card holders and largely operating using the ATMs.

Even if we had the numbers pertaining to usage of RuPay cards, most likely these would be the non-PMJDY account holders, as there is enough evidence to suggest that a large portion of them are dormant, and there are not many RuPay-enabled devices at the BM level. The MicroSave study found that almost 80% of their sample preferred to carry out transactions through BMs. Hence, to get a more comprehensive idea of the level of activity in PMJDY accounts, it becomes important to take a look at the transactions at the level of BM.

The study conducted by MicroSave found the average number of transactions per BM per month to have increased from 209 in wave II (April–May 2015) to 301 in wave III (October–November 2015). This 44% increase in transactions over a period of about six months paints a positive picture. Increased focus by BMs on customer retention leading to customer transactions has led to this rise. A closer analysis of these transactions reveal that cash withdrawals and deposits form the core of a BM's day-to-day business, with a BM conducting on an average about 127 cash withdrawals and 173 cash deposits per month.[11] Thus, a more effective way of tracking the information pertaining to usage of the facilities is to look at transactions at the BM level. In addition, it is strongly advised that the RBI also track information on use of alternative channels and put the data out in the public domain for analysis. While the RBI tracks the use of alternative channels for interbank transactions, the data pertaining to the intrabank transactions remain with the bank and do not get escalated to a centralized database.

Overdraft

Apart from offering basic deposit and withdrawal facilities, PMJDY accounts also provided credit in the form of OD. As per PMJDY mission statement, OD up to ₹5,000 would be provided to the customers after six months of satisfactory performance of saving/credit history. The rate of interest on these accounts is 2% more than the base rate or 12%, whichever is lower (including the fee to be paid to credit guarantee fund). The government has called for the creation of a credit guarantee fund in phase 2 of PMJDY implementation to provide guarantee against defaults in ODs in basic banking accounts. This credit guarantee fund is to begin with a corpus of ₹1,000 crores funded by the FIF being maintained by NABARD.

The OD facility was envisaged as an exigency fund for the poor borrowers. But a look at the numbers (Table 4.5) shows that this is not really taken off on scale yet.

Of the total PMJDY account holders, only 2.8% of them have been offered an OD and a small proportion have been sanctioned. Even among the ones that have been sanctioned, nearly half of them do not avail the facility. The reasons for the low offtake of the OD are related to how actively the PMJDY account is being used on the savings side, and whether it has been linked with the Aadhaar number. The design of the OD is linked to the average balance in the savings as well as the need to de-duplicate the account, for which Aadhaar seeding has been made a primary condition. Thus, we can see that even with the accounts that have availed the OD facility, the average borrowing is only around ₹1,350 per account.

Table 4.5 Report on Overdraft Under PMJDY

Report on Overdraft as of May 27, 2016	
Total number of accounts offered for OD	6,316,424
Total number of accounts OD sanctioned	3,584,329
Total number of accounts OD availed	1,920,290
Amount of total OD availed (in ₹million)	2,591.81

Source: Report on Overdraft, http://pmjdy.gov.in/files/od/od/od.pdf, accessed on June 8, 2016.

[10] NPCI Press Release, http://www.npci.org.in/documents/RuPay_insuranc_program.pdf, accessed on June 1, 2016.

[11] PMJDY Wave III Assessment, http://www.microsave.net/files/pdf/PMJDY_Wave_III_Assessment_MicroSave.pdf, accessed on May 27, 2016.

Insurance and Pension

A significant initiative undertaken by PMJDY was to widen the scope of financial inclusion to ensure access to basic social security schemes such as insurance and pension. By linking insurance and pension to PMJDY accounts, the government was providing a single one-stop service. Besides ensuring activity in these accounts, this measure seeks to provide hitherto excluded people the cover of basic social security net. During the year, there were changes in the norms pertaining to bundled insurance on the RuPay cards. In the past, the RuPay card provided an insurance cover of ₹1 lakh subject to the condition that the cardholder used the card at least once in a 45-day window. This stipulation was introduced to encourage the use of RuPay cards. However, in November 2015, NPCI extended the 45-day usage condition to 90 days.[12] This stipulation was further modified to include branch transactions performed by the customers as well.[13] This relaxation of criteria would not have made sense if the focus was on ensuring activity in accounts. Rather, this seemed to indicate that the goal was to ensure that people have access to social security schemes.[14]

In addition to this, 2015 also saw the rolling of micro-insurance and pension schemes as a part of implementing phase 2 of PMJDY in a move that can has been termed 'Jan Dhan se Jan Suraksha'. Three ambitious Social Security Schemes pertaining to the Insurance and Pension Sectors, namely Pradhan Mantri Jeevan Jyoti Bima Yojana (PMJJBY), Pradhan Mantri Suraksha Bima Yojana (PMSBY), and Atal Pension Yojana (APY) were launched in May. The schemes were undertaken with the objective to move toward creating a universal social security system, targeted especially for the poor and the underprivileged. See Table 4.6 for the progress under these schemes and Figure 4.1 for a break-up of the rural and urban segmentation.

Of all the social security schemes, the PMSBY seemed to have a greater acceptance than the other schemes. Both life insurance and pension schemes had lesser subscribers, possibly pointing toward the need for creating awareness and financial literacy to expand the time horizons of the poor. Figure 4.2 gives the details of the claims settled under

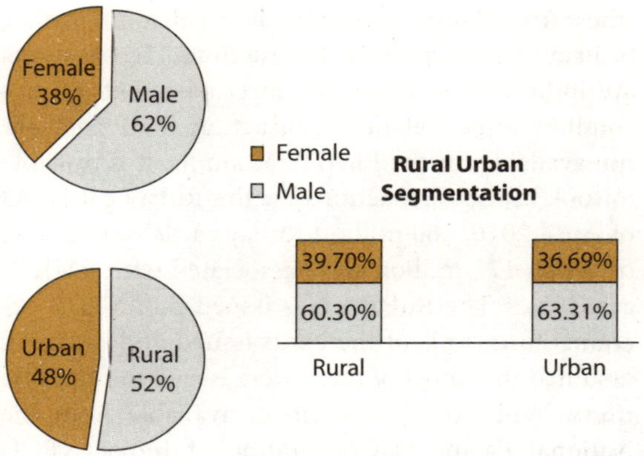

Figure 4.1 Composition of the Schemes as of May 2016

Source: Summary of APY/PMJJBY/PMSBY, http://jansuraksha.gov.in/Files/Reports/02.06.2016-P2P.pdf, accessed on June 8, 2016.

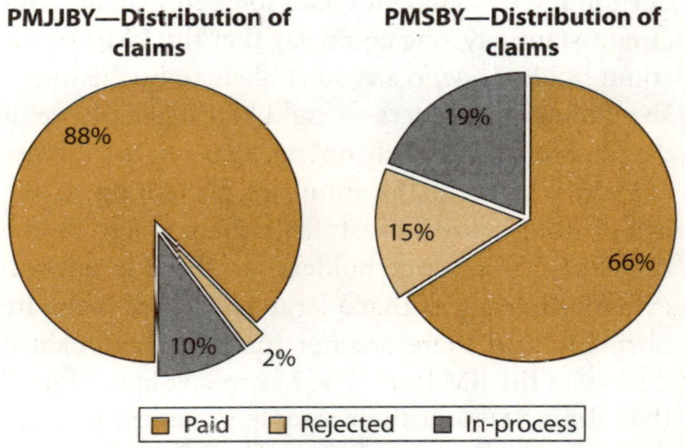

Figure 4.2 Distribution of Claims as of May 2016

Source: Daily Progress of Claims under PMJJBY and PMSBY, http://jansuraksha.gov.in/Files/Claims-Report/Claims_Reported_08062016.pdf, accessed on June 8, 2016.

Table 4.6 Summary of APY/PMJJBY/PMSBY as of May 2016

Scheme Name	Rural Male	Rural Female	Urban Male	Urban Female	Grand Total
APY	860,427	451,302	854,225	523,179	2,689,133
PMJJBY	9,173,466	5,682,101	9,454,369	5,353,435	29,663,371
PMSBY	29,734,761	20,053,478	28,186,464	16,427,632	94,402,335
Grand total	39,768,654	26,186,881	38,495,058	22,304,246	126,754,839

Source: Summary of APY/PMJJBY/PMSBY, http://jansuraksha.gov.in/Files/Reports/02.06.2016-P2P.pdf, accessed on June 8, 2016.

[12] Press release, http://pib.nic.in/newsite/PrintRelease.aspx?relid=131915, accessed on June 1, 2016.

[13] NPCI Press Release, http://www.npci.org.in/documents/RuPay_insuranc_program.pdf, accessed on June 1, 2016.

[14] As on November 20,2015, out of 697 claims lodged under accidental insurance under RuPay debit card in PMJDY accounts, 644 claims have been disposed off (http://pib.nic.in/newsite/PrintRelease.aspx?relid=131915, accessed on October 10, 2016). Due to inability to find statistics for the current year analysis of the same has not been included in the article.

these schemes. However, it is to be noted that these schemes like the PMJDY were universal in nature. While they were targeted at the poor, there was nothing in the scheme that prevented from the non-poor subscribing to these schemes. Both the insurance schemes had more takers in rural areas when compared to urban areas. However, in case of APY, there were more urban subscribers.

The survey conducted by MicroSave (Sharma, Giri, and Chadha 2016) found APY to be more popular among literate and high-income customers. Low-income customers found APY scheme costlier as compared to both PMSBY and PMJJBY, and also found it a burden to make regular monthly contribution over a long period (minimum 20-year period). Further, customers who were receiving old age pension under National Social Assistance Programme (NSAP) did not want to pay for another pension scheme.

LAST-MILE CONNECTIVITY

Ultimately, the success of the opening the accounts of the poor and pushing benefits into the accounts will take the initiative to one level, but the meaning in all this will come when the poor can easily transact using these facilities. That happens with the smooth functioning of the last-mile touchpoint. There has been recognition of this issue throughout, but the infrastructure to address this problem has not received the right ideas. The solution is a ubiquitous interoperable BC. But, this needs significant coordination in the back-end infrastructure between the government, banks, the payment systems, the telecom companies, and the authentication bridge of Aadhaar.

The policy approach of understanding the economics, the readiness, and the technology was started in right earnest during the year and it is expected that this will show some interesting results, going forward. The new architecture of the PBs may also help in having some disruptive ideas in this space.

The sticking point is that the BC commissions continue to be low and the government is not willing to reconsider this aspect. In January 2015, the finance ministry fixed DBT commissions at 1% for rural schemes, subject to an upper limit of ₹10 per transaction.[15] This has turned out to be far too low than the 3.14% DBT commission estimated by the Task Force on Aadhaar-Enabled Unified Payment Infrastructure.[16] A detailed analysis conducted by MicroSave earlier this year estimated the minimum cost to be 2.63% (which would reduce with an increase in transaction volumes).[17] However, the commission stipulated by the finance ministry is much lower, making it difficult for BMs to cover operational costs. The end result: shift in BM's focus to alternative sources of income. This negatively impacts their effectiveness in providing last-mile connectivity. Considering the current trend of BM dormancy, measures to rectify the situation have to be urgently taken. Therefore, the viable model of a BC that would eventually emerge is a multipurpose customer service point, where the fixed costs are shared by an array of services that go beyond payments. Something like a *kirana* store looks like an obvious choice.

Being the closest link available, BMs are more often than not the chief source of information for customers. Hence training of BMs is of paramount importance. The initiative of the RBI to involve IBA and the banks to proactively look at training and certification of BCs and the initiative of maintaining a registry of BCs is a welcome step.[18] This will add to the capacity-building of BCs.

CONCLUSIONS

Since its launch on August 28, 2014, PMJDY has come a long way. It is arguably one of the most exhaustive projects undertaken in the direction of financial inclusion. It is currently at a critical juncture where it has made significant inroads toward spreading access and awareness of financial services. However, PMJDY continues to face a lot of hurdles that it needs to overcome to attain the goal of financial inclusivity. At this point, we need to take a look at the strengths of the program as well as its weaknesses. The Aadhaar Act giving statutory backing to Aadhaar is likely to turn the situation

[15] Office Memorandum, Ministry of Finance, http://finmin.nic.in/the_ministry/dept_expenditure/plan_finance2/Revised_DBTL_Commission.pdf, accessed on June 9, 2016.

[16] Report of the Task Force on an Aadhaar-Enabled Unified Payment Infrastructure, http://finmin.nic.in/reports/Report_Task_Force_Aadhaar_PaymentInfra.pdf, accessed on June 9, 2016.

[17] MicroSave Policy Brief #12, http://www.microsave.net/files/pdf/1430745205_PB_12_How_a_1_DBT_Commission_Could_Undermine_India_s_Financial_Inclusion_Efforts.pdf, accessed on June 9, 2016.

[18] First Bi-monthly Monetary Policy Statement, https://www.rbi.org.in/scripts/BS_PressReleaseDisplay.aspx?prid=36654, accessed on July 3, 2016.

around. It will hopefully give the necessary push to Aadhaar-seeding and subsequent reduction of account dormancy.

With account enrolments reaching saturation, the focus is slowly shifting to the level of transactions. Expanding the scope of DBT and conversion of DBT accounts to PMJDY accounts are significant steps in this direction. The next step would be to encourage states to bring in their schemes into the fold of DBT. There is already movement in this direction with states increasingly bringing in more schemes under the scope of DBT.

Flaws in last-mile connectivity infrastructure prove to be operational bottlenecks for the successful implementation of PMJDY. While the condition of agent networks is improving, they still have a long way to go. Increased commission and ensured support would help in reducing the current BC dormancy. Low-cost solution based on mobile technology, increased adoption of mobile wallets, and so on are some of them. Swift implementation of these recommendations is likely to improve the last-mile delivery scenario.

While high levels of enrolment and increasing transaction volumes denote the success of PMJDY, there are other aspects that mar its success as we have already seen. By building on its strengths and working on its weaknesses, the project can scale unprecedented heights in financial inclusivity and this is precisely what the next focus should be.

REFERENCES

RBI (Reserve Bank of India). 2016. *Reserve Bank of India Annual Report, 2015-16*. Mumbai: RBI. Available at: https://rbidocs.rbi.org.in/rdocs/AnnualReport/PDFs/0RBIAR2016CD93589EC2C4467793892C79FD05555D.PDF (Accessed on September 2, 2016).

Sharma, M., A. Giri, and S. Chadha. 2016. *Pradhan Mantri Jan Dhan Yojana: Wave III Assessment*. Lucknow: MicroSave.

Digital Financial Inclusion[1]

5

Chapter

INTRODUCTION

Digital financial inclusion has occupied an important space in the discourse on financial inclusion. With the ubiquitous rollout of both Internet and mobile technology, the digital medium is now seen as the most powerful medium in cutting the divide between the haves and the have nots. The movement toward digital is not only about reducing transaction costs and back-end processing, it is also about moving expensive cash-based transactions out in favour of cashless settlements. In addition, there are big business opportunities now seen in analytics-based businesses that use the traces left by the digital transaction subjecting it to big data analysis. Therefore, it is not surprising that it has caught the attention of not only players in India who want to ride on the IndiaStack story that is being built, but also has grabbed global attention to the extent that a recent meeting of the finance ministers and central bank governors of the G20 at China thought it fit to discuss, articulate, and release the high-level principles for digital financial inclusion (see Box 5.1). This high-level attention can be said to be the most important highlight of the year in digital financial inclusion.

During the year, the RBI also put out a concept paper[2] on card acceptance infrastructure which focussed more on digital transactions at the terminal point to reduce the usage of cash. The issues raised in the concept paper were at two levels. The first was to improve the infrastructure of card acceptance infrastructure and who should bear the cost. One of the options discussed was the setting up of an acceptance

Box 5.1 G20 High-level Principles for Digital Financial Inclusion

The G20 stands at an unprecedented time when our leadership has the potential to drive the growth of inclusive economies by promoting digital financial services. Two billion adults globally do not have access to formal financial services and are excluded from opportunities to improve their lives. While tremendous gains in financial inclusion have already been achieved, digital financial services, together with effective supervision (which may be digitally enabled), are essential to close the remaining gaps in financial inclusion.

Digital technologies offer affordable ways for the financially excluded—the majority of whom are women—to save for school, make a payment, get a small business loan, send a remittance, or buy insurance. The 2010 G20 Principles for Innovative Financial Inclusion spurred initial efforts and policy actions. These 2016 High-Level Principles for Digital Financial Inclusion build on that success by providing a basis for country action plans reflecting country context and national circumstances to leverage the huge potential offered by digital technologies.

PRINCIPLE 1: Promote a Digital Approach to Financial Inclusion

Promote digital financial services as a priority to drive development of inclusive financial systems, including through coordinated, monitored, and evaluated national strategies and action plans.

[1] This chapter is co-authored with Ms. Hasna Ashraf, student of MA in Development Studies, Indian Institute of Technology, Madras.

[2] https://rbidocs.rbi.org.in/rdocs/PublicationReport/Pdfs/MDRDBEDA36AB77C4C81A3951C4679DAE68F.PDF, accessed on September 20, 2016.

PRINCIPLE 2: Balance Innovation and Risk to Achieve Digital Financial Inclusion
Balance promoting innovation to achieve digital financial inclusion with identifying, assessing, monitoring and managing new risks.

PRINCIPLE 3: Provide an Enabling and Proportionate Legal and Regulatory Framework for Digital Financial Inclusion
Provide an enabling and proportionate legal and regulatory framework for digital financial inclusion, taking into account relevant G20 and international standard setting body standards and guidance.

PRINCIPLE 4: Expand the Digital Financial Services Infrastructure Ecosystem
Expand the digital financial services ecosystem—including financial and information and communications technology infrastructure—for the safe, reliable and low-cost provision of digital financial services to all relevant geographical areas, especially underserved rural areas.

PRINCIPLE 5: Establish Responsible Digital Financial Practices to Protect Consumers
Establish a comprehensive approach to consumer and data protection that focuses on issues of specific relevance to digital financial services.

PRINCIPLE 6: Strengthen Digital and Financial Literacy and Awareness
Support and evaluate programs that enhance digital and financial literacy in light of the unique characteristics, advantages, and risks of digital financial services and channels.

PRINCIPLE 7: Facilitate Customer Identification for Digital Financial Services
Facilitate access to digital financial services by developing, or encouraging the development of, customer identity systems, products and services that are accessible, affordable, and verifiable and accommodate multiple needs and risk levels for a risk-based approach to customer due diligence.

PRINCIPLE 8: Track Digital Financial Inclusion Progress
Track progress on digital financial inclusion through a comprehensive and robust data measurement and evaluation system. This system should leverage new sources of digital data and enable stakeholders to analyze and monitor the supply of—and demand for—digital financial services, as well as assess the impact of key programs and reforms.

These eight principles are based on the rich experience reflected in G20 and international standard-setting bodies' standards and guidance. They also recognize the need to support innovation while managing risk and encouraging development of digital financial products and services.

Source: Global Partnership for Financial Inclusion, http://www.gpfi.org/sites/default/files/documents/G20%20High%20Level%20Principles%20for%20Digital%20Financial%20Inclusion%20-%20Full%20version-.pdf, accessed on September 17, 2016.

development fund—contributed by all the players in the market but independently managed. The second option placed was the mandating of opening of acceptance infrastructures (ATMs and PoS devices) which are in proportion to the cards issued.

On the other hand, the concept paper also discussed how to drive transaction on the digital platform from the consumer end. The proposals largely discussed the appropriate fees to be charged by the merchants as merchant discount rate, keeping in mind that there could be smaller transactions.

Both the above questions ensure that the ecosystem would become more friendly for digital transactions to happen. While this in itself does not assure a faster offtake of digital financial inclusion, it certainly does provide a good ecosystem for players to come on board.

Nandan Nilekani, former chairman of UIDAI, declared that the Indian financial sector is undergoing the 'WhatsApp' moment. This was not done once, but he repeated it in several talks across the country, where he talked about the digital revolution that is going to come, fundamentally changing how transaction processing happens, how cash would be handled, and how banking itself might change. Nilekani's talk was not isolated, but there were several conferences, workshops, and events where the digitization of cash was discussed. There are two aspects to digitization of the financial space—the first is about transaction efficiency and the second is about inclusion. While most of the buzz is on getting better transaction efficiencies, the important piece in this jigsaw will always be the inclusive space. The digitization project assumes greater importance in the light of the government wanting to shift more and more schemes that benefit the poor to a DBT framework. This implies that technology has to be used from the source account to reach the benefits to the destination account in the most efficient manner. While the ideal situation would imply a cashless settlement, that dream seems to be a distance, while most of the intermediary steps have already been digitized.

ECOSYSTEM FOR DIGITAL BANKING

The basic foundation for digitization was laid long before when, with the prodding of the government and the RBI, the banks aggressively went in for CBS platform, thereby digitizing the back-end. This ensured that the banking system's back operations were ready. At the client level, while the banks were moving to cashless transactions by using debit and credit cards and Internet banking, those were happening on local platforms with handshakes between institutions provided by the backend switch operated by the NPCI. With the roll out of Aadhaar, one big hurdle in inclusion—that of providing a identity document—was addressed. While the banking system had its own mechanisms of dealing with the identity, with reduced requirements of basic accounts, what Aadhaar did was to create a buzz around having a common identity document, the cost of which was borne by the state. With the additional features of biometric capture, it also promised de-duplication and thus added a significant value to a plain vanilla identity document. This second piece was very important in the roll out of the PMJDY (discussed in Chapter 4).

So, the back-end eco-system was there; the front-end customer enrolment had happened. The challenge now was to ensure that both these are put to adequate use, and DBT was an effective way of increasing the usage of the channel. However, both these necessary conditions did not solve the last-mile problem, that the customer ultimately had to convert the balance available in the bank account into cash in order to transact—purchase essentials, pay for the bills, and carry out day to day transactions. While there were card-based transactions that enabled cashless trade, the usage was somewhat limited. The statistics indicate that the number of debit cards outnumbered the credit cards by 27 times and while credit cards were used more at the PoS, the debit cards were used more in the ATMs, thus showing the preference for converting the outstanding balances to cash before expending it.

TECHNOLOGY-ENABLED TOUCHPOINTS

A look at the numbers on how the technology enabled transactions are growing gives an idea of the geometric growth that this segment is going to have. ATMs and PoS devices are the most commonly

Box 5.2 Fintech and Digital Innovation—Opportunities, Challenges, and Risks

Financial services, including banking services, are at the cusp of a revolutionary change driven by technological and digital innovations. Fintech is an umbrella term coined to denote new competitors (typically nonfinancial firms) bringing technological innovations having a bearing on financial services. Digital banking, block chain technology, distributed ledgers, big data, and person-to-person (P2P)/business-to-business (B2B)/business-to-consumers (B2C) platforms which bring together lenders and borrowers are some of the more recent innovations in Fintech. These offer tremendous opportunities and benefits for the financial sector. Convenience and speed of performance, real-time transactions, lower transaction costs, distributed ledger data availability for information and decision-making, product tailoring, and absence of intermediaries are some of the benefits of Fintech.

Fintech is of particular relevance in India given the national aspiration for universal financial inclusion, ensuring last mile reach of finance at affordable costs. A combination of cloud computing, hand-held devices and mobile smartphones have aided the expansion of Fintech in India. The newly introduced PBs are expected to be important players in the arena of Fintech given the central role of technology in their operations.

However, Fintech brings with it several challenges for the regulator given its departure from the traditional process of financial intermediation. The risks entailed therein are not just limited to technology but could, inter alia, involve: issues arising from transactions in financial products by unregulated financial and non-financial entities; outsourcing of products/services; and acquisition of software solutions without access to/awareness about source codes.

In view of the 'disruptive' potential of Fintech, it is necessary to examine the need for regulation and design an appropriate regulatory framework, if required. Hence, the RBI has set up the Inter-regulatory Working Group on Fin Tech and Digital Banking (Chairman: Shri S. Sen) in July 2016. The group, inter alia, will assess the opportunities and risks from Fintech for customers and other stakeholders. Furthermore, it will examine the implications and challenges of Fintech for various financial sector functions, including intermediation, clearing, and payments being taken up by non-financial entities, and suggest appropriate regulatory response, if any.

Source: RBI (2016) Annual Report.

Table 5.1 Data on Technology-enabled Touchpoints and Transactions over the Years

Detail	2012	2013	2014	2015	2016	Growth
Infrastructure						
Onsite ATMs	47,545	55,760	83,379	89,061	101,950	114%
Offsite ATMs	48,141	58,254	76,676	92,337	97,149	102%
Online PoS	647,869	840,983	1,050,323	1,126,389	1,385,342	114%
Offline PoS	13,051	13,307	15,661	346	326	–98%
Total touchpoints	756,606	968,304	1,226,039	1,308,133	1,584,767	109%
Credit Cards						
Outstanding credit cards	17,653,818	19,538,329	19,181,567	21,110,653	24,505,219	39%
Transactions at ATMs	202,106	225,770	296,548	437,278	612,531	203%
Transactions at PoS	28,744,710	35,616,482	46,105,415	56,906,942	72,220,394	151%
Amnts ₹ million at ATM	1,209	1,493	1,662	2,344	2,803	132%
Amnts ₹ million at PoS	88,374	111,217	145,487	178,988	226,943	157%
Debit Cards						
Outstanding debit cards	278,282,839	331,196,720	394,421,738	553,451,553	661,824,092	138%
Transactions at ATMs	471,031,623	482,004,645	571,497,661	624,205,135	731,722,405	55%
Transactions at PoS	30,668,922	45,376,619	56,981,333	76,105,726	112,868,336	268%
Amnts ₹ million at ATM	1,317,168	1,556,406	1,796,099	1,987,480	2,245,822	71%
Amnts ₹ million at PoS	46,534	66,873	85,771	108,283	134,632	189%

Source: ATM/PoS/Card Statistics, https://rbi.org.in/scripts/ATMView.aspx?atmid=61, accessed on July 14, 2016.
The overall ATM statistics are available at the National Payments Corporation of India website, http://www.npci.org.in/nfsatm.aspx, accessed on August 28, 2015.

Notes: 1. The above numbers pertain to the ATMs of 56 scheduled commercial banks in the following ownership category—foreign banks, public sector banks (including IDBI Bank), and old and new private sector banks. However, some foreign banks, Bharatiya Mahila Bank, RRBs, and all the co-operative banks (both rural and urban) were left out. Totally there were 226,816 ATMs as of August 2016.

2. Of these, 1024 ATMs belonged to RRBs, 2442 ATMs were with urban co-operative banks, and 14,169 were white label ATMs—independent stand-alone entities providing just the ATM service to the banking sector. The number of ATMs owned by RRBs and co-operative banks are discussed in the respective chapters.

accessed touchpoints (see Table 5.1). Over the years there has been a continuous increase in the number of ATMs and PoS. However, given the scale and diversity of India, the acceptance infrastructure is still largely underdeveloped with 15 ATMs per 100,000 adults and 1.2 million PoS terminals for an estimated 14 million merchants (J. M. Financial 2015). By 2020 around 40% of merchants are expected to have electronic payment acceptance devices. The issuance gap that exists in PoS terminals is quite high. This would ultimately lead to acceptance problems. One way to tackle this would be to take advantage of the existing infrastructure of smartphones and work toward a virtual mobile point of sale (mPoS) solution that converts a merchant's smartphone into a virtual PoS device.

Table 5.2 shows the indicators for the payments systems, which clearly indicates the increase in volumes of digital transactions both in terms of the channels used for digital transactions and the number of transactions as well as the volumes. As the new innovations come into the field, it is possible that there is going to be a greater decline in the use of cash and the overall economy would move toward cashless.

Several players are eying the space of payments. In 2015, RBI granted in-principle license to 11 players to set up PBs (out of which three of them have withdrawn). An interesting fact here is that as many as four of these are clearly identifiable to groups having interests in the telecom space. Payments banks will provide banking access to the poorer customers, enabling them to perform domestic remittance to the remotest part of the country. It will drive cashless transaction in geographically inaccessible and sparsely populated parts of the country. Apart from

Table 5.2 Payment System Indicators

Item	Volume (million)			Value (₹ billion)		
	2013–14	2014–15	2015–16	2013–14	2014–15	2015–16
1	2	3	4	5	6	7
Systemically Important Financial Market infrastructures (SIFMIs)						
1. RTGS	81.1	92.8	98.3	734,252	754,032	824,578
Total Financial Markets Clearing (2+3+4)	**2.6**	**3.0**	**3.1**	**621,570**	**672,456**	**721,094**
2. CBLO	0.2	0.2	0.2	175,262	167,646	178,335
3. Government Securities Clearing	0.9	1.0	1.0	161,848	179,372	183,502
4. Forex Clearing	1.5	1.8	1.9	284,460	325,438	359,257
Total SIFMIs (1 to 4)	**83.7**	**95.7**	**101.4**	**1,355,822**	**1,426,488**	**1,545,672**
Retail Payments						
Total Paper Clearing (5+6+7)	**1,257.3**	**1,195.8**	**1,096.4**	**93,316**	**85,439**	**81,861**
5. CTS	591.4	964.9	958.4	44,691	66,770	69,889
6. MICR Clearing	440.1	22.4	0.0	30,943	1,850	0
7. Non-MICR Clearing	225.9	208.5	138.0	17,682	16,819	11,972
Total Retail Electronic Clearing (8+9+10+11+12)	**1,108.3**	**1,687.4**	**3,141.6**	**47,856**	**65,366**	**91,408**
8. ECS DR	192.9	226.0	224.8	1,268	1,740	1,652
9. ECS CR	152.5	115.3	39.0	2,492	2,019	1,059
10. NEFT	661.0	927.6	1,252.9	43,786	59,804	83,273
11. Immediate Payment Service (IMPS)	15.4	78.4	220.8	96	582	1,622
12. National Automated Clearing House (NACH)	86.5	340.2	1,404.1	215	1,221	3,802
Total Card Payments (13+14+15)	**1,261.8**	**1,737.7**	**2,707.2**	**2,575**	**3,325**	**4,484**
13. Credit Cards	509.1	615.1	785.7	1,540	1,899	2,407
14. Debit Cards	619.1	808.1	1,173.5	955	1,213	1,589
15. Prepaid Payment Instruments (PPIs)	133.6	314.5	748.0	81	212	488
Total Retail Payments (5 to 15)	**3,627.4**	**4,620.9**	**6,945.2**	**143,748**	**154,129**	**177,752**
Grand Total (1 to 15)	**3,711.1**	**4,716.6**	**7,046.6**	**1,499,570**	**1,580,617**	**1,723,425**

Source: RBI (2016) Annual Report.
Notes: 1. Real time gross settlement (RTGS) system includes customer and inter-bank transactions only.
2. Settlement of collateralised borrowing and lending obligation (CBLO), government securities clearing and forex transactions are through the Clearing Corporation of India Ltd. (CCIL).
3. Consequent to total cheque volume migrating to the cheque truncation system (CTS), there is no magnetic ink character recognition (MICR) cheque processing centre (CPC) location in the country as of now.
4. The figures for cards are for transactions at point of sale (POS) terminals only.
5. The National Automated Clearing House (NACH) system was started by the National Payments Corporation of India (NPCI) on December 29, 2012, to facilitate inter-bank, high volume, electronic transactions which are repetitive and periodic in nature.
6. ECS: Electronic clearing service; DR: Debit; CR: Credit; NEFT: National electronic funds transfer.
7. Figures in the columns might not add up to the total due to rounding off.

this, there are about 46 players operating prepaid payment instruments (PPIs) (see Table 5.3). These players can be believed to eventually redefine the payments space. The innovations and architecture that they are likely to bring about would immensely benefit the cause of financial inclusion. Also in the ecosystem are white label ATM players, specialised in setting up and operating ATMs with a revenue model based on transaction fee. Clearly the space is getting interesting and lucrative, and it is possible for banking to expand beyond the infrastructural constraints laid out by the banks themselves.

Table 5.3 List of PPI Licencees, Payments Bank Licencees, and White Label ATM Operators

	Prepaid Payment Instruments	Payments Banks Entities
1	Aircel Smart Money Limited	Aditya Birla Nuvo Limited
2	Airtel M Commerce Services Ltd.	Airtel M Commerce Services Limited
3	Atom Technologies Limited	Department of Posts
4	Card Pro Solutions Pvt. Ltd.	Fino PayTech Limited
5	Citrus Payment Solutions Pvt. Ltd.	National Securities Depository Limited
6	Delhi Integrated Multi- Modal Transit System Limited	Reliance Industries Limited
7	DigitSecure India Private Limited	Vijay Shekhar Sharma—Paytm
8	Edenred (I) Private Limited—nee Accor Services Pvt. Ltd.	Vodafone m-pesa Limited
9	Eko India Financial Services Private Limited	
10	Freecharge Payment Technologies Private Limited	White Label ATM Operators
11	Fino Paytech Ltd.	AGS Transact Technologies Ltd.
12	FX Mart Pvt. Ltd.	BTI Payments Pvt. Ltd.
13	GI Technology Private Limited	Hitachi Payment Services Pvt Limited
14	Hip Bar Private Limited	Muthoot Finance Ltd.
15	Idea Mobile Commerce Services Ltd.	RiddiSiddhi Bullions Limited
16	India Transact Services Limited	SREI Infrastructure Finance Ltd.
17	Itz Cash Card Ltd.	Tata Communications Payment Solutions
18	Kedia Infotech Ltd.	
19	LivQuik Technology (India) Private Limited	Vakrangee Limited
20	MMP Mobi Wallet Payment Systems Limited	
21	Mpurse Services Pvt. Ltd.	
22	Muthoot Vehicle & Asset Finance Ltd.	
23	My Mobile Payments Limited	
24	One97 Communications Ltd.	
25	One Mobikwik Systems Private Limited	
26	Oxigen Services (India) Pvt. Ltd.	
27	Paul Fincap Pvt. Ltd.	
28	PayMate India Pvt. Limited	
29	PayU Payments Private Limited	
30	Pay Point India Network Private Limited	
31	Premium eBusiness Ventures Private Limited	
32	Pyro Networks Private Ltd.	
33	QwikCilver Solutions Pvt. Ltd.	
34	Reliance Payment Solution Limited	
35	Smart Payment Solutions Pvt. Ltd.	
36	Sodexo SVC India Pvt. Ltd.	
37	Spice Digital Ltd.	
38	Tech Mahindra Limited	
39	Transaction Analysts (India) Private Ltd.	
40	TranServ Private Limited	
41	UAE Exchange & Financial Services Ltd.	
42	UTI Infrastructure Technology and Services Ltd.	

	Prepaid Payment Instruments	Payments Banks Entities
43	Vodafone m-pesa Limited	
44	Weizmann Impex Service Enterprise Limited	
45	Y-Cash Software Solutions Private Limited	
46	ZipCash Card Services Pvt. Ltd.	

Source: RBI, https://rbi.org.in/SCRIPTs/PublicationsView.aspx?id=12043, accessed on July 18, 2016.

DIGITAL 'INCLUSION'

Digital financial inclusion can be defined as the digital access to and use of formal financial services by excluded and underserved populations. Such services should be suited to the customers' needs and delivered responsibly, at a cost both affordable to customers and sustainable for providers (Lauer and Lyman 2015). One of the key concerns of most schemes aimed at financial inclusion has been the infeasibility of small transactions. Digital channels bring down the costs significantly. Greater access to digital channels would ensure that transaction costs no longer remain a problem. Despite these, banks continue to be the primary means of financial access in India, and, thus, it is necessary to have a human interface between the banking outlet and the customer. This was initially tried as a business correspondent, with limited success. While experiments on the BC are going on, the government in the last year's budget announced that they would be working on the basis of a JAM trinity. This meant two aspects had to happen. First, the ecosystem should have an affordable and simple back-end technology and second, the mobile phone and usage penetration should be deep. Both are happening. The most significant policy event was the merger of the Financial Inclusion Technology fund with the Financial Inclusion fund to provide a holistic support for inclusion (see Box 5.3).

Box 5.3 FITF Merged with FIF

Financial Inclusion Technology Fund

During the year the Financial Inclusion Technology Fund (FITF) was merged with the FIF and the corpus was set at ₹20 Billion. While the objectives of the FITF fund was focused, the new, merged FIF had much broader objectives. In an era where the market outside of the institutions eligible for being funded are moving toward digitization, it was a bit surprising that the focused FITF was merged into a general FIF. The objectives of the FIF shall be to support "developmental and promotional activities" including creating of financial inclusion infrastructure across the country, capacity-building of stakeholders, creation of awareness to address demand side issues, enhanced investment in green information and communication technology (ICT) solution, research and transfer of technology, and increased technological absorption capacity of financial service providers/users with a view to securing greater financial inclusion. The fund shall not be utilized for normal business/banking activities.

The eligible activities/purposes included the support for funding the setting up and operational cost for running financial inclusion and literacy centers. The setting up of such centers are in sync with the objective of GoI for setting up financial literacy centers up to the block level under the PMJDY. The cost of technical manpower employed by banks for running the financial inclusion and literacy centres (as banks have manpower shortages) will be funded from the fund. The scope of activities to be carried out by these centers would be as follows:

- Providing financial literacy training to all individuals/households of the area.
- Providing counseling services for opening of bank accounts and for operating banking and other financial products and services.
- Providing training to BCs about various banking and other financial products and services and also training them in use of technological devices so as to ensure smooth servicing of customers.
- Redressal of customer grievances by attending to customer complaints, if necessary, by taking up with banks and other institutions.

Eligible institutions with whom banks can work for seeking support from the FIF:

- NGOs
- SHGs
- Farmer's Clubs
- Functional Cooperatives

- I.T.-enabled rural outlets of corporate entities
- Well-functioning Panchayats
- Rural Multipurpose kiosks/Village Knowledge Centers
- Common Services Centres (CSCs) established by Service Centre Agencies (SCAs) under the National e-Governance Plan (NeGP)
- Primary Agricultural Societies (PACs)

Source: RBI Notification, https://rbidocs.rbi.org.in/rdocs/notification/PDFs/F20626C9DE770E5145738FADC7A72EF47DE8.PDF, accessed on September 29, 2016.

In addition to the architectural ecosystem, there have been more innovations on the institutional ecosystem as well. Already prepaid wallets have taken off and companies like Paytm have been aggressively marketing the 'use' of wallets. The wallets with strategic tie-ups have also addressed the pain points for payments. With eight of the players getting to be PBs—which helps them to do cash in and cash out transactions—the flexibility in operations will increase and these players will be light on touchpoints and heavy on technology, and will use the unified payment interface (UPI) infrastructure to the hilt.

So far so good. But how does the above help the cause of financial inclusion? The answer for that question is a bit more involved. That is because, as of now the applications of these technologies have been mostly set in the middle-class urban settings. However, very much the way the setting up of the mobile phone network architecture helped us to reach more than a billion mobile connections, this architecture will find applications in the inclusive space sooner than later. With the DBT flows going through the banking system, with 10 new SFBs and 8 new PBs looking at the inclusive space with disruptive technology, we are bound to see more action in this space. However, there are issues to be addressed.

So what is the scope for digital financial inclusion in India? Studies point toward a trend of rapid adoption of digitization in India. The younger the individual, the greater is the inclination to adopt digitization. India's demographic dividend is highly favourable in this regard, considering that the median age of an Indian is expected to be 29 years by 2020, with 900 million of the population falling in the age group of 15–60 years by 2025 (KPMG 2015). Spurring digitization on is the fact that there is an increase in mobile and Internet penetration across the country. With financial inclusion slowly moving onto a digital platform, the benefits of owning a mobile are also increasing. There seems to exist a cycle of increased digitization of financial inclusion leading to increased mobile penetration, which in turn again widens the scope of digital financial inclusion. This scenario adds momentum to the journey toward financial inclusion. Given that the number of financially excluded is still high, digital channels have a high potential that could be effectively used to further financial inclusion.

One factor that has acted as a disincentive to the adoption of card accepting infrastructure by merchants, especially small merchants, is merchant discount rate (MDR). In order to encourage all categories of merchants to deploy card acceptance infrastructure and also to facilitate acceptance of small-value transactions through card payments, the RBI rationalized the MDR for debit cards with effect from September 2012. Since then, the MDR for debit card transaction has been capped at 0.75% for transaction values up to ₹2,000 and at 1% for transaction values above ₹2,000.[3] However, the central bank observed that following the cap, the growth in number of PoS terminals had slowed and, therefore, the infrastructure for card acceptance facility failed to keep pace with the growth in retail electronic payments. In order to improve the current scenario, the RBI has proposed a rationalization of MDR (RBI 2012). The dilemma that RBI faces in this regard is that while a reduction of MDR is required to make the system more appealing to merchants, it becomes less appealing to banks. Keeping this in mind, the RBI is looking at multiple options for rationalization of MDR. What policy changes may ultimately come about and what impact they may have needs to be seen.

Last-mile connectivity of most financial inclusion schemes including the mammoth-sized PMJDY is still dependent on agents or BC or as in the case of PMJDY, BM. When we look at technology-enabled touchpoints, it hence becomes important to look at the device penetration amongst agents. As per a study conducted by MicroSave, the transaction readiness of agents is dependent on the availability of transaction devices with them. The study found 81% of agents to be transaction ready (Sharma, Giri, and Chadha 2016). Increasing dormancy of BMs is becoming a cause for concern. This is slightly problematic considering the fact that a vast majority of the population, especially in rural India, is highly dependent on agents for basic banking services. In

[3] RBI Notification at https://rbidocs.rbi.org.in/rdocs/Notification/PDFs/CEMD28062012.pdf, accessed on July 18, 2016.

Box 5.4 Former Governor Subbarao on Telcos and Banks

MSS: Dr Chakrabarty was very articulate arguing that inclusion should be the bank led and other players in the financial system were necessary but only incidental. He argued that the push for inclusion should come from banks. Is there a justification for it being predominantly with the banks?

Dr Subbarao: The justification is quite straight forward. It is only banks that can give all the four components of financial inclusion that we just spoke about—credit, micro-insurance, savings and remittance. In fact, telecom companies used to complain that the RBI was biased against them. There was no such thing. RBI was quite open to allowing telecom companies to ride on their comparative advantage and contribute to FI. But we have to recognize that by themselves, telecoms cannot deliver the full gamut of financial inclusion. Only banks can do that.

MSS: In fact, famously you held out telecom companies are a threat to the banking companies in you CAB speech, if I remember right.

Dr Subbarao: It's possible I said that, but that must be seen in the context in which I said it. The point though, is that the banks are trusted, be they public sector banks or private banks. A telecom company, on the other hand, is typically a private enterprise. In order to get people outside the system to come in, we need that trust. Only banks can inspire that trust.

Now with payments banks coming in, telecoms have an opportunity to get into the banking space. They can leverage on their technology and penetration while RBI too will have comfort as the telecom company sponsored banks will come within its regulatory purview.

such a scenario, digital platform could be seen as a viable alternative that can be utilized to provide last-mile connectivity.

MOBILE AND INTERNET

Mobile phones, as a medium for extending banking services, have attained great significance. The rapid growth of mobile users in India, through wider coverage of mobile phone networks, has made this medium an important platform for extending banking services especially to the unbanked sections of the society. A look at the numbers in Table 5.4 shows that we are on the cusp of an exponential growth in mobile-based transactions. From a million transactions in 2011 to almost 50 million transactions on mobile; less than a billion rupees worth of transactions to almost ₹600 billion of transactions shows a steep growth and the rate of growth is increasing by the year. With the simplification of the interface through UPI this number is expected to grow even faster.

Table 5.4 Data on Transactions on the Mobile

Year	Volume (Millions of Transactions)	Growth	Value (₹ Billion)	Growth
March 2011	1.05		0.84	
March 2012	3.12	197%	2.32	176%
March 2013	6.40	105%	9.91	327%
March 2014	10.74	68%	34.07	243%
March 2015	19.76	84%	169.14	396%
March 2016	49.47	150%	572.80	238%

Source: RBI, https://rbi.org.in/scripts/NEFTView.aspx, accessed on August 28, 2016.

Both the number and value of mobile-based transactions have been rising rapidly. To understand this growth and its potential, it is imperative to look at the physical and regulatory infrastructure of mobile banking in India. However, it is important to note the digital divide between the urban and the rural areas (Table 5.5). The urban tele-density is at 148%, indicating almost 1.5 connections per individual where as in case of the rural areas, it is touching 51%. Most likely, these subscribers are expected to be men, while the inclusive customers are generally women. This is corroborated by a research carried out by Grameen Foundation in UP (Ramanathan 2015).

What is interesting to note is the region-wise penetration of Internet. Even here we see that the South

Table 5.5 Details of Wireless Connections (Millions)

Detail	April 16
Wireless subscribers	1,034.25
Urban subscribers	586.41
Rural Subscribers	447.84
Urban tele-density	147.9
Rural tele-density	51.19
Broadband subscribers	134.04

Source: Telecom Regulatory Authority of India, http://www.trai.gov.in/WriteReadData/WhatsNew/Documents/Press_Release_No.49_20_june_2016_Eng.pdf, accessed on August 29, 2016.

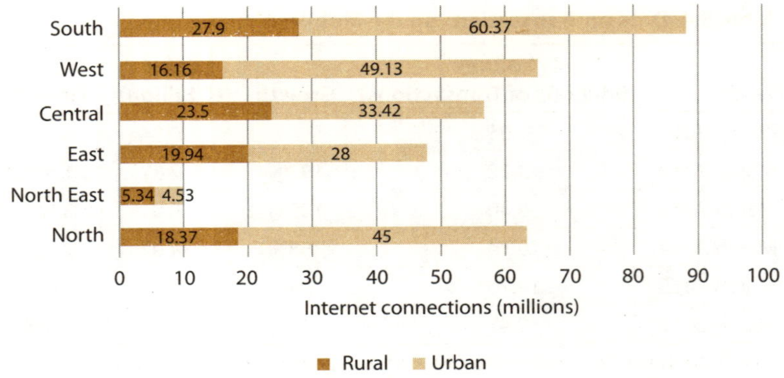

Figure 5.1 Regional Penetration of Internet

Source: TRAI (2016).

dominates in terms of overall share (Figure 5.1). The story of financial inclusion that has been discussed in the previous chapters seems to continue to play out even in somewhat unrelated field of usage of Internet, but this certainly has implications for how the digital financial inclusion story will pan out. The thought that digital solutions may be more viable in areas where physical facilities are a challenge need to be checked carefully, as infrastructure for digital inclusion turns out to be crucial in going beyond the comfort zones.

According to InterMedia India FII Tracker survey, 90% of the population had access to a mobile phone (93% in urban and 88% in rural areas). However, only 60% of them owned one. The growth in the usage of mobile money has been extremely slow (current mobile money use is 1%). The awareness of mobile money is also low at 10%. See Box 5.5 for highlights of the study.

Box 5.5 Highlights of Mobile Money Use

Mobile money use and awareness remain low.

- Mobile money awareness is at 10% and use is at just 0.5%.
- As of August 2015, licenses for PBs had been issued by the Indian Central Bank. Some observers expect these to help spur mobile money growth. Survey fieldwork concluded before these changes could have any potential market impact.

Registered use of mobile money services is growing at a slow place.

- Overall mobile money use grew from 0.3% to 0.5% of adults between 2014 and 2015.
- The longer individuals use mobile money services, the more likely they are to be registered mobile money account holders.

Mobile phone competency, especially with regards to sending and receiving text messages, corresponds to higher rates of financial inclusion through banks, but only slightly higher rates of mobile money usage.

- The number of adults who have used a mobile phone to send or receive text messages (SMS capable) and have a mobile money account in their name (1%) is not much higher than the number of adults who have never sent or received an SMS (0.1%).
- The difference between these two groups in other financial account ownership is much larger, though in opposite directions for banks and NBFIs: SMS capable adults are more likely to have a bank account (73% vs. 62%) than their counterparts, whereas SMS capable adults are less likely to have an NBFI account than the SMS incapable.

Source: InterMedia (2016).

Mobile money account holders are primarily men under 35 years living in urban locations. Low awareness of mobile money and low SIM card ownership seem to be the most prominent barriers to using mobile phones for financial services (InterMedia 2016).

Of the type of mobile phones owned, basic phones are the most common (67%). Smartphone penetration in India stands at 12% (InterMedia 2016). While smartphone penetration in India is on the rise, it is still quite low. Total 14% of the users use mobile phones for advanced functions and out of these 74% are financially included. The younger the individual, the more likely they are to use advanced functions (see Table 5.6). With the median age of Indian population expected to be 29, this looks positive for the future of financial inclusion in India.

While analyzing the status of mobile supported financial services it is also important to look at the access of Internet as a number of these services are Internet based. While the number of mobile subscribers in India is quite high, the number of mobile Internet subscribers lags far behind. As of December 2015, the total number of Internet subscribers is 331.65 million (TRAI 2016). Internet density is currently low at 12.89% (Indicus Centre

Table 5.6 InterMedia Financial Inclusion Tracker Survey

INDIA
FSP INDICATORS

Main FSP Indicator	2013 %	2014 %	2015 %
Adults (15+) that have a bank account	47%	55%	63%
Adults (15+) that have ever accessed a mobile money account	0.3%	0.3%	1%
Adults (15+) with active accounts	25%	29%	45%
Adults (15+) below the poverty line with active accounts	20%	24%	40%
Males (15+) with active accounts	32%	36%	50%
Females (15+) with active accounts	18%	21%	39%
Rural males (15+) with active accounts	26%	30%	45%
Rural females (15+) with active accounts	15%	19%	36%
Adults (15+) actively using accounts beyond basic wallet, P2P and bill pay	9%	9%	10%
Adults (15+) below the poverty line actively using accounts beyond basic wallet, P2P and bill pay	7%	7%	8%
Males (15+) below the poverty line actively using accounts beyond basic wallet, P2P and bill pay	12%	12%	10%
Females (15+) below the poverty line actively using accounts beyond basic wallet, P2P and bill pay	6%	6%	9%
Rural Males (15+) below the poverty line actively using accounts beyond basic wallet, P2P and bill pay	10%	10%	8%
Rural Females (15+) below the poverty line actively using accounts beyond basic wallet, P2P and bill pay	5%	6%	8%

Source: Intermedia India Financial Tracker Surveys: Wave 2 (N=45,087 15+); Wave 3 (N=45,036, 15+), June–October 2015, http://finclusion.org/uploads/file/reports/InterMedia%20FII%20Wave%203%202015%20India.pdf accessed on August 28, 2016.

for Financial Inclusion 2015). While there is improvement in this scenario with the Internet density expected to rise 39% by June 2016, inclusion schemes dependent on Internet have less chances of being effective.

This physical infrastructure of mobile banking is well supplemented by a regulatory infrastructure. RBI has established a set of operative guidelines for mobile banking services. These guidelines, based on industry best practices, aim to bring in greater standardization across mobile services offered by various banks. This regulatory framework helps in bringing about a sense of confidence and trust in mobile based financial services.

It is important to look at other initiatives implemented by the government that will help take this digital financial inclusion forward. One such key initiative is the Digital India program launched by the NDA government in July 2015. As a part of the initiative, the government plans to implement a Comprehensive Telecom Development Plan which aims at bringing connectivity to the most isolated regions of India by 2019 through expansion of mobile and Internet services including 55,669 villages and areas affected by left-wing terrorism. This will be a major shot in the arm for digital financial inclusion in India.

A number of mobile-based financial services have been implemented over the years that have managed to have a significant impact. For instance NPCI has introduced an important service: The *99# service for mobile banking without Internet. This service was introduced taking into account the need for immediate low-value remittances, expanding financial inclusion. Banking customers can avail this service by dialing *99# on their mobile phone and transacting through an interactive menu displayed on the mobile screen. It is currently offered by 51 banks and all global system mobile service providers and can be accessed in 12 different languages including Hindi and English. The service also offered through BC Micro-ATMs to serve the rural populace making it the most promising platform for financial inclusion.

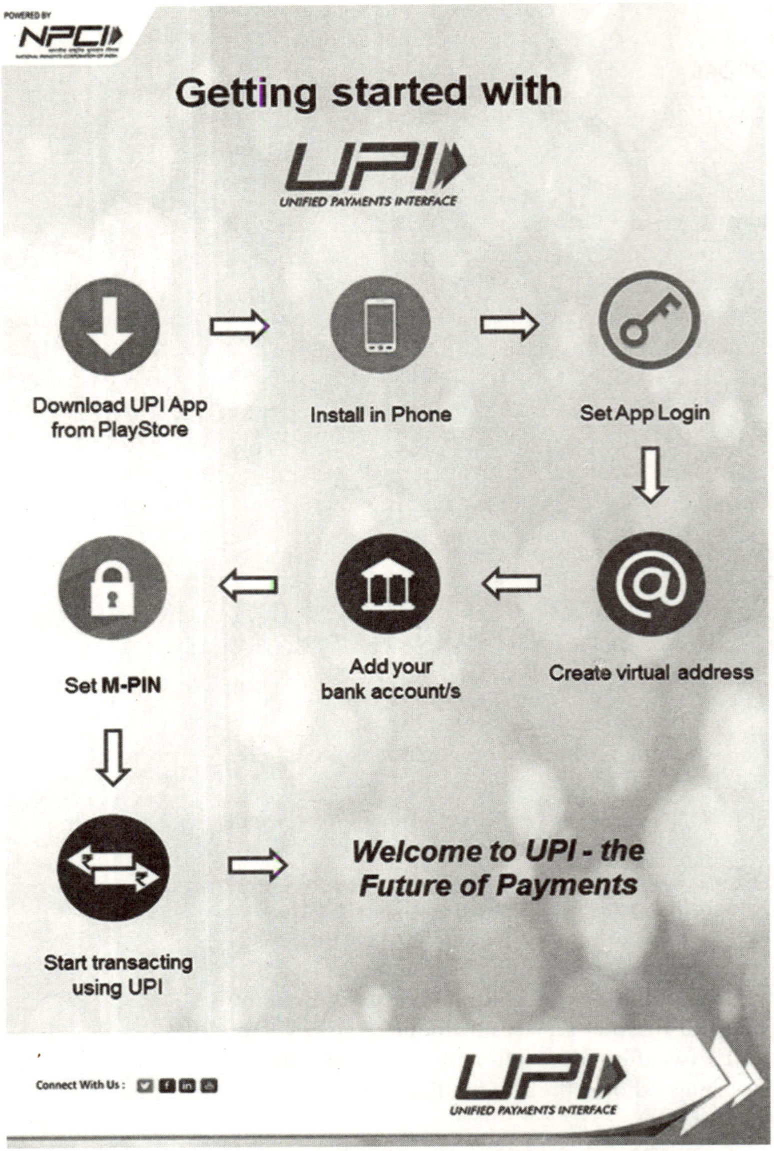

Figure 5.2 NPCI's Five-step Process for UPI

Source: National Payments Corporation of India.

Table 5.7 Pricing Model for UPI P2P Transactions

S. No.	Particulars	Amount	Paid By	Paid To
1	UPI switching fee	25 p	Remitter Bank	NPCI
2	IMPS switching fee	50 p	Remitter Bank	NPCI
3	PSP fee	50 p	Remitter Bank	Remitter PSP
4	Transaction amount	Variable	Remitter Bank	Beneficiary Bank
5	Interchange fee	IMPS P2P Pricing#	Remitter Bank	Beneficiary Bank

Source: NPCI.
Note: # In IMPS:
Up to a value ₹25,000—Interchange payable is ₹1.0.
Upward of ₹25,000 to ₹200,000—Interchange payable is ₹5.0.

Immediate Payment Service (IMPS) launched by NPCI is one such service offered. IMPS offers instant 24×7 interbank electronic fund transfer service through mobile, Internet and ATMs. There are currently 169 members including banks and prepaid instrument issuers on the platform. The growth in IMPS transactions is in fact astounding. Approximately 200 million transactions have been carried out in the year 2015 up from 60 million in 2014 (Axis Capital 2016).

Nilekani correctly identifies the growth of the mobile phone penetration and the increase in smartphone usage in his presentation. The launch of the UPI by the NPCI is a potential game changer on how payments could be done. The simple architecture developed by NPCI makes the interface for payments easy (Figure 5.2).

Mobile wallet offered by PPI players is yet another important service offered. These are basically used for money transfers, banking transactions, bill payments, and so on. The Indian mobile wallet market is expected to be more than ₹12 billion by 2019, a significant increase from approximately ₹3.5 billion at the end of 2014 (KPMG 2016).

With the launch of UPI, the debate has shifted to whether the new UPI will pose a threat to the prepaid wallets. While the ease of operation of UPI makes it simpler to make payments, and therefore there are arguments that there would be stiff competition for wallets. The pricing model for UPI is competitive both for the bankers and for the merchants (see Tables 5.7 and 5.8). Moreover, some of the wallet players are themselves becoming niche banks. Therefore, in days to come, it is quite possible that we see new innovative models emerging, as well as some consolidation happening in this sector.

AADHAAR

While we have discussed Jan Dhan (in detail in Chapter 4) and mobile (earlier in the chapter) in the JAM trinity, it is important to note the developments on Aadhaar as well. During the past year, the controversies around Aadhaar were discussed. This year, however, the Aadhaar (targeted delivery of financial and other subsidies, benefits, and services) Bill, 2016 was passed, giving the project a legal sanctity. This was a significant development, as the entire exercise of enrollment and use of Aadhaar was constantly being questioned in the courts of law. With the passage of the bill, the continuance of enrollments is not under question, though there might still be issues pertaining to privacy that may be adjudicated in future.

Table 5.8 Pricing Model for Merchant Transactions

Particulars	Amount	Paid By	Paid To
UPI switching fee	25 p	Remitter Bank	NPCI
IMPS switching fee	50 p	Remitter Bank	NPCI
PSP fee	50 p	Beneficiary Bank	Remitter PSP
Transaction amount	Transaction value	Remitter Bank	Beneficiary Bank
Interchange fee	IMPS merchant pricing*	Beneficiary Bank	Remitter Bank

Source: NPCI.
Note: * In IMPS:
Up to a value ₹2,000—Interchange payable is ₹0.40%.
Upward of ₹2,000—Interchange payable is ₹0.65%.

Table 5.9 Aadhaar Saturation

Aadhaar saturation as of June 30, 2016	
Number of Aadhaars assigned	1,026,098,560
Percentage of total population covered	80.20%
Percentage of population (0–5 years) covered	20.60%
Percentage of population (5–18 years) covered	63.40%
Percentage of population (above 18 years) covered	97%
Percentage of Aadhaar seeded PMJDY accounts	47.83%

Source: UIDAI, https://uidai.gov.in/images/news/aadhaar_saturation_30Jun2016.pdf, accessed on July 14, 2016.

As of June 2016, more than a billion Aadhaar numbers have been assigned, accounting for more than 80% of the total population (Table 5.9).

The fact that only about 47.8% of PMJDY accounts have been linked to Aadhaar, while many more account holders actually have Aadhaar numbers, indicates the distance to be travelled in completing this loop. There might even be reluctance amongst some customers in linking the account with the number on the concern of privacy. This issue is controversial and has to be tackled with tact and maturity. The unique identity provided by Aadhaar stands to act as a mode of authentication which is important when it comes to the implementation of schemes. One question is about why Aadhaar seeding did not pick pace? The answer partly was in the fact that Aadhaar did not have a statutory backing. With the act being passed and notified, the mapping of Aadhaar numbers with the bank account may improve, though the act does not really make Aadhaar mandatory. From a perspective of ease of opening the account, Aadhaar as an electronic KYC (eKYC) document serves a useful purpose. The use of Aadhaar for verification in real-time online transactions is to be tested at scale and we would know its efficacy in due course.

Apart from being a document aiding identification, Aadhaar is the key enabler of the Aadhaar Enabled Payment System (AEPS). AEPS is a bank-led model which allows online, interoperable financial inclusion transactions at PoS through BCs of any bank using the Aadhaar authentication. The services offered on AEPS include balance enquiry, cash withdrawal/deposit, Aadhaar-to-Aadhaar fund transfer, and gateway authentication services.

Yet another important function of Aadhaar is aiding the Aadhaar Payment Bridge System (APBS). APBS has been successful in channelizing government subsidies and benefits to intended beneficiaries using Aadhaar numbers. APBS links the government departments and their sponsor banks on one side and beneficiary banks and beneficiary on the other side. In a sense, the real intent of Aadhaar lies not in providing a proof of identity but rather in targeted delivery of services. This role has become even stronger with the launch of PMJDY and the JAM trinity.

DIGITAL FINANCE AT THE FRONTIER

There are multiple efforts from the ecosystem to ensure that the digital financial system turns out to be inclusive. The Bill and Melinda Gates Foundation (BMGF) has launched the Level One Project which works with all elements of the ecosystem to make digital finance inclusive. The idea is to create an ecosystem that provides easy and seamless, and cost effective access to the financial system. The framework of Level One Project is described in Figure 5.3.

There are two elements that need to be addressed at the cutting edge of digital finance. The first is about customer habits and reliability. It is evident that at the customer level, the way they transact is a

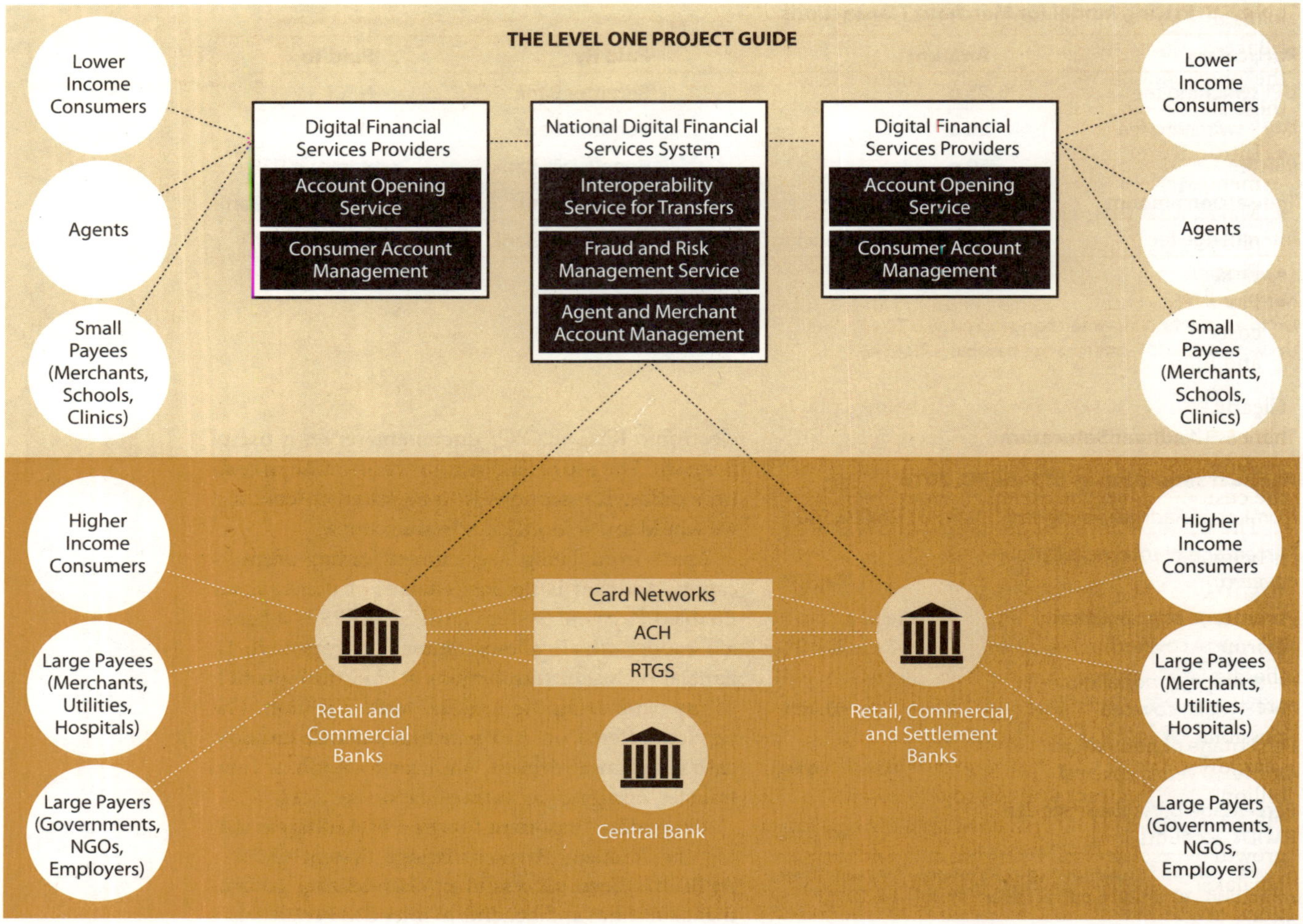

Figure 5.3 Level One Project of BMGF

Source: The Level One Project Guide: Designing a New System for Financial Inclusion (2015).

function of old habits as well as the reliability of the technology. It would be difficult to expect customers to shift to digital cash/transactions if the ATM links fail, if online authentication does not work, if network signals are weak, and if technology itself intermittently fails to sow doubts on the reliability. Therefore, as the agenda of digital finance goes further, it is important to ensure that the back-end technology is robust and failsafe. Usually the digital divide comes because the remote areas where there are small ticket and small number of transactions are the ones that are likely to get negatively affected. If these areas which do not have a natural physical advantage also lose on the digital advantage the divide increases. Therefore, enough attention needs to be paid on recourse and operating systems for recourse. A paper by the Consultative Group to Assist the Poor (CGAP) discusses the models of recourse for transactions in new touchpoints, user-led versus agent-led touchpoints, and models for advanced financial products (Mazer and Garg 2015). The issues discussed in the paper are important to ensure that the user experience is great in order to effect a behavioural change from conventional finance to digital finance.

In addition to just the experiential concerns, there are also concerns about the whether the targeting is appropriate and in spite of the failsafe technology, would the usage be appropriate. For instance, is having money on the mobile safe? Would it encourage impulsive financial decisions? What would be the gender balance—would the money in the hands of the woman get transferred to the mobile of the man? These are questions that were raised in a research by Grameen Foundation as they rolled out mobile money in UP (Ramanathan 2015). It is interesting that the customers of Sonata with whom the experiment was carried out adopt to repaying the loans through a mobile wallet—Oxygen. The experience recounts the steps that are needed in getting the poor women to be digitally comfortable, and these steps include:

- Introduce a third party agent as a venue for payments.
- Make sure that clients associate their mobile phones with these payments.
- First proceed with *fully agent-assisted* transactions.
- Pay agents commission in lieu of transportation costs to reach the group meeting venue (Anand and Ramanathan 2015).

Clearly, bringing about a behavioral change that enhances the customer experience needs a significant amount of investment in handholding and assuring the customers that the digital channel is safe.

The second element is about how the technology is being put to use to make the services more inclusive. While much action is happening on the digital finance space at the roll out level, there are many disruptive experiments at work the world over on the digital finance. What we have discussed above are the experiments that look at the conventional possibilities. Janalakshmi for instance, during the year, drew up a multi-year contract valued at ₹5.5 billion.[4] The contract was to provide an end to end IT and analytics solution that will fuel the aggressive growth of Janalakshmi. Using big data and analytics, Janalakshmi and IBM would offer customised solutions at the client level, by generating alternatives for future financial planning. This will be done by matching the customer profile with the data generated from matching experiences of people moving up the value chain through intelligent financial investments and entrepreneurial ventures. A technology using natural language processing and machine learning and is termed as a cognitive system.[5] A presentation seems to indicate that this would not only revolutionise how financial institutions deal with risk, but would be a breakthrough in financial counselling and literacy programs as well.[6]

One aspect that possibly deserves attention is the level of big data mining that can happen, the algorithms that can be built, and the use of machine learning in order to expand the market. For instance, look at Figure 5.4 where organisations like Lenddo

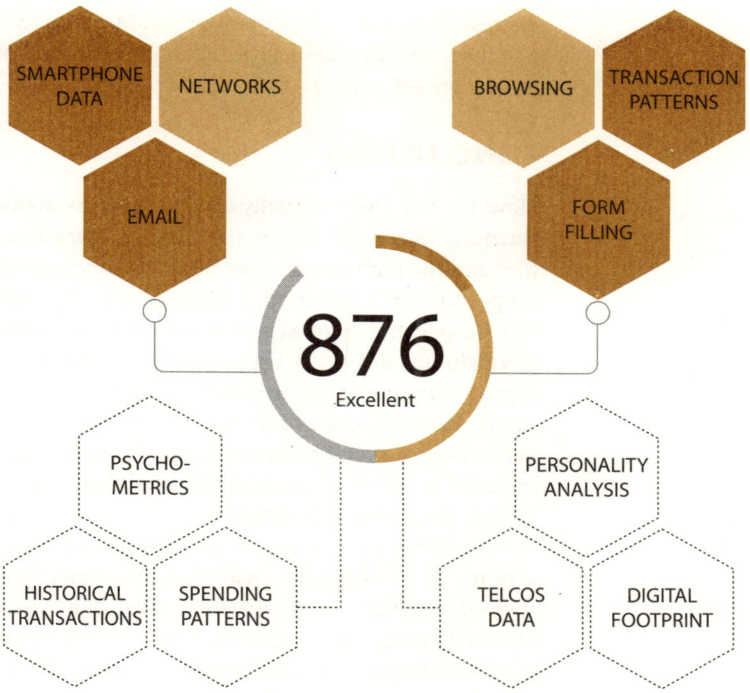

Figure 5.4 Lendoo's Credit Scoring Model

Source: https://www.lenddo.com/pdfs/Lenddo-Scoring-Factsheet-201608.pdf, accessed on October 7, 2016.

use data from multiple sources to map out and allot a credit score for a potential borrower. There are organisations like Cignifi who also do credit scoring. Organisations like the Entrepreneurial Finance Lab administer a psychometric test (lasting about 30 minutes), online or offline to get a credit score instantly. Organisations like RevolutionCredit also use multiple data aspects in assessing the customers behavioural pattern. There are many more companies like Lendoo that are building models using publicly available private data to profile the potential customers. Companies like Segovia use satellite imaging, machine learning, biometrics, and adaptive fraud detection techniques to monitor government-to-person (G2P) (or DBT) payments.

However, the models raise significant concerns about data privacy and how customers could be targeted at their vulnerabilities. First, most of the date that is used assumes informed consent, which is questionable. Second, if this data that is mined is used to target customers into getting into a debt cycle that encourages consumption behaviour that is not matched by the overall growth in the income behaviour, the sector would be pushing the borrowers toward a greater stress. While a greater amount of digitisation is going to help in the cause of inclusion, would it create stressed customers due to the

[4] Reported in Economic Times, accessed from http://articles.economictimes.indiatimes.com/2014-07-14/news/51484974_1_ibm-india-janalakshmi-financial-microfinance-firm, accessed on September 11, 2016.

[5] http://www.ibm.com/watson/

[6] https://www.youtube.com/watch?v=J9o0hvEpVvE

aggressive growth of technology enabled microfinance sector? This has happened in the past and has to be guarded against.

CONCLUSIONS

How far has India actually come about in digital financial inclusion? Given the existing infrastructure and the high demand for financial services, the scope for digital financial inclusion is quite high. But despite the high scope, a shift to the digital platform has not really happened. The potential of digital channels in furthering the agenda of financial inclusion has not really been fully utilized. The percentage of the population that has been digitally included is still only around 49% (InterMedia 2016). Where does the problem lie?

Both in terms of number and volume of transactions, technologically enabled touchpoints have showed marked improvements over the years. However, acceptance infrastructure is not keeping pace with the rise in requirements. An increased focus on innovations based on existing infrastructure (mPoS for example) is likely to improve this scenario.

When it comes to the use of mobile technology, the physical infrastructure is well in place. Mobile phones are currently marked by high access across the country. However, low ownership of mobile phones and SIM cards are turning out to be significant barriers to effective digital financial inclusion. Another major concern is the lack of awareness regarding mobile based financial services. When it comes to Internet-based services the problem lies in access itself. Internet does not seem to be having the same reach that mobile has. Low penetration of smartphones is another factor that should be noted. While the situation is rapidly changing for the better, in the current context, schemes that are less dependent on advanced functions have better chances of being successful. The use of multilingual voice-based interaction accessible even through basic sets is one way to effectively take digital financial inclusion forward.

While the reach of telecom sector is unparalleled, the quality of the service is often questionable. Weak telecom connectivity and bandwidth limits digital transactions, especially in rural areas. Hence, looking at the expansiveness of mobile networks alone is not going to be of help if the quality of services in not monitored. The tele-density metrics that we currently have are insufficient to monitor quality of financial services.

In terms of numbers, Aadhaar has made significant progress. However, effective implementation of financial inclusion schemes are dependent on Aadhaar-seeding of bank accounts and in terms of Aadhaar seeding there is still a long way to go. The legal backing that Aadhaar recently received is hoped to enhance the pace of Aadhaar seeding. The security concerns revolving around Aadhaar continue to persist. These concerns cannot be taken lightly and a privacy law to allay them is the need of the hour.

The regulatory infrastructure is also well in place, however, banks, telecoms, and payment service providers are yet to exploit synergies in serving the same customers owing to multiple domain regulators. There is also the problem of overlapping jurisdictions. There is a rising need for a regulatory framework that will encourage cross-sector partnerships with clearly defined roles for each of the players involved.

While both regulatory and physical infrastructure seems to be in place, it does not mean that they are not without flaws. Identifying and addressing these flaws is the next step. Raising awareness about digital financial transactions is of utmost importance and all the players involved need to step up to the task. Encouraging new schemes to utilize the digital platform will ensure increased adoption. This will also prevent banks from being overburdened.

The year 2015 has seen remarkable improvements in terms of digital financial inclusion. It is slowly proving to be the future of financial inclusion in India. The detailed numbers of transactions on digital medium are provided in Appendices 5.1 and 5.2. However, the progress made so far should not lead to complacency as there is still have a long way to go before the target of financial inclusion is fully achieved.

APPENDIX 5.1
Retail Payments Statistics on NPCI Platforms: Financial Transactions

S. No.	NPCI Operated Systems Financial Transactions:	2014–15 Volume (in Mn)	2014–15 Value (in Bn)	2015–16 Volume (in Mn)	2015–16 Value (in Bn)
1	NFS inter-bank ATM cash withdrawal	2,374	8,312	2,837	9,993
2	NACH—National Automated Clearing House	325	1,197	1,367	3,706
2.1	APBS Cr. (disbursement based on UIDAI No.)	168	61	713	177
2.2	ACH debit	3	58	24	504
2.3	ACH credit	81	52	487	879
2.4	NACH credit	72	1,025	115	1,998
2.5	NACH debit			28	148
3	CTS cheque clearing	926	66,010	920	69,889
4	IMPS	78	582	221	1,622
5	RuPay Card usage at (PoS)	5	11	25	45
6	RuPay Card usage at (eCom)	1	0.5	10	6
7	AEPS (inter-bank) transactions over micro ATM (e.g., cash withdrawal/cash deposit)			0.36	0.86
	Total financial transactions	3,709	76,111	5,381	85,262

Source: http://www.npci.org.in/stats.aspx, accessed on August 28, 2016.

APPENDIX 5.2
Retail Payments Statistics on NPCI Platforms: Non-financial Transactions

S. No.	NPCI Operated Systems Non-financial Transactions:	2014–15 Volume (in Mn)	2015–16 Volume (in Mn)
1	NFS inter-bank transactions over ATM (e.g., balance inquiry/Mobile No. registration, etc.)	694	863.00
2	AEPS (inter-bank) transaction over micro ATM (e.g., balance inquiry/mini statement, etc.)		0.33
3	AEPS (intra-bank) UIDAI authentication over micro ATM		94.30
2.2	eKYC verification (successful transaction)		12.63
4	Demographic queries (authenticated UID)		12.98
5	Archieval query on CTS (Print+Retrieve request) (NAS)		0.92
6	Account No. verification service under ACH	61	37
6.1	Old account confirmation (OAC) service under ACH		7.65
6.2	Customer NACH (earlier ECS) mandate processed	1.16	4.53
6.3	Aadhaar Mapper-Enabled Services (AMES)		118.11
6.4	Aadhaar Status Verification Services	30.54	315.62
6.5	Aadhaar Overdraft Verification Services (AOVS)	0.02	2.99
6.6	Aadhaar Seeding Queries	25.22	28.90
7	Total Non-Financial Transactions (B)	812	1,499

Source: http://www.npci.org.in/stats.aspx, accessed on August 28, 2016.

REFERENCES

Anand, P. and S. Ramanathan. 2015, November 12. "Steady and Sustainable Behaviour Change – Lessons from Sonata." Grameen Foundation Insights Blog. Lucknow: Grameen Foundation. Available at: http://www.grameenfoundation.org/blog/steady-and-sustainable-behaviour-change-%E2%80%93-lessons-sonata#.V8OIPph942w (Accessed on August 29, 2016).

Axis Capital. 2016. *NPCI: Driving Digital Payment Revolution*. Mumbai: Axis Capital.

Indicus Centre for Financial Inclusion. 2015. *Service Quality Standards in Telecom Connectivity for Financial Inclusion*. Delhi: Indicus Centre for Financial Inclusion.

InterMedia. 2016. *India Wave Report: FII Tracker Survey*. Washington DC: InterMedia (Accessed on August 28, 2016).

JM Financial. 2015. *NPCI-UPI to Usher E-Payments Revolution*. Mumbai: JP Financial.

KPMG. 2015. *Role of Digital Banking in furthering Financial Inclusion*. Gurgaon: KPMG.

———. 2016. Digital Banking: Banking on the Go.

Lauer, K. and T. Lyman. 2015. Digital Financial Inclusion: Implications for Customers, Regulators, Supervisors, and Standard-Setting Bodies. Washington DC: CGAP.

Mazer, R., and Garg, N. 2015, December. "Recourse in Digital Financial Services: Opportunities for Innovation." C Gap Brief. Washington: CGAP.

Ramanathan, S. 2015, June 15th. "The Cash to Mobile Money Transition: Insights from Uttar Pradesh Microfinance Clients." Grameen Foundation Insights Blog. Grameen Foundation. Available at: http://www.grameenfoundation.org/blog/cash-mobile-money-transition-%E2%80%93-insights-uttar-pradesh%E2%80%99s-microfinance-clients#.V8ODwZh942w (Accessed on August 29, 2016).

RBI. 2012. Banking Structure in India: The Way Forward (Discussion Paper). Mumbai: RBI

Sharma, M., Giri, A., and Chadha, S. 2016. *Pradhan Mantri Jan Dhan Yojana Wave 3 Assessment*. Lucknow: MicroSave.

TRAI. 2016. *The Indian Telecom Services Performance Indicators (Oct–Dec 2015)*. Delhi: TRAI.

Rural Cooperatives[1]

6
Chapter

INTRODUCTION

Is the glory of the rural cooperatives over? Or is the cooperative system reinventing itself? If this question were to be examined, it is evident that there are some initiatives that indicate that the show is not over yet. The most significant announcement this year was the announcement of the Kerala government that they would be amalgamating all the District Cooperative Central Banks (DCCBs) and the State Cooperative Banks (StCBs) into a single Kerala Bank, after setting up a committee to study it (ToI 2016). While this is yet to result in tangible action, if it does, this might just be the beginning of fundamental changes in the rural cooperative sector. In a way the report packages the spirit of the recommendations of the Prakash Bakshi Committee (RBI 2013), which had amongst other things suggested that the PACS that were not commercially viable become agents of the upper-tier institutions and work as service delivery points. There was much objection to the Bakshi Committee, particularly in the fact that it violated the spirit of mutuality that comes from a member-owned proximate institution which provides a friendly entry point for the poor and the marginalized. While parts of the cooperative system are in trouble, it is important to ensure that the autonomy of these institutions is protected. It is therefore very important to track the changes in the rural cooperative space.

In terms of the coverage that the cooperative system is getting, it appears that there is little to cheer about. Even the Inclusive Finance India reports over the years have not paid attention to the rural cooperative sector. This chapter would be the first in this series, and hopefully the sector will be tracked. The rural cooperative sector possibly is as important as the postal department in terms of its physical outreach. While PACS were the most powerful and immediate institutions that were providing formal financial services, the primacy of the cooperatives has eroded over a period of time, with other institutional innovations—the quotas given to commercial banks to open rural branches, the spread of RRBs, and the explosive growth of the microfinance sector—have displaced the PACS. However, it is still important to track the developments in this sector to ensure that the primacy of the cooperative system is not completely eroded in favor of the market-based systems.

There has been much action in the rural cooperative credit structure after the Vaidyanathan Committee submitted its report in 2005. The states drew up memorandums of understanding with the central government, some of the laws were changed, and the central government pumped-in money to the sector, both for recapitalization of cooperatives as well as for upgradation of technology and human resources. However, in spite of all the interventions, there is hardly any data about cooperatives in the public domain. The National Federation of State Cooperative Banks (NAFSCOB) presents the data about primary cooperatives with a lag and the current data that is available for the cooperatives is for the year 2014–15. It has been a while since the RBI and later NABARD put out data on cooperatives: Till about mid-1980s the *Statistical Tables Relating to the Cooperative Movement in India* came out in two volumes—one dedicated to the credit cooperatives

[1] The author is thankful to Mr B. Subrahmanyam, MD NAFSCOB, for providing the data on primary cooperatives at a very short notice and for the feedback on a draft of this chapter. The author is also thankful to Mr Y.C. Nanda for useful feedback on the draft chapter.

and one to the non-credit cooperatives. That volume has not been published in the digital era, where it should be easier to collate and integrate the data. This year, NABARD published provisional statistics on cooperative banks, something that should be welcomed. The statistics pertain only to the upper tier cooperatives—the StCBs and the DCCBs. While welcoming this volume, it is important to articulate the expectation that similar data for primary cooperatives should also brought out. In fact, the Vaidyanathan Committee in its report had made the following observation:

> The secondary data used in this chapter and elsewhere, are from two sources—the NABARD and the NAFSCOB. Ideally, the Task Force would have preferred to rely on data put out by NABARD. It was not able to do so, partly because NABARD's database was mainly focused on the intermediate and apex tiers, and partly because it did not have the break up required by the Task Force.
>
> While using the data it soon became apparent to the Task Force that the statistical data reporting and compilation relating to the cooperative sector leaves much to be desired. (NABARD, 2004)

Box 6.1 Former Governor of RBI D. Subbarao on Agricultural Cooperatives

MSS: One initiative, not from the RBI, but following the report of the All India Rural Credit Survey Committee Report, we had state partnership with cooperatives. This effort was a decentralized effort and led by states. The data of the 1960s and 1970s show that there is reason to celebrate to achievement of cooperatives, but later they fell into sickness followed by the first all-India debt waiver. This is corroborated by the All-India Debt and Investment Survey data for the later decades. Do you think cooperatives continue to have relevance in the current day?

DS: The story of cooperatives has been a very sad and disheartening one. In the early years of our development, we set a lot of store by the cooperatives; they were seen as an inclusive and cost effective way of reaching credit to the needy. Except in select parts of the country, cooperatives have failed to live up to those expectations. When I was working in the field in the 1980s, malpractices in cooperatives were quite common. There used to be complaints of capture by vested interests, of corruption and casteism. We have failed to keep cooperatives apolitical and honest.

Therefore, any data coming out of NABARD should be welcomed. While the last year's report did not discuss the rural cooperative structure, the current report adds a chapter based on the data available.

PRIMARY AGRICULTURAL COOPERATIVE SOCIETIES

The data on primary cooperative societies is currently collected and disseminated by the NAFSCOB. The latest data available for the cooperative sector was for the year 2014–15, and this has been organized according to the same zonal classification as the database of the RBI with one exception. Sikkim is classified in the Eastern sector in the RBI data, and is classified under the northeastern sector in the NAFSCOB data. However, the numbers of Sikkim are relatively small and do not affect the larger set of arguments. While the numbers show significant penetration at over 92,000 PACS, as per the NAFSCOB numbers, only about 67,000 PACS are effective and are in the viable range and may be actually providing some services to the members.

However, it is important to note that these PACS are all in the rural and semi-urban locations. This number is significantly higher than the 45,359 unique rural and semi-urban locations that have bank branches. Similarly, the postal network operates out of around 25,000 departmental post offices with owned or rented offices, whereas the other postal touchpoints are provided by the Grameen Dak Sevaks from other premises including their own residences. Even if we assume that the cooperatives have a reduced and weakened presence, cooperatives still have the best physical reach within the country and every effort needs to be made to ensure that these institutions are at least protected to the extent that they are operating.

The membership numbers of these cooperatives give another indication of the reach. All the cooperatives were having 121 million members with a significant proportion of the membership coming from the disadvantaged sections of the society. On the other hand, the commercial banks have about 100 million SBAs up to a ticket size of ₹200,000, and these cover both the rural and the urban areas. The exposure of the banking system to agriculture (direct) was about 60 million accounts.

While the outreach and the membership numbers look very promising, the detail of the actual number of borrowers, portfolio performance, and other parameters do not make very encouraging reading. Overall, the overdue percentage for the PACS across the country is at 22.42% with northeast having the worst performance of 64.49% overdues.

Table 6.1 Number of Primary Agricultural Cooperative Societies as of March 2015 (in '000s)

Region	Total PACS	Viable PACS	Potentially Viable PACS	Dormant PACS	Defunct PACS	Others
North	12.80	9.14	2.94	0.20	0.34	0.18
Northeast	3.50	1.82	0.50	0.68	0.38	0.12
Eastern	18.57	13.98	3.00	0.59	0.41	0.60
Central	13.39	10.78	1.99	0.39	0.16	0.07
West	29.88	21.02	8.08	0.61	0.10	0.07
South	14.66	10.28	3.42	0.37	0.20	0.40
Total	92.79	67.02	19.93	2.82	1.59	1.43

Source: Performance of PACS 2014–15. Mumbai: NAFSCOB.

Table 6.2 Membership Details of Primary Agricultural Cooperative Societies as of March 2015 (Number in Millions)

Region	Membership	Scheduled Castes	Scheduled Tribes	Small Farmers	Rural Artisans	Marginal Farmers and Others
Northern	15.33	2.57	1.57	5.99	0.97	4.23
Northeast	3.55	0.48	0.71	0.88	0.12	1.35
Eastern	27.24	2.69	3.30	6.88	0.72	13.64
Central	8.00	2.93	1.15	2.34	0.28	1.30
West	17.04	1.09	1.06	4.39	0.41	10.10
South	49.93	6.95	1.51	19.92	4.15	17.40
Total	121.09	16.72	9.30	40.40	6.65	48.02

Source: Performance of PACS 2014–15. Mumbai: NAFSCOB.

Table 6.3 Position of Advances and Overdues from PACS as of March 2015 (₹ in Billion)

Region	Loans Disbursed	Loans Outstanding	Demand	Collection	Balance	Overdue Percentage
Northern	212.08	185.55	216.35	158.78	57.57	26.61%
Northeast	0.38	0.63	0.50	0.18	0.32	64.49%
Eastern	53.19	49.28	59.98	35.67	24.31	40.53%
Central	55.35	55.14	72.03	49.55	22.47	31.20%
West	239.10	224.20	282.23	183.59	98.64	34.95%
South	1,030.40	957.46	965.17	810.58	154.59	16.02%
Total	1,590.50	1,472.26	1,596.26	1,238.35	357.91	22.42%

Source: Performance of PACS 2014–15. Mumbai: NAFSCOB.

Even on this parameter, the cooperatives in the south are much better off, but the performance of cooperatives on the whole is much to be desired. As of now, the disbursement of ground-level agricultural credit by cooperative structure even with all its weaknesses is higher than the RRB structure. These two institutions that are actually reaching out to the last mile in the crucial part of our economy need to be sustained. Even now, the share of the cooperatives in catering to the needs of the small and marginal farmers is the highest from all the institutional sources. However, the relative share of the cooperatives is reducing significantly in favor of RRBs and there is a need to revisit the institutional form, which has traditionally been most proximate to the poor and the disadvantaged.

This shows that even after the implementation of the reform package, as suggested by the Vaidyanathan Committee, the ground-level situation of the cooperatives have not significantly improved. The impressive numbers of outreach and membership can be put in a more realistic

Table 6.4 Details of Performance of PACS and Physical Infrastructure, March 2015

Region	Profit-making PACS	Loss-making PACS	PACS with Godowns	Number of Villages Covered	Staff Strength	Societies with Full-time Secretary
Northern	8,393	3,460	7,657	107,366	29,094	8,276
Northeast	612	931	1,186	33,780	8,849	1,926
Eastern	4,169	10,026	11,728	196,010	37,828	11,869
Central	6,689	4,097	12,007	167,153	24,521	4,095
West	15,053	13,847	11,346	48,595	14,150	6,785
South	8,737	5,079	11,531	76,874	49,990	12,359
Total	43,653	37,440	55,455	629,778	164,432	45,310

Source: Performance of PACS 2014–15. Mumbai: NAFSCOB.

Box 6.2 Former RBI Governor Dr Y.V. Reddy on Vaidyanathan Committee and Agricultural Cooperatives

MSS: You were enthusiastically supporting the recommendations of the Vaidyanathan Committee on agricultural cooperatives, and possibly that was a good chance to get them on track.

Dr Reddy: Yes, there was the cooperative system. One major area where I thought we can push reforms in the cooperative institutions was through the recommendations of the Vaidyanathan committee. This started in my first year as governor.

MSS: Now that nothing much has happened, do you see cooperatives as sunset institutions—particularly given the political economy of interest rate caps on loans, subventions, and write offs. Is there a way in which we could save these institutions that provide decentralized financial services to the farming class?

Dr Reddy: I was really hopeful about the cooperative system. After agreeing to chair the implementation committee I saw that the political will to implement disappeared, I could see the non-cooperation from the state governments—they wanted to dilute the conditions for government of India to give money to the states. Then it became clear that the most powerful instrument for providing rural credit was impossible politically. So that was a failure.

The other failure was in loan waivers, which naturally, I opposed. The only thing which we could do at that point of time was to say this time the government should bear the burden and I made it a condition that earlier some of the losses due to these waivers were to be absorbed by the banks.

But this also had another effect, the banks found it easy to clean up their balance sheets, so they entered into a phase which we did not visualize where there was a convergence of interests between the bankers and the government. It is a short term solution with a huge long term cost, and now the government of India has a problem in disciplining the states. So, we lost the moral authority to impose the credit culture.

perspective when we look at the functional numbers of these PACS. Effectively, while there might be many viable and potentially viable PACS, the real proof of performance comes from the PACS that have some infrastructure (Godowns), are in profits, and have a full-time secretary. Assuming that there would be a significant overlap between the three parameters, the indications are that these could be around 40,000 in number across the country. That is the operational number that one should work with.

Overall, PACS continued to perform their role as the basic link with the customer. However, with the increasing concern that the three-tier structure of PACS, DCCBs, and StCBs there were questions on whether the entire structure could be viable with thin margins, and high defaults leading to imbalances between the structures. One of the suggestions that was made was to redesignate PACS as BCs and the primary point of contact, while all the transactions could be done on the books of the DCCB, thereby disintermediating one tier. This proposal faced some resistance with successful PACS and, therefore, there might be a need to look at a hybrid approach between the self-sustaining successful PACS that have member deposits and multiple streams of income, and the stressed cooperatives.

As a part of the development activities, NABARD established the Centre for Professional Excellence in Cooperatives at its Bankers Institute of Rural

Development, in order to provide training and support services to cooperatives. In addition,

> [T]o enable PACS deliver more efficient financial and non-financial services in a viable manner to their members, PACS Development Cells (PDCs) have been created in DCCBs and StCBs. The PDCs, currently established and functional in 94 DCCBs have identified 2,198 PACS operating in 20 states to strengthen them through training, handholding, guiding, exposure visits and other suitable interventions. With the help of PDCs, 1,328 PACS have prepared business development plans. (NABARD 2016)

DCCBs AND StCBs

While the Vaidyanathan Committee recommendations were made to strengthen the cooperative sector across tiers, it appears that the task of reviving the large number of widespread primary cooperatives was too complicated with all the conditionalities imposed by the committee. However, the impact of the Vaidyanathan Committee seems to have had a much better effect on the upper tiers. One of the recommendations of the committee was that all the upper-tier institutions, the DCCBs and the StCBs, should function as proper licensed banks and the State should infuse capital into these structures to ensure that they had capital adequacy. As a result of the initiatives, all the StCBs which were 17 were all licensed and of the 296 DCCBs that were unlicensed, only 23 remained unlicensed by 2013. With the infusion of capital from the central government, the respective state governments, and NABARD, with stiff performance criteria imposed on these institutions, the number of unlicensed DCCBs was brought down to 11 as of June 2016 (RBI 2016).

The broad parameters of performance of the StCBs and DCCBs are given in Table 6.5.

Table 6.5 Performance Indicators of StCBs and DCCBs (₹ in Billion)

	State Cooperative Banks		DCCBs	
Particulars	**2014–15 (Audited)**	**2015–16 (Unaudited)**	**2014–15 (Audited)**	**2015–16 (Unaudited)**
Number of banks	32	33	370	370
Number of banks reporting	32	33	370	369
Number of branches	1,029	1,089	13,583	13,943
Share capital	53.55	47.12	130.45	141.29
Reserves	128.88	136.49	163.07	268.63
Deposits	1,028.59	1,112.92	2,573.16	2,968.04
Borrowings	687.21	679.14	798.26	1,266.39
Investments	751.23	535.34	1,360.34	1,534.89
Total loans outstanding	1,145.45	1210.91	2,189.47	2,739.71
Number of banks in profit	28	27	300	326
Amount of profit	11.05	8.65	18.20	19.26
Number of banks in loss	4	6	59	44
Amount of losses	0.25	0.23	10.44	3.65
Accumulated losses	6.17	6.75	38.21	48.04
NPA % to loans outstanding	5.02	4.55	9.42	7.86
CD ratio	108.00	108.80	85.1	92.31
ID ratio	74.7	48.10	52.7	51.71
Branch productivity	2.09	1.97	0.37	0.39
Recovery %	94.91	95.14	76.53	80.36
Total demand	500.78	689.20	1,345.56	1,952.82
Total collection	476.33	655.74	1,029.74	1,569.29
Balance (including overdue)	24.45	33.46	311.62	381.19
Aggregate net worth	151.34	151.91	314.04	351.66

Source: Key Statistics on Cooperative Banks (STCCS). Mumbai: NABARD.
Notes: DCCBs from West Bengal were not included; Only 359 DCCBs reported profit/loss figure for 2014–15.

From the data, it is clear that the upper-tier structures are in much better health with greater recovery and a healthy portfolio. While detailed data for this structure is available that shows the break-up of region-wise deployment of portfolio, this would be mirroring the data for PACS that has already been discussed. What is important to note is that while the credit data would largely be reflected in the ground-level credit data for agriculture in case of StCBs, an outstanding of ₹212 billion was in the nonpriority sector (possibly directly financed by them to the clients) as against a total book size of ₹1,031 billion. Similarly, DCCBs together had given loans of ₹344 billion for non-priority sector purposes as against a total outstanding of ₹1,780 billion.

ECOSYSTEM INVESTMENTS

In terms of investments being made in the development of the sector, it also appears that the trend is moving toward significant investments in the upper tiers. Apart from recapitalization of DCCBs, there have been significant investments made in the technological upgradation, of bringing all the banks on a common CBS platform. NABARD has facilitated the setting up of computer labs and CBS in more than 200 DCCBs. The idea is to make DCCB the pivotal point in the chain. These banks equipped with modern technology could not only raise resources from the borrowers of PACS but also from the general public, by virtue of being in urban locations. This will add to the net resources available to the cooperative structure. One of the reasons for encouraging the deposits at the DCCB level rather than the PACS level is also to ensure that the depositors are protected with deposit insurance, which is at present available only to banks (and thus DCCBs) and not to societies (PACS).

On the other hand, the PACS are being encouraged to be agents of the DCCBs as envisaged by the Prakash Bakshi Committee, and thus the financial support to the PACS are more to enable this function, by providing them with PoS devices that enable them to carry on transactions on behalf of the DCCBs seamlessly. The commission to be given to the PACS to make this activity viable and to ensure that the staff are adequately compensated is being worked out. NABARD has also provided financial support for maintenance of the CBS systems till 2016–17. Most of the banks are provided with pooled bandwidth negotiated centrally by NABARD to ensure that connectivity is not an issue. While there is also a window for computerization of PACS, the effort seems more in terms of integrating the banks into the mainstream banking system. In this regard, the StCB are encouraged to become members of the payment systems, have ATMs, and be present in the mainstream systems.

In the districts that are affected by left wing extremism and where connectivity is a problem, NABARD has instituted a scheme to ensure that banking services are provided. This scheme subsidises the branch by providing significant financial assistance for a period of five years helping the branches with connectivity and solar powered very small aperture terminals.

CONCLUDING NOTES

From the data provided by NABARD and NAFSCOB, it is clear that the cooperative system at the primary level is not doing well and much attention needs to be paid. However, over a period of time, there is also a realization that this is a very difficult problem to solve. The overall trend in the cooperative system seems to be to protect and strengthen the upper tier, so that they are intact and healthy, and using their power and muscle, the primaries could be light-touch member contact points. Whether this, or the Kerala experiment of delayering the cooperatives, is desirable is a debatable point. It is not that de-layering has not happened elsewhere. The Desjardins movement in Quebec, Canada, went through the process and was able to bring in some systemic efficiency. However, in the process of de-layering it is not wise to remove the primary touchpoint. Instead it may be better to consolidate the intermediary structures. However, the investments and energies seem to be going in the direction of disempowering the primaries. While this is the overall movement of the cooperatives sector across the country, what should be watched is the experiment being undertaken by the government of Kerala to integrate all the cooperative finance institutions into a single bank—currently called the Kerala Cooperative Bank. If this experiment rolls out, that might well be the template for the future of rural cooperatives in India. Again, whether this is desirable from a distributional point is not clear. But going forward, the action on the cooperative front would be very important to track.

REFERENCES

NABARD (National Bank for Agriculture and Rural Development). 2004. *Draft Final Report of the Task Force on Revival of Co-operative Credit Institutions.* Mumbai: NABARD.

———. 2016. *Annual Report 2015–16.* Mumbai: NABARD.

RBI (Reserve Bank of India). 2013. *Report of the Expert Committee to examine Three Tier Short Term Co-operative Credit Structure*. Mumbai: RBI. Available at: https://rbidocs.rbi.org.in/rdocs/PublicationReport/Pdfs/EEPERC240113_F.pdf (Accessed on September 13, 2016)

———. 2016. *Annual Report, 2015–16*. Mumbai: RBI. Available at: https://rbidocs.rbi.org.in/rdocs/AnnualReport/PDFs/0RBIAR2016CD93589EC2C4467793892C79FD05555D.PDF (Accessed on September 2, 2016).

ToI. 2016. "'Kerala Bank' Will Be Launched Next Year: Cooperation Minister." *Times of India*, Tiruvanathapuam edition. Available at: http://timesofindia.indiatimes.com/city/thiruvananthapuram/Kerala-Bank-will-be-launched-next-year-Cooperation-minister/articleshow/53334587.cms (Accessed on September 13, 2016).

Urban Cooperative Banks[1]

7

Chapter

INTRODUCTION

Urban cooperative banks (UCBs) are small and neighborhood banks, and usually cater to a large section of population that is left out of the mainstream banking system. During the previous year, a committee of the RBI, chaired by Deputy Governor R. Gandhi, submitted a report suggesting that there could be a few of the cooperative institutions that are "too big to be cooperative" and, therefore, it would be a good idea to convert them into commercial banks. The experience of Europe clearly indicates that the concept of "too big to be a cooperative" is not true. However, the structure that has helped the Western cooperatives into large umbrella brands, with local autonomous—locally governed units—needs to be considered seriously, even when the RBI takes a rather narrow regulatory perspective.

POLICY DISCOURSE

The discourse of the RBI following the report of the committee has been somewhat worrisome in the context of the principles on which the cooperatives work, as against the commercial banks. The cooperatives are expected to work on the principles of mutuality and open membership. The principle of open membership makes it unfair to transfer any residual amounts on liquidation to the existing membership and, therefore, the law prohibits distribution of accumulated surpluses. The RBI seems to indicate that this universally accepted principle needs to be revisited. This comes, not from an inadequate appreciation of the cooperative form of organization but from a zealous regulatory concern.

The questions asked by the deputy governor in an address at a conference on UCBs are worth engaging with, to clear the gaps in perception of how cooperatives are seen by the regulator. Deputy Governor Gandhi posed the following questions:

> We need to reflect on certain soul searching questions. It may cause certain shock to several of you, the veterans of co-operative movement, to undertake this search. Because, you need to find answers to some inconvenient questions. They are as follows:
>
> 1. Has the co-operative movement retained its relevance after its 130 years existence in India?
> 2. Has the Indian psyche grown beyond the need for 'one person one vote for mutual benefit' idiom?
> 3. Has the co-operative movement captured the imagination of younger generation?
> 4. Has it produced enough qualified and energetic young leaders to carry forward the movement?
> 5. How the movement can insulate itself from the trends that as the CAB study pointed out reduce the cooperativeness of co-operatives?
>
> (Gandhi 2016)

The discourse of the RBI pertaining to the urban cooperative banks was in continuation of the thoughts expressed first by the Malegam Committee (Malegam 2011) and later reinforced by the Gandhi Committee (RBI 2015). However, there was no significant action in either converting the existing urban cooperative banks to small finance banks or issuing new licenses for new cooperative banks. This issue may be addressed positively if the RBI recognizes the fundamental differences in how cooperatives are structured and, therefore, need a distinct

[1] The author is thankful to Ms Anita Bhattacharya of Reserve Bank of India for clarifying some issues pertaining to the data and to Shri D. Krishna, former CEO of National Federation of State Cooperative Urban Banks, for useful feedback on the draft of this chapter.

regulatory framework, rather than look at the cooperative structure as creating a regulatory arbitrage. In the questions posed by the deputy governor, it may be important to add two more questions:

1. Has the cooperative movement captured the imagination of younger generation?
2. Has it produced enough qualified and energetic young leaders to carry forward the movement?

A majority of the 1,570 urban banks are laggards in technology adoption and are wanting in professionalism as well as ability to adopt quickly to changes (Krishna 2016).

The urban cooperative banking sector is divided into three segments. The urban cooperative thrift and credit societies form the base of this structure. While statistics for this sector are not readily available, these are expected to be small and run on the principle of mutuality. They are not expected to seek deposits from nonmembers, and loaning is also amongst the members themselves. However, in practice, these cooperative societies might be seeking nonmember deposits by enrolling the customers as nominal, nonvoting members.

REGULATION AND SUPERVISION

There were some internal changes in the RBI and a new department of cooperative bank regulation was established. This brings the central bank's focus on to a very important segment of the banking system. The new department would not only be responsible for supervision and regulation of urban cooperative banks, which the extant department was doing, it will also be responsible for the state cooperative banks and the district cooperative central banks which are a part of the rural cooperative architecture.

OTHER DEVELOPMENTS

In a recent development, the interministerial group on deposit-taking has submitted a draft bill for banning unregulated deposits (called the Banning Bill). The proposed bill has implications on a very wide canvas, including the urban thrift and credit cooperative societies. The bill put up on the finance ministry website for comments proposes two important aspects with regard to cooperative societies (Ministry of Finance, GOI 2016).

First, only regulated deposits should be permitted in all forms of institutions. The bill has proposed elaborate processes for anybody who violates the clauses. The definition of regulated deposits includes deposits in cooperatives under the various state legislations, but only to the extent that these deposits are placed by full-fledged voting members of the cooperative, thereby preventing the cooperative from seeking deposits from nonmembers or nominal members. If this bill is passed, then it is a welcome step, purely from the perspective of what the cooperative is all about: A business unit that caters to the needs of its members and not of others.

Second, the bill seeks to bring an amendment to the multi-state cooperative societies' act—which comes under the purview of the central government—to prevent those cooperatives incorporated under the multi-state act from accepting any form of deposit, including member deposit. The reason: Multi-state cooperatives are being used as back door instruments to garner large-scale public funds. The implication of this proposal is that there would be no multi-state financial cooperatives, and example of a knee-jerk reaction without a clear rationale in passing statues.

Only cooperatives within a state, with voting rights for the depositors will operate. If as per the Gandhi Committee large cooperatives can opt for applying for small finance bank licenses, the Banning Bill reduces the possibility of cooperative societies becoming large. From the perspective of the cooperative principles, this may be a welcome step.

The second segment in the cooperative structure consists of the cooperatives that have been accorded a license by the RBI, but do not have a scheduled status. The third segment consists of the scheduled urban cooperative banks. The structure is given in Figure 7.1.

While there has been much talk about the UCBs, it is clear from the data that activity-wise nothing significant has been happening. There have been no new licenses issued after the Malegam Committee submitted its report in 2011, though the recommendation was to set-up new UCBs. Similarly, the growth numbers of the existing UCBs have also been moderate both in terms of outreach as well as portfolio as seen in Table 7.1.

REGIONAL SPREAD

In terms of regional spread, the UCBs are concentrated in the western and southern parts of India. The UCBs in the western part not only are the highest in number, but are also represented by the highest number of branches and spread. Only three districts in the western part of India are uncovered—they do not have a UCB branch. While the western zone represents about 50% of the UBCs incorporated across the country; the number of service touchpoints (branches and extension counters) are 68% and ATMS are 85%. The western zone represents almost 75% of all business carried out by UCBs.

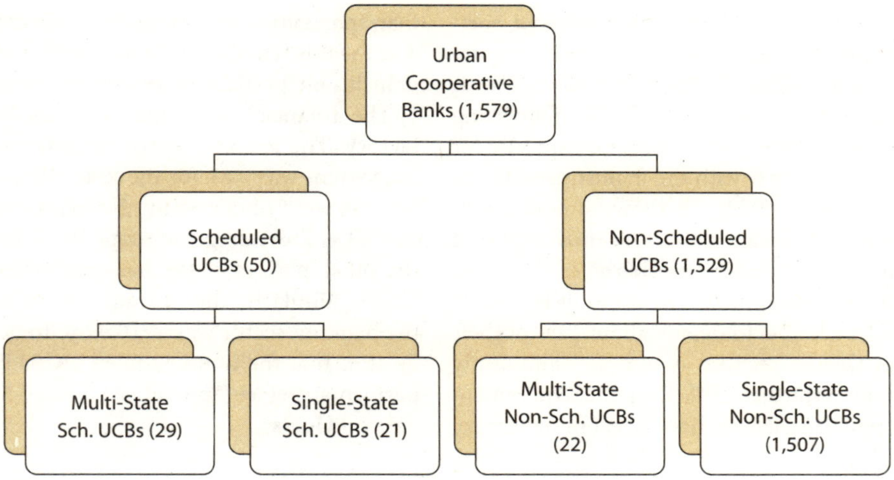

Figure 7.1 Structure of Urban Cooperative Banks in India (as of March 31, 2015)

Source: RBI (2016).

Table 7.1 UCBs in the Recent Years

Year	No. of UCBs	Deposits (₹ Billion)	Advances (₹ Billion)
2011	1,645	2,118.80	1,364.98
2012	1,618	2,386.41	1,577.93
2013	1,606	2,768.30	1,810.31
2014	1,589	3,155.03	1,996.51
2015	1,579	3,551.35	2,251.06

Source: RBI (2016).

How Inclusive Are UCBs?

In the 2015 report it was adequately demonstrated that the UCBs actually represent the smaller customer. A comparison made by the Gandhi Committee indicated that the largest UCBs were generally comparable in size to the smaller private-sector banks. Thus, it was possible to create a continuum of size in the private sector between the new generation private-sector banks, which were substantially large and comparable to the nationalized banks, the smaller old generation private-sector banks overlapping in size with the large scheduled cooperative banks. However it is important to recognize that the UCBs served the small finance needs, if we go by the definition taken by the RBI for SFBs. The Gandhi Committee had indicated that 96.84% of the advances of scheduled commercial banks were in loan account size of less than ₹2.5 million. The figure for nonscheduled banks was 99.24% of the accounts, which were of a size less than ₹2.5 million.

It is clear that the UCBs are operating in the same space as the SFBs in terms of portfolio composition by size. However, when we examine the purposes for which the UCBs lent, there may be some significant

Table 7.2 Region-wise Spread of UCBs as of March 2015

Region	No. of UCBs	No. of Branches (Including HO)	No. of Extension Counters	No. of ATMs	No. of Districts with a UCB Branch	No. of Districts Without a UCB Branch	Deposits (₹ Billion)	Advances (₹ Billion)
North	72	384	14	64	68	54	117.70	77.07
Northeast	16	54	1	2	16	82	12.22	7.22
East	58	169	6	8	32	87	49.60	25.70
Central	135	500	21	91	95	71	124.88	67.02
West	742	6,572	172	2,353	71	3	2,652.40	1,667.55
South	556	2,043	23	223	100	4	594.55	398.73
All-India	1,579	9,722	237	2,741	382	301	3551.35	2,243.28

Source for 2015: Primary (Urban) Co-operative Banks Outlook. 2016. Mumbai: RBI, http://dbie.rbi.org.in/DBIE/dbie.rbi?site=publications#!4, accessed on May 3, 2016.

differences in terms of spread of branches and portfolio under priority sector. The SFB norms require that 25% of the branches of SFBs be in rural areas with population up to 9,999 and 75% of the portfolio being for priority-sector loans, with targets for exposure for agriculture being on par with the mainstream banks. The data available in Table 7.3 shows almost a 50% exposure to priority sector, with a very small exposure to agriculture. This is understandable given that these banks are by definition urban. However, it is evident that the UCBs are able to deploy about 14% of their portfolio to weaker sections, which is significantly higher than the stipulated 10%. Even the requirement for deployment to weaker sections is recommendatory than mandatory. Therefore, it is important to recognise the role that the UCBs play in the larger mandate of inclusion, particularly in the urban areas.

The financial performance of UCBs was satisfactory. The average return on assets of the banking system was 0.81 for the year 2014–15. The best returns were obtained by the private sector banks at 1.68%, indicating the scope for improvement of the other players in the banking system including UCBs. Similarly, the average return on equity of the banking sector was at 10.42%. In general, it can be seen that the nonscheduled UCBs have a better performance (see Appendices 7.1 to 7.5 for detailed data on UCBs).

Table 7.3 Composition of Credit to Priority Sectors by UCBs (as of End March 2015)

Advances of UCBs to Priority Sector and Weaker Section (Amount ₹ Billion)						
	Composition of Total Priority Sector Credit			Of Which, Composition of Credit to Weaker Sections		
Sector	March 31, 2014	March 31, 2015	Percentage to Total (2015)	March 31, 2014	March 31, 2015	Percentage to Total (2015)
1. Agricultural credit	58	56	2.5	24	23	1.0
1.1 Direct agricultural credit	23	21	0.9	9	9	0.4
1.2 Indirect agricultural credit	35	34	1.5	15	14	0.6
2. Micro and small enterprises	461	523	23.3	78	95	4.2
2.1 Direct credit to micro and small enterprises	398	434	19.3	62	74	3.3
2.2 Indirect credit to micro and small enterprises	62	89	4.0	17	21	0.9
3. Microcredit	32	49	2.2	11	19	0.8
4. State-sponsored organizations for SC/ST	2	1	0.1	1	3	0.1
5. Education loans	17	17	0.8	7	7	0.3
6. Housing loans	206	229	10.2	70	79	3.5
7. Others	200	233	10.4	65	86	3.8
All priority sectors	976	1108	49.4	257	311	13.9

Source for 2014: Statistical Statements Relating to Banks in India, 2014. Mumbai: RBI (2015), http://dbie.rbi.org.in/DBIE/dbie.rbi?site=publications#!3, accessed on September 14, 2015.

Source for 2015: Primary (Urban) Co-operative Banks Outlook. Mumbai RBI (2016), http://dbie.rbi.org.in/DBIE/dbie.rbi?site=publications#!4, accessed on May 3, 2016.

Notes: 1. Percentages are with respect to total credit of UCBs.

2. Components may not add up to the total due to rounding off.

Table 7.4 Select Financial Indicators of UCBs (as of March 31)

(%)

	All SCBs*	Scheduled UCBs		Nonscheduled UCBs		All UCBs	
Financial Indicators	2014–15	2013–14	2014–15	2013–14	2014–15	2013–14	2014–15
Return on assets	0.81	0.71	0.70	0.90	0.97	0.81	0.84
Return on equity	10.42	8.96	8.94	8.80	10.65	8.87	9.91
Net interest margin	2.64	2.68	2.50	3.43	3.39	3.08	2.97

Source: Mumbai: RBI database, http://dbie.rbi.org.in/DBIE/dbie.rbi?site=publications#!4, accessed on May 3, 2016.

Note: *Data for 2014–15 are provisional.

Table 7.5 Non-Performing Assets of UCBs

As of March 31st, Amount in Rupees Billion

S. No.	Items	As of March 31 2014	2015
1	Gross NPAs	115.00	135.01
2	Gross NPA ratio (%)	5.74	6.02
3	Net NPAs	41.46	57.11
4	Net NPA ratio (%)	2.17	2.66
5	Provisioning	73.53	77.90
6	Coverage ratio (%)	63.94	57.70

Source: Mumbai: RBI database, http://dbie.rbi.org.in/DBIE/dbie.rbi?site=publications#!4, accessed on May 3, 2016.
Note: Data for 2015 are provisional.

UCBs: THE WAY FORWARD

The question of the future of UCBs remains somewhat uncertain. The Gandhi Committee recommendations seem to indicate the path shown in Figure 7.2.

When cooperative banks become large, there are multiple concerns. One concern is whether they are losing their cooperative nature, and the second is whether they have become large enough, from a regulatory perspective, to be regulated under a different framework. The Gandhi Committee did engage with both these issues and was in favor of bringing the banks into the mainstream regulatory framework and sacrificing the cooperativeness of the banks. The committee did not consider the possibility of large cooperatives retaining the umbrella brand, but being broken up into smaller neighborhood units with a hybrid model of cooperatives at the member/client level, but a corporation at the upper tier, though such models have made cooperative banks a formidable force to reckon with in European countries

While the above was the path laid out, no action has been taken yet in implementing this proposal. However, an analysis of the data seems to indicate that of the scheduled UCBs, 36 of them have adequate capital of more than ₹1 billion—which is the minimum requirement to become a small finance bank. If we were to consider the business size considerations articulated by the committee—that banks having a total business of ₹20 billion—were considered to be too big to be cooperative, then, only three UCBs fall into this threshold as per the data of March 2015.

An alternative proposal that the Gandhi Committee considered was to create clusters of cooperative banks with a common umbrella brand for very large cooperatives. However, the committee did not consider it appropriate. Given that there are only three large banks that are causing regulatory concern of "too large to be cooperative", it may be a good idea to re-visit the path laid out by the committee to see that the cooperative nature of the banks are not lost.

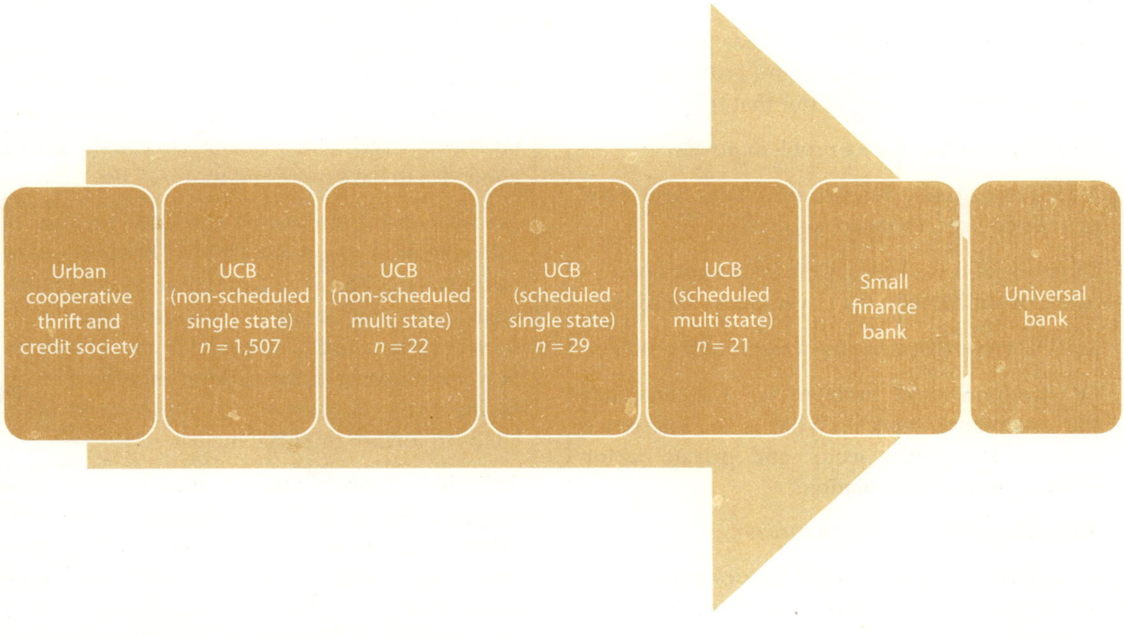

Figure 7.2 Pathways for Urban Cooperatives

Box 7.1 Former RBI Governor Dr Y.V. Reddy on Urban Cooperative Banks

MSS: Let us talk about UCBS. The latest approach of RBI seems to be to convert UCB to SFBs. They want UCBs to be under mainstream regulation.

Dr Reddy: Even now, are they not under mainstream regulation?

MSS: Yes but it involves a state government MoU.

Dr Reddy: As far as the regulations of the financial operations are concerned, they are with RBI. There is no issue there.

MSS: The Gandhi Committee suggests something interesting, and being a student of co-operation, I am personally uncomfortable with it. They are saying that there should be a path—you set up a cooperative society, when it is of a decent size we will convert you to an UCB, and when that becomes larger we'll convert it to an SFB. Now personally, I am even uncomfortable with the UCB concept because cooperative society is a mutual. The moment you bring the word "Bank" you are dealing with public at large.

Dr Reddy: Exactly! That is the issue. In essence you are absolutely right. Either it is a cooperative society or it is a bank. Cooperative bank is a misnomer. We inherited it. We should have clarified it long back.

Second, what is the problem that you are trying to solve? Are you trying to solve the problems of UCBs and if yes what is the problem you are facing in UCBs now?

MSS: What they are saying is that they are not very well regulated and they are growing in size and once they grow it is better that they …

Dr Reddy: But are they a problem now?

MSS: I don't think they are a problem right now, neither do I see a simmering problem.

Dr Reddy: If it is a bank, is the institutional structure compatible with the governance of a bank?

MSS: Correct, that is the most significant problem.

Dr Reddy: Second problem is, who regulates the governance aspects. What is the difference between the public sector and private sector banks in terms of regulation?

MSS: The governance structure is …

Dr Reddy: The government decides governance for public sector banks. For private sector, though it is under company law, the governance aspect has to be cleared by the RBI under the Act. RBI has to be satisfied with the standards of governance. In the case of UCBs, the governance aspects are with the state government.

MSS: No but my own discomfort is with cooperatives being converted to corporations. They are under different incorporations right? As a one-time measure it may be okay, but as a continuing policy, where you start as a cooperative …

Dr Reddy: If you have a standard procedure for conversion of cooperative society into a bank, and pre-conditions for conversion are set, I see no problem. As long as everybody knows, a cooperative society can potentially become a bank, provided you increase to this size, I see no issue.

I totally agree that a cooperative society is based on the principle of mutuality. If it is not mutual, then you are a separate body, you are financial intermediary. I think the fundamental difference is when a mutual is also an intermediary. Cooperative society is mutual and so the risk is totally internal.

Box 7.2 Former RBI Governor Dr D. Subbarao on Urban Cooperative Banks

MSS: I would like to know your views on UCBs. It was during your time that the Malegam Committee was set up for UCBs. Recently RBI got a report from the Gandhi committee. Both committees suggest encouraging new UCBs. Malegam Committee even suggested a lower capital requirement for UCBs being set up in the northeast. But a cooperative bank is an oxymoron. A bank by definition has public deposits, which are nonmember transactions. There is conflict of interest as the borrowers largely run the bank. Do you think it's a good idea to have more and more UCBs?

Dr Subbarao: I am not so sure, not because of the oxymoron you point out, but because urban banks have not been uniformly successful or uniformly efficient across the country. They have served certain urban areas well and elsewhere they have been a failure. What exactly are you asking? Are you suggesting that we need more UCBs to further financial inclusion?

MSS: In fact, the Gandhi Committee seems to suggest a road map. The roadmap is to start with urban cooperative societies, when they reach a certain size, hand over a UCB license, when they become a bigger convert them to an SFB, get them into mainstream banking as they achieve certain milestones. If they do not achieve the milestones they remain where they are. There is also an ideological problem of a cooperative becoming a commercial institution, that I will leave for the moment. But thinking this of a road map is it a …

Dr Subbarao: No. The Gandhi Committee Road Map looks reasonable, indeed well thought out. At the beginning of this interview we talked about how urban areas get neglected in financial inclusion. Maybe this road map is the way to go to achieve urban financial inclusion. So if an institution starts off as a thrift society and succeeds, maybe it should be allowed to grow into a bank.

MSS: But what about the ideological issues of cooperatives being converted to for-profit entities?

Dr Subbarao: I am not so concerned about the 'ideological shift' you are talking about as about the track record of cooperatives, about whether they have been a force for the good. Sadly, I remain disheartened. In some sense, the cooperatives symbolize everything that has been wrong with our rural milieu. As I told you earlier, during my field career as an IAS officer in the 1980s, I saw cooperatives being highly politicized, being casteist, riven by factions, being captured by vested interest and even exploiting the weaker sections. I thought maybe I was making too harsh a judgement, that I shouldn't judge the entire cooperative movement by my own admittedly limited experience and offered to go for a one week training on cooperatives in Pune. My impression did not change even after this training. Gandhijee articulated the cooperative movement as a means of decentralized self-help that would buttress the foundations of our economy. Sadly, cooperatives have not evolved as Gandhijee visualized.

MSS: It certainly did not work everywhere. We do not have a Rabobank or a Desjardins type of a story to narrate. Those institutions integrated into the mainstream banking system but were able to retain the cooperative character.

Dr Subbarao: Neither did we succeed in replicating the successful model of credit unions of the west.

APPENDIX 7.1
Financial Performance of UCBs (as of March 31, 2015)

Profit and Loss Account of Urban Cooperative Banks (as of March 31, Amount in ₹ Billion)

Item	Scheduled UCBs		Nonscheduled UCBs		All UCBs		% Growth
	2013–14	2014–15	2013–14	2014–15	2013–14	2014–15	
1. Interest/discount received [2 + 3 + 4 + 5]	153.29	173.39	205.63	232.89	358.91	406.28	13.20
2. Interest/discount received on loans and advances (other than from banks	109.25	119.89	141.66	159.56	250.91	279.45	11.38
3. Interest on market lending (to banks, if any)	1.06	1.21	1.39	2.36	2.46	3.57	45.31
4. Interest on investments	38.79	44.40	54.91	61.96	93.69	106.36	13.52
5. Interest on additional balance with RBI, inter-bank deposits, placements and credits	4.18	7.89	7.67	9.01	11.85	16.91	42.65
6. Other income	16.81	20.93	10.56	12.81	27.38	33.74	23.25
7. Total income [1 + 6]	170.10	194.32	216.19	245.71	386.29	440.02	13.91
8. Interest paid	106.95	124.22	138.27	158.03	245.22	282.25	15.10
9. Operating expenses	17.11	20.02	27.15	30.33	44.25	50.36	13.80
10. Other operating expenses	18.26	20.26	19.08	21.95	37.34	42.21	13.03
11. Total expenses [8 + 9 + 10]	142.31	164.50	184.50	210.31	326.81	374.81	14.69
12. Operating profit (+)/loss (–) [7 – 11]	27.79	29.81	31.69	35.40	59.48	65.21	9.64
13. Provision against risks/contingencies	11.18	9.23	8.23	7.52	19.40	16.75	–13.66
14. Net profit (+)/loss (–) before taxes [12 – 13]	16.61	20.58	23.46	27.88	40.07	48.46	20.92
15. Provisions for taxes	4.38	6.80	5.85	6.55	10.23	13.35	30.53
16. Net profit (+)/loss (–) after taxes [14 – 15]	12.23	13.77	17.61	21.33	29.84	35.11	17.63

Source: RBI Data Warehouse, http://dbie.rbi.org.in/DBIE/dbie.rbi?site=publications#!4, accessed on May 3, 2015.

Notes: 1. Data for 2014–15 are provisional. 2. Components may not add up/subtract to the whole due to rounding off. 3. Percentage variation could be slightly different because absolute numbers have been rounded off to rupees billion. 4. Value zero indicates nil or negligible.

APPENDIX 7.2
Liabilities and Assets of Urban Co-op Banks

Balance Sheet of Urban Cooperative Banks (as of March 31) (Amounts in ₹ Billion)

Items	Scheduled UCBs 2014	Scheduled UCBs 2015	Nonscheduled UCBs 2014	Nonscheduled UCBs 2015	All UCBs 2014	All UCBs 2015	Growth (%)
Liabilities							
1) Capital	27.99	30.81	61.73	68.73	89.72	99.54	10.94
	(1.54)	(1.51)	(2.95)	(2.97)	(2.29)	(2.29)	
2) Reserves and surplus	115.79	131.47	127.75	142.29	243.53	273.75	12.41
	(6.37)	(6.46)	(6.10)	(6.14)	(6.22)	(6.29)	
3) Deposits	1,456.04	1,642.21	1,721.65	1,909.13	3,177.69	3,551.34	11.76
	(80.07)	(80.65)	(82.18)	(82.44)	(81.20)	(81.60)	
4) Borrowings	21.27	19.01	4.25	3.44	25.52	22.46	–12.00
	(1.17)	(0.93)	(0.20)	(0.15)	(0.65)	(0.52)	
5) Other liabilities and provisions	197.28	212.64	179.55	192.25	376.82	404.89	7.45
	(10.85)	(10.44)	(8.57)	(8.30)	(9.63)	(9.30)	
Total liabilities	1,818.37	2,036.14	2,094.92	2,315.84	3,913.29	4,351.97	11.21
	(100.00)	(100.00)	(100.00)	(100.00)	(100.00)	(100.00)	
Assets							
1) Cash in hand	8.76	10.80	25.04	26.93	33.80	37.74	11.63
	(0.48)	(0.53)	(1.20)	(1.16)	(0.86)	(0.87)	
2) Balances with RBI	80.77	84.30	8.46	12.94	89.23	97.24	8.98
	(4.44)	(4.14)	(0.40)	(0.56)	(2.28)	(2.23)	
3) Balances with banks	107.02	142.37	185.89	216.17	292.91	358.54	22.40
	(5.89)	(6.99)	(8.87)	(9.33)	(7.49)	(8.24)	
4) Money at call and short notice	4.95	7.32	9.77	12.53	14.72	19.85	34.88
	(0.27)	(0.36)	(0.47)	(0.54)	(0.38)	(0.46)	
5) Investments	483.95	515.07	669.15	716.00	1,153.10	1,231.07	6.76
	(26.61)	(25.30)	(31.94)	(30.92)	(29.47)	(28.29)	
A) SLR investments	437.37	474.49	635.27	677.75	1,072.64	1,152.24	7.42
	(24.05)	(23.30)	(30.32)	(29.27)	(27.41)	(26.48)	
i) Investments in approved securities	428.74	464.66	475.59	505.87	904.33	970.53	7.32
	(23.58)	(22.82)	(22.70)	(21.84)	(23.11)	(22.30)	
ii) Balances with central/state cooperative banks	8.63	9.83	159.68	171.87	168.31	181.71	7.96
	(0.47)	(0.48)	(7.62)	(7.42)	(4.30)	(4.18)	
B) NonSLR investments	46.58	40.58	33.88	38.25	80.46	78.83	–2.03
	(2.56)	(1.99)	(1.62)	(1.65)	(2.06)	(1.81)	
6) Loans and advances	938.33	1,057.71	1,065.19	1,185.58	2,003.52	2,243.29	11.97
	(51.60)	(51.95)	(50.85)	(51.19)	(51.20)	(51.55)	
7) Other assets	194.59	218.56	131.41	145.69	326.00	364.25	11.73
	(10.70)	(10.73)	(6.27)	(6.29)	(8.33)	(8.37)	
Total assets	1,818.37	2,036.14	2,094.92	2,315.84	3,913.29	4,351.97	11.21
	(100.00)	(100.00)	(100.00)	(100.00)	(100.00)	(100.00)	

Source: RBI Data Warehouse, http://dbie.rbi.org.in/DBIE/dbie.rbi?site=publications#!4 accessed on May 3, 2016.

Notes: 1. Data for 2015 are provisional; 2. Figures in brackets are percentages to total liabilities/assets.

3. Components may not add up to the whole due to rounding off. 4. Percentage variation could be slightly different because absolute numbers have been rounded off to rupees billion.

APPENDIX 7.3
Distribution of UCBs by Size of Deposits and Advances as of March 31, 2014

	Distribution Based on Deposits				Distribution Based on Advances				
	No. of UCBs		Deposits			No. of UCBs		Advances	
Deposits	No.	% Share to Total	Amount	% Share to Total	Advances	No.	% Share to Total	Amount	% Share to Total
1	2	3	4	5	6	7	8	9	10
0.00 ≤ D < 0.10	137	8.68	7.81	0.22	0.00 ≤ A < 0.10	304	19.25	16.60	0.74
0.10 ≤ D < 0.25	287	18.18	47.59	1.34	0.10 ≤ A < 0.25	392	24.83	64.38	2.87
0.25 ≤ D < 0.50	338	21.41	119.68	3.37	0.25 ≤ A < 0.50	279	17.67	95.79	4.27
0.50 ≤ D < 1.00	260	16.47	175.44	4.94	0.50 ≤ A < 1.00	240	15.20	165.33	7.37
1.00 ≤ D < 2.50	302	19.13	447.11	12.59	1.00 ≤ A < 2.50	202	12.79	308.90	13.77
2.50 ≤ D < 5.00	128	8.11	445.34	12.54	2.50 ≤ A < 5.00	83	5.26	274.35	12.23
5.00 ≤ D <10.00	70	4.43	458.48	12.91	5.00 ≤ A < 10.00	45	2.85	287.81	12.83
10.00 ≤ D	57	3.61	1,849.89	52.09	10.00 ≤ A	34	2.15	1,030.57	45.94
Total	1,579	100.00	3,551.34	100.00	Total	1,579	100.00	2,243.29	100.00

Source: RBI Data Warehouse, http://dbie.rbi.org.in/DBIE/dbie.rbi?site=publications#!4, accessed on May 3, 2015.
Notes: 1. Data are provisional. 2. Components may not add up to the whole due to rounding off.

APPENDIX 7.4
Rating-wise Distribution of UCBs as of March 31, 2015

(Amount in ₹ Billion)

Ratings	No. of UCBs	% Share in Total	Deposits	% Share in Total	Advances	% Share in Total
A	449	28.44	1490.85	41.98	942.85	42.03
B	791	50.09	1557.97	43.87	999.83	44.57
C	263	16.66	382.83	10.78	238.24	10.62
D	76	4.81	119.68	3.37	62.36	2.78
Total	1579	100.00	3,551.34	100.00	2,243.29	100.00

Source: RBI Data Warehouse, http://dbie.rbi.org.in/DBIE/dbie.rbi?site=publications#!4, accessed on May 7, 2015.
Notes: 1. Data are provisional. 2. Components may not add up to the whole due to rounding off. 3. Ratings are based on the inspection conducted during the financial years 2013–14 to 2014–15. 4. Percentage variation could be slightly different because absolute numbers have been rounded off to ₹ billion.

APPENDIX 7.5
Bank-wise Select Financial Parameters of Scheduled UCBs as of March 31, 2015

S. No.	Bank Name	Average Cost of Deposits (%)	Average Yield on Advances (%)	NII to TA (Spread) (%)	NII to WF (%)	Non-II to WF (%)	Return on Assets (ROA) (%)	CRAR (%)	B/E	P/E
1	Abhyudaya Cooperative Bank Ltd., Mumbai	7.87	11.07	2.02	2.05	1.72	0.29	12.81	57.97	0.13
2	Ahmedabad Mercantile Co-Op Bank Ltd.	7.23	11.32	3.37	3.43	0.36	1.20	29.95	59.48	0.61
3	Amanath Cooperative Bank Ltd. Bangalore	8.97	4.64	1.00	1.87	0.82	0.00	−142.3	0.00	0.07

(Continued)

(Continued)

S. No.	Bank Name	Average Cost of Deposits (%)	Average Yield on Advances (%)	NII to TA (Spread) (%)	NII to WF (%)	Non-II to WF (%)	Return on Assets (ROA) (%)	CRAR (%)	B/E	P/E
4	Andhra Pradesh Mahesh Cooperative Urban Bank Ltd.	8.15	15.05	3.51	3.53	0.38	1.04	21.66	40.87	32.78
5	Bassein Catholic Cooperative Bank Ltd.	7.62	12.37	3.28	3.32	0.35	1.64	21.38	144.42	1.63
6	Bharat Cooperative Bank (Mumbai) Ltd., Mumbai	8.60	13.65	2.76	2.78	1.27	1.38	12.68	118.50	1.03
7	Bharati Sahakari Bank Limited.	7.41	12.37	2.90	3.07	1.38	1.77	15.85	65.24	0.78
8	Bombay Mercantile Cooperative Bank Limited	6.07	11.50	1.96	2.86	2.57	0.11	11.34	24.52	1.14
9	Citizen Credit Cooperative Bank Ltd., Mumbai	7.10	12.20	3.28	3.30	0.54	0.83	20.76	68.80	0.44
10	Cosmos Cooperative Urban Bank Ltd.	8.31	12.20	2.00	2.09	2.03	0.30	11.25	91.35	0.20
11	Dombivli Nagari Sahakari Bank Ltd.	7.80	12.17	2.59	3.07	1.27	0.95	13.07	101.73	0.58
12	Goa Urban Cooperative Bank Limited	7.19	11.26	2.82	2.93	0.36	0.52	15.55	61.95	0.24
13	Gopinath Patil Parsik Janata Sahakari Bank Ltd., Thane	6.19	12.50	4.09	4.11	0.59	1.13	19.47	56.50	0.50
14	Greater Bombay Cooperative Bank Limited	7.53	13.18	0.23	0.23	1.28	0.54	13.25	64.34	0.23
15	Indian Mercantile Cooperative Bank Ltd., Lucknow	7.00	13.86	4.09	4.17	0.20	9.75	11.16	5.87	0.03
16	Jalgaon Janata Sahakari Bank Ltd.	8.04	13.38	0.50	0.61	1.42	0.60	11.67	47.05	0.20
17	Janakalyan Sahakari Bank Ltd., Mumbai	7.34	12.07	2.47	2.47	0.47	0.29	11.23	77.17	0.40
18	Janalaxmi Cooperative Bank Ltd., Nashik	8.01	12.57	2.10	3.69	2.34	2.46	4.66	10.60	1.18
19	Janata Sahakari Bank Ltd., Pune.	8.59	13.68	2.74	2.79	0.46	0.82	11.64	115.78	0.63
20	Kallappanna Awade Ichalkaranji Janata Sahakari Bank Ltd.	8.36	13.47	2.84	3.10	0.82	0.66	13.46	48.01	0.21
21	Kalupur Commercial Coop.Bank Ltd.	7.79	11.96	2.59	2.72	0.65	1.37	16.45	108.47	1.75
22	Kalyan Janata Sahakari Bank Ltd., Kalyan	7.62	12.86	2.98	3.05	1.17	1.03	12.31	63.55	0.49
23	Karad Urban Cooperative Bank Ltd.	8.46	13.46	2.44	2.49	0.94	0.37	11.1	53.20	0.13
24	Mahanagar Cooperative Bank Ltd., Mumbai	7.99	13.68	3.27	3.40	0.76	0.87	12.98	63.34	0.38
25	Mapusa Urban Cooperative Bank of Goa Ltd., Mapusa	7.35	14.58	2.60	3.19	1.07	0.38	–7.56	35.77	0.09
26	Mehsana Urban Co-Op Bank Ltd.	8.38	12.86	2.71	2.71	0.29	0.91	12.03	122.09	0.70
27	Nagar Urban Cooperative Bank Ltd., Ahmednagar	8.51	15.07	3.74	3.94	1.40	0.83	15.32	46.89	0.28
28	Nagpur Nagrik Sahakari Bank Ltd.	7.19	11.81	2.94	3.07	1.39	0.87	20.75	36.04	0.24
29	Nasik Merchant's Cooperative Bank Ltd.	7.46	15.21	4.65	4.76	1.08	2.32	28.32	39.59	0.72
30	New India Cooperative Bank Ltd., Mumbai	7.22	12.30	2.73	2.76	0.78	2.86	12.35	103.67	0.30
31	NKGSB Cooperative Bank Ltd., Mumbai	8.03	12.52	2.31	2.35	0.87	0.66	12.62	85.12	0.38

S. No.	Bank Name	Average Cost of Deposits (%)	Average Yield on Advances (%)	NII to TA (Spread) (%)	NII to WF (%)	Non-II to WF (%)	Return on Assets (ROA) (%)	CRAR (%)	B/E	P/E
32	Nutan Nagarik Sahakari Bank Ltd., Ahmedabad	7.55	12.00	2.49	2.50	2.50	0.66	14	75.40	0.36
33	Pravara Sahakari Bank Ltd.	7.89	12.66	2.82	2.87	2.87	0.97	12.22	31.12	21.67
34	Punjab & Maharashtra Cooperative Bank Ltd.	8.64	15.08	3.18	3.19	0.85	1.09	12.43	83.15	0.55
35	Rajkot Nagrik Sahakari Bank Ltd.	8.18	12.92	1.78	2.43	0.93	1.35	12.37	60.18	0.60
36	Rupee Cooperative Bank Ltd.	5.62	5.33	–0.48	–1.18	0.11	0.00	–222.1	25.75	-0.69
37	Sangli Urban Cooperative Bank Ltd., Sangli	8.69	14.19	2.54	2.81	0.41	0.25	12.31	27.33	0.60
38	Saraswat Cooperative Bank Ltd., Bombay	7.76	11.52	1.68	1.86	1.07	0.61	12.57	106.01	0.45
39	Sardar Bhiladwala Pardi Peoples Coop Bank Ltd.	6.42	11.11	3.10	3.22	0.26	0.68	20.56	62.55	0.30
40	Shamrao Vithal Cooperative Bank Ltd.	8.15	12.66	2.26	2.50	0.88	0.93	12.66	87.20	0.49
41	Shikshak Sahakari Bank Ltd., Nagpur.	7.70	12.36	2.56	2.95	0.46	0.32	13.75	33.17	0.07
42	Solapur Janata Sahakari Bank Ltd.	8.68	14.78	3.31	3.42	0.46	0.78	11.17	67.82	0.37
43	Surat Peoples Coop Bank Ltd.	7.92	13.03	3.70	3.70	0.36	1.55	14.13	125.48	1.35
44	Thane Bharat Sahakari Bank Ltd.	7.15	12.67	3.18	3.30	0.72	0.48	12.27	49.43	0.17
45	The Akola Janata Commercial Cooperative Bank Ltd., Akola.	7.76	13.58	3.25	3.34	0.82	1.50	14.21	37.75	0.23
46	The Akola Urban Cooperative Bank Ltd., Akola.	8.31	12.99	1.52	1.73	0.69	–1.34	9.32	38.13	–0.36
47	The Kapol Cooperative Bank Ltd., Mumbai	7.99	11.49	2.26	0.18	0.12	–1.28	–7.08	33.28	–0.37
48	The Khamgaon Urban Cooperative Bank Ltd., Khamgaon.	6.49	14.79	3.75	4.11	1.26	1.77	20.02	26.54	0.38
49	TJSB Sahakari Bank	7.81	13.11	3.03	3.10	0.61	1.28	14.96	109.95	0.96
50	Zoroastrian Cooperative Bank Ltd., Bombay	7.06	12.75	3.66	3.68	0.39	1.38	15.87	59.11	0.83

REFERENCES

Gandhi, R. 2016. Whither Co-operative Banking? Maharashtra Urban Cooperative Banks Conference 2015. Nagpur: Reserve Bank of India, 14. Available at: https://rbidocs.rbi.org.in/rdocs/Speeches/PDFs/UCSP5FF5A1E3B6A94B9EA19733C1433C425C.PDF (accessed on April 4, 2015).

Malegam, Y. 2011. *Report of the Expert Committee on Licencing New Urban Cooperative Banks*. Mumbai: RBI. Available at: https://rbidocs.rbi.org.in/rdocs/PublicationReport/Pdfs/MFR120911RF.pdf (accessed on April 1, 2016)

Ministry of Finance, GOI. 2016. *Report of the Inter Ministerial Group on Deposit Taking. Ministry of Finance*. New Delhi: Government of India. Available at: http://financialservices.gov.in/Public%20Comments%20on%20the%20Report%20of%20the%20Inter-Ministerial%20Group%20on%20Deposit%20Taking.pdf (Accessed on May 7, 2016).

RBI (Reserve Bank of India). 2015. *Report of the High Powered Committee on Urban Cooperative Banks*. Mumbai: RBI.

———. 2016. *Primary (Urban) Cooperative Banks' Outlook 2014–15*. Mumbai: Reserve Bank of India.

India Post and the Inclusion Agenda[1]

8

Chapter

Over the years, a number of schemes have been implemented by both the Government of India and the RBI to further the agenda of financial inclusion. But a lack of synergy often led to duplication of efforts and underutilization of existing networks. The underutilization of the postal network is an example of this. But this scenario is changing. The potential of the postal network in extending crucial financial services to underserved sections of Indian population is slowly being realized.

PHYSICAL OUTREACH OF THE POSTAL NETWORK

What makes the postal network ideal for carrying the agenda of financial inclusion forward is the very extensiveness of the network (see Figure 8.1). The department of posts, with its network of 154,939 post offices, is the largest postal network in the world. Nearly 90% of this network is located in rural India. On an average 8,354 people are served by a post office in the country. In rural areas, a post office serves 6,258 people and in urban areas a post office serves 26,922 people.

India Post has more than double the number of branches of all the commercial banks operating in India. None of the financial institutions have such a big network to reach to the bottom of population as India Post has. Table 8.1 gives the details of the reach of the postal network broken down into regions.[2]

The number of postal outlets has plateaued over the years and there are only marginal differences in the number of outlets year-on-year. Unlike the banking system, which is increasing its footprint, the postal outlets have not grown. This is something worth pondering. While the opening of Gramin Dak Sewak (GDS) post offices has played a significant role in the expansion of postal network in the country, especially in rural areas, there is no evidence that these offices are over time being upgraded to departmental post offices.

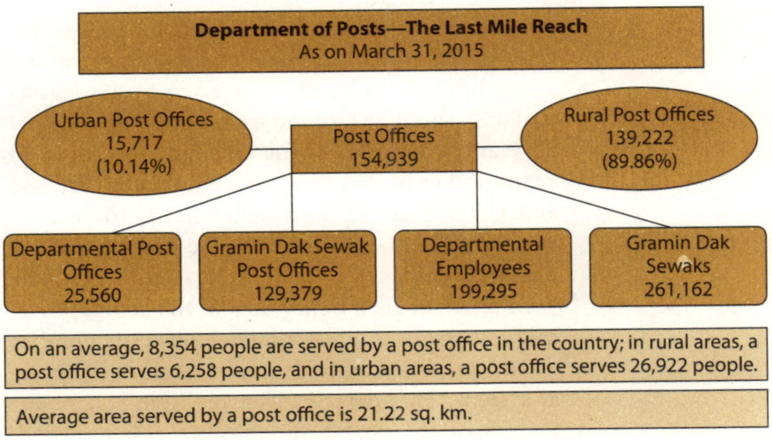

Figure 8.1 India Post: Reach

Source: Government of India. (2016). Annual Report 2015–16, New Delhi: Department of Posts, Ministry of Communications and Information Technology, Government of India.

[1] This chapter is coauthored with Ms Hasna Ashraf, student of MA in Development Studies, Indian Institute of Technology, Madras. Hasna's contribution in collection of data and drafting of this chapter is substantial and is gratefully acknowledged. The authors are also thankful to Ms Madhumita Das, DDB India Post and Professor Chinmay Tumbe, IIM, Ahmedabad, for the feedback on the first draft of this chapter.

[2] The data is organized into six regions (North, Northeast, East, Central, West, and South and two classifications (rural and urban), to have a comparison with the banking network which is also organized into six regions. In the later chapters when we discuss banking, we have consolidated the banking statistics into comparable classifications by merging rural and semi-urban into one basket and urban and metropolitan to another).

Table 8.1 Number of Postal Outlets as of March 2015

	Departmental Post Offices			GDS Post Offices			Total Post Offices		
Region	Rural	Urban	Total	Rural	Urban	Total	Rural	Urban	Total
North	1,679	2,063	3,742	17,983	169	18,152	19,662	2,232	21,894
Northeast	585	376	961	5,754	217	5,971	6,339	593	6,932
East	2,275	2,191	4,466	24,687	250	24,937	26,962	2,441	29,403
Central	1,498	2,848	4,346	27,115	387	27,502	28,613	3,235	31,848
West	1,674	1,880	3,554	18,084	204	18,288	19,758	2,084	21,842
South	4,525	3,966	8,491	33,363	1,166	34,529	37,888	5,132	43,020
Total	12,236	13,324	25,560	126,986	2,393	129,379	139,222	15,717	154,939

Source: Government of India (2016) Annual Report 2015–16, New Delhi: Department of Posts, Ministry of Communications and Information Technology, Government of India.

There is a qualitative difference between a bank branch, which is a proper brick and mortar structure under the control of the bank with some basic specifications of area and facilities, and a postal outlet, which is predominantly operating out of premises that are non-standardized, largely out of the residences or work places of GDS. The GDS post offices function for a period of three hours up to a maximum of five hours. These are manned by GDSs who are paid time-related continuity allowance for the services they render. As of March, there were 261,162 GDSs working in 126,986 GDS post offices, broadly indicating that for every GDS post office, there were two persons operating. Some limited evidence from Karnataka suggests that only about 28% of the workforce is aged below 30 years, while 37% of the GDS are aged over 50 years, and only 5% of them are graduates (Fargose and Utkarsh 2016). This factor needs to be considered when we talk of using the potential of the postal network.

In order to get a better idea of the actual physical footprint, it is interesting to look at the number of outlets owned, rented, or in control of the postal system. This data is given in Table 8.2. About a sixth of the postal outlets were either owned, or rented, or in the custody of India Post. Rest of the outlets were operating out of the premises of GDSs. Therefore, it is important to consider the touchpoints managed by the GDS as similar to the BCs or BC Agents or the customer service centers of the banks.

What these numbers indicate is that the postal network has managed to seep into rural India like no banking network has ever been able to. The progress the postal network has made, especially in the northeast region, when compared to banking networks is significant.

A comparison with the postal networks of other developed and developing countries (Table 8.3) will give us a better idea of India Post's reach.

Another advantage of the postal network is the strength of its last-mile connectivity. Last-mile

Table 8.2 Properties Under the Control of India Post, Region-wise

	Owned	Rented	Free	Total
North	822	2,658	357	3,837
Northeast	264	646	82	992
East	730	3,683	385	4,798
Central	648	3,477	371	4,496
West	652	2,871	181	3,704
South	1,325	6,846	328	8,499
	4,441	20,181	1,704	26,326

Source: Government of India (2016) Annual Report 2015–16, New Delhi: Department of Posts, Ministry of Communications and Information Technology, Government of India.

Table 8.3 Comparison with Other Postal Networks

Country	Total Number of Permanent Post Offices (2014)	Avg. Area Covered (km²)	Avg. Number of Inhabitants Served
China	51,774	185,363	26,902,801
Brazil	12,225	696,446	16,548,602
US	30,088	320,031	10,593,728
Russia	41,450	411,952	3,400,001
Germany	25,000	14,281	327,447
France	17,075	32,299	3,746,362

Source: Postal Statistics from Universal Postal Union, http://www.upu.int/en/resources/postal-statistics/about-postal-statistics.html, accessed on June 24, 2016.

connectivity has often proven to be a bane for most financial inclusion schemes. The inability of the existing BC network to actually reach out to the masses and gain their trust is a major issue faced. This is where we see the significance of postal networks. Over the long years of service provision, postal networks have time and again proven their trustworthiness. Hence the usage of postal networks to deliver financial services would be a very viable solution to overcome the current hurdles to last-mile delivery.

In terms of reach, it can be agreed that the postal network is quite extensive. But in a world that is fast becoming electronic and connected, the relevance of the postal network depends on its ability to innovate and change with the times. To achieve this, the information technology modernization project of the department of posts was taken up. It was approved by the Government of India in November 2012 as a mission mode e-governance project with an outlay of ₹49.09 billion. The project aims at transforming the department of posts into a totally technology driven department. Currently, the project is in implementation stage and is expected to be completed by 2017.

As a part of this project, all the departmental post offices (DPO) in the country including north-eastern region have been computerized. A data center has been established and has started functioning at Navi Mumbai. As of March 2016, 27,736 DPOs including mail offices and administrative offices were networked under a single wide area network (WAN) and connected to the data center. CBS was in operation in more than 22,000 post offices and ATMs that have been installed in more than 800 locations.[3] Extension of CBS increases the scope of inter-post office transactions increasing their effectiveness. Rural ICT project has been launched in three pilot circles, namely Rajasthan, Bihar, and Uttar Pradesh in December 2015.

To further the outreach of the postal network, the postal department has begun giving 4,000 handheld devices to the rural postmen on a pilot basis in six circles which will help them sell third-party products, make e-commerce deliveries, and so on. By 2017, this facility is expected to be available to every postman. Hopefully this will dovetail with the expansion of the India Post Payments Bank (IPPB). IPPB may derive synergies from the postal network in using the network as an agency for its outreach program.

With the physical outreach of the postal network being quite strong, the government is gradually realizing the massive potential of the network to further the agenda of financial inclusion. With the modernization process well on track, the quality as well as the effectiveness of last-mile delivery was becoming a factor that could be counted on. Where most schemes have last-mile delivery as a bottleneck, it is pretty much the strength of the postal network. This aspect was also endorsed by Dr Bimal Jalan, former governor of RBI (see Box 8.1).

Box 8.1: Former Governor Dr Bimal Jalan on Postal Network

MSS: Post offices have been collecting small savings through NSS, Kisan Vikas Patra, postal deposit accounts. They have by definition been dealing with deposits of the poor because there is a cap of ₹450,000 that they can collect per depositor. They also have a formidable network. But when it came to a banking license, the RBI somehow thought that they were not ready for a universal bank license yet, even though they dealing with money on one side …

Dr Jalan: So far as post offices are concerned, it is extremely desirable to use the vast postal network for transfer of deposits and funds to the people. However, a full-fledged banking system through the post offices is not feasible. Of course, the Postal Department can use the vast expansion of post offices by creating a special subsidiary which is managed and regulated by the Postal Department under the supervision of the RBI.

When I look at them in terms of financial services, there is a lot that they can do. Transfer of funds from the government to the people. We must give an opportunity for people to be able to deposit, to have access to the banking system, or financial institution structure. However on the matter of credit, it has to be ensured that the appraisal system for credit in its place. It takes time to establish an appropriate institutional structure.

MSS: Now with these differentiated payments bank that the postal department will set up, and the postal network that is available, it would be a formidable network, much more deeply penetrated than the banking system. And also

[3] Statistics on CBS and ATMs are based on newspaper reports:

Indian Express (2016), 'Fresh Ownership Model to Run India Post Payments Bank Professionally: Ravi Shankar Prasad,' http://indianexpress.com/article/business/banking-and-finance/fresh-ownership-model-to-run-india-post-payments-bank-professionally-ravi-shankar-prasad-2822580/, accessed on June 14, 2016.

through their GDSs, they have something equivalent to the business correspondent which is time tested you know. So lot of payments could happen through that, the government payments, DBT etc. But my question is whether we are creating multiple parallel systems one for just remittances and small savings and another for credit and other banking services and not using the full potential of the postal network?

Dr Jalan: The two are not to be seen as exclusive. They are additional. This transfer mechanism is extremely important but if we can create a vast infrastructure of deposit taking institutions which are transferring funds to credit worthy individuals, that is the thing to do, and that is why we are expanding the banking system also. Regional banks, small banks, payments banks, so on.

MSS: In fact, in the last 3–4 years the expansion of banking system in the rural areas has been much more.

Dr Jalan: Yes you should look at that fact also. Both sides of the equation are equally important. If you have to attach weights, the depositor's side of the equation, the depositors safety is of utmost importance, particularly in the rural areas.

MSS: Because they are much more vulnerable

Dr Jalan: Yes. And the second part of the equation is credit.

FINANCIAL SERVICES

The post office has had a long tradition of offering financial services to the masses. It first launched the money order service in 1880 (Tumbe 2015). Through the provision of services such as savings, remittances, and insurance through its extensive network, the postal department adds to the cause of financial inclusion in a significant manner. The trustworthiness of the postal department makes it a reliable financial partner for the masses.

Savings

Over the years, India Post has been offering multiple savings products catering to different requirements. Post office savings account, recurring deposit account, time deposit account, monthly income account scheme, senior citizen savings scheme, public provident fund account, national savings certificates, Kisan Vikas Patra, and so on. An addition was made to this last year with the introduction of the Sukanya Samrudhi Account which was intended for the welfare of the girl child. As of March 2016, a total of 399 million were there under various schemes. The details of the savings schemes are given in Table 8.4. The low average balances when compared to average bank account balances and low balance requirements for most schemes indicate that the postal department is serving significantly smaller customers.

Table 8.4 Balance Outstanding with India Post on Savings Schemes as of March 31, 2016 (₹ in Billion)

Region	Savings Bank	Recurring Deposit	Time Deposits Including NSS	Public Provident Fund	Monthly Income Scheme	Senior Citizen	Total
North	87.33	175.91	6.42	203.30	276.80	48.33	910.56
Northeast	17.72	23.88	0.20	7.58	39.35	1.70	95.60
East	100.71	95.16	12.68	44.34	643.83	33.76	1,106.74
Central	121.53	174.45	2.76	63.25	261.07	16.87	734.10
West	60.36	77.06	15.58	131.34	469.69	34.14	860.00
South	79.47	195.79	6.98	76.77	311.59	44.67	765.50
BASE	1.35	2.92	0.12	0.90	3.24	0.28	11.02
Total Savings Balances	468.48	745.15	44.73	527.48	2,005.55	179.75	4,483.51
Add NSC* and KVP**							1,704.42
Total							6,187.93

Source: Government of India (2016) Annual Report 2015–16, New Delhi: Department of Posts, Ministry of Communications and Information Technology, Government of India.

Notes: * NSC—National Savings Certificate. **KVP—Kisan Vikas Patra.

Remittances

India Post is a major player in remittances, both domestic and international. The money order is the oldest financial product offered by the postal department. It continues to be a significant instrument for domestic remittance, though it has lost substantial market share in recent years on account of high transaction costs. The government uses this service for the disbursement of the amounts for various social security schemes. The past year saw a total of 135.2 million inland money orders carrying a total value of ₹141.80 billion, out of which ₹54.7 billion were disbursed by the government for various social security schemes.

Apart from traditional money orders, India Post also offers instant money order (iMO) which allows the instantaneous remittance of money. Under this service, a person can send an amount from ₹1,000 up to ₹50,000 in one transaction. Money will be disbursed to the payee at any of the designated iMO post office in India on presentation of a 16-digit iMO number and a photo identity proof. As of March, the service is available in 16,785 post offices across the country.[4]

Mobile money transfer service is another facility offered by India Post in association with Bharat Sanchar Nigam Limited. It enables instant money transfer from one place to another using mobiles through post offices. This service is a boon for those sections of the society who regularly remit money to their homes at faraway places and who have no access to bank accounts. The service is currently available in 15,000 post offices across the country.

Apart from domestic remittances, India Post also plays a major role in international money transfer as a partner of leading money-transfer operators. The service enables instant international money remittance to customers in India sent from around 195 countries on a real time basis. India Post has been operating this service in association with Western Union from 9,942 post office locations and with MoneyGram through 6,070 post office locations.

Insurance

A major contribution of India post to financial inclusion is the provision of insurance services. The major insurance types offered by India Post are Postal Life Insurance (PLI) and Rural Postal Life Insurance (RPLI). PLI, introduced in 1884, is the oldest life insurance scheme for the benefit of the government and semi-government employees. RPLI on the other hand was introduced in 1995 for the benefit of rural populace to extend insurance cover to the people living in rural areas, with special emphasis on weaker sections and women workers, thus, playing a direct role in financial inclusion. The maximum sum assured under RPLI has been raised from ₹500,000 to ₹1 million. Rural India, despite its immense potential does not have many sources offering insurance services. This is where we see the significance of India Post. RPLI caters to the needs of rural India. However, considering how even now only a small fraction of rural India has been covered by insurance, India Post still has a long way to go.

Apart from these two schemes (Table 8.5), India Post also helps in the provision of the Jan Suraksha Schemes. The Jan Suraksha schemes, PMSBY and PMJJBY have been launched with effect from September 7, 2015 in all CBS post offices. The schemes are available to all post office savings accountholders. The use of the extensive network of the postal department for the distribution of the Jan

Table 8.5 Details of Postal Life and Rural Postal Life Insurance Policies

Name of the Scheme	No. of Policies Procured (in '000s)	Sum Assured (₹ Billion)	Aggregate No. of Active Policies (in '000)	Aggregate Sum Assured (₹ Billion)	Premium Income (₹ Billion)	Claims (in '000s)	Claims (₹ Billion)
PLI	324	142.77	5,442	1,091.06	59.63	198	21.59
RPLI	477	46.52	15,245	828.22	19.83	164	6.92
Total	801	189.29	20,687	1,919.29	79.47	362	28.51

Source: Government of India (2016) Annual Report 2015–16, New Delhi: Department of Posts, Ministry of Communications and Information Technology, Government of India.

[4] Last year's report indicated that the service would be extended to an additional 7,036 post offices. However, this does not seem to have happened.

Suraksha schemes is a well-thought-out way to get the schemes to more people. As of February 1,06,784 subscribers have been enrolled under PMSBY and 9,140 under PMJJBY.

Pension

India Post is a point of presence for the National Pension System (NPS) for Indian citizens. Under this scheme, any subscriber who intends to open a pension account will be provided the facility at all head post offices in the country. Through the provision of pension as a third=party product, India Post in a way adds to the diversity of financial products offered to the masses.

Apart from NPS, India Post currently also offers APY. APY was launched in CBS head post offices from December 1, 2015, and 25,398 subscribers had enrolled in this scheme by February 2016.

THIRD-PARTY SERVICES: IMPLEMENTATION OF GOVERNMENT SCHEMES

The department of posts was entrusted with implementation of various government sponsored social security schemes under MGNREGA, Indira Gandhi National Old Age Pension Scheme, Indira Gandhi National Widow Pension Scheme, and Indira Gandhi National Disability Pension Scheme. Through this, India Post has contributed to the inclusion of nearly 85 million rural citizens. These schemes are being made either through money orders or post office savings bank (POSB) Accounts depending upon the choice of implementing agency and beneficiaries. During 2014–15, ₹36.31 billion was disbursed through POSB and ₹54.69 billion through money orders.

India Post has taken the responsibility to disburse the wages through post offices by opening savings bank accounts in the names of MGNREGA beneficiaries (in all states with the exception of Jammu and Kashmir). As of March 2015, the scheme is operational through 96,774 post offices across the country. The details are given in Table 8.6. However, while the number of accounts that are under India Post for payments has marginally gone up, the amounts have fallen significantly. This could be because of dormant accounts, and possibly because the customer base may have shifted to one of the banks under the PMJDY mission of opening accounts. Clearly, as they go forward, India Post will have to regain its market share in the government business.

Indira Gandhi Matritva Sahyog Yojana (IGMSY), a conditional cash transfer for addressing maternal undernutrition was introduced in 52 selected districts. Postal network in these districts is contributing to the success of the scheme by opening accounts for the beneficiaries and facilitating transfer of cash to them under the scheme. As of March 2015, more than 510,000 accounts were opened through which ₹1.07 billion were disbursed.

Table 8.6 MGNREGA Accounts and Amounts Disbursed

	Number of Accounts (₹ Million)	Amount (₹ Billion)
2008–09	29.2	38.63
2009–10	42.5	79
2010–11	49	91.79
2011–12	53.8	78.65
2012–13	57.4	120.14
2013–14	64.2	114.03
2014–15	68.2	76.88

Source: Government of India (2016) Annual Report 2015–16, New Delhi: Department of Posts, Ministry of Communications and Information Technology, Government of India.
Note: Includes both live and silent accounts.

India Post has also been extending a hand of support in the disbursement of various social security payments under DBT. The effectiveness of India Post's last-mile delivery is what makes it ideal for this. The existing role is expected to be extended with the complete implementation of Rural Information Communication Technology (RICT) Solution and CBS. Currently, the potential of the postal network is not well utilized for the implementation of DBT. This situation is expected to change with the massive reboot planned in the implementation of DBT. This DBT 2.0 envisages the use of post offices and roping in postmen as delivery agents for door-to-door disbursal of payments, including wages for rural jobs and subsidy for fuels, food, and fertilizers. The current hurdle faced by the DBT scheme, that of last-mile delivery, can be overcome with the better utilization of the postal infrastructure for the delivery of DBT. The revised scheme is expected to be brought into effect by March 2017.[5]

[5] While this aspect is drawn from the annual report of India Post, it has not been possible to get other documents supporting this. A decision was also taken to convert all DBT accounts to PMJDY accounts. There have been reports of how IPPB would be used for the delivery of DBT. In the light of these, it is not known how the implementation of DBT 2.0 may actually take place.

THE NEXT STEP: INDIA POST PAYMENTS BANK

So far we have been looking at the financial services that India Post has traditionally been offering. Through this, India Post has managed to bring financial services closer to people who lack access to formal banking set-ups. While the services currently offered by India Post are similar to those offered by a formal banking set up, it got a major boost in the direction of formal banking when the union finance minister announced the government's intention to set up the PB by India Post in the 2015–16 Budget speech. What does this mean for India Post?

Formed based on the recommendations of the Nachiket Mor Committee, PBs are differentiated banks that offer most of the services offered by commercial banks except for loans and credit card products. They can raise deposits up to ₹1 lakh and also enable transfers and remittances through a mobile phone. The basic idea behind their formation is to push the agenda of financial inclusion forward by providing current and savings accounts, and payments or remittance services to migrant labor workforce, low income households, small businesses, unorganized sector workers, and other users. Through low transaction costs these seek to enable poorer citizens to take their first step into formal banking.

The department of posts got an 'in-principle' approval from the RBI to set up the PB in September 2015. The IPPB is proposed to be set up with a corpus of ₹8 Billion, of which ₹4 billion would be equity and ₹4 billion a grant. Under the IPPB, the initial plan is to have 650 main branches where the department has head post offices or bigger post offices. Subsequently, 25,000 'spoke' branches will be set up while the other 130,000 post offices will act as BCs. This does not, however, mean that the previous financial services offered by India Post will be merged with the new payments bank. IPPB is to be set up as a separate entity, a public limited company under the department of posts that will make use of the existing postal network. The IPPB will be set up on a lean operating model. It will focus on financial inclusion by harnessing low-cost technology based solutions to extend access to formal banking especially in rural areas and among unbanked and under banked segments of the society. The PB is expected to receive its license from the RBI by March and all 650 branches start their operations by September 2017.[6]

[6] *Business Standard*. (2016). India Post Payments Bank to Be a Reality, http://www.business-standard.com/article/economy-policy/india-post-payments-bank-to-be-a-reality-116060101947_1.html, accessed on June 14, 2016.

Ever since the 'in-principle' approval from the RBI to set up a PB, India Post has received proposals for partnerships from about 50 companies. What is it about India Post that makes it ideal to become a payments bank? The most important factor would be the extensiveness of the network. As has already been discussed, the reach of the postal network is unparalleled. Not just in terms of extensiveness but also in terms of quality, this network is strong. With the IT modernization project well on track, the last-mile connectivity of the network is ever-improving. And unlike the BC model that seems to be having numerous lacunae, the postal network has adopted the GDS model that has proven to be effective and trustworthy over time. Hence by adopting the postal network, IPPB already has a very strong infrastructure in place.

Besides this, the experience India Post has in managing remittances and small savings deposits also adds to its advantage. In fact, given its history in providing financial services, transformation into a PB is the next logical step.

For India Post, this transformation becomes a significant step toward its foray into banking. Through this step, India Post gets the scope to play directly in the mainstream market system. In order to fulfill the Universal Service Obligation (USO), subsidy is provided to all branch post offices in rural areas, which ranges from 66.66% in normal rural areas to 85% in hilly, tribal, desert, and inaccessible areas. With the functions of the PB added to this network, there would be better utilization or existing resources and a reduction in departmental losses.

India Post, being a significant player in the savings and remittances market, was already carrying out the functions of a PB. What makes the transformation to a PB different is that it gives the existing set-up a proper structure, clear accounting, and proper segregation of functions. The transformation to a PB is indeed a step forward. But how big a step is it? Given the advantages that India Post has in terms of infrastructure and experience, the role of IPPB can be possibly expanded. Provision of credit is an important financial service, access to which would be a shot in the arm for the financial upliftment of unbanked population. However, credit does not form a function of a PB. Extension of microcredit through IPPB is a possibility that can be considered once the PB becomes operational. Considering the reach of the postal network, this would allow for an effective inclusive finance. Other details of IPPB is discussed in

Chapter 12 where the PBs and their plans are discussed in detail.

CONCLUDING NOTES

India Post has traditionally been offering financial services. The detailed numbers of the services offered and the network of the postal department are given in Appendices 8.1 to 8.4. The potential that the postal network has in furthering financial inclusion is slowly being realized. The formation of India Post PB is an indication of this. How it ultimately pans out is to be seen.

Given the experience that India Post has in providing financial services and the high demand for microcredit in rural and unorganized sectors, the possibility of introducing a credit component in post office savings banks should be considered. The report submitted by the Expert Committee on Harnessing the India Post Network for Financial Inclusion explores this possibility. The committee has suggested a workable mechanism through which the India Post network can deliver short-duration, fixed-size, non-collateralized microloans (of ₹500 for one month) without using public money.[7] It is high time these recommendations be taken up and implemented to bring in credit into the picture.

Another factor that needs focus is the synergy of existing projects to avoid duplication of efforts. Once it is launched, IPPB can be used as a platform for the distribution of government schemes, thus reducing the burden that currently falls on public sector banks. The PB can also be used to execute existing projects in financial inclusion, PMJDY, for example. The use of the extensive postal network for the implementation of an exhaustive scheme like PMJDY is guaranteed to maximize the impact.

India Post is slowly gaining prominence in the area of financial inclusion. Its contribution to the cause over the years has been by no means small. With its potential being realized, the dynamics is shifting and India Post is a player that is slowly becoming indispensable.

[7] Report of the Expert Committee on Harnessing the India Post Network for Financial Inclusion, http://www.indiapost.gov.in/pdf/iief-indiapostreport.pdf, accessed on June 21, 2016.

APPENDIX 8.1

Scheme-wise/Year-wise Details of Outstanding Balance of Saving Accounts with India Post

(₹ in Billion) as of March 31

Scheme	2009	2010	2011	2012	2013	2014	2015
Post Office Savings Bank	226.90	264.58	301.01	340.70	378.50	430.17	474.28
1 Year Term Deposit	144.93	180.49	182.76	168.69	213.36	273.43	361.53
2 Year Term Deposit	11.12	12.30	13.68	13.11	14.75	17.67	20.31
3 Year Term Deposit	36.90	37.81	42.68	42.07	39.89	39.15	41.42
4 Year Term Deposit	69.70	45.13	45.33	50.04	62.09	76.89	94.31
5 Year Term Deposit	650.72	628.18	612.50	626.61	679.62	741.49	745.13
National Savings Certificate 1987	38.62	38.74	42.31	40.58	39.63	38.69	36.89
National Savings Certificate 1992	5.65	5.77	4.78	4.07	3.26	2.77	2.32
Monthly Income Scheme 1987	1,795.04	2,016.93	2,186.74	2,052.88	2,017.87	2,020.85	2,005.57
Senior Citizen	206.51	249.89	309.13	267.63	240.93	224.92	179.75
MGNREGA			0	56	0	0	0
Post Office CTD			0	6	0	6	8
Others	49	44	36	22	22	22	22
Total	3,186.58	3,480.26	3,741.28	3,607.22	3,690.12	3,866.31	3,961.81
National Savings Certificate VI	–60	–69	–66	–69	–75	–77	-82
National Savings Certificate VII	–43	-51	–43	–49	-64	-50	-53
National Savings Certificate VIII	553.09	547.76	546.42	550.69	647.19	750.86	856.08
Indira Vikas Patra	10.31	10.22	10.20	8.94	9.07	8.96	8.87
Kisan Vikas Patra	1475.17	1,539.33	1,585.84	1,539.60	1,283.75	1,067.54	848.41
Kisan Vikas Patra 2014							26.71
Others	59	56	60	65	20.25	56.49	95.38
Total	2,038.13	2,096.67	2,141.97	2,098.70	1,958.87	1,882.58	1,834.10
Public Provident Fund	234.02	260.96	315.83	359.93	411.21	466.08	527.48
Grand Total	5,458.73	5837.89	6,199.08	6,065.85	6,060.20	6,214.97	6,323.39

Source: Director, Financial Services, India Post.

APPENDIX 8.2
Number of Accounts of Various Savings Schemes as of March 31, 2015

(in numbers)

Circle	Savings Bank	Recurring Deposit	Time Deposit	Fixed Deposit	Cumulative Time Deposits	Public Provident Fund	Monthly Income Scheme	National Saving Scheme 87	National Saving Scheme 92	Senior Citizen	Sukanya Samridhi Account	Mahila Samridhi Yojana	Mahatma Gandhi National Rural Employment Guarantee Act*	Total
Andhra Pradesh	15,559,080	18,109,644	540,407	0	1,130	93,611	1,137,842	11,101	3,237	47,323	219,439	15,727	24,589,582	60,328,123
Assam	4,512,042	1,900,288	181,222	0	1,084	41,983	371,945	2,252	335	4,330	48,451	0	1,380,161	8,444,093
Bihar	14,268,945	3,421,886	1,594,598	0	688	49,217	1,205,436	2,299	202	26,860	12,974	0	6,707,904	27,291,009
Chhatisgarh	2,870,218	867,916	69,677	0	1,303	32,477	124,928	1,547	133	5,303	7,868	0	5,399,961	9,381,331
Delhi	1,463,047	621,732	153,112	2	10,069	221,311	596,807	26,985	1,100	84,099	25,629	2,094	0	3,205,987
Gujarat	6,374,586	5,298,183	2,187,683	0	5,678	226,239	2,095,543	31,261	255	91,720	63,948	0	2,262,577	18,637,673
Haryana	3,173,161	1,870,540	1,268,305	0	83,879	93,746	455,241	11,014	305	20,730	70,889	129,679	67,359	7,244,848
Himachal Pradesh	1,891,628	2,183,863	488,917	22	4,615	23,286	203,843	1,514	75	4,756	23,141	0	98,359	4,924,019
Jammu & Kashmir	1,282,199	283,152	256,268	0	5,676	7,628	93,446	1,509	50	2,294	25,947	21,262	3,991	1,983,422
Jharkhand	5,292,403	2,022,431	363,590	0	1,877	40,956	416,167	3,481	0	15,696	109,445	0	3,914,247	12,180,293
Karnataka	14,398,705	6,209,844	301,388	4	8,373	105,092	644,017	15,473	1,671	51,972	501,860	0	669,670	22,908,069
Kerala	6,142,153	5,150,876	207,252	298	–42,710	18,629	450,376	5,714	2,094	6,866	123,615	6	312,963	12,378,132
Madhya Pradesh	11,445,784	10,153,376	593,515	59	10,533	55,398	629,972	6,954	327	22,054	78,641	1,108,431	2,087,904	26,192,948
Maharashtra	7,927,560	21,632,124	1,534,911	0	20,705	466,169	2,191,683	77,457	2,337	138,417	0	0	3,496,733	37,488,096
Northeast	1,440,712	680,677	53,771	4	1,447	5,725	60,326	883	116	2,090	9,151	19,530	681,649	2,956,081
Orissa	8,113,358	3,998,822	394,093	0	9,317	19,683	466,482	4,782	326	13,404	54,884	23,455	1,608,472	14,707,078
Punjab	3,630,646	1,622,352	877,034	127	13,206	178,543	773,857	14,594	689	42,168	59,385	31,768	244,269	7,488,638
Rajasthan	10,155,648	4,607,976	399,589	0	4,600	209,856	815,435	7,772	801	26,446	35,852	102,295	3,720,999	20,087,269
Tamilnadu	13,728,456	11,805,868	711,760	0	7,270	142,327	804,931	17,188	5,604	70,217	606,385	17,668	0	27,917,674
Uttar Pradesh	15,092,187	14,163,666	1,822,316	0	23,916	181,361	1,796,524	18,521	413	105,018	176,763	369,098	377,636	34,127,419
Uttarakhand	3,762,839	1,581,705	290,854	0	8,887	32,033	175,181	2,694	185	8,668	63,732	6,903	222,901	6,156,582
West Bengal	13,001,480	4,343,864	1,945,879	0	0	165,000	5,533,388	–1,851	36,373	163,271	168,006	0	7,037,265	32,392,675
Base Post Office	441,349	407,319	2,762	0	91	14,714	30,438	374	28	475	0	0	0	897,550
Total	165,968,186	122,938,104	16,238,903	516	181,634	2,424,984	21,073,808	263,518	56,656	954,177	2,486,005	1,847,916	64,884,602	399,319,009

Source: India Post Annual Report.

Note: *Including of both MGNREGA (with Balance) and MGNREGA (Zero Balance).

APPENDIX 8.3
Outstanding Balances in Various Savings Schemes

As of March 31, 2015 (₹ in Billion)

Circle	Saving Bank	Recurring Deposit	Time Deposit	Fixed Deposit	Cumulative Time Deposit	Public Provident Fund	Monthly Income Scheme	NSS 87	NSS 92	Senior Citizen	Total
Andhra Pradesh	17.17	40.00	22.24	0.00	0.00	16.24	110.84	1.07	–0.05	11.84	219.35
Assam	12.45	14.70	1.27	0.00	0.00	6.31	28.33	0.13	–0.07	1.03	64.16
Bihar	25.00	30.28	58.54	0.00	0.01	7.58	74.34	9.49	2.21	1.13	208.58
Chhatisgarh	7.43	17.58	5.51	0.00	–0.04	6.29	18.85	0.49	–0.10	2.26	58.29
Delhi	17.35	25.97	14.29	–0.01	–0.01	88.20	80.75	1.61	0.55	25.04	253.74
Gujarat	26.80	25.35	43.54	0.00	0.04	62.73	178.10	3.43	–1.78	19.37	357.57
Haryana	13.38	31.00	15.86	0.00	–0.06	20.73	36.27	0.81	0.00	5.85	123.85
Himachal Pradesh	11.97	27.46	10.22	0.00	0.01	6.37	23.42	0.11	0.00	1.64	81.18
Jammu and Kashmir	4.31	5.00	11.25	0.00	0.03	1.53	8.30	–0.07	0.11	1.38	31.85
Jharkhand	–1.82	6.67	15.14	0.00	0.02	1.19	53.05	–0.02	–0.19	3.40	77.45
Karnataka	24.95	41.31	7.37	0.00	0.02	24.66	67.05	0.65	1.35	15.66	183.03
Kerala	10.31	64.31	2.59	0.00	0.00	4.92	26.26	0.46	0.01	3.31	112.18
Madhya Pradesh	32.51	39.19	8.15	0.01	–0.01	10.95	43.14	0.41	–0.19	3.80	137.96
Maharashtra	33.56	51.70	29.02	0.00	0.01	68.61	291.59	13.34	–0.18	14.77	502.43
Northeast	5.27	9.16	3.97	0.00	0.00	1.27	11.02	0.09	–0.01	0.67	31.44
Orissa	17.41	20.73	11.70	0.00	–0.01	3.47	34.08	0.21	–0.06	1.69	89.23
Punjab	22.93	36.00	42.16	0.00	0.00	49.41	67.21	1.03	0.90	10.86	230.50
Rajasthan	17.39	50.46	19.83	0.00	0.01	37.06	60.85	0.46	–0.21	3.57	189.43
Tamil Nadu	27.03	50.17	18.54	0.00	0.00	30.95	107.43	2.68	0.28	13.86	250.95
Uttar Pradesh	69.58	97.68	71.05	–0.02	–0.02	40.08	173.71	0.98	0.51	8.32	461.88
Uttarakhand	12.01	20.00	10.40	0.00	0.00	5.93	25.37	–0.12	–0.10	2.49	75.97
West Bengal	60.11	37.49	92.66	0.26	0.06	32.10	482.35	–0.13	–0.95	27.53	731.48
Base	1.35	2.92	2.24	0.00	0.00	0.90	3.24	0.07	0.02	0.28	11.02
Total	468.48	745.15	517.55	0.24	0.07	527.48	2,005.55	37.18	2.06	179.75	4,483.51

Source: India Post Annual Report.

APPENDIX 8.4
Distribution of Postal Outlets

Distribution of Rural and Urban Post Offices as of March 31, 2015

(in number)

	Departmental Post Office									Gramin Dak Sewak Post Office									Total Post Office		
	Head Post Office			Sub Post Office			Total			Sub Post Office			Branch Post Office			Total					
Circle	Rutal	Urban	Total	Rural	Urban	Total	Rural	Urban	Total	Rural	Urban	Total	Rural	Urban	Total	Rural	Urban	Total	Rural	Urban	Total
Andhra Pradesh	4	91	95	1,379	971	2,350	1,383	1,062	2,445	–	–	0	13,417	293	13,710	13,417	293	13,710	14,800	1,355	16,155
Assam	0	19	19	396	211	607	396	230	626	–	–	0	3,251	135	3,386	3,251	135	3,386	3,647	365	4,012
Bihar	1	30	31	622	398	1,020	623	428	1,051	–	–	0	7,971	45	8,016	7,971	45	8,016	8,594	473	9,067
Chhatisgarh	0	10	10	99	238	337	99	248	347	–	–	0	2,780	20	2,800	2,780	20	2,800	2,879	268	3,147
Delhi	0	12	12	4	387	391	4	399	403	–	–	0	79	69	148	79	69	148	83	468	551
Gujarat	0	34	34	645	660	1,305	645	694	1,339	–	–	0	7,549	95	7,644	7,549	95	7,644	8,194	789	8,983
Haryana	0	16	16	180	301	481	180	317	497	–	–	0	2,152	28	2,180	2,152	28	2,180	2,332	345	2,677
Himachal Pradesh	3	15	18	351	97	448	354	112	466	–	–	0	2,310	6	2,316	2,310	6	2,316	2,664	118	2,782
Jammu & Kashmir	0	9	9	93	163	256	93	172	265	–	–	0	1,409	25	1,434	1,409	25	1,434	1,502	197	1,699
Jharkhand	0	13	13	222	221	443	222	234	456	–	–	0	2,613	30	2,643	2,613	30	2,643	2,835	264	3,099
Karnataka	0	58	58	837	817	1,654	837	875	1,712	–	–	0	7,776	179	7,955	7,776	179	7,955	8,613	1,054	9,667
Kerala	6	45	51	977	480	1,457	983	525	1,508	–	–	0	3,223	337	3,560	3,223	337	3,560	4,206	862	5,068
Madhya Pradesh	0	43	43	332	688	1,020	332	731	1,063	–	–	0	7,156	104	7,260	7,156	104	7,260	7,488	835	8,323
Maharashtra	1	60	61	1,028	1,126	2,154	1,029	1,186	2,215	–	–	0	10,535	109	10,644	10,535	109	10,644	11,564	1,295	12,859
North - East	0	9	9	189	137	326	189	146	335	–	–	0	2,503	82	2,585	2,503	82	2,585	2,692	228	2,920
Orissa	0	35	35	660	502	1,162	660	537	1,197	1	–	1	6,915	56	6,971	6,916	56	6,972	7,576	593	8,169
Punjab	0	22	22	331	409	740	331	431	762	–	–	0	3,080	14	3,094	3,080	14	3,094	3,411	445	3,856
Rajasthan	1	47	48	716	585	1,301	717	632	1,349	–	–	0	8,953	27	8,980	8,953	27	8,980	9,670	659	10,329
Tamil Nadu	0	94	94	1,322	1,410	2,732	1,322	1,504	2,826	–	–	0	8,947	357	9,304	8,947	357	9,304	10,269	1,861	12,130
Uttar Pradesh	0	72	72	867	1,604	2,471	867	1,676	2,543	–	–	0	14,863	249	15,112	14,863	249	15,112	15,730	1,925	17,655
Uttarakhand	0	13	13	200	180	380	200	193	393	–	–	0	2,316	14	2,330	2,316	14	2,330	2,516	207	2,723
West Bengal	0	47	47	770	945	1,715	770	992	1,762	–	–	0	7,187	119	7,306	7,187	119	7,306	7,957	1,111	9,068
Total	16	794	810	12,220	12,530	24,750	12,236	13,324	25,560	1	0	1	126,985	2,393	129,378	126,986	2,393	129,379	139,222	15,717	154,939

Source: India Post Annual Report.

REFERENCES

Fargose, V. and Utkarsh. 2016, August. *Expanding the Scope of India Post Payments Bank*. Bengaluru: Indian Institute of Management Bangalore.

Tumbe, C. (2015). "Towards Financial Inclusion: The Post Office of India as a Financial Institution, 1880–2010." *Indian Economic and Social History Review*, 52(4): 409–37.

Review of SHG-Bank Linkage Programme[1]

9

Chapter

INTRODUCTION

Dr Rangarajan, former Governor RBI, has been a big supporter of diversity of institutions (see Box 9.1) and this was a year where this community-based initiative grew in strength. The SHG movement continued to grow in 2015–16, largely due to the push given by the government program of the NRLM. While in the past year, it was noted that the formation of groups has plateaued out, possibly reaching a saturation point, the activity within the groups continued to grow both in terms of savings collected from women members as well as in terms of the loans disbursed to them. In addition, there was an increasing effort of mainstreaming the SHG data. On the one hand the NABARD continued its project of digitising the SHG data, so that it is easily accessible to bankers and others for monitoring purposes, on the other hand the RBI laid out a road-map for all SHG credit data to be collected and uploaded with the credit information companies (CICs) so that the individual-level indebtedness could be monitored. As we go forward, it is possible that the NBFC-MFI norms may be applied to the microfinance sector as a whole, given that the stress on indebtedness is being talked about.

While there was much progress in the PMJDY (discussed in detail in Chapter 4), and there has been significant efforts to ensure that women open the accounts, the policy discourse did not indicate any convergence between the SHG program or the NRLM program with the PMJDY scheme. Neither were there any thoughts or discussion on integrating PMJDY accounts with the KCC. Going forward, it would be important to look at the convergence possibilities.

Box 9.1 Dr C. Rangarajan on SHGs

We should experiment with all types of institutions. I don't think there is any particular institution alone on which we should focus. But then there is a particular issue of how to reach out to the extremely small borrowers. That segment is not going to be met by the banking system. The only route available to the banking system is through the SHGs. In that case, the loans can become extremely small. Otherwise, individually providing credit of that size will become extremely difficult.

The approval for SHGs as an instrument or an institution through which lending can be given was given during my time. In fact there was a lot of confusion at that time on whether they should be registered and if we should frame rules to deal with the groups. There was an important circular of NABARD, which we approved during my time, which paved the way for groups to link with banks through an inter-se agreement.

Source: Interview with the author.

REVIEW OF DEVELOPMENTS IN SELF-HELP GROUP BANK LINKAGE PROGRAMME

In the past few years we have seen the following trend:

The presence of the government schemes in the Self-help Group Bank Linkage Programme (SHGBLP) is increasing. While the actual number

[1] The author is thankful to Ms Girija Srinivasan and Mr C.S. Reddy who read the early draft of this chapter and gave constructive feedback.

of new SHGs promoted has somewhat plateaued—growing at 1.53%, 3.59%, and 2.68% in the past few years, the amounts saved and the loans availed by these groups have been increasing. However, this growth is coming more and more from the governmental schemes, particularly the NRLM.

With the launch of NRLM (replacing SGSY), the thrust has moved from providing access to finance to a livelihoods approach. Thus, NRLM is involved not only in augmenting credit, but also in organising groups, federating them, providing them with support services, and much more through specialized vehicles such as the state livelihood missions and dedicated teams. Therefore, NRLM has been able to take under is fold a substantial number of groups that were originally promoted by civil society organizations. In 2011–12, in the early days of launch of NRLM, around 30% of the SHGs were associated with the government programs. In 2015–16, this proportion has gone up to around 45%. Given that the number of groups is not growing at that pace, it is evident that the government program is taking over the groups that were promoted by the civil society, banking, and other organizations. The credit extended under concessional norms under NRLM to any group is counted as NRLM. Otherwise, the groups largely remain where they are and, therefore, this number is a good indication of the involvement of the state in this agenda.

In the past years, there was little convergence between the work of NABARD through its own developmental programs—of providing financial support for capacity building, group formation, and the work of NRLM. The past year's report discussed the recommendations of the Usha Thorat Committee that examined the need to set up a separate developmental financial institution for SHGs, where the committee had called for a greater convergence between the Ministry of Rural Development. Following the recommendations, a strategic advisory board was set up with the deputy managing director of NABARD as the chair of the board and multiple stakeholders from the department of financial services (DFS), Ministry of Finance (MOF); NRLM; bankers; and domain experts was set up. The strategic advisory board also ensures greater field convergence than before. The results could be seen in the 2015–16 numbers where there is an increased share of NRLM-related groups in all the activities.

Apart from the large organizations such as Dhan Foundation, Sanghamithra, NABARD Financial Services (NABFINS) and SKDRDP that continue their work in this area and grow, many of the smaller civil society organizations have, over a period of time, embraced the MFI model and moved toward commercial microfinance. So, a trend is now getting clear—the community-based model is veering toward becoming a state-driven program, while the MFI model is veering toward a private enterprise format.

The MFI model (discussed in Chapter 10) is aggressively growing. As we could see, the growth in the private sector MFIs is worrisomely fast, and the discipline is lacking in the SHGBLP format. This trend is to be spotted in the way the non-performing assets are panning out in the SHGBLP.

The growth and developments in the SHGBLP is to be understood keeping the above context in mind.

PROGRESS UNDER SHGBLP

As stated earlier, the group formation as plateaued out, but there has been significant growth in the amount of savings (24% growth) and the relative share of groups under NRLM and NULM growing. Similarly, while loans disbursed to SHGs have grown by 35%, the loans disbursed to the NRLM groups have disproportionately grown. Table 9.1 gives the numbers on SHGs for the past four years, and we can see that while there is little action on group formation, the activities of savings and loaning within the groups are showing growth.

REGIONAL SPREAD OF SHGs

The role of NRLM in the renewed interest of SHGBLP cannot be wished away. The number of active SHGs (which had some savings) was at a peak of 7.9 million in March 2011. This fell to about 7.32 million in March 2012. But ever since, there has been an increase in active SHGs, and by March 2016, the number of groups with some savings activity had reached the high levels of March 2011. While the number of groups went back to the peak number, the amount of savings collected was always growing year-on-year at around 20%, which is an important factor to be noted. However, the numbers given by the database represent only savings of the members deposited in the banks and remaining as balance. If we count the savings amounts within the groups that are circulating, this amount may be higher. In some states with the SHG loans being subsidized by the government (such as Andhra Pradesh (AP) and Telangana), the incentive to leave savings at bank and borrow loans at

Table 9.1 Overall Progress Under SHG Bank Linkage for Last 4 Years

(Amount in Billion/Numbers in Million)

		2012–13		2013–14		2014–15		2015–16	
	Particulars	**No. of SHGs**	**Amount**	**No. of SHGs**	**Amount**	**No. of SHGs**	**Amount**	**No. of SHGs**	**Amount**
SHG savings in banks	Total SHGs	7.32 (−8.1%)	82.17 (25.4%)	7.43 (1.53%)	98.97 (20.45%)	7.70 (3.59%)	110.60 (11.74%)	7.90 (2.68%)	136.91 (23.79%)
	NRLM/SGSY/Govt programs	2.05 (−3.6%)	1821.65 (30.6%)	2.26 (10.46%)	24.78 (36.01%)	3.05 (34.92%)	44.24 (78.56%)	3.46 (13.27%)	62.45 (41.16%)
	%NRLM/SGSY/	28.0	22.2	30.45	25.03	39.65	40.00	43.70	45.61
	NULM/SJSRY	NA	NA	NA	NA	0.43	10.72	0.45 (3.00%)	10.06 (6.12%)
	% NULM/SJSRY	NA	NA	NA	NA	5.63	9.69	5.64	7.35
	All women SHGs	5.94 (−5.7%)	65.15 (27.6%)	6.25 (5.27%)	80.13 (22.99%)	6.65 (6.38%)	92.64 (15.61%)	6.76 (1.68%)	120.35 (29.92%)
	% women groups	81.1	79.3	84.15	80.96	86.41	83.77	85.58	87.91
Loans disbursed to SHGs in the year	No. of SHGs extended loan	1.22 (6.3%)	205.85 (24.5%)	1.37 (12.02%)	240.17 (16.67%)	1.63 (19.03%)	275.82 (14.84%)	1.83 (12.67%)	372.87 (35.18%)
	NRLM/SGSY/Govt programs	0.18 (−13.8%)	22.07 (−16.5%)	0.23 (24.56%)	34.81 (57.67%)	0.64 (28.45%)	94.88 (27.26%)	0.82 (26.91%)	167.86 (76.92%)
	%NRLM/SGSY/	14.8	10.7	16.52	14.49	39.54	34.40	44.54	45.02
	NULM/SJSRY	NA	NA	NA	NA	0.11	18.72	0.11 (5.71%)	26.20 (40.00%)
	%NULM/SJSRY	NA	NA	NA	NA	6.46	6.79	6.06	7.03
	All women SHGs	1.04 (12.4)	178.54 (26.3%)	1.15 (11.02%)	210.38 (17.83%)	1.45 (25.69%)	244.20 (16.07%)	1.63 (12.50%)	344.11 (40.92%)
	% women groups	85.1	86.7	84.3	87.6	89.05	83.53	88.92	92.29
SHG loans outstanding	Total SHGs	4.45 (2.2%)	393.75 (8.4%)	4.20 (−5.71)	429.28 (9.02%)	4.47 (6.46%)	515.46 (20.06%)	4.67 (4.59%)	571.19 (10.81%)
	NRLM SGSY/Govt programs	1.19 (−1.9%)	85.97 (6.7%)	1.31 (9.55%)	101.77 (18.38%)	1.85 (41.24%)	197.53 (94.08%)	2.19 (18.69%)	266.10 (34.72%)
	%NRLM SGSY	26.8	21.8	31.1	23.7	41.32	38.32	46.89	46.59
	NULM/SJSRY	NA	NA	NA	NA	0.32	34.63	0.32 (−1.57%)	39.80 (14.93%)
	% NULM/SJSRY	NA	NA	NA	NA	7.12	6.72	7.00	6.97
	All women SHGs	3.76 (2.9%)	328.40 (7.8%)	3.40 (−9.34)	361.52 (10.08%)	3.86 (13.27%)	459.02 (26.97%)	4.04 (4.61%)	514.29 (12.04%)
	% women groups	84.4	83.3	81.2	84.2	86.35	89.05	86.37	90.04

Source: Status of Microfinance in India 2015–16. Mumbai: NABARD, 2016.
Note: Figures in parenthesis indicate growth/decline over the previous year.

very low interest is also possible. Therefore, the fluctuations in this number should be tempered with the happenings at the local level.

The bank loans to SHGs also saw a fall both in the number of accounts and the amounts disbursed in 2010–11 and 2011–12. However, both these have seen a smart recovery in the past four years. While it is true that only a fraction of the groups that are formed are a part of the bank linkage program for loans, with the NRLM coming in, the offtake of credit for the group seems to have improved. While there is much ground to be covered, the turnaround from the negative zone to the positive zone is to be celebrated.

Table 9.2 Number of SHGs with Savings and Amount of Savings Collected: 2012 and 2016

Region	March 31, 2012			March 31, 2016		
	SHGs (Millions)	Savings (₹ Billion)	Ave. Savings/ Group	SHGs (Millions)	Savings (₹ Billion)	Ave. Savings/ Group
North	0.41	2.53	6,175	0.39	4.50	11,440
Northeast	0.37	1.53	4,159	0.43	1.90	4,426
East	1.63	9.47	5,827	1.70	24.84	14,608
Central	0.81	6.14	7,549	0.82	8.41	10,312
West	1.06	8.72	8,210	1.02	10.57	10,383
South	3.58	37.13	10,362	3.55	86.69	24,449
Total	7.86	65.51	8,335	7.90	136.91	17,324

Source: Status of Microfinance 2012 and 2014. Mumbai: NABARD.

Savings

The data in Table 9.2 shows that the average savings per group is dramatically improving. In the past four years, it has almost grown by 2.5 times in the Eastern sector and the savings amounts have doubled if we look at the average statistics for the country as a whole. The only region where the growth in absolute savings is low is the northeastern region. Whether this growth is because of the increase in voluntary savings of the poor or because of pumping in of revolving and group funds from NRLM is to be investigated. Given the amount of investments that the NRLM is making in this sector, the possibility of the growth triggered by external grant and revolving fund-based instrument cannot be ruled out. A study on the impact of SHGs conducted across six states by AP Mahila Abhivruddhi Society (APMAS) has an interesting counter view (see Box 9.2).

However, the data for the SHG sector has shown an interesting trend which is discussed later. The role of NRLM can clearly be seen in this data. The data on targets versus achievements for NRLM shows that in most states the target for bank linkage has been achieved. States such as Telangana, Uttar Pradesh, and Uttarakhand are slightly short of targets. The states where the target is falling significantly short are Madhya Pradesh (54.26%), Meghalaya (5.27%), Mizoram (1.67%), Nagaland (28.15%), and some union territories (UTs).[2] It is clear that there is a problem in the spread of the SHGs in the northeast and the numbers show this.

While it is possible to acknowledge the growth due to NRLM, what is not evident is that the regional variation continues. The data for 2012 and 2016 on the regional spread is given in Figure 9.1 and the charts are self-evident.

The proportions of the presence of SHGs still favour the south, with 45% of the groups belonging to the region. A percentage point difference between 2012 and 2016 has resulted in the Eastern zone relatively gaining while the North and the northeastern region continue to have the same proportions.

While this is the story with the physical presence, the data on the business aspect shows that from 2012 to 2016, the amounts of savings generated by the SHGs in the South are relatively greater. South accounted for 57% of the amounts saved in 2012 and this has gone up to 63% in 2016 (Figure 9.2). The Eastern zone, while increasing the relative share of SHGs, has not been able to retain the relative share of amounts of savings.

Box 9.2 Reasons for Large Savings Account Balances

Multiple reasons for large funds in SHG-SB accounts: During focus group discussions, the SHGs were reported the reasons for lying large funds in SB account as (a) banks not allowing SHGs to withdraw savings once the group got credit linkage, (b) payment of loan installment through SB account where there is no separate account for loan, (c) large amount of monthly savings in the recent years, (d) no lending with own funds, and (e) the practice of distribution of group funds once in a year or at the time of bank linkage loan disbursement.

Large funds in SHG-SB accounts have mixed implications: The SHGs are unable to use own funds optimally; unable to provide credit to members, despite the fact that there is a high demand for credit from the members; dependent on traditional credit sources even for small loans to meet contingency needs; and banks pay marginal interest rate on savings (3%), whereas SHG charges 12–24% to their members, consequentially less earnings to SHGs.

Source: Draft Report of Impact Study of SHGs Across Six States: Hyderabad, APMAS, 2016.

[2] http://www.nrlmbl.aajeevika.gov.in/NRLM/UI/Achievement/ProjectWiseAchievement.aspx, accessed on August 22, 2016.

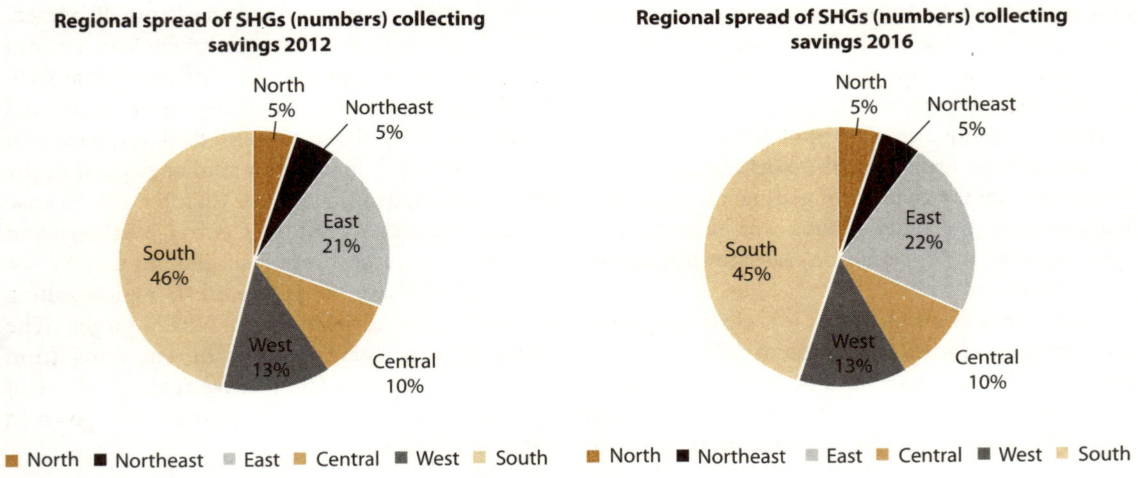

Figure 9.1 Region-wise Distribution of SHGs Collecting Savings, 2012 and 2016

Source: Status of Microfinance 2012 and 2014. Mumbai: NABARD.

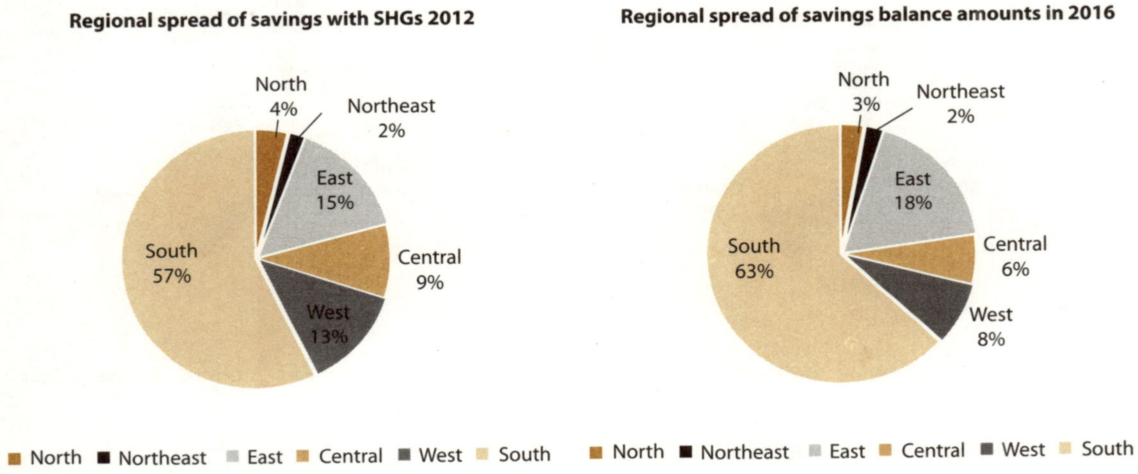

Figure 9.2 Region-wise Savings Balances with SHGs in 2012 and 2016

Source: Status of Microfinance 2012 and 2014. Mumbai: NABARD.

This may be because after 2010 the MFIs are no longer having a vibrant business in the state of AP and Telangana and that might have helped in refocussing all the financial inclusion efforts through either SHGs or banks, while the other states/regions had the luxury of MFIs as well. While this argument helps in explaining the credit story much better—because MFIs deal only with credit—there might be an argument for savings as well because the amount that a member can borrow is also a function of the overall group fund available with the SHG. If we look at the raw numbers, we find that while the overall savings in SHGs grew by 108% over the 2012 base, the savings of AP and Telangana put together grew at by 278% over the same base. These two states obviously have contributed significantly to the numbers in the Southern region. However, one of the reasons for the possible rise in savings may be because the groups may not be lending from the group funds—keeping them in deposit and earning an interest, while borrowing from the bank for their credit needs, given that both the states have a 0% interest loans being offered to SHGs.

Loans

While savings is just the beginning of the group formation, it is only when the loans start flowing that the linkage with the banks becomes meaningful. Clearly, it is easy to open an account with the bank and deposit savings and it is much more difficult to get a loan from the bank. Therefore, while we see the pattern where the number of groups, and the groups with savings in banks having a significant overlap, it is only a small proportion of the groups that actually get loans. And the older the groups are, the greater are the chances of getting a formal bank loan, because the older groups will have transactions to show and it would be easier for the banker to assess them.

From the data given below, it is clear that while we can see significant impact of NRLM in the growth of bank linkage and portfolio, the benefit has veered toward the South. While the Southern region has 63% of the SHG loan accounts (up from 61% in 2012), it has 81% of the loans disbursed. This clearly indicates that the average loan amount in the Southern region is significantly high as well. While a part of the story may be the AP-Telangana argument made above, it is still difficult to explain this growth. While we see a similar pattern in the growth of microfinance (see Chapter 10), in case of microfinance at least the Central, Northern and the Eastern sectors were also picking up. We see the relative share of northeastern region falling because of nonachievement of NRLM targets. The other growth story seems to be emerging from the Eastern region. The relative regional share of loan disbursements in 2012 and 2016 is given in Figures 9.3 to 9.6.

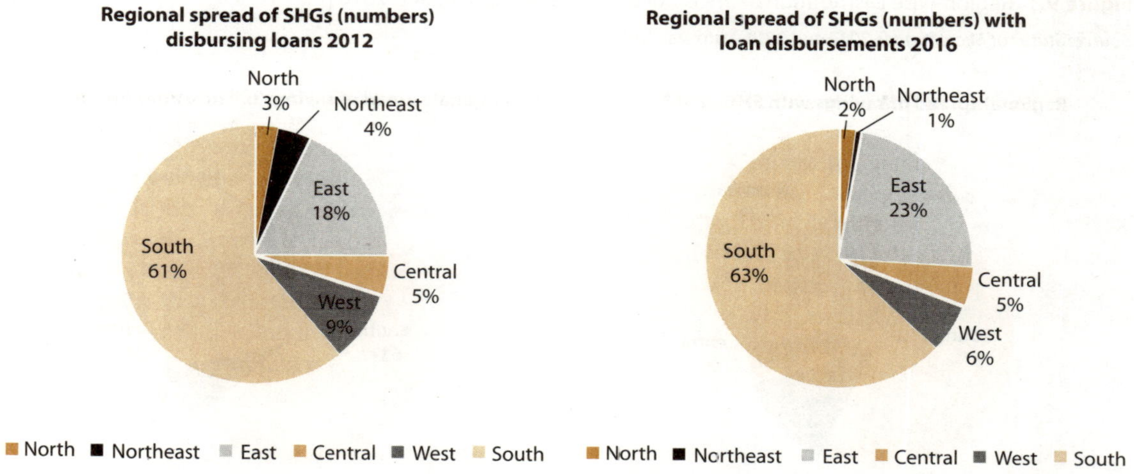

Figure 9.3 Loans Disbursed to SHGs in 2012 and 2016

Source: Status of Microfinance 2012 and 2014. Mumbai: NABARD.

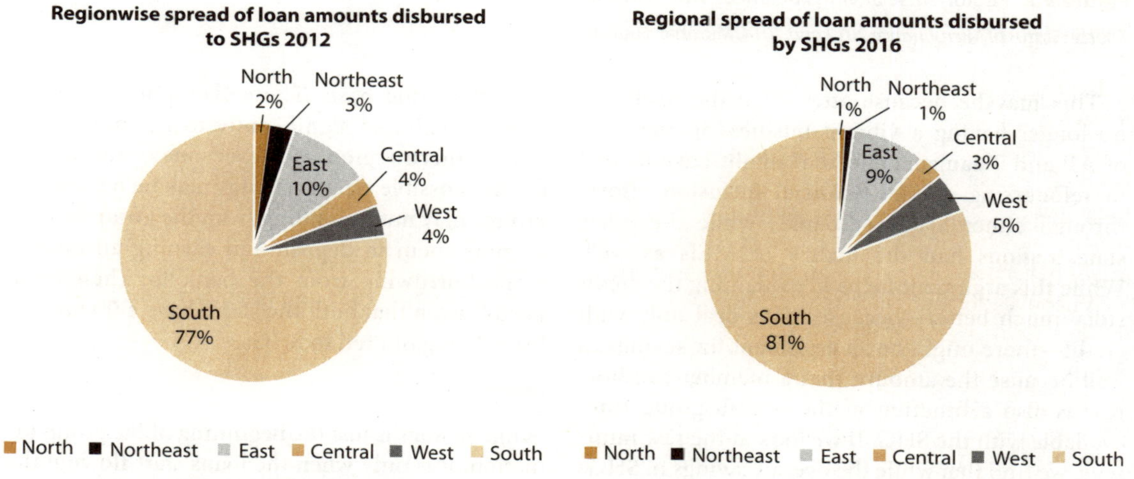

Figure 9.4 Loan Amounts Disbursed to SHGs in 2012 and 2016

Source: Status of Microfinance 2012 and 2014. Mumbai: NABARD.

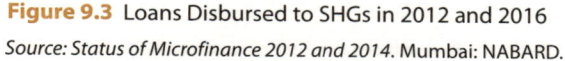

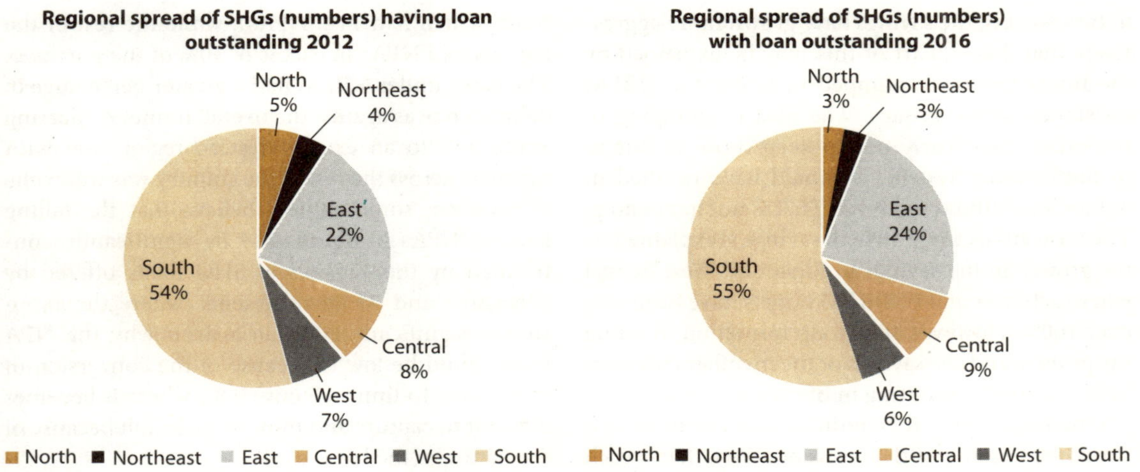

Figure 9.5 Number of SHGs Accounts Outstanding as of March 31, 2012 and 2016
Source: Status of Microfinance 2012 and 2014. Mumbai: NABARD.

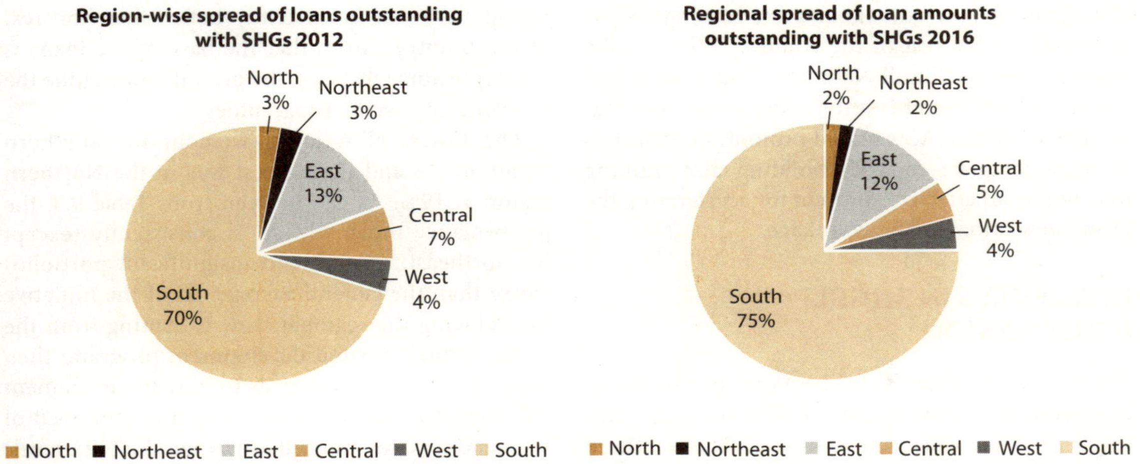

Figure 9.6 Loan Amounts Outstanding with SHGs as of March 31, 2010 and 2015
Source: Status of Microfinance 2012 and 2014. Mumbai: NABARD.

Experts offer one caveat in interpreting the data for which we do not have complete information. Over a period of time, thanks to the circular of the NABARD, the banks have moved away from granting a term loan to the SHG to granting a limit from which the amounts may be drawn. These limits might have bloated up the loan amounts.[3]

When we look at how much leverage (Figure 9.7) the banking system is willing to give on the savings on the poor, the statistics are interesting. The leverage (or the credit multiplier) has actually reduced between 2012 and 2016. This only points

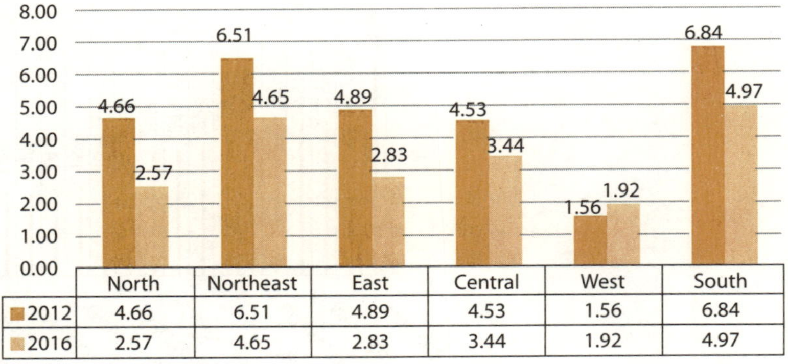

	North	Northeast	East	Central	West	South
2012	4.66	6.51	4.89	4.53	1.56	6.84
2016	2.57	4.65	2.83	3.44	1.92	4.97

2012 2016

Figure 9.7 Region-wise Credit Multiple of Savings in SHGs in 2016
Source: Status of Microfinance 2012 and 2014. Mumbai: NABARD.

[3] Reddy, C. 2016, September 1. Personal Communication; Srinivasan, G. 2016, August 29. Personal Communication.

to two aspects; the savings have grown more aggressively than loans. Part of this may be explained by the funds that were pumped in under the NRLM assistance to the groups. The idea of pumping in resources was clearly not to keep those resources in the banking system. It should have resulted in higher loan offtake of credit. That is not happening. The Eastern-sector growth of savings is explained by the growth in the savings in Bihar and West Bengal where achievement of NRLM targets have been way over 100%. However, the group formation, funding the groups, and the savings of the members may not be concurrently resulting in offtake of credit.

One reason why the credit offtake might be low would be because of the levels of NPAs. States such as Arunachal, Manipur, Meghalaya, and Tripura have had very high NPAs. A high level of NPAs would make the bankers wary of further lending, and thus reduce the credit multiplier number. Uttar Pradesh and Uttarakhand also had high NPAs compared to the rest of the country. While in the Southern region, Tamil Nadu and Puducherry had the worst NPA numbers, the other states had reasonable numbers. Accelerated promotion of groups without adequate capacity building and training may not be an effective shortcut for accelerating the group formation and bank linkage.

NPA LEVELS IN SHGBLP: A DISCUSSION

The average NPA levels of the entire portfolio was at around 6.23% (as against 7.40% last year) cutting across the source of the loans. The Southern region had the best performance (except for Tamil Nadu which had 11% NPAs), while the rest of the regions had NPAs in excess of 10% of the portfolio. The loans under NRLM had a greater percentage of delinquency as against the overall numbers. Barring South and to an extent Western region, the NPA numbers across the rest of the country was worrying.

However, some experts believe that the falling level of NPAs in South may be significantly contributed by the writeoff of SHG loans offered by Telangana and AP governments, where the exposure is significant. Another reason why the NPA levels could be low is because of the conversion of term loans to limits (Figure 9.8), where it becomes difficult to capture and monitor a default because of the nature of the loan.

Given that the SHGBLP is trying to break the jinx of focussing excessively on the south and move toward the rest of the country, the performance of the portfolio reaffirms the faith that Southern region performs consistently better than the rest of the country. Given that the base of the loans is disproportionately large, the overall figures hide the problems of specific geographies.

The lowest NPA levels were in the Southern region at 6% and the highest was in the Northern region at 19%. As can be seen from Table 9.3, the performance under NRLM is consistently (except for northeast, a small and insignificant portfolio) worse than the general average. So, if the initiative for reducing the regional skew is coming from the state, through is rural development program, then there is a cause for worry as to how the movement will spread in regions that are so direly in need of financial services, particularly when the NPA levels are high.

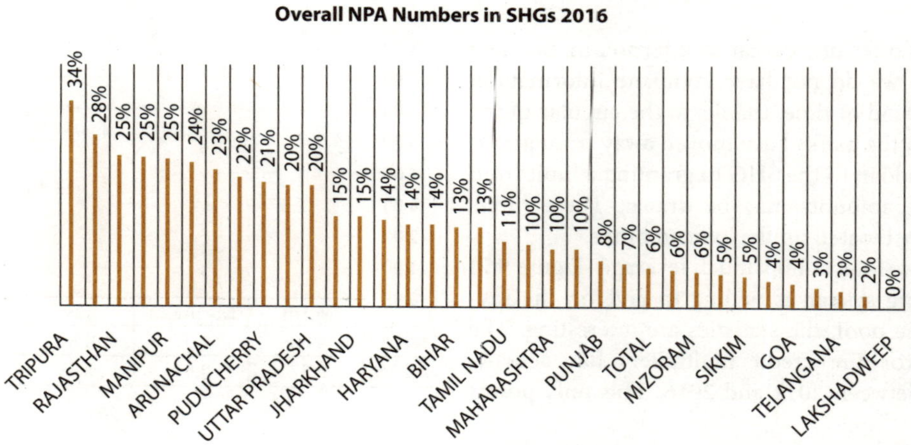

Figure 9.8 NPA Levels in SHGs Stacked According to States

Source: Micro Credit Innovations Department (MCID), NABARD.

Table 9.3 Regional Spread of NPA by Source of Loan

Source →	Public Sector Banks		Private Sector Banks		RRBs		Coop		Total	
Region ↓	**Total NPAs**	**NPAs from NRLM Loans**	**Total NPAs**	**NPAs from NRLM Loans**	**Total NPAs**	**NPAs from NRLM Loans**	**Total NPAs**	**NPAs from NRLM Loans**	**Total NPAs**	**NPAs from NRLM Loans**
North	28%	30%	3%	15%	22%	11%	17%	25%	19%	22%
Northeast	18%	18%	2%	100%	15%	10%	17%	19%	16%	15%
East	17%	18%	0%	28%	12%	6%	6%	4%	13%	11%
Central	19%	19%	0%	17%	21%	22%	35%	30%	16%	21%
West	1%	13%	1%	13%	9%	14%	24%	26%	9%	15%
South	2%	4%	2%	48%	3%	3%	3%	8%	4%	4%
Total	6%	6%	1%	19%	7%	6%	8%	10%	6%	6%

Source: Status of Microfinance in India, 2016. Mumbai: MCID, NABARD, 2016.

In general, the RRBs, being regional and local institutions, had lower level of NPAs than the commercial banks except for the Central region, which brought their overall averages down. This was the case last year also. What is surprising is that the NPA numbers of the private sector banks are no better than the public sector banks when it comes to NRLM portfolio, while their NPA levels in the overall portfolio is low and very manageable. Clearly the amounts that go toward NRLM are so low that they possibly account for the entire NPA levels. There has to be some deep introspection on the methodology of NRLM to see if, due to targets and scale, the quality of the groups and the credit program is being compromised.

The NPA stress is clearly visible, particularly in the NRLM segment. One aspect that needs serious consideration is in the process of group formation. While the SHGs in the South took a long time to go through the four-stage process of forming, storming, norming, and performing to develop their own internal processes and discipline, the groups aggressively promoted by NRLM are putting money into the process much faster. The financial resources are not only coming in for the ecosystem, but also at the group and the transaction level.

In general, any intervention at the level of transactions has been found to be counterproductive to the credit discipline, including on writeoffs and interest subventions. Dr Rangarajan in an interview with the author had this to say:

> I think we should take the approach of supporting the institutions. The better thing is to provide institutional support rather than interest subvention. Interest rates in some of these institutions are already low. Some refinance may be provided if an economic activity is not viable at the rates that are normal in the organized financial system. We should not have a structure whose viability is seriously in question. Institutions don't come up on their own. Even in the case of SHGs, a lot of spade work had to be done initially to create the institutions.

Therefore, there needs to be a rethink at the NRLM level if the model that they are adopting is going to be a national model or whether it would be tweaked to suit the local conditions, and if the subventions will be invested smartly.

A recent report by Indiaspend[4] indicated a much higher levels of NPA based on the data put up by the management information systems maintained by NRLM. Coupled with the concerns that we may have about the possible stress due to MFI loans, it is quite possible that the inclusive finance sector is sitting on top of a crisis that may hit sooner than later. Clearly, at the field level, there needs to be a greater understanding of client portfolio and behaviour - including borrowings from nonformal sources and sources from which data does not go to the CICs. Pending complete mapping and digitization of data, each one of the anecdotal reports of stress should be thoroughly investigated and corrective steps taken. The last thing that the inclusive finance sector can afford now is a negative publicity resulting in a crisis-like situation.

On its part, the RBI issued detailed instructions for the banks to monitor their SHG portfolio,

[4] http://www.indiaspend.com/cover-story/banks-race-to-targets-rural-womens-groups-to-defaults-68113, accessed on August 23, 2016.

particularly on the NPA situation. Asking the banks to monitor NPA levels in the SHG segment on an ongoing basis, the RBI asked the banks to collect detailed information from members availing loans in excess of ₹20,000 in case the gross NPA of SHGs exceeded 10% or is higher than the total gross NPA of the bank by five percentage points.[5]

OTHER/NEW INITIATIVES

One of the issues that has been of concern to the RBI has been the uploading of credit information to the CIC. This is not only important from the view of monitoring the NPAs, but also would lead to eventual convergence. If the information on indebtedness of individuals is not adequately captured, then it is possible that the NBFC-MFI norms which lay down a limit on the overall indebtedness of the individual borrowers are breached in spirit and are rendered ineffectual. It has negative effects both on SHG lending and MFI lending given that there could be significant number of overlapping customers. In this regard, the RBI has taken a considered stance which was articulated in the notification discussed in Box 9.3.

Box 9.3 Notification on Sharing SHG Credit Information with CICs

However, the circular issued in June 2014[6] has not been effectively implemented due to issues of the format of data capture and the level of digitization of SHG records. Both these elements are important. NABARD has undertaken an ambitious project of digitising SHG records and has completed the pilot project. The details of the next phase are discussed further. Given the complexity of the issue, the RBI issued a new notification on phased information provision to CICs.

The first phase is being implemented from July 1, 2016, where the data of SHGs which avail of a loan of more than ₹100,000 from the banking system is to be reported to the CICs. However, the banks are instructed to collect all non-credit information from the groups—irrespective of the loan amount—at the time of the application. In addition, the notification prescribes collection of more detailed information from individuals who are borrowing more than ₹30,000 from the groups. The interloaning details from the savings of SHG members were exempted from this notification. In fact, the notification goes one step further by encouraging the banks to open individual accounts of all SHG members at the time the SHG opens the account with the bank, without making it a precondition.

The circular also requires the CICs to make changes in their systems to capture the information with regard to the indebtedness of the SHG members. While the tone of the notification indicates that none of the elements prescribed in the notification should be made a precondition for an SHG to avail a loan from the banks, it encourages the banks to adhere to all the formats and indicates that the nonadherence will result in exclusion of the noncompliant SHG accounts in the reckoning of the priority sector lending targets.

Source: https://www.rbi.org.in/Scripts/NotificationUser.aspx?Id=10227&Mode=0, accessed on September 20, 2016.

While there were the usual concerns about the performance of SHGs, there have been very interesting experiments happening in the field (see Boxes 9.4 and 9.5). This section tries to capture some of these interesting initiatives. Most of these are not at scale, but certainly look at the art of the possible once a strong group is built up.

- In addition to the digitization effort, there were two other initiatives undertaken by the Indian Railway Catering and Tourism and Corporation where there were effort to rope in SHGs to cater food to the passengers of trains under the e-catering project. Some select stations would be allotted to SHG women and the kitchen would be allotted to them. Based on the orders received through e-booking of food, the women would have to supply food at a specified time to the railways. This was being piloted in Sindhudurg and, if successful, it will effectively link the local economy with the mainstream effortlessly and capture the markets with the fleeting population.
- There is also a proposal to operate water vending machines in about 4,000 railway stations and on a pilot basis these vending stations are offered to the group to manage this facility. The groups would get a commission on the basis of the overall vending done through the stations.

[5] https://www.rbi.org.in/Scripts/NotificationUser.aspx?Id=10227&Mode=0, accessed on September 20, 2016.

[6] https://www.rbi.org.in/Scripts/NotificationUser.aspx?Id=8968&Mode=0, accessed on September 20, 2016.

Box 9.4 Digitization of SHGs

The digitization of SHGs is a project that was initiated last year continued with significant financial inputs from the FITF. While the project was thought of by NABARD, there was greater convergence during the year where NRLM and a set of NGOs were roped in as implementing agencies. In areas where digitization has been complete, such as Dhule in Maharashtra and Ramgarh in Jharkhand, NABARD claims that the group linkage has gone up. In phase II of the digitization program, the project will be rolled out in Nalbari (Assam), Muzaffarpur (Bihar), Rajnandgaon (Chhattisgarh), Mehsana (Gujarat), Mandi (HP), Ambala (Haryana), Udhampur (J&K), Mysuru (Karnataka), Kasaragod (Kerala), Indore (MP), Wardha (Maharashtra), West Garo Hills (Meghalaya), Jagatsinghpur (Odisha), Bikaner (Rajasthan), Jhalawar (Rajasthan), West Tripura (Tripura), Barabanki (UP), Varanasi (UP), Dehradun (Uttarakhand), West Midnapur (West Bengal), Hazaribagh (Jharkhand), and UT of Puducherry. In all, about 250,000 groups have been digitised. The financial data is initially collected in an excel sheet and then subjected to an audit to check the accuracy between the group records and the sheets. Then the data gets into the server.

This database is available as an app on a tablet as well. Going forward, this data would also naturally feed into the grading of the group and the grading chart gets updated every time there is a meeting and transactions take place. The increased level of information and the information being available on a real-time basis helps the group to access greater credit, based on the transaction history. The banks with whom the SHGs are banking would be given viewing rights through an exclusive login id. The banker, for instance, can drill down on the database till the customer level. In general, the attempt is to make the data fully Aadhaar-based, so that the de-duplication and matching of the indebtedness data could be done.

It is expected that the digitization of SHG data would be completed by 2019. While the initial investments are happening from the funds that are available in the FITF, the feedback is that SHGs are willing to pay for the costs that will improve the accuracy of recording the data and make the transactions more efficient.

Another imperative that will make this an important effort is following the RBI circular on uploading SHG data on to the databases of CICs. Bankers are finding it difficult to upload this detailed customer-level data to the database and it is turning out to be transaction intensive. With the digitization project, it would be easier to upload the data to the CICs as well.

Of course, beyond all this, data capture would help in undertaking bid data analysis and tailor the policies much better. In all, the success of the digitization of SHG records is expected to have all-round benefits.

The digitization process is expected to bring in the following benefits:

- Advantage of the grading reports auto-generated by the system was taken by many bank branches in Ramgarh and Dhule.
- Grading reports are being used by banks for appraising SHGs before credit linkage.
- Large number of first as well as subsequent linkages for many SHGs.
- Increase in credit flow to SHGs.
- Increased levels of awareness amongst bank branches about the functioning of SHG dealing with them through MIS generated from the system.
- The real time SMS alerts brought transparency in the operations/transactions and confidence among the SHG members.

Source: *Status of Microfinance in India, 2016*. Mumbai: MCID, NABARD, 2016.

Box 9.5 AKRSPI's Community-based Savings Groups

Aga Khan Rural Support Programme-India (AKRSP-I) has a set of unique groups called the Community-Based Savings Groups (CBSG) functioning in Bihar and these predate the roll out of the NRLM project Jeevika. The design of these groups are very distinct from the joint liability groups (JLG) promoted by the MFIs and the groups promoted by Jeevika. In general, there is a token savings of ₹10 per meeting collected by the Jeevika groups. There are group funds given from the mission to kick-start the livelihoods activity and link the groups to the banking system. The mission is also creating an intermediary structure such as the village organizations and district federations. These intermediary layers are expected to provide the transaction volumes for the banks to get interested in the SHGs and provide linkage. However, the complaint is that the credit linkage does not take off, or when it does take off, it results in a greater level of NPAs.

This is a difficult chicken-and-egg problem. We can see from data where the regions are economically backward, heavily agrarian in nature that the usual credit deposit ratio of the banking system is low. The ability to access and use credit effectively is linked to the access to markets and to a set of diversified livelihoods which increase the transaction intensity and monetization of transactions. That is largely happening in southern and western regions. However, in places like Bihar, which traditionally has a low credit deposit ratio, the focus of a livelihoods mission should be to create market linkages and livelihood diversification opportunities and allow the credit market to grow organically. The AKRSP's CBSG model shows that if there is a flexible system that is responsive to the client needs, there could be vibrancy in the activity.

The CBSGs largely collect savings and are not under pressure to link with the bank. The savings units are decided by the groups and are usually higher than the Jeevika groups. Once the savings units (say ₹50 or ₹100) are decided, then the members are free to save in multiples of those units. The groups are encouraged to borrow from within the group fund at an interest rate that is nearer the informal rates, but decided by the groups. At the end of a savings cycle, the accumulated group fund (including the interest collected) is shared out and the groups start savings once again. Some of the groups that are mature and have livelihood activities that need enhanced credit then are going to the banking system for linkage. Possibly, regions that are not linked to the markets need a savings first model before the credit linkage model takes off.

While there is much written about convergence, we need to think whether convergence would remove the innovation that AKRSPI groups are providing. There are insights and learnings to be gained from innovations and, therefore, the timing of convergence is something that needs to be thought about.

Source: Author's primary research.

CONVERGENCE VERSUS INNOVATION

Over the years, there have been several opinions expressed on trying to seek convergence between multiple groups promoted by different agencies. While the government has a particular approach to group promotion and growth, and under the NRLM, even though the efforts are presumably bottom-up, there is a template under which the groups get formed and operate. There is a process of identification of the poor, forming women into groups and federating the groups at the village level through village organizations, and later federating them at the district level. This ensures some level of standard operating procedure, with timelines, and it is possible to scale these efforts seamlessly. However, the question is whether convergence and standardization is a good thing.

The issues of convergence are addressed through a counter juxtaposition of innovation and out-of-the box thinking. If we look at the geographic variation in the NPA numbers across districts, it is possible to surmise that this could be because the standardized approach did not build in adequate localization and, therefore, was inappropriate—which resulted in adverse usage and defaults. Alternately, it could also be surmised in the implementation of the project, standard operating procedures were not adopted, and therefore it is an implementation failure.

On the other hand, when there are multiple state led programs, including the programs that are designed to do cash transfer, there might be a need for converging the institutional architecture to ensure that the point of transaction that the citizen has with an formal sector outlet is interoperable and gives him/her access to all the facilities that they are entitled to.

CONCLUDING NOTES

While the SHGBLP has grown significantly over the years, it is clear from the data that the meaningful linkage is happening only in the southern part of the country. The detailed data are available in Appendices 9.1, 9.2, 9.3, and 9.4. This report does not discuss the activities happening elsewhere in terms of federating structures. There are examples of the federal structures working, however, the federal structures add to layers of cost and bureaucracy. It may be better to make the transactions at the groups and at the village-level large enough to deal with the mainstream banking system. As we go forward, it is the same client who is a member of an SHG, a JLG of an MFI, a customer of the SFB, and an account holder of the PMJDY account and possibly somebody in the family having a KCC. So the question is whether we are opening up multiple channels with a trickle in each channel, or whether at the household level there is scope for rationalization of the channel, while providing for innovation at the back-end. Those answers would be found in future years.

APPENDIX 9.1
Progress Under SHG Bank Linkage Programme—Savings of SHGs with Banks

(₹ in Millions)

	Commercial Banks		Regional Rural Banks		Cooperative Banks		Total	
Region/State	**No. of SHGs**	**Savings Amount**	**No. of SHGs**	**Savings Amount**	**No. of SHGs**	**Savings Amount**	**No. of SHGs**	**Savings Amount**
Northern Region								
Chandigarh	225	12.79	0	0.00	0	0.00	225	12.79
Haryana	21,987	1,371.00	17,031	184.40	3,903	33.75	42,921	1,589.14
HP	14,976	141.74	9,649	78.60	19,560	120.77	44,185	341.11
J & K	3,772	103.85	3,927	135.53	687	1.67	8386	241.05
New Delhi	3,221	46.46	0	0.00	447	7.13	3668	53.59
Punjab	15,246	276.18	7,966	69.84	6,759	51.80	29,971	397.82
Rajasthan	94,710	653.89	81,882	709.84	87,527	502.18	264,119	1,865.91
Total	154,137	2,605.91	120,455	1,178.20	118,883	717.29	393,475	4,501.40
Northeastern Region								
Assam	87,045	561.29	221,073	523.21	25,568	28.32	333,686	1,112.82
Arunachal	1,652	22.37	1,496	10.13	1,469	9.24	4,617	41.73
Manipur	3,947	20.17	7,129	13.31	2,544	2.22	13,620	35.70
Meghalaya	1,406	12.59	4,194	54.58	2,596	26.61	8,196	93.78
Mizoram	203	1.19	7,327	46.55	542	1.97	8,072	49.71
Nagaland	3,037	29.78	801	0.05	7,594	40.00	11,432	69.82
Sikkim	1,186	29.19	–	–	356	10.46	1,542	39.64
Tripura	9,261	84.38	29,285	323.50	10,112	51.55	48,658	459.43
Total	107,737	760.94	271,305	971.33	50,781	170.36	429,823	1,903
Eastern Region								
A & N	341	2.58	–	–	4,134	63.47	4,475	66
Bihar	154,216	2,064.08	124,392	1,536.55	–	–	278,608	3,601
Jharkhand	62,490	673.19	36,769	282.04	67	0.62	99,326	956
Odisha	218,514	2,359.97	184,452	1,863.83	83,720	634.97	486,686	4,859
West Bengal	259,085	3,791.27	207,401	4,986.46	364,525	6,576.15	831,011	15,354
Total	694,646	8,891.08	553,014	8,668.89	452,446	7,275.21	1,700,106	24,835
Central Region								
Chhattisgarh	43,826	506.49	98,070	1,013.10	18,565	85.05	160,461	1,605
MP	138,100	1,802.70	97,995	598.72	12,523	81.69	248,618	2,483
UP	129,172	2,593.34	233,625	1,223.01	1,182	4.28	363,979	3,821
Uttarakhand	13,740	278.62	22,696	159.30	6,159	64.57	42,595	502
Total	324,838	5,181.14	452,386	2,994.13	38,429	235.59	815,653	8,411
Western Region								
Goa	3,928	66.52	–	–	3,613	87.87	7,541	154
Gujarat	136,431	1,142.02	51,287	458.96	33,632	240.45	221,350	1,841

(Continued)

(Continued)

Region/State	Commercial Banks		Regional Rural Banks		Cooperative Banks		Total	
	No. of SHGs	Savings Amount	No. of SHGs	Savings Amount	No. of SHGs	Savings Amount	No. of SHGs	Savings Amount
Maharashtra	336,380	4,013.65	104,400	556.96	348,378	4,003.96	789,158	8,575
Total	476,739	5,222.19	155,687	1,015.92	385,623	4,332.28	1,018,049	10,570
Southern Region								
AP	613,603	35,729.51	270,560	4,986.98	17,354	739.71	901,517	41,456
Karnataka	605,154	7,987.92	137,921	1,613.29	219,371	4,823.01	962,446	14,424
Kerala	176,301	4,766.23	54,527	754.80	42,031	769.69	272,859	6,291
Lakshadweep	2	0.01	–	–	–	–	2	0
Puducherry	9,062	325.47	3,961	57.69	1,740	25.81	14,763	409
Tamil Nadu	640,316	6,575.44	42,497	438.14	169,221	2,186.74	852,034	9,200
Telangana	337,576	12,293.05	194,498	2,163.45	10,201	456.51	542,275	14,913
Total	2,382,014	67,677.61	703,964	10,014.34	459,918	9,001.48	3,545,896	86,693
Grand Total	4,140,111	90,338.88	2,256,811	24,842.81	1,506,080	21,732.21	7,903,002	136,914

Source: Status of Microfinance in India 2015–16. Mumbai: MCID, NABARD, 2016.

APPENDIX 9.2
Progress Under SHG-Bank Linkage Programme—Bank Loans Disbursed in 2015–16

(Amounts in Millions)

Region/State	Commercial Banks		Regional Rural Bank		Cooperative Banks		Total	
	No. of SHGs	Loans Disbursed	No. of SHGs	Loans Disbursed	No. of SHGs	Loans Disbursed	No. of SHGs	Loans Disbursed
Northern Region								
Chandigarh	5	1	–	–	–	–	5	1
Haryana	2,649	425	1,168	108	52	7	3,869	540
HP	1,093	167	669	100	1,464	186	3,226	453
J & K	1,778	120	1,049	98	2	0	2,829	218
New Delhi	263	22	–	–	8	0	271	22
Punjab	1,636	294	763	63	257	21	2,656	378
Rajasthan	12,932	2,314	3,816	284	8,502	620	25,250	3,218
Total	20,356	3,342	7,465	653	10,285	835	38,106	4,830
Northeastern Region								
Assam	7,772	536	14,306	1,017	547	34	22,625	1,587
Arunachal	27	4	6	1	24	2	57	7
Manipur	88	10	214	22	80	4	382	36
Meghalaya	41	4	149	13	14	2	204	18
Mizoram	4	0	315	46	8	1	327	47
Nagaland	123	23	47	0	1,085	113	1,255	136

	Commercial Banks		Regional Rural Bank		Cooperative Banks		Total	
Region/State	**No. of SHGs**	**Loans Disbursed**	**No. of SHGs**	**Loans Disbursed**	**No. of SHGs**	**Loans Disbursed**	**No. of SHGs**	**Loans Disbursed**
Sikkim	12	6	–	–	22	3	134	9
Tripura	626	42	21	297	406	19	1,053	357
Total	8,793	625	15,058	1,395	2,186	177	26,037	2,197
Eastern Region								
A & N	29	4	–	–	223	36	252	40
Bihar	31,675	2,296	66,933	3,810	–	–	98,608	6,106
Jharkhand	7,303	460	3,494	190	21	13	10,818	662
Odisha	32,315	4,484	25,399	3,548	5,950	571	63,664	8,603
West Bengal	99,085	6,195	40,508	7,098	99,641	6,245	239,234	19,538
Total	170,407	13,438	136,334	14,646	105,835	6,865	412,576	34,949
Central Region								
Chhattisgarh	6,616	655	3,220	224	1,249	85	11,085	964
MP	35,469	5,457	7,625	442	91	10	43,185	5,909
UP	18,173	2,394	7,692	550	43	0	25,908	2,944
Uttarakhand	1,611	188	1,101	73	1,392	1,830	4,104	2,090
Total	61,869	8,693	19,638	1,288	2,775	1,925	84,282	11,907
Western Region								
Goa	501	136	–	–	202	62	703	198
Gujarat	17,248	2,036	5,127	456	1,263	171	23,638	2,663
Maharashtra	64,119	13,949	8,380	998	15,685	1,056	88,184	16,003
Total	81,868	16,121	13,507	1,454	17,150	1,289	112,525	18,863
Southern Region								
AP	290,983	83,054	107,761	30,499	5,327	1,502	404,071	115,055
Karnataka	195,477	48,374	43,056	6,516	42,856	7,701	281,389	62,591
Kerala	58,677	9,897	8,592	2,109	11,999	2,062	79,268	14,069
Lakshadweep	–	–	–	–	–	–	–	–
Puducherry	620	122	493	143	295	77	1,408	343
Tamil Nadu	121,937	35,655	20,738	6,745	27,684	5,862	170,359	48,262
Telangana	121,294	32,529	97,757	26,201	3,251	1,075	222,302	59,805
Total	788,988	209,630	278,397	72,213	91,412	18,280	1,158,797	300,124
Grand Total	1,132,281	251,850	470,399	91,649	229,643	29,370	1,832,323	372,869

Source: MCID, NABARD.

APPENDIX 9.3
Progress Under SHG Bank Linkage Programme—Bank Loans Outstanding

(As of March 31, 2016)

Region/State	Commercial Banks		Regional Rural Banks		Cooperative Banks		Total	
	No. of SHGs	Loans Outstanding	No. of SHGs	Loans Outstanding	No. of SHGs	Loans Outstanding	No. of SHGs	Loans Outstanding
Northern Region								
Chandigarh	211	20	–	–	–	–	211	20
Haryana	11,894	1,308	6,248	685	770	59	18,912	2,051
HP	5,761	435	6,808	233	5,692	449	18,261	1,117
J & K	2,186	146	1,437	101	18	3	3,641	250
New Delhi	549	50	–	–	9	0	558	50
Punjab	8,508	1,262	4,768	235	1,758	88	15,034	1,584
Rajasthan	52,076	3,950	16,536	986	29,495	1,582	98,107	6,518
Total	81,185	7,170	35,797	2,240	37,742	2,181	154,724	11,591
Northeastern								
Assam	42,495	3,221	59,991	3,293	4,651	89	107,137	6,603
Arunachal	232	24	58	6	118	7	408	37
Manipur	912	42	1,149	52	2	0	2,063	93
Meghalaya	424	24	669	67	480	25	1,573	117
Mizoram	80	8	1,038	144	1,038	144	2,156	296
Nagaland	1,108	78	98	0	2,142	218	3,348	296
Sikkim	610	60	–	–	22	2	632	62
Tripura	6,000	401	20,398	671	7,145	272	33,543	1,343
Total	51,861	3,858	83,401	4,233	15,598	756	150,860	8,847
Eastern Region								
A & N	87	6	–	–	536	50	623	55
Bihar	101,236	5,088	166,102	4,936	–	–	267,338	10,025
Jharkhand	31,832	2,933	33,138	724	29	1	64,999	3,669
Odisha	106,002	9,149	81,377	8,327	26,492	1,358	213,871	18,834
West Bengal	194,321	10,911	167,018	17,844	222,732	9,039	584,071	37,794
Total	433,478	28,086	447,635	31,831	249,789	10,460	1,130,902	70,377
Central Region								
Chhattisgarh	14,802	1,064	63,589	1,862	2,937	59	81,328	2,984
MP	70,679	7,207	44,889	2,397	3,358	125	118,926	9,729
UP	82,543	8,469	133,963	6,735	653	52	217,159	15,257
Uttarakhand	7,490	511	6,807	253	3,087	225	17,384	989
Total	175,514	17,251	249,248	11,248	10,035	460	434,797	28,959

Region/State	Commercial Banks		Regional Rural Banks		Cooperative Banks		Total	
	No. of SHGs	Loans Outstanding	No. of SHGs	Loans Outstanding	No. of SHGs	Loans Outstanding	No. of SHGs	Loans Outstanding
Western Region								
Goa	1,082	206	–	–	709	100	1,791	306
Gujarat	33,278	2,348	12,323	554	2,586	165	48,187	3,067
Maharashtra	124,988	12,681	39,846	2,856	43,307	1,436	208,141	16,973
Total	159,348	15,235	52,169	3,411	46,602	1,701	258,119	20,346
Southern Region								
AP	553,081	121,856	231,841	48,437	17,305	1,915	802,227	172,208
Karnataka	448,290	53,020	106,262	13,137	77,885	8,590	632,437	74,747
Kerala	112,859	16,296	24,002	2,480	41,019	2,537	177,880	21,313
Lakshadweep	2	0	–	–	–	–	2	0
Puducherry	3,004	349	1,389	160	440	73	4,833	582
Tamil Nadu	307,738	49,573	32,063	5,442	93,092	8,576	432,893	63,590
Telangana	300,004	58,763	181,669	38,476	11,274	1,393	492,947	98,632
Total	1,724,978	299,857	577,226	108,131	241,015	23,085	2,543,219	431,073
Grand Total	2,626,364	371,456	1,445,476	161,093	600,781	38,643	4,672,621	571,192

Source: MCID, NABARD.

APPENDIX 9.4
State-wise and Bank Type-wise NPA Levels of SHGs

(₹ in Million)

Region/State	Public Sector Commercial Banks			Private Sector Commercial Banks			Regional Rural Banks			Cooperative Banks			Total		
	Loan Amt OS Against SHGs	Amt of GNPA Against SHGs	NPA % age to Loan OS	Loan Amt OS Against SHGs	Amt of GNPA Against SHGs	NPA % age to Loan OS	Loan Amt OS Against SHGs	GNPAs Against SHGs	NPA % age to Loan OS	Loan Amt OS Against SHGs	GNPA Against SHGs	NPA % age to Loan OS	Loan Amt OS Against SHGs	Amt of GNPA against SHGs	NPA % age to Loan OS
North															
Chandigarh	20	5	24%	–	–	0%	–	–	0%	–	–	0%	20	5	24%
Haryana	1,067	210	20%	240	–	0%	685	28	4%	59	44	75%	2,051	283	14%
HP	405	43	11%	30	–	0%	233	26	11%	449	83	19%	1,117	152	14%
J & K	79	5	6%	67	0	0%	101	4	0%	3	2	50%	250	11	4%
New Delhi	50	11	22%	–	–	0%	–	–	0%	0	–	0%	50	11	22%
Punjab	1,028	84	8%	234	0	0%	235	19	8%	88	20	23%	1,584	123	8%
Rajasthan	2,009	937	47%	1,941	81	4%	986	404	41%	1,582	213	13%	6,518	1,635	25%
Total	4,657	1,293	28%	2,513	81	3%	2,240	482	22%	2,181	362	17%	11,591	2,219	19%
Northeast															
Assam	3,217	530	16%	5	0	2%	3,293	298	9%	89	44	50%	6,603	872	13%
Arunachal	24	4	16%	0	–	0%	6	3	43%	7	2	31%	37	8	23%
Manipur	42	18	44%	–	–	0%	52	4	9%	0	0	0%	93	23	25%
Meghalaya	24	10	42%	–	–	0%	67	14	21%	25	9	36%	117	33	28%
Mizoram	8	2	27%	–	–	0%	144	14	10%	144	1	1%	296	17	6%
Nagaland	78	22	28%	0	0	54%	0	0	6%	218	22	10%	296	44	15%
Sikkim	60	3	5%	–	–	0%	–	–	0%	2	–	0%	62	3	5%
Tripura	401	120	30%	–	–	0%	671	287	43%	272	51	19%	1,343	458	34%
Total	3,853	709	18%	5	0	2%	4,233	620	15%	756	130	17%	8,847	1,459	16%
East															
A & N	6	1	12%	–	–	0%	–	–	0%	50	7	15%	55	8	14%
Bihar	4,639	932	20%	450	0	0%	4,936	396	8%	–	–	0%	10,025	1,328	13%
Jharkhand	2,897	447	15%	36	–	0%	724	97	13%	13	–	0%	3,669	544	15%
Odisha	7,176	1,944	27%	1,973	2	0%	8,327	2,537	30%	1,358	214	16%	18,834	4,696	25%
W Bengal	10,335	958	9%	575	–	0%	17,844	945	5%	9,039	425	5%	37,794	2,328	6%
Total	25,053	4,282	17%	3,033	2	0%	31,831	3,975	12%	10,460	646	6%	70,377	8,904	13%

Central															
Chhattisgarh	928	166	18%	136	0	0%	1,862	111	6%	59	9	15%	2,984	286	10%
MP	3,153	621	20%	4,054	21	1%	2,397	343	14%	125	14	11%	9,729	999	10%
UP	6,635	1,208	18%	1,834	4	0%	6,735	1,843	27%	52	14	27%	15,257	3,069	20%
Uttarakhand	411	67	16%	101	–	0%	253	53	21%	225	79	35%	989	200	20%
Total	11,127	2,063	19%	6,125	25	0%	11,248	2,350	21%	460	115	25%	28,959	4,554	16%
West															
Goa	148	8	5%	58	0	0%	–	–	0%	100	4	5%	306	12	4%
Gujarat	1,849	137	7%	499	6	1%	554	36	7%	165	46	28%	3,067	225	7%
Maharashtra	5,664	925	16%	7,017	72	1%	2,856	286	10%	1,436	351	24%	16,973	1,635	10%
Total	7,661	1,070	14%	7,574	78	1%	3,411	323	9%	1,701	402	24%	20,346	1,872	9%
South															
AP	121,819	4,269	4%	37	2	6%	48,437	1,245	3%	1,915	38	2%	172,208	5,555	3%
Karnataka	45,650	808	2%	7,370	50	1%	13,137	513	4%	8,590	195	2%	74,747	1,567	2%
Kerala	15,231	894	6%	1,065	25	2%	2,480	75	3%	2,537	151	6%	21,313	1,144	5%
Lakshadweep	0	–	0%	–	–	0%	–	–	0%	–	–	0%	0	–	0%
Puducherry	349	107	31%	–	–	0%	160	6	3%	73	8	11%	582	121	21%
Tamil Nadu	31,828	5,088	16%	17,744	358	2%	5,442	547	10%	8,576	914	11%	63,590	6,907	11%
Telangana	58,763	2,010	3%	–	–	0%	38,476	508	1%	1,393	43	3%	98,632	2,561	3%
Total	273,640	13,176	5%	26,217	435	2%	108,131	2,893	3%	23,085	1,350	6%	431,073	17,854	4%
Grand Total	325,990	22,594	7%	45,466	620	1%	161,093	10,643	7%	38,643	3,005	8%	571,192	36,862	6%

Source: MCID, NABARD.

Review of Microfinance[1]

10

Chapter

INTRODUCTION: MICROFINANCE DURING THE YEAR

By June 2016, there were 71 institutions licensed by the RBI as NBFC-MFIs (as against 65 institutions listed last year). While collectively their footprint was across the country, it is interesting to note the regional spread of the headquarters of the MFIs (see Table 10.1).

In addition to the above-mentioned institutions, there were another 95 institutions that were operating as non-NBFC-MFIs across the country. These institutions were incorporated as trusts, societies, cooperatives, and not-for-profit companies (Sa-Dhan 2016).

The MFIs were operating all across the country and had penetrated to the length and breadth of the country. As against 430 districts last year, in 2016 there were 507 districts that had 5 or more entities giving loans with joint liability as a feature. While most of them were NBFC-MFIs (captured by MFIN), there were also other players in the market who uploaded their data to Sa-Dhan and to the CICs. Table 10.2 gives the details of the lender penetration across the country.

Table 10.1 MFIs in India

Headquarters	Number of MFIs
South (Bangalore, Srinivasapur, Haveri, Shivamogga, Chennai, Tiruchirappalli, Madurai, Theni, Coimbatore, Hyderabad)	30
East (Kolkata, Howrah, Michael Nagar, Bhubaneswar, Rajgangpur)	10
West (Mumbai, Pune, Latur, Ahmedabad, Vadodara)	13
North (Delhi, Jaipur, Jalandhar)	10
Central (Varanasi, Lucknow)	3
Northeast (Guwahati, Chaygaon)	5
Total	71*

Source: RBI, http://rbidocs.rbi.org.in/rdocs/content/DOCs/NMFI012014FL.xls, accessed on August 14, 2016.
Note: *Includes Bandhan, Janalakshmi, Ujjivan, Disha, Suryoday, Equitas, Utkarsh, ESAF, and RGVN(NE), all of which are/will be converted into a bank during the year/next year.

Table 10.2 Number of Districts with Lender Penetration

Number of Active Lenders		NA (Districts in AP and TL)	0	<=2	3–5	>5	Total
MFIN 2016	Number of Districts	23	84	24	97	448	676
All 2016	Number of Districts	23	53	43	50	507	676
All 2015	Number of Districts	23	88	50	85	430	676

Source: CRIF High Mark.

[1] The author is thankful to Mr N. Srinivasan, microfinance expert, Ms Rathna Vishwanathan, CEO MFIN, and Mr Parijat Garg, CRIF High Mark, for useful inputs on the draft of the chapter.

STRUCTURAL ISSUES

To say that the year has been interesting for microfinance would be an understatement. There has been much action with investments coming in, strategic investments by banks and other NBFCs in the sector, consolidation, and tremendous growth. The main highlights during the year were as follows:

- This was a year in which one of the largest MFIs that converted into a universal bank had stabilized operations—on both the loan book side and the deposit side. While as a bank, Bandhan continued to remain close to an MFI in terms of its asset portfolio, on the deposits side, it was able to generate deposits that surpassed its own targets. The fact that while continuing to be a bank Bandhan remained true to its founding customers is to be celebrated. While Bandhan's gross loan portfolio (GLP) grew by 56% when it was an NBFC in 2014–15, the growth in its microfinance portfolio as a bank in 2015–16 was moderated at 28%. Details of Bandhan's operations are captured in Chapter 11.
- This was a year in which eight MFIs were given an in-principle license to become SFBs. Together they represented 44% of the GLP of the for-profit MFIs that reported their data to MFIN. If we were to consider Bandhan's portfolio as a part of the NBFC-MFI numbers for the year end and remove all the NBFC-MFIs (including Bandhan) that were becoming banks, overall about 63% of the GLP classified as MFIs would be moving to the banking sector.
- Grama Vidiyal, with a GLP of ₹15 billion and representing about 3% of the NFBC-MFI space, was acquired by IDFC Bank to be converted into a wholly owned subsidiary, and functions as a BC, thereby transferring its portfolio to the banking system. Grama Vidiyal had 1.2 million customers and branches in 319 locations across 65 districts in 6 states.[2]
- IDFC Bank also picked up a stake of 9.99% for a sum of ₹85 million in ASA International India Microfinance Private Limited. This would give IDFC Bank access to markets in the northeast and give a board position in the company.[3]
- DCB Bank acquired a 5.81% stake in Odisha-based Annapurna Microfinance for ₹99.9 million,[4] largely to fuel its financial inclusion goals.
- RBL Bank acquired a 30% stake in Mumbai-based Swaadhar Finserve, and followed it up by taking a stake of nearly 10% in Utkarsh Microfinance which is in transition to a small finance bank.
- Kotak Mahindra Bank acquired BSS Microfinance in an all-cash deal in September 2016.[5]
- Muthoot Finance Limited (different from Muthoot Fincorp, which owns the Muthoot Microfinance) picked up a significant stake in Belstar Investment and Finance Private Limited. As of June 30, 2016, Muthoot was having a stake of 46.83% in Belstar.[6]
- During the previous year, Manappuram (another gold loan company) had acquired a majority stake in Asirvad Microfinance and during the year, Asirvad continued to operate as a subsidiary of Manappuram.
- There is an increasing interest in the banking sector for having strategic alliances with the MFIs as well as acquiring the MFIs. At least two MFIs were said to be in talks with a private sector bank for an outright buyout and a strategic investment with exclusive arrangements as a business correspondent.

The interest of the banking sector in the MFI sector was largely driven by the imperative of priority sector advances. Two changes in the regulatory regime might have prompted these moves. The priority sector lending norms were changed to introduce two subtargets—8% of the ANBC to be deployed to small and marginal farmers and 7.5% of the ANBC to be deployed to microenterprises. While these targets in themselves could be achieved through a combination of securitization deals, portfolio buyouts, retaining the shortfall, and buying RIDF and Small Industries Development Bank of India (SIDBI) bonds as a penalty, the requirement that the targets should be met every quarter makes the

[2] http://www.livemint.com/Industry/r4gXcsaj8zo5q6X-vaiZavI/IDFC-Bank-buys-microfinance-firm-Grama-Vidiyal.html, accessed on August 15, 2016.

[3] http://www.vccircle.com/news/banking/2016/01/12/idfc-bank-picks-10-stake-asa-international-india-13m, accessed on August 14, 2016.

[4] http://www.vccircle.com/news/micro-finance/2016/03/02/dcb-bank-buys-581-stake-annapurna-microfinance accessed on August 14, 2016.

[5] http://www.vccircle.com/news/micro-finance/2016/09/30/kotak-mahindra-bank-acquires-bss-microfinance, accessed on October 17, 2016.

[6] http://www.muthootfinance.com/muthoot/assets/new/1469775347MFIN%20Q1%20FY17%20investor%20presentation.pdf, accessed on October 7, 2016, 40–41.

transactions complicated and messy. It is, therefore, not surprising that the banks—particularly the private sector banks—are resorting to a source that is more continuous in nature.

In addition, the stipulation that banks have to open 25% of the incremental branches in unbanked rural areas also requires them to look for locations. Given that some of the MFIs have stabilized operations in several locations, it makes sense for the banks to take them over and convert some of the MFI branches into bank branches. The availability of the MFIs that are working at a low cost and are profitable also enhances the banks' ability to trade obligations across the banking system through the PSLC.

In general, we can see that the MFI sector is getting more and more mainstreamed—the interest in the sector is no longer restricted to people who have been working in the sector for long with specialized knowledge. In fact, it is the mainstream NBFCs and the banking sector that are showing increasing interest in the sector. While a large number of them that have not achieved scale have remained with the original promoters, the larger ones are under some churn—transformation to a banking architecture, consolidation, strategic investments from mainstream NBFCs/banks, change of ownership/management, and so on. Table 10.3 gives the brief journey of all the registered NBFC-MFIs that are listed with the RBI.

Table 10.3 NBFC-MFIs[7] and Their Journey Through the Times

S. No.	MFI Name	Description
1	Bandhan http://www.bandhanbank.com/	Started as an NGO, converted into an NBFC-MFI, currently a universal bank. Original promoter still in operational control.
2	ESAF http://www.esafmicrofin.com/	Started as NGOs, converted into NBFC-MFIs, currently transforming to SFBs. Original promoters still in operational control.
3	RGVN (Northeast) Microfinance Ltd http://www.rgvnnemfl.com/	
4	Janalakshmi http://www.janalakshmi.com/	Started as NBFCs, professionally run, operational control with the initial promoters, and currently having SFB licenses.
5	Ujjivan http://www.ujjivan.com/	
6	Equitas http://www.equitas.in/	
7	Suryoday http://suryodaymf.com/	
8	Utkarsh http://utkarshmfi.com/	
9	Disha Microfin http://www.dishamicrofin.com/	Disha started as an NBFC-MFI and has now received an SFB license. Currently operationally controlled by the Fincare group. Future started as an NGO, transformed into an NBFC-MFI, and now is a part of the Fincare group. Both will fold into SFBs.
10	Future http://future.ifapl.com/ http://www.fincare.com/	
11	Grama Vidiyal http://www.gvmfl.com/	Started as an NGO, transformed into an NBFC-MFI, taken over by IDFC Bank to be a wholly owned subsidiary. Had applied for an SFB license.
12	BSS Microfinance http://www.bssmicrofinance.co.in/	Started as an NGO, transformed into an NBFC-MFI, taken over by Kotak Mahindra Bank.

(Continued)

[7] The category NBFC-MFI was introduced only in 2011 after the Malegam Committee submitted its report and a large part of the report was accepted. Prior to 2011, these organizations were classified as just NBFCs.

(Continued)

S. No.	MFI Name	Description
13	Swadhaar FinServe http://www.swadhaar.com/	NGO background, transformed into an NBFC-MFI, currently 30% owned by RBL Bank.
14	Annapurna Microfinance http://ampl.net.in/	Started as an NGO, transformed into an NBFC-MFI. Currently operationally controlled by promoters. The DCB Bank has taken 5.81% stake in the organization.
15	Belstar http://www.belstar.in/ http://www.muthootfinance.com/	Started as an NGO (hand in hand), transformed into an MFI, and taken over by Muthoot Finance.
16	Asirvad Microfinance http://www.asirvadmicrofinance.co.in/	Started as an NBFC-MFI and controlling stake taken over by Manappuram, a gold loan company.
17	S.M.I.L.E Microfinance Limited http://www.smileltd.in/	Promoted by N. Sethuraman as an NBFC-MFI. Operational control with the nominees of DWM Investments who hold a majority stake. Not under the operational control of the original promoter.
18	SKS (currently known as Bharat Financial Inclusion) http://www.bfil.co.in/	Started as an NGO, transformed into an NBFC-MFI, listed on the exchanges after an IPO. The promoter has exited and is professionally managed. Had applied for an SFB license.
19	Grameen Koota http://www.grameenkoota.org/	Started as an NGO, converted into an NBFC-MFI. The company is currently significantly owned by CreditAccess Asia NV and operationally controlled by nonpromoters.
20	Satin Creditcare Network Limited http://www.satincreditcare.com/	Started as an NBFC and later converted into an NBFC-MFI. Run by the promoters and listed on the exchanges. Had applied for an SFB license.
21	Arohan http://www.arohan.in/	Set up as an NBFC-MFI by a professional. Controlling stake acquired by Intellecap, an NBFC. The stake was acquired with a view to consolidate the two businesses. Had applied for an SFB license.
22	Agora Microfinance http://www.amil.co.in/	Started as NBFC-MFIs, continue under the operational control of the promoters and are professionally run.
23	Sahayog Microfinance http://www.sahayogmicro.com/	
24	Midland Microfin http://midlandmicrofin.com/	
25	Samasta Microfinance Limited http://www.samasta.co.in/	
26	Jagaran Microfinance http://www.jagaranmf.com/	
27	Growing Opportunity Finance(India) http://www.gopportunity.net/	
28	Uttrayan Financial Services http://www.uttrayan-mfi.com/	

S. No.	MFI Name	Description
29	Shree Marikamba https://www.tofler.in/companyinfo/U67100KA2014PTC073382/shree-marikamba-micro-finance-private-limited	
30	Vedika Credit Capital https://www.zaubacorp.com/company/VEDIKA-CREDIT-CAPITAL-LTD/U67120WB1995PLC069424	
31	Shroff Capital and Finance Pvt. Ltd https://www.zaubacorp.com/company/SHROFF-CAPITAL-AND-FINANCE-PVT-LTD/U65910GJ1995PTC025418	
32	MSM Microfinance http://www.msmmicrofinance.com/	
33	Vizhuthugal Development Finance Private Limited https://www.zaubacorp.com/company/VIZHUTHUGAL-DEVELOPMENT-FINANCE-PRIVATE-LIMITED/U65922TN2008PTC069707	
34	Shikhar Microfinance Private Limited https://www.zaubacorp.com/company/SHIKHAR-MICROFINANCE-PRIVATE-LIMITED/U74899DL1993PTC052165	
35	SV Creditline http://www.svcl.in/	
36	Fusion Microfinance http://fusionmicrofinance.com/	
37	Altura Financial Services https://www.zaubacorp.com/company/ALTURA-FINANCIAL-SERVICES-LIMITED/U65100DL2013PLC259294	
38	Grameen Development & Finance Private Limited http://grameensahara.org/GDFPL/index.html	
39	Digamber Capfin Ltd http://www.digamberfinance.com/	
40	Anik Financial Services http://anikfin.blogspot.in/	
41	Intrepid Finance and Leasing Pvt. Ltd https://www.zaubacorp.com/company/INTREPID-FINANCE-AND-LEASING-PVT-LTD/U65921MH1994PTC216496	
42	Svatantra Microfin Limited https://www.svatantramicrofin.com/	Professionally run by Ananya Birla, a part of the Aditya Birla family.
43	Nabard Financial Services http://nabfins.org/	A subsidiary of NABARD.

(Continued)

(Continued)

S. No.	MFI Name	Description
44	Madura Microfinance http://maduramicrofinance.co.in/	Started as an NBFC-MFI with roots in banking and developmental work. Continues to be with the promoters.
45	Muthoot Microfin http://www.muthootmicrofin.com/	A part of the Muthoot Fincorp (Pappachan) group.
46	Namra Finance http://www.armanindia.com/	An NBFC-MFI wholly owned by Arman Finance, a mainstream NBFC.
47	Repco Microfinance http://repcomsme.co.in/	Promoted by REPCO Bank. Operational control with the promoters. Had applied for an SFB license.
48	Saija Finance http://saija.in/	Active NBFC-MFIs; they had applied for SFB licenses.
49	Light Microfinance http://www.lightmicrofinance.com/	Active NBFC-MFIs; they had applied for SFB licenses.
50	Sonata Finance Private Limited http://www.sonataindia.com/	Active NBFC-MFIs; they had applied for SFB licenses.
51	Village Financial Services http://village.net.in/	Started as an NGO, transformed into an NBFC-MFI. Had applied for an SFB license.
52	Chaitanya India http://www.chaitanyaindia.in/	Started as an NGO, transformed into an NBFC-MFI. Had applied for an SFB license.
53	IDF Financial Services http://www.idf-finance.in/	Started as NGOs, transformed into NBFC-MFIs, and are continuing to be operationally controlled by promoters.
54	Nirantara FinAccess http://www.finaccess.nirantara.co.in/	Started as NGOs, transformed into NBFC-MFIs, and are continuing to be operationally controlled by promoters.
55	YVU Finance http://www.yvumf.com/about-us.html	Started as NGOs, transformed into NBFC-MFIs, and are continuing to be operationally controlled by promoters.
56	Adhikar http://www.adhikarindia.in/	Started as NGOs, transformed into NBFC-MFIs, and are continuing to be operationally controlled by promoters.
57	Sambandh Finserve http://www.sambandhfin.com/	Started as NGOs, transformed into NBFC-MFIs, and are continuing to be operationally controlled by promoters.
58	Navachetana Microfin http://www.navachetana.in/	Started as NGOs, transformed into NBFC-MFIs, and are continuing to be operationally controlled by promoters.
59	Varam Capital http://varam.in/	Started as NGOs, transformed into NBFC-MFIs, and are continuing to be operationally controlled by promoters.
60	RORS Finance http://www.rors.in/	Started as NGOs, transformed into NBFC-MFIs, and are continuing to be operationally controlled by promoters.
61	Virutcham Microfinance http://www.virutcham.org/	Started as NGOs, transformed into NBFC-MFIs, and are continuing to be operationally controlled by promoters.
62	Nightingale Finvest http://www.nightingalefinvest.in/	Started as NGOs, transformed into NBFC-MFIs, and are continuing to be operationally controlled by promoters.
63	Arth Microfinance http://www.arthfinance.com/	Started as NGOs, transformed into NBFC-MFIs, and are continuing to be operationally controlled by promoters.
64	Margadarshak http://www.margdarshak.org.in/	Started as NGOs, transformed into NBFC-MFIs, and are continuing to be operationally controlled by promoters.

S. No.	MFI Name	Description
65	Share Microfin http://www.sharemicrofin.com/	NGO background, transformed into NBFC-MFIs, were in financial trouble due to the AP crisis, and are still operating as NBFC-MFIs with significant investments from private equity players.
66	Asmitha Microfin Limited http://www.asmithamicrofin.com/	
67	Spandana Sphoorty http://www.spandanaindia.com/	
68	Pahal (Ahmedabad) http://www.pahalfinance.com/	The infrastructure was owned by an NGO, taken over by an NFBC-MFI, and is operationally controlled by the company.
69	Unnati Trade and Fincon http://www.companywiki.in/company/unnati-trade-and-fincon-pvt-limited/u65910wb1992ptc055152	Taken over the portfolio of Sarala Women Welfare Society and operates as an NBFC-MFI.
70	Pahal (Mumbai)	No information available in the public domain.
71	Satra Development Finance limited	

Source: Data from the respective companies' websites and associated websites, accessed on August 15, 2016.

INVESTMENTS IN MFI SECTOR

During the year (from August 2015 to July 2016), the MFIs raised a significant amount of resources through equity, subdebt, debentures, and preference shares (Table 10.4). Just two IPOs of Ujjivan and Equitas mopped up an incremental amount of ₹19 billion (including investments by anchor investors prior to the IPO), in addition to ₹6.6 billion mopped up by exiting investors in these organizations. Janalakshmi raised around ₹10 billion incremental amounts through debentures and Tier 2 capital. Another amount of ₹5 billion was raised by MFIs which were not in the list of firms given in-principle licenses. The faith of the investors and markets in the microfinance and small finance sector continues to be unwavering. However, it is to be seen that only a few larger MFIs have been raising resources continuously, while the medium and smaller ones do not figure in the list. Even when we look at the individual NBFC-MFIs, barring the top 20 MFIs (including the ones that are getting to be banks), the others neither have a significant amount of institutional investment nor do they access the markets on a continuing basis.

Table 10.4 Fund Infusion in MFIs—August 2014 to July 2015

Month of Announcement	MFI Name	Infusion (₹ in Million)	Exit[8]	Investors
November 2015	SV Creditline	100		Preference shares.
December 2015	SV Creditline	520		Debentures from Blue Orchard.
February 2016	Satin Creditcare	250		Debentures from the Institute of Financial Management and Research (IFMR) Investment Adviser Services.
June 2016	Satin Creditcare	2,500		Karvy Capital. Nonconvertible redeemable cumulative preference shares.
June 2016			Exit 3.13% of 12.23% held for ₹3,760.	Equator Capital for four times return on investment over six years.

(Continued)

[8] Exits are neutral on the company as the sellers are replaced with new buyers. It is only an indication of the value that was generated for the investors at the time of exit.

(Continued)

Month of Announcement	MFI Name	Infusion (₹ in Million)	Exit[8]	Investors
July 2016			Exit 3.5% of 7.5% held for ₹4,600.	Danish Microfinance for five times return on investment over six years.
February 2016	Saija	200		Debentures from IFMR Investment Adviser Services.
January 2016	Janalakshmi	3,300		CDC—Tier 2 capital.
April 2016		6,000	Exit ₹4,000	TPG Asia new investments with a concurrent exit of unspecified investors.
June 2015		300		IFC, senior debt.
May 2016	Grameen Koota	1,350		IFC, debt.
April 2016	Ujjivan	2,650		Investment by anchor investors ahead of IPO.
May 2016	Ujjivan	3,580	Exit of ₹5,270 through offer for sale by Elevar, IFC, Sarva Capital, and WWB Capital partners.	IPO.
April 2016	Equitas	6,530		Investment by 16 anchor investors ahead of IPO.
April 2016	Equitas	7,200	Exit of ₹1,450 through offer for sale by private equity investors.	IPO.

Source: http://www.vccircle.com/search?search_api_views_fulltext=microfinance, accessed on August 14, 2016.

IPOS BY EQUITAS AND UJJIVAN

In addition to the deals, there were two public offerings of shares which were met enthusiastically by the markets. Equitas issue was oversubscribed by 17 times and Ujjivan which followed suit had an oversubscription of 41 times the offer. Both listed on a smart premium to the issue price. The biggest players in the microfinance sector are all heavily funded by international equity. However, due to the fact that both Equitas and Ujjivan had received in-principle licenses to set up SFBs, there were restrictions on foreign holding. The public issues showed that even the Indian investors had an appetite for the microfinance-like sector. Although one could argue that being a potential bank, they could attract more capital, but the experience of Bharat Financial Inclusion (formerly SKS) which raised capital from the Indian markets indicates that there is an appetite for local capital to flow into this sector. Till March 2016, Bharat Financial Inclusion had about 67% foreign equity—fairly moderate compared to the large NBFC-MFIs which have a greater proportion of foreign equity. Similarly, Satin Creditcare, another listed company, had around 63% of its equity held by foreign sources.

More discussion about Equitas and Ujjivan is available in Chapter 11 where the SFB model is discussed in detail.

FUNDING BY THE BANKING SYSTEM

During the year, the MFIs received a funding of ₹337.06 billion from the banking system, as against a funding of ₹72 billion in 2012–13. In addition, there were about ₹96 billion of loans securitized. Given that the banking system has restructured about ₹60 billion of debts under a corporate debt restructuring scheme following the aggressive growth of MFIs in the state of AP, the banks seem to be reposing greater faith in the sector outside of AP. In a year where there have been talks of the banks taking a hit due to NPAs and sluggish credit growth, to report a growth of 55% on the MFI portfolio as well as 91% growth in the securitization deals indicates the immense amount of faith that the mainstream financial system is reposing in the MFI sector. While it might be true that a large portion of the bullishness on MFIs may be driven by the need to satisfy priority sector lending targets, a portion may also be driven by the fact that NBFC-MFIs are raising a risk capital and showing a fair amount of capital adequacy which might be giving a level of comfort for the banking system. However, the aggressive growth rates of the sector need to be considered.

CLIENT PROTECTION: REGULATORY CHANGES

For all practical purposes, 2010 was the year that redefined the microfinance sector significantly. The AP crisis led to an ordinance and later a law, where the vulnerability of the client was put at the core. The Malegam Committee report and the NBFC-MFI guidelines thereafter also ensured that the client was brought to the center of the argument. In general, the regulatory approach has been favoring depositors to ensure that the depositors are not fleeced. On the lending side, the regulators have largely been benevolent except in cases of usury. However, in the report of 2008, the author had argued that

> The small borrowers do not have any past resources; when they take a loan they virtually mortgage their future to the lender. Vulnerable sections of people will be much more affected if credit availability is disrupted or credit terms are altered to their detriment. Unlike in the case of saver, small borrowers lose a part of their future if credit relationship is impaired. In such a context, protection from the regulator should possibly address the requirements of borrowers more than the savers. The regulatory stance in respect of microfinance sector should be reformulated to encompass the interests of small borrowers who have more to lose if the linkage with credit institution is disrepute. (Srinivasan 2008)

We need to see the regulatory changes in the context discussed above. On the regulatory side, during the last year the definition of the permissible limit of total indebtedness while granting loans was raised from ₹60,000 to ₹0.1 million. The effects of this were seen during the year as the average ticket size of MFI loans went up significantly. Otherwise, there were minor changes in the notification, allowing the MFIs to lend up to ₹30,000 per client (as against the cap of ₹15,000 per client) with a tenor less than 24 months.[9] Clearly, this was exposing the clients to higher risks. The self-regulatory organizations (SROs)—MFIN and Sa-Dhan—modified their code of conduct to introduce a subclause which addressed some effects of contagion in the case of rapid expansion.

This clause was added to ensure one more level of customer protection:

> MFIs after due verification of credit bureau reports will ensure that loans given on the basis of joint liability of group of borrowers (JLG loan) is restricted to ₹60,000 per borrower. Where the loan to a specific borrower exceeds ₹60,000, or the loan takes the total debt of the borrower above ₹60,000, such a loan should be given as an individual loan without involving the JLG. (MFIN and Sa-Dhan 2015)

The RBI also came up with a notification that mandated the banks to collect data from SHGs at the member level to be shared with the credit information companies. This notification suggested that the banks should start collecting and sharing the credit information from the SHGs from July 2016 with detailed formats in which the information should be collected and shared with CICs. While the first phase lasting up to June 2017 will collect information and report where the individual indebtedness of the member is more than ₹30,000, it was envisaged that in the second phase starting June 2017 complete information would be shared with the CICs (RBI 2016).

With this information coming in, and with the need being articulated that all bank lending that is MFI-like should also be a part of the CIC database and should be subject to the overall two-lender and lending amount caps, there might be a greater level of customer protection as we go forward. As of now, while these norms are strictly applicable to NBFC-MFIs, they are not applicable to banks, thereby creating some distortions.

Till now, the credit data of only the banks and MFIs were being collected, but with this additional information, the data will provide a better insight into the client-level indebtedness, allowing the banks to make a more informed credit decision, while preventing

[9] http://www.vccircle.com/news/micro-finance/2015/11/26/rbi-doubles-short-term-loan-cap-mfis, accessed on August 15, 2016.

the MFIs from making further loans beyond the permissible level of indebtedness. As of now, when the MFIs access credit data, CICs give data of indebtedness to a microlender (not restricted to NBFC-MFIs) and to an individual member. The microlender includes NBFC-MFIs, NBFCs, banks, and other lenders operating in JLG lending space.

Over a period of time, if the issue of client protection (against over-indebtedness by ambitious MFIs) is to be addressed, then it might be necessary to realistically map the indebtedness of the family and provide one integrated report containing the overall indebtedness and the number of loans from multiple sources. We are at a distance from achieving this, but with the gradual tightening on the amount and the quality of information to be uploaded to the CICs, there would be better information-sharing and risk assessment at least at the secondary level. The recommendations of the Aditya Puri Committee will also provide a broad framework for information-sharing by the CICs.

In addition to the above, one of the issues regularly faced is that the borrowers may use multiple identity documents and changes in spelling in order to access multiple loans without getting into the radar of the CICs. Therefore, MFIN and Sa-Dhan in the revised code also introduced the following clause:

> To reduce the errors in identification of borrowers in credit bureau reports, MFIs will move toward adoption of UIDAI number (Aadhaar number) based KYC within a two year period (from the day this COC comes into effect). As an initial measure, MFIs will ensure that while providing second and subsequent cycle loans the borrowers are identified with their Aadhaar number as part of KYC. The Aadhaar numbers will then be used by the Credit Bureaus for producing CIR. (MFIN and Sa-Dhan 2015)

At a structural level, the SROs are putting in a framework of code, outlets for complaints, investigation, and reporting both to the organization and to the RBI. However, the question of the effectiveness of the SROs needs to be considered. This needs to be considered essentially because SROs cannot take any effective penal action on their own. The penal action has to emanate from the RBI, and within RBI the enthusiasm to act on smaller events and on diagnostics may be limited as is evidenced by the concern that the RBI could be concerned more about financial stability than customer protection in the case of NBFCs (see Box 10.1). Therefore, the regulation of MFIs falls between the responsibility devolved on the SROs and the regulatory action vesting with the RBI.

On the other hand, there was an increasing concern that the non-NBFC-MFIs did not fall under a regulatory framework. While many of them were voluntarily members of Sa-Dhan and reporting their numbers, it still left them vulnerable to action by the local law enforcement agencies. These institutions are caught between the registered NBFC-MFIs and the unregistered and unregulated organizations. There were issues with local law enforcement agencies in the case of Cashpor in Bihar and Chhattisgarh. The longstanding demand of a microfinance bill by the sector seems to have fallen by the wayside, given that there is little action. Even the proposed Micro Units Development and Refinance Agency (MUDRA) Act did not find traction.

Box 10.1 Former Governor Subbarao on NBFC-MFIs

MFIs and Lessons from the AP Episode

MSS: You mentioned that the AP episode was around three big issues. Is there any other way in which it could have been tackled? I mean in hindsight we can always be very wise.

Dr Subbarao: Can you please be more specific about it?

MSS: There was possibly an early signal in 2006. There was enough market buzz that there was overlending. Interest rates were something Sa-Dhan had discussed with SERP and the state government in 2006, but MFIs had not lived up to their commitments. Self-regulation did not work. That indication was also there. And what we used to call as social collateral and social pressure can now be termed as coercive recovery. But from the indications available, including the suicide cases, there was much more than just social pressure being applied on the customers.

Dr Subbarao: I get your question. I am thinking on my feet and cannot recall sufficient detail to corroborate or contest your comments. The only point I want to make is that the RBI's regulation is guided by two main objectives—consumer protection and financial stability. Banks are tightly regulated because they are important for both dimensions. NBFCs are typically less tightly regulated than banks in order not to overconstrain their business model. MFIs are a category of NBFCs. It is possible that the

RBI was guided more by financial stability concerns with the result that consumer protection in the MFI sector got relegated as a secondary objective.

But there is also a special AP dimension to the blowout in the MFI sector in the state. I know because I am from the AP cadre of the IAS. The state government is very proactive; it had its own very successful 'Velugu' program; and there may have been some rivalry or overlap which caused friction. Admittedly, I cannot rule out the fact that the RBI may have been blindsided to the developments in the MFI sector but in evaluating the blowout in the sector, you cannot ignore the unique AP dimension.

MSS: There was also a larger political picture at that time, which cannot be easily brought into equation.

Dr Subbarao: You are right. Political differences are omnipresent in our system, and by definition, they are intangible. As I said, several factors including the RBI's preoccupation with financial stability to the relative neglect of consumer protection have together triggered the AP MFI crisis.

Going beyond the genesis of the problem, resolving it also became a big challenge for me. In the wake of the AP MFI agitation, we appointed a committee headed by Mr Malegam, a veteran and respected director on the board of the RBI. The committee made a comprehensive set of recommendations. By far the most significant one was to cap the interest rate that MFIs can charge. On the face of it, it looks like a straightforward remedy given that the usurious interest rate charged by MFIs was the main grievance in the entire agitation. But implementing this recommendation posed an intellectual challenge to me.

Let me explain. There was a time when the RBI used to regulate the entire structure of interest rates in the system, both on the deposit and lending sides. As part of the reform process, that entire structure of administered interest rates has been dismantled. This happened over the tenure of several governors. It was finally during my term that we brought the curtain down on the administered interest rate structure by deregulating the interest rate on the saving deposit account. It was widely hailed as it had the potential to benefit millions of middle-class households in the country whose only saving avenue is a savings deposit account. Some even said that this would be my lasting legacy as governor! And here I was, in the wake of the MFI agitation, called upon to reverse regulation of interest rates, reversing as it were a historic process. I was quite torn in reaching a decision on this.

MSS: In fact, that is interesting. If you look at the entire discourse of RBI pre-Malegam not only during your time, but during Dr Reddy's time as well, it had a very encouraging attitude toward the MFI sector; the notification asked the banks to report progress on lending to MFIs on quarterly basis and also proactively treated the joint liability loans as secured loans, for provisioning and prudential norms.

Dr Subbarao: Yes, possibly we went a little overboard, but we learnt from the AP episode. So, there is always a silver lining!

MICROFINANCE PERFORMANCE DURING THE YEAR

Microfinance sector grew at a sharp pace during the year. The highlights are given in Box 10.2. The sector continued to be profitable and as the numbers below indicate, the growth happened with the deepening of the engagement.

Box 10.2 Highlights of MFI Performance, March 2016

- As of March 31, 2016, MFIs on aggregated basis have a branch network of 9,669 and employee base of 85,888 of which 62% are loan officers (i.e., 53,834) who provide doorstep credit to low-income clients served by MFIs.
- As of March 31, 2016, MFIs provided microcredit to 32.5 million clients*, an increase of 44% over financial year (FY) 2014–15.
- The aggregate GLP of MFIs stood at ₹532 billion (excluding nonperforming portfolio, i.e., Portfolio at Risk (PAR) > 180 days in AP). This represents a year-on-year growth of 84% over FY 2014–15 and an increase of 24% over the last quarter.
- Annual loan amount disbursements in FY 2015–16 reached ₹619 billion, representing an increase of 65% compared to that in FY 2014–15.
- Total number of loans disbursed by MFIs grew to 34.7 million crore, an increase of 36% in FY 2015–16 compared to that in FY 2014–15.

- PAR figures remained under 1% for FY 2015–16.
- Average loan amount disbursed per account last year was ₹17,805. The figure for FY 2014–15 was ₹14,731.
- MFIs now cover 30 states/union territories.
- In terms of regional distribution (for GLP), south is at 35%, east at 15%, north at 25%, and west at 25%.
- Productivity ratios for MFIs continued to move upward. Average GLP per branch is now at ₹55 million, up by 51% over FY 2014–15 and average GLP per loan officer ₹9.9 million, 33% more from the last year, that is, FY 2014–15.
- Insurance (credit life) to over 37 million clients with sum insured of ₹598 billion was extended through MFIN.
- Pension accounts were extended to 2.3 million clients through MFIN.

Source: MFIN MicroMeter, Issue 17, http://mfinindia.org/wp-content/uploads/2016/05/Micrometer%20Issue%2017_Q4%20FY%2015-16_27th%20May%202016_print.pdf, accessed on August 15, 2016.
Note: * Client numbers may not represent 'unique' clients given that a client might have borrowed from multiple institutions.

GROWTH OF MFIs DURING THE YEAR[10]

The spread of MFIs across the country was impressive. As per the data made available by MFIN (Table 10.5), MFIs were present in 32 states and union territories. In about 21 states, there were more than 5 MFIs. Apart from the geographic spread, the year witnessed very significant growth in the loan disbursals by MFIs, and as of March 31, 2016, the MFIs had a GLP of over ₹530 billion. A part of this portfolio—about ₹113 billion—was not in the books of the MFIs but was under the management of the MFIs. Of ₹113 billion, ₹24.84 billion was originated by the MFIs acting as business correspondents to a bank.

The increased investment in the microfinance sector and the general bullishness was not without a reason. After the 2010 crisis, the sector that went into a bit of a setback bounced back on very strong growth numbers. From a GLP of ₹168.13 billion in 2011–12, the portfolio grew more than three times (see Figures 10.1 and 10.2).

Branch Network and Clients

When we look at the regional spread of physical branch network and clients as detailed in Table 10.6, we find that south continues to dominate in the footprint, though in two of the southern states—Telangana and AP—there is hardly any microfinance activity. While the relative share of south in branch network remained at 33% of all the branches, the overall growth in branches in south was dominated by Kerala, where the branch network grew by 72%, while the growth in branches across the country was at 30%. The relative share of the eastern region was down from 30% to 20% and that of northeast was down from 4% to 2%. This was largely attributable to the migration of Bandhan out of this dataset as it became a bank. Bandhan was not only the largest MFI but also had a very high presence in these regions. In spite of the withdrawal of Bandhan, there was strong growth in the east on absolute numbers—particularly in Bihar and Jharkhand. The northern, central, and western regions increased their relative proportions. The strongest growth came from Haryana in north, Chhattisgarh, Madhya Pradesh, and Uttar Pradesh in central, and Maharashtra in the west.

While the branches captured in Figure 10.3 represent the NBFC-MFI branches drawn from the MFIN database and numbered 9,669 across the country, the database of Sa-Dhan which included non-NBFC-MFIs showed 11,644 branches. There was a minor difference between the NBFC-MFI branches reported by MFIN and Sa-Dhan, possibly pertaining to the variation in the organizations that were reporting to the two agencies.

Portfolio

The portfolio numbers are largely in sync with the physical outreach and the clients. The southern region has a relatively higher portfolio outstanding (see Figure 10.4). The eastern region has shown some shrinkage in relative share explained by Bandhan getting out of the database. However, it is important to notice that the overall pie of loan outstandings and loan disbursements has grown significantly in comparison to the past year. The disbursements have grown at 83% and the outstandings have

[10] This segment solely relies on the data of the 56 MFIs that form the database of MFIN. Together these 56 MFIs represent 90% of the NBFC-MFI business in the country and are subject to the oversight of MFIN as an SRO. In addition, there are others who are offering microfinance like JLG products, including banks which are not discussed in this chapter. The SHG segment of the business is discussed in a separate chapter.

Table 10.5 **State-wise Details of MFIs for 2014–15 and 2015–16**

		Gross Loan Portfolio (₹ Billion)		Number of Clients (Million)		Number of Branches		Number of Employees		Loans Disbursed (₹ Billion)		No. of Accounts (Million)	
State/Region	MFI (Nos.)	2014–15	2015–16	2014–15	2015–16	2014–15	2015–16	2014–15	2015–16	2014–15	2015–16	2014–15	2015–16
Delhi	8	3.65	5.82	21.2	55.6	47	41	1,226	1,370	4.07	6.17	18	22
Haryana	14	4.21	11.65	28.6	49.1	100	169	989	1,670	5.3	14.48	30	65
Punjab	10	9.88	0	0	56.2	0	128	0	1,199	0	13.42	0	65
Rajasthan	14	7.05	12.59	55.8	75.4	188	217	1,562	1,990	9.18	16.2	56	84
North		24.79	30.06	105.6	236.3	335	555	3,777	6,229	18.55	50.27	105	235
Assam	10	3.56	7.73	32.5	53.2	133	203	943	1,306	4.77	9.51	29	47
Tripura	5	0	0.4	0	3.4	0	22	0	152	0	0.68	0	4
Northeast		3.56	8.13	32.5	56.6	133	225	943	1,458	4.77	10.19	29	51
Bihar	21	15.34	29.21	120.6	193.1	427	629	3,136	5,087	20.74	39.2	138	220
Jharkhand	9	3.85	8.98	33.4	56.6	124	239	943	1,850	5.8	12.53	41	71
Odisha	13	16.49	31.41	139	213.5	437	510	3,034	4,525	22.9	41.68	167	250
West Bengal	14	16.59	30.75	168.7	219.1	536	643	4,088	5,541	24.48	43.79	178	261
East		52.27	100.35	461.7	682.3	1,524	2,021	11,201	17,003	73.92	137.2	524	801
Chhattisgarh	17	4.45	8.77	37.2	58.6	189	263	1,161	1,826	6.13	11.23	38	59
Madhya Pradesh	27	22.54	40.84	183.5	280.5	706	984	4,797	7,494	29.64	49.73	181	257
Uttar Pradesh	19	30.71	56.45	211.6	312.7	699	988	5,645	8,717	36.74	67.58	212	318
Uttarakhand	11	3.42	5.93	22.9	33.1	70	82	493	726	4	7.18	23	32
Central		61.12	111.99	455.2	684.9	1,664	2,317	12,096	18,763	76.51	135.72	454	666
Gujarat	19	10.28	20.64	91.3	123.4	334	433	2,453	3,360	12.21	22.41	68	98
Maharashtra	32	33.62	63.29	257.4	371.1	755	1,174	6,888	10,224	42.94	79.42	298	442
West		43.9	83.93	348.7	494.5	1,089	1,607	9,341	13,584	55.15	101.83	366	539
Andhra Pradesh	5	0.78	0.82	12.7	11.5	639	361	2,716	2,135	2.13	1.17	13	7
Karnataka	24	41.09	71.65	273.8	382.3	944	1,198	9,248	11,475	53.63	90	455	625
Kerala	10	11.5	24.34	67	122.3	204	350	1,994	3,630	14.39	31.02	100	173
Puducherry	10	1.13	1.93	9.2	12.2	18	20	176	230	1.42	2.29	9	11
Tamil Nadu	19	50.8	86.87	444.4	565	1,162	1,352	9,743	12,665	61.19	102.65	441	551
South		105.3	185.61	807.1	1,093.3	2,967	3,281	23,877	30,135	132.76	227.13	1,018	1,368
Total		290.94	520.07	2,210.8	3,247.9	7,712	10,006	61,235	87,172	361.66	662.34	2,495	3,661

Source: MFIN MicroMeter, Issue 17, March 31, 2016, http://mfinindia.org/wp-content/uploads/2016/05/Micrometer%20Issue%2017_Q4%20FY%2015-16_27th%20May%202016_print.pdf, accessed on August 16, 2016.

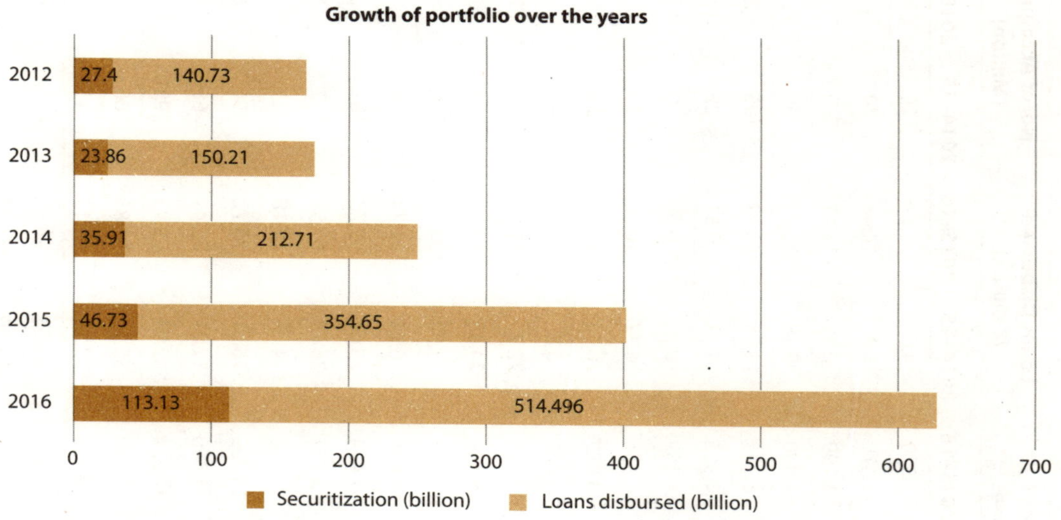

Figure 10.1 Growth of MFI Portfolio Post-2010

Source: Microfinance Institutions Network.

Indicators: MFI Models	2016	2015	Change
Client outreach	39.9 million	37.1 million	↑
Women clients	97%	97%	No change
SC/ST clients	30%	28%	↑
Other minorities	27%	18%	↑
Rural clients	38%	33%	↑
Gross outstanding portfolio	638 billion	488 billion	↑
Own portfolio	469 billion	390 billion	↑
Managed portfolio	169 billion	98 billion	↑
Avg. loan per borrower	114 billion	131 billion	↓
Income generation loan	94%	80%	↑
Female staff in MFIs	15%	16%	↓
ABCO	440	419	↑
OER	10.22%	11.45%	↑
FCR	13.3%	12.42%	↓
Yield	21%	24%	↓
Margin	10.00%	10.20%	↓
OSS	113%	113%	↓
ROA	2.2%	1.73%	No change
ROE	11.6%	8.19%	↑
CAR	19.39%	19.10%	↑
Leverage	3.2	2.9	↑
Fund flow outstanding	448 billion	408 billion	↑
Equity outstanding	45 billion	41 billion	↑
NPA	0.15%	0.215	↑
SHG model			

Total No. of SHGs linked	7.9 million	7.7 million	↑
No. of families reached	103 million	101 million	↑
Total savings of SHGs	136 billion	113 billion	↑
Total No. of SHGs credit linkage	1.83 million	1.62 million	↑
Gross loan outstanding	571 billion	517 billion	↑
Total loan disbursed	372 billion	303 billion	↑
Avg. loan disbursed per SHG	203,526	186,556	↑
Avg. loan outstanding per SHG	122,258	115,759	↑
NPA	6.45%	7.40%	↓

Figure 10.2 Performance Highlights of MFIs—Including Non-NBFC-MFIs

Source: The Bharat Microfinance Report 2016.

Table 10.6 Year-on-Year Growth Rates of MFI Activities, 2014–15 and 2015–16

State/Region	MFI (Nos.)	GLP (%)	Client (%)	Branches (%)	Employees (%)	Loans Disbursed (%)	Loan Accounts Disbursed (%)	Average Loan Disbursed per Account (%)
Delhi	8	59	162	−13	12	52	23	24
Haryana	14	177	72	69	69	173	117	26
Rajasthan	14	79	35	15	27	76	48	19
North		21	124	66	65	171	125	20
Assam	10	117	64	53	38	99	61	24
Northeast		128	74	69	55	114	74	22
Bihar	21	90	60	47	62	89	59	19
Jharkhand	9	133	69	93	96	116	75	23
Odisha	13	90	54	17	49	82	49	22
West Bengal	14	85	30	20	36	79	47	22
East		92	48	33	52	86	53	21
Chhattisgarh	17	97	58	39	57	83	54	19
Madhya Pradesh	27	81	53	39	56	68	42	18
Uttar Pradesh	19	84	48	41	54	84	50	23
Uttarakhand	11	73	45	17	47	80	40	29
Central		83	50	39	55	77	47	21
Gujarat	19	101	35	30	37	84	44	28
Maharashtra	32	88	44	55	48	85	48	25
West		91	42	48	45	85	47	25
Andhra Pradesh	5	5	−9	−44	−21	−45	−45	0
Karnataka	24	74	40	27	24	68	37	22
Kerala	10	112	83	72	82	116	74	24
Puducherry	10	71	33	11	31	61	27	27
Tamil Nadu	19	71	27	16	30	68	25	34
South		76	35	11	26	71	34	27
All India		79	47	30	42	83	47	25

Source: Computed by the author from Table 1.5 above.

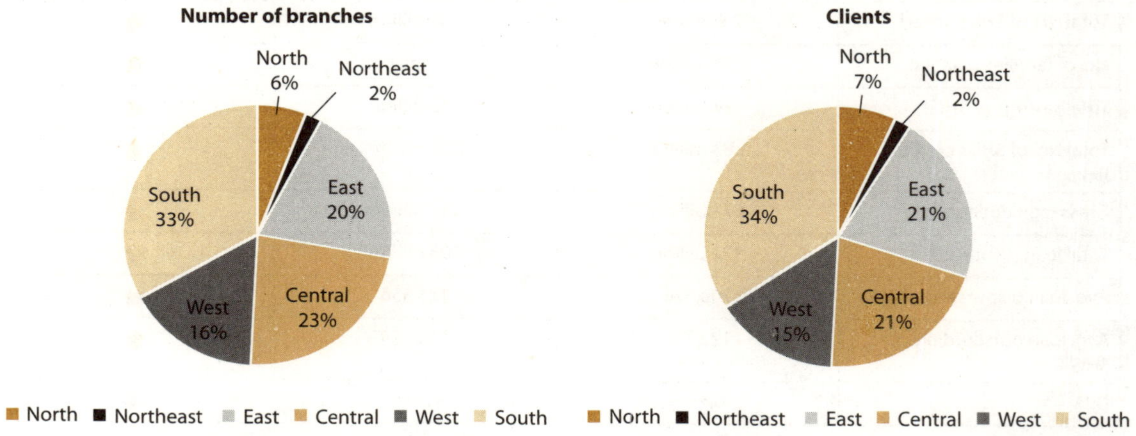

Figure 10.3 Regional Spread of the MFI Branches and Clients

Source: Microfinance Institutions Network.

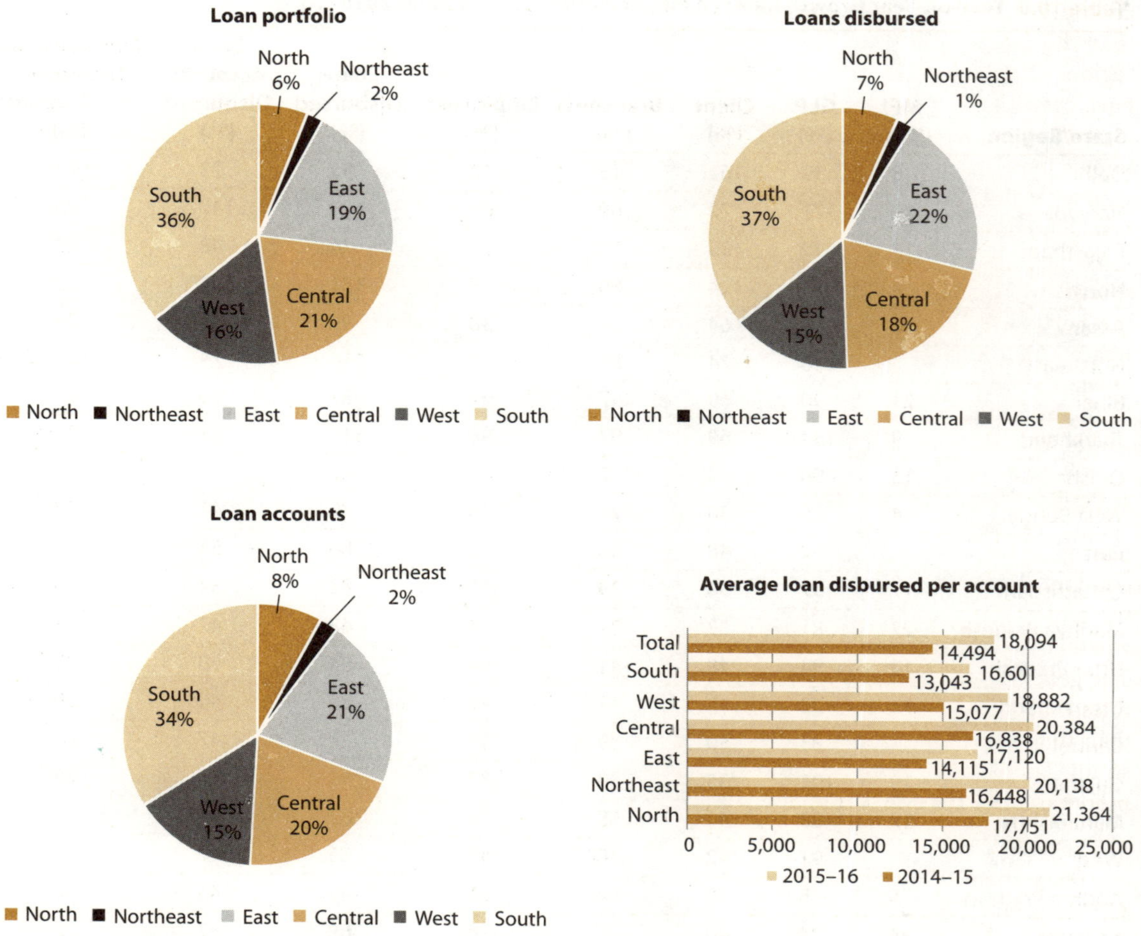

Figure 10.4 Regional Spread of the Loan Portfolio and Loan Accounts

Source: Microfinance Institutions Network.

grown by 79% compared to the past year. Haryana in north, Assam in northeast, Chhattisgarh in central, Jharkhand in east, Gujarat in west, and Kerala in south have shown a disproportionate growth in portfolio outstanding—all these states have more than doubled their outstandings with strong disbursements during the year. Even on these parameters, the south leads with the central region following suit.

While the growth in disbursements and portfolio shows a strong growth across the board in all regions, these have been partly a result of expansion of branch offices which grew at 30% across the country and employees which grew at 44% across the country. However, a significant portion of the value add is also because of deepening with the clients—or because of larger loan sizes. On an average, the loan size grew by ₹3,600. What is more interesting is that the average loan size in northern, northeastern, central, and eastern regions was significantly higher than the average loan size in southern and western regions. Traditionally, south and west are known to have been better in banking parameters as well as loan offtake. This aggressive growth in the areas not known for a capacity for credit absorption should be seen with a bit of awe and a bit of concern because it is so counter-intuitive.

While it is important to look at the regional spread, what is equally important is the spread of the portfolio between rural and urban India. The Bharat Microfinance Report brought out by Sa-Dhan indicates that 78% of the portfolio comes from the urban areas, while a smaller percentage comes from the rural areas (Sa-Dhan 2016).

A DEEPER LOOK AT THE DATA

During the interactions with sector specialists, the constant question that cropped up was whether the growth rates of the MFIs were sustainable and whether the sector is heading for a 2010-like crisis. The general consensus seems to be that the growth rates that the MFIs are seeing are more aggressive than they should have been, and there are signs of strain. Therefore, it is important to look at the data more carefully. Here are the topline numbers:

- The portfolio growth rate in the last year has been a phenomenal 84% (previous year, it was 63%).
- This growth in portfolio comes with a concurrent growth in loan disbursements which grew at 45% (previous year, it was 55%).

However, the interesting numbers are as follows:

- The number of branches of MFIs grew by 22% (previous year, it was 8%).
- The staff strength of MFIs grew by 38% (previous year, it was 20%).
- The number of clients grew by 44% (previous year, it was 29%).
- The number of loans grew by 45% (previous year, it was 37%).

From the numbers and Figure 10.5, it is clear that the portfolio managed by the MFIs (both off and on the balance sheet) is growing disproportionately to the base—branches, employees, and clients. This clearly shows deepening of engagement with the same client, either through higher loan amounts or through multiple loan accounts, or both. For a longer term representation, see Figure 10.6.

Clearly, an employee is managing many more clients, with greater amount of indebtedness. This stress is accentuated in some MFIs and some geographies more than others. It becomes even more of a matter

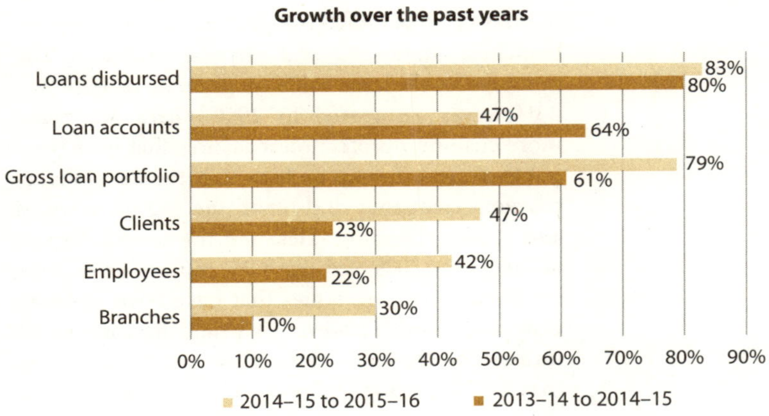

Figure 10.5 Growth of MFIs

Source: Microfinance Institutions Network.

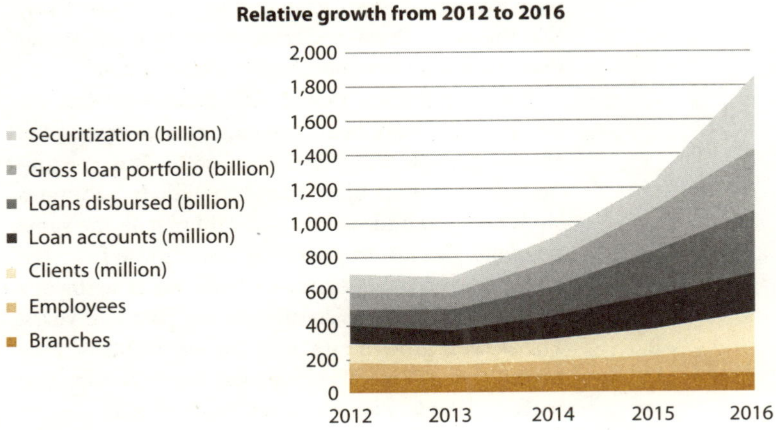

Figure 10.6 Relative Growth of Various Parameters

Source: Computed from MFIN databases of various years.

Table 10.7 Movement of Performance Parameters

Parameter	Year 2011–12	Year 2015–16	Year 2015–16 (for Large MFIs)	Year 2015–16 for Janalakshmi[11]
Average amount outstanding per client	7,533	16,394	16,601	23,773
Average loan disbursed per account	12,232 (figure for 2013)	17,805	17,603	29,634
Average clients per branch	2,135	3,358	3,723	13,547
Average GLP per branch (₹ million)	16	55	55	322
Average clients per loan officer	491	603	621	592
Gross loan portfolio per employee (₹ million)	3.7	9.9	10.3	14.07

Source: MFIN MicroMeter, Issue 17, http://mfinindia.org/wp-content/uploads/2016/05/Micrometer%20Issue%2017_Q4%20FY%2015-16_27th%20May%202016_print.pdf, accessed on August 17, 2016.

of concern in 22 MFIs, each of which has a GLP of more than ₹5 billion. These represent 90% of the size of MFIs on all parameters—portfolio, disbursements, branches, employees, and physical outreach. The numbers for the large MFIs are given in Table 10.7.

However, compared to 2010, there are many more customer protection measures that have been put in place—the cap on loan size, the detail on repayment frequency and tenor, the cap on margins and absolute lending rates, and the need to report all loans to CICs and use CIC reports in making credit decisions are issues that have been systemically addressed. However, it would be difficult to understand the stress particularly because the stress may be happening under the radar. If very aggressive (almost 100%) growth is coming in from states that have traditionally not been known for credit offtake and nonfarm activities and states that have a very large base and a robust banking system are also showing tremendous growth, then it is most likely that this is being pushed from the supply side rather than a surge of demand from the customers.

A look at the individual MFI data shows that the top 10 MFIs have been growing at a compounded annual growth rate (CAGR) of 66%. This calculation does not include Bandhan which became a bank last year and has a significant play in the same segment. The fastest growth is coming also from the largest player Janalakshmi—which was growing at a CAGR of 137% consistently for the past five years. The slowest growth rate from the top 10 MFIs came from Grama Vidiyal which was recently acquired by IDFC Bank. Possibly at a CAGR of 30%, Grama Vidiyal was unable to attract investments for fueling its further growth. In the past five years, Grama Vidiyal's equity has been static, and only in 2014–15 it raised some cumulative nonconvertible preference shares. In one sense, the growth cycle might be a cycle that requires more capital, capital requires greater efficiency and performance, which can be achieved by scale, and to scale, one needs more capital. Are the large microfinance agencies riding this tiger of extremely ambitious growth?

Where are the concerns coming from? In January 2016, a report in the online periodical *The Wire* (Dogra 2016) indicated that there were suicides in the Azamgarh district of UP. Dogra documented the plight of overindebted borrowers—but also documented how easy it is to get a loan and how deeply indebted the borrowers are, with a large portion of the loans going for consumption purposes. At the same time, an article about brewing microfinance crisis (Sriram 2016) drew much attention and was acknowledged as a red flag with advisories on preventive action.[12] A report by market analyst Ambit put a negative report on microfinance and called the rates of growth unsustainable.[13] A well-known sector expert Ramesh

[11] Janalakshmi Financial Services is the largest MFI (after Bandhan became a bank) and its numbers are significantly at variance from the rest of the industry. We decided to put these numbers of a model that is growing more aggressively than anybody else in the industry.

[12] See http://m2iconsulting.com/wp-content/uploads/2016/01/Reputational-Risk-Event-for-MFIs.pdf, accessed on August 17, 2016.

[13] Report by Ambit, https://forum.valuepickr.com/.../62760d8ddfce398b73fd3a6bbe6c4c37aa9a42fc.pdf, accessed on August 17, 2016.

Arunachalam also indicated that microfinance was in for an AP-like crisis.[14] In addition, stock market players like Daljeet Kohli[15] and Ramesh Damani[16] have questioned the basic model of microfinance. Given that this is so mainstream and being talked about by so many players, the reputational risks are higher than they were in 2010. It is in this context that we need to look at the issues that microfinance sector may be facing.

A white paper issued by industry association MFIN released in May 2016 put several red flags on the stress (MFIN 2016). The report flagged the following issues:

- Ambitious targets for field staff which do not take into account issues such as overpenetration and concentration in concerned geographies.
- Undue influence exerted by members/leaders due to a tendency to rely on certain people repeatedly such as center leaders, who, over a period of time, assume a much larger and important role in the scheme of things. Being entrusted with the responsibility of group formation, they start manipulating group behavior and use members of the group to borrow on their behalf. Consequently, if they choose to default, it is the client who has borrowed on their behalf who comes under stress.
- Inadequate time spent by MFI staff on compulsory group trainings (CGTs) of MFI staff which is an important tool for knowledge dissemination and strengthening group cohesion. Dilution of this process impacts the robustness of the group.
- Challenges in identifying proxy clients and ghost lending.

In addition to the above, the paper also put out some data to indicate the anecdotal incidents that could potentially snowball into a crisis, given in the seriousness of these instances. The details of the instances included suicides or attempts to suicide, obstruction of repayment by ring leaders, mass default, media reports, and closure of branches by local administration.

While there were articles that expressed the contrary view, a blog by IFMR[17] responded to the article cited above in *The Wire*. This blog, using extensive data both from MFIs and CICs, indicated that the concerns expressed by the article was not borne out by data analysis and these instances of suicides, pipelining, and default were not significant in order to cause a systemic risk. Similarly, an article in *The Economic Times* in April 2016[18] indicated that the MFIs were out of an unprecedented crisis and credited the mood to better regulations and diligent borrowers that there was much scope for hope and growth. The same sentiment was expressed in research reports by Anand Rathi and Nirmal Bang where they advised to buy microfinance stocks. Clearly, the jury is not out on this yet.

In the last year, the report had discussed why it was difficult for 2010 to repeat itself and during the year it is important that those points be revisited.

Box 10.3 Why Is It Difficult for 2010 to Repeat Itself (But Still We Need to Be Concerned)

The improvements (reproduced from the report last year):

While there is much discussion on whether the industry is growing at an unstainable pace, the situation has changed fundamentally in the larger ecosystem that might provide adequate checks and balances from the situation going out of hand. Some of the factors that preceded the MFI crisis in AP in 2010 can be seen—high levels of investment coming in at high valuations and large number of MFIs operating in a single area. Therefore, the rumblings that the growth rates, the valuations, etc. could be leading to aggressive lending and client-level indebtedness may be well founded.

However, there are multiple mitigating factors that can provide a corrective framework. As an RBI-recognized SRO, MFIN is charged with undertaking the following functions:

1. Surveillance
2. Dispute resolution

[14] http://microfinance-in-india.blogspot.in/2016/03/2010-andhra-pradesh-microfinance-crisis.html, accessed on October 10, 2016.

[15] http://rakesh-jhunjhunwala.in/the-stock-picks-of-daljeet-kohli-of-indianivesh, accessed on October 10, 2016.

[16] http://rakesh-jhunjhunwala.in/ramesh-damani-junks-business-model-of-micro-finance-stocks-even-as-they-surge-breach-upper-circuits, accessed on October 10, 2016.

[17] http://www.ifmr.co.in/blog/2016/01/22/microfinance-through-a-data-lens, accessed on October 10, 2016.

[18] http://articles.economictimes.indiatimes.com/2016-04-19/news/72453400_1_sks-microfinance-s-dilli-raj-ap-crisis, accessed on October 10, 2016.

3. Grievance redressal
4. Knowledge dissemination and training
5. Managing data

MFIN already has a robust system of collecting and disseminating data with fair degree of granularity. The data cuts are available in the public domain with a two-month lag and at a granularity of a state and MFI. Going forward, MFIN is working on collecting data at the district level. MFIN also has a helpline and is able to track complaints and has field presence. MFIN has a self-regulation committee which is firewalled from the regular function as an industry association.

In addition to MFIN, there are at least two credit bureaus that are working actively in this space and all loans being given out are being queried. CRIF High Mark, for instance, has shared the data on high percentages of inquiries being rejected for being noncompliant which in itself is a strong indicator of aggressive behavior and this could be tracked down.

The most important aspect is that with Bandhan moving out of the space to become a universal bank and with eight other MFIs getting an in-principle license to set up SFBs—particularly the ones that were growing aggressively and fast—there would be a bit of a slowdown as these institutions gear up for the transition phase. Therefore, it is quite likely that in spite of the aggressive growth, there are some natural circuit breakers that slow down the industry and help the MFI sector to take a pause and reflect.

The Concerns

While the above arguments given during the last year continue to be valid, there are reasons why the safeguards might fail. These are the issues on which the safeguards might fail.

- The macro growth numbers in terms of deepening the engagement with the clients (greater amounts of loan being given to the clients, including top-up loans) may be indicative of evergreening.
- The moving away of Bandhan takes one of the largest player out of the two-lender norm applicable to NBFC-MFIs. While the relative share of the east is reduced in the overall pie, we still see aggressive growth in areas where Bandhan was strong—West Bengal, Bihar, Jharkhand, and Northeast.
- The CICs largely give MFIs data on indebtedness on the JLG product and have not completely integrated the data with individual indebtedness with the bank on a non-JLG product. This is a matter of concern with Bandhan becoming a bank and eight other MFIs being on their way to be a bank.
- While the CICs are moving toward a single nonrepudiable identity document of Aadhaar, it is at quite a distance from being completely implemented. Therefore, it is quite possible that the aggressive growth may also be with multiple identity papers being presented and duplication of loan accounts.
- There are reports (such as the one in *The Wire* discussed earlier) where identities are being traded in return for a small consideration to a leader/agent. This practice will not show up in the database, but anecdotal evidence shows pipelining.
- With loan ticket size increasing, there has to be some involvement of the family in the larger enterprise and we do not see a greater involvement of men as clients.

The only aspects that might mitigate the concerns above are as follows:

- A significant movement of the MFI portfolio from rural to urban centers where entrepreneurship activities are available and larger ticket loans make economic sense.
- A significant growth in the nonfarm economy in the areas where microfinance is aggressively growing and is, therefore, able to absorb the credit.
- A significant improvement in the quality of data available to enable credit decisions based on data rather than physical interaction.
- Modeling of the past data to see patterns and replacing artificial intelligence in decision-making to ensure that automation has led to an aggressive growth.

Source: The Author.

WHAT THE DATA DOES NOT TELL US

With all the systems in place and the granular data available with MFIN, it is found that it is extremely difficult to predict stress purely from data. For instance, from the district-level data collected by MFIN in its MicroSpread, the following aspects come out:

- While MFIs are present in 509 districts (600 as per CRIF High Mark report, which include non-NBFC-MFI lenders as well), about 50% of the entire portfolio of the MFIs are concentrated in 80 districts; about 50% of the entire branch network was concentrated in about 100 districts; and 50% of the accounts were concentrated in 85 districts. These districts in all represented 15 states/union territories as against the MFI presence in 32 states/union territories.
- There were 10 districts that had a portfolio outstanding of more than ₹5 billion, spread across 4 states and representing 10% of the GLP, 10% of the loan accounts, and 7% of the branch network.
- There were another 50 districts that had a portfolio between ₹2.5 billion and ₹5 billion, spread over 13 states (including the 4 states mentioned above) and these represented about 32% of the GLP, 30% of the accounts, and 24% of the branches.

When we look at the data above, it would tell us that the top districts have too much of concentration of portfolio, lesser branch network in comparison to the other areas, and much higher average loan amount. In one sense, these are the areas that are to be monitored for concentration risks, multiple lending, and stress. One would assume that the districts where the portfolio is relatively lesser, the scope for stress and multiple lending will be limited.

However, when we look at these districts where there is a heavy exposure, the alarm bells need not necessarily ring. For instance, Bengaluru district has the highest GLP but being a large district, there may be ample opportunities to lend. Also being a city, there might be scope for diversified livelihoods. While the average loan ticket size as per the CRIF High Mark data (which is at variance with the MFIN data because it is more broad-based and covers all JLG type loans) in Bengaluru is ₹27,000, it may not be as worrying as the same amount elsewhere, say in Nagpur or Wardha. Also, the fact that 78% of the overall MFI portfolio is now in urban areas (Sa-Dhan 2016) might mean that MFIs are in areas that have ample livelihood opportunities and cash flows.

Using the CRIF High Mark data of the top 100 districts by GLP size (details in Table 10.8), the areas showing worrying signs have been identified based on multiple criteria.

Table 10.8 Districts Where the Average Loan Size Is High (₹ in Billion)

Previous Rank	District	Portfolio Rank	GLP March 2016	GLP March 2015	Active Lenders	Active Loans (Million)	Average Loan (2015–16; Thousand)	% Loans for Income Generation	% of Economically Active Women (2016)	% of Economically Active Women (2015)
3	South 24 Paraganas (WB)	3	10.57	6.94	59	0.592	27–35	31.01	17.15	14.29
4	Koch Bihar (WB)	13	7.13	5.79	9	0.334	27–35	39.96	28.27	30.97
12	Hooghli (WB)	9	7.59	5.09	30	0.405	27–35	28.5	15.6	12.84
13	Jalpaiguri (WB)	15	7.01	5.04	10	0.361	27–35	32.96	21.55	19.38
22	North Dinajpur (WB)	30	4.94	3.61	16	0.276	27–35	39.36	20.09	18.73
33	Malda (WB)	38	4.27	2.9	18	0.241	27–35	29.64	14.64	12.29
75	Darjeeling (WB)	71	3.29	2.19	11	0.158	27–35	31.23	17.59	15.59
76	Nagaon (AS)	44	4.02	2.18	15	0.17	27–35	27.35	17.05	13.75
61	Kamrup (AS)	54	3.74	2.36	17	0.182	27–35	17.79	35.54	27.11
60	Kamrup Metro (AS)	64	3.54	2.42	17	0.168	27–35	12.51	39.68	30.49
	Sonitpur (AS)	73	3.23	1.96	11	0.132	27–35	28.14	20.04	14.67
57	Bulandshahr (UP)	59	3.64	2.45	14	0.194	27–35	5.46	16.93	10.28
	Meerut (UP)	78	3.13	1.73	15	0.156	27–35	7.14	14.11	7.63
21	Ghaziabad (UP)	91	2.99	3.64	23	0.156	27–35	13.86	10.15	12.12

Source: CRIF High Mark.

In West Bengal, the districts of South 24 Paraganas, Koch Bihar, Hooghli, Jalpaiguri, North Dinajpur, Malda, and Darjeeling have very high outstandings per account and have a high exposure from the lending institutions. The same criteria apply to Kamrup, Kamrup Metro, Nagaon, and Sonitpur districts of Assam. Three districts of Bulandshahr, Ghaziabad, and Meerut in Uttar Pradesh show similar signs, though it is possible that we can disregard Ghaziabad due to its urban nature and its proximity to Delhi. Table 10.8 has the details.

On the other hand, there is a set of districts where the average loan outstanding is not that high, but the levels of penetration are—where the proportion of economically active women covered by a loan is very high (see Table 10.9). These are also districts which have a very high exposure from MFIs. The districts are Nagpur and Wardha in Maharashtra, Coimbatore, Madurai, Nagapattinam, Thanjavur, Namakkal, Thiruvarur, and Pudukkottai in Tamil Nadu, and Mysore in Karnataka. These are the districts to be watched carefully.

However, from *The Wire* report, the stress seems to be emanating out of eastern Uttar Pradesh, Madhya Pradesh, Chhattisgarh, and Jharkhand. These states and the districts which have been mentioned as hot zones do not figure in the list of districts that have very large MFI exposure. One parameter that might throw some light is the number of MFI accounts as a proportion of the number of households in the district. That will give an indication of penetration and pervasiveness of microfinance, even if the district is small and may not come up on the absolute amount of GLP. For instance, in the MicroSpread data, one district that tops the list in terms of MFI loan saturation is Chamarajanagar in Karnataka where there have been some complaints.

Interestingly, Azamgarh district that was in the news does not even feature in the top 100 districts of exposure and the other parameters. Clearly, stress has to do with the ability to cope, which may change from context to context. We possibly need not panic as long as the exposure is in urban areas, areas connected to markets, and areas that have significant nonfarm enterprises. Areas that are agrarian are the ones that are vulnerable to a greater stress for the same absolute amounts of indebtedness.

POSSIBILITIES

If we put the above concerns in perspective, there might be three scenarios—all of which are important to consider, given that there are increasing signs of excessive growth and stress and warning signals are coming in from multiple sources.

Table 10.9 Districts Where the Customer Penetration Levels Are High (₹ in Billion)

Previous Rank	District	Portfolio Rank	GLP March 2016	GLP March 2015	Active Lenders	Active Loans (Million)	Average Loan (2015–16; Thousand)	% Loans for Income Generation	% of Economically Active Women (2016)	% of Economically Active Women (2015)
10	Nagpur (MH)	5	8.28	5.13	33	0.613	20–23	16.9	35.53	24.72
	Wardha	92	2.97	1.99	31	0.231	20–23	17.59	47.68	31.38
5	Coimbatore (TN)	6	7.98	5.47	35	0.575	20–23	24.64	43.95	34.33
14	Thanjavur (TN)	11	7.31	4.99	28	0.563	20–23	27.08	62.27	45.61
19	Madurai (TN)	24	5.42	3.73	28	0.442	17–20	30.84	40.58	32.74
72	Nagapattinam (TN)	48	3.88	2.24	24	0.3	17–20	30.15	50.05	35.5
50	Thiruvarur (TN)	51	3.79	2.55	28	0.286	20–23	27.43	61.82	42.34
58	Namakkal (TN)	66	3.43	2.44	33	0.268	20–23	28.01	42.41	32.21
	Pudukkottai (TN)	94	2.92	1.95	30	0.244	20–23	25.89	38.72	27.19
15	Mysore (KA)	14	7.02	4.74	22	0.586	17–20	36.04	39.58	28.05

Source: CRIF High Mark.

Scenario 1: There may be stress in a given MFI because of excessive growth, stress on the loan officers to fulfill both acquisition and collection targets which are incentivized, and inadequate appraisals and default. If the default happens with an isolated MFI, then the contagion should not be too difficult to manage. However, if such an institution happens to be systemically important and its products are difficult to differentiate, then the problem might spread to other MFIs as well. The problem would be worse if the institution in trouble happens to be a license holder of an SFB. The reputational risks are high.

Scenario 2: There may be stress in isolated geographies as was reported in *The Wire*, which may be investigated and controlled. For instance, before the 2010 AP crisis happened, we had isolated incidents of default and stress in Kolar, Krishna, and Nizamabad which were brought under control before it spread. However, we also need to remember that Krishna and Nizamabad were precursors of the 2010 AP crisis as well. So any such instance of isolated stress events should ring alarm bells for the MFI sector as a whole.

Scenario 3: A stress in a geographical area that spreads with a domino effect like the AP crisis. Uttar Pradesh, where we have seen an aggressive growth and from where the anecdotal reports have come from, is going in for an election in the near future should be under the watch of the MFI sector. Similarly, the sector should be under the watch for any negative news that could have a political or journalistic fallout.

What is more important is that the data that are being monitored and examined are largely from the regulated mainstream MFIs. However, the players in the microfinance space are much larger than the NBFC-MFIs. We have the SHG programs being run, and they are coming into the database of the CICs in due course. Whether that would be late is for us to wait and watch. Similarly, there are a range of providers who are regulated by the state law (co-ops, Nidhis, and chit funds) and some providers who are pretending to be mainstream but might be unincorporated entities. The negative contagion from their actions—since they might call themselves MFIs—will hit the MFIs. This is an aspect that the MFIs should consider.

Having had a dream run in growth, great valuations, two successful IPOs, eight SFB licenses, one universal bank license, almost no default in spite of the overall stress in the banking sector, and continuous droughts across the country with an agrarian crisis around, the microfinance sector should now be wary, careful, take a breather, and pause. Otherwise, the worst might come true.

THE NEXT GENERATION MFIs

With many large MFIs becoming SFBs, and with the RBI indicating that the bank licenses will be available on tap, it appears that as MFIs grow, the natural progression would be to become an SFB, thereby offering a bouquet of services to the clients. As the MFIs grow to SFBs, they may enter the space for MUDRA as there would be a ceiling of ₹2.5 million only to the extent of 50% of the portfolio, while the rest has no limits. Clearly, there may be some space vacated for the newer entrants and smaller customers. In this sense, it is important to continue to look at smaller institutions that innovate and are reinventing the field. It may be recollected that the current large MFIs were all nurtured initially by the funding and capacity-building by Friends of Women's World Banking (FWWB) and later by SIDBI through its MicroCredit Innovations Department and SIDBI Foundation for Micro Credit. In this regard, Sa-Dhan has taken the initiative to nurture new generation MFIs with the help of SIDBI.

The nurturing will be done by identifying organizations that have a portfolio of less than ₹500 million. In the first stage, the following criteria are tested:

1. Whether these organizations are relevant?
2. Whether their existence will be sustainable?
3. What are the future options for growth and viability?
4. What are the areas of growth and transformation?

Once the information is obtained, there would be a road map for each individual institution looking at a strategic vision plan. These plans would be implemented after examining the growth in portfolio, scope to grow as a BC, and scope for business development. Based on the strategic plan, the following activities are undertaken:

1. Capacity-building through mentor engagement and leveraging the mentor for greater funding opportunities.
2. Human resource component that trains and empathizes people toward the clients.
3. Technical capacity-building program.
4. Facilitating the flow of funds.

SIDBI through its India Microfinance Equity Fund (IMEF) will be making investments in these selected organizations. Sa-Dhan is working with about 25 new generation MFIs in the 4 states selected for the Poorest State Inclusive Growth (PSIG) program, funded by UK Aid and implemented by SIDBI. The PSIG program is being rolled out in Madhya Pradesh, Bihar, Uttar Pradesh, and Orissa. In addition, the IMEF will also be supporting another 25 emerging MFIs in other states as well.

IN CONCLUSION

There is much action on the MFI front:

- Small organizations are being nurtured.
- Unprecedented investments are coming into the sector.
- Loan funding continues to flow from the banking sector, while the rest of the credit offtake in the rest of the economy is moderate.
- There is a policy support that is allowing MFIs to morph into banks and the first generation MFIs are moving toward becoming banks.
- And at the same time, there is concern that the sector is growing too fast, experiencing stress, and may be on the verge of another crisis.

These are times to tread cautiously and with great amount of thought.

REFERENCES

Dogra, C.S. 2016, January 15. "Why Microfinance Is Becoming a Bad Word All Over Again." *The Wire*. Available at: http://thewire.in/18937/why-microfinance-is-becoming-a-bad-word-all-over-again (Accessed on August 17, 2016).

MFIN (Microfinance Institutions Network). 2016. "Microfinance Industry: Growth and Stress." White Paper. Gurgaon: MFIN.

MFIN and Sa-Dhan. 2015. *Code of Conduct for Microfinance Industry.* Gurgaon: MFIN.

RBI (Reserve Bank of India). 2016, January 14. "Credit Information Reporting of all SHGs." Notification. Mumbai: RBI. Available at: https://rbidocs.rbi.org.in/rdocs/notification/PDFs/C29131BD0B179E4747D-099BB4F72394F5FEE.PDF (Accessed on August 25, 2016).

Sa-Dhan. 2016, September. *Bharat Microfinance Report 2016*. New Delhi: Sa-Dhan.

Srinivasan, N. 2008. *Microfinance India: State of the Sector Report 2008*. New Delhi: SAGE Publications. Available at: http://inclusivefinanceindia.org/uploads/publication_link_files/state-of-the-sector-report-2008.pdf (Accessed on October 16, 2016).

Sriram, M.S. 2016, January 26. Murmurs of a Fresh Crisis in the Microfinance Sector. *Mint*. Available at: http://www.livemint.com/Opinion/Gn7z2lGvfvw-goyjxByRHpO/Murmurs-of-a-fresh-crisis-in-the-microfinance-sector.html (Accessed on August 17, 2016).

MFIs to Banks: The Continuing Story of Transformation[1]

11

Chapter

INTRODUCTION

The last year had seen the announcement of a two new categories of differentiated banks being announced, of which SFBs created an excitement in the inclusive finance space. Following the final guidelines (see Box 11.1), 10 players were given an in-principle approval to set up SFBs. They were expected to adhere to all the conditions of the licensing in an 18-month timeframe and convert the in-principle license into a final license. Of the 10 players, 8 players were NBFC-MFIs, 1 was a LAB, and another was an NBFC. The Capital Local Area Bank was the first to get the final license and they also started operating as an SFB from April 2016. Equitas was also accorded a final license, and they have started operating as a bank from September 2016. The other players are in the process of going through all the preparatory work in order to launch their respective SFBs in due course, before the end of the financial year. This report will cover the process of moving from an NBFC to an SFB, and the issues, concerns, and plans of all the players.

Box 11.1 Deputy Governor of RBI N.S. Vishwanathan on SFBs

If you have noticed, our draft guidelines for these banks were initially titled as small banks—basically signaling that the size of the institution would be small, such as the RRBs and the LABs. But the final guidelines and the in-principle licenses were given to SFBs, thereby signaling that it was not the size of the institution, but the nature of the portfolio that we were expecting the new institutions to target. It is not that financial inclusion is seen as an obligation to these institutions, but it is seen as the core business for the institutions. Therefore, in most matters, the SFBs enjoy similar privileges as the universal banks, including the ability to grow geographically and on the balance sheet. All minor changes in the regulatory design should be seen as intended to ensure that the SFBs keep focus on their core business and maintain local touch even while having a national footprint.

CONCEPTUAL ISSUES[2]

Unlike the other institutions which have a well-settled format, SFBs are new and, therefore, some of the design principles need to be addressed. First, it is a significant leap from the traditional MFI business. While the MFI business helped the institutions to acquire customers who would affect the assets side of the balance sheet, a bank gave access to customers who would deposit their savings, which affected the liabilities side of the balance sheet as well. And, in case of a bank, the safety of the deposits of small and diverse set of savers (on the liabilities side) needs to be protected by ensuring that the assets side of the balance sheet is safe. Any lending institution would be exposing itself to some credit

[1] The author is thankful to Professor Janat Shah, Director, IIM Udaipur, for organizing a workshop of SFBs where much of the issues were discussed. Thanks are also due to N. S. Vishwanathan, Deputy Governor, RBI, who spent a day with all the SFB licensees and clarified much of the regulatory aspects.

[2] Based on an address by N.S. Vishwanathan, Deputy Governor, RBI, in an interaction with the chief executives of organizations that have received in principle licenses to set up SFBs.

risks. Credit risk could take the nature of having a geographic concentration risk, asset concentration risk, or a portfolio risk. In case of MFIs, post-AP crisis in 2010, most MFIs focused on addressing the geographic concentration risk. The asset concentration risk was never there because the MFIs never lent a significant amount to a single borrower. Even the NBFC-MFI regulations which imposed a loan limit per borrower of ₹0.1 million prohibited this from happening. However, this risk would become real as they become banks and as they are permitted to lend any amount for half of their portfolio. The one risk that the MFIs suffered was the portfolio risk—this was termed as "though not putting all the eggs in the same basket, but keeping all the baskets in the same place."

In addition to this, there are market risks which emanate from the mismatch between the cost of funds and the yield from the deployment. The cost of funds is a function of the tenor of the deposits as well as the rate at which they are contracted, and tend to be sticky because mid-tenor correction of interest rates is not possible. However, the assets may be repriced in a floating rate scenario, thereby making income generating assets more volatile in movement compared to the liabilities. The mismatch in the tenor of assets and liabilities also adds another layer of risks.

Then there are operational risks which get heightened in case of SFBs because of the need to realign from the existing systems as an MFI to a new system of banking. This could be not only human resource related re-alignment problem, but also information technology related realignment problem. In addition there could be other operational risks.

The most important would be the liquidity risk. Banking is one business where the liquidity risk could quickly convert itself into a solvency risk as there could be a run on the bank. While there are systems to have adequate liquidity through statutory liquidity ratios and cash reserve ratios, these will trigger themselves in crisis situation, but still may not be sufficient to prevent a collapse. Therefore, it is necessary for institutions exposed to such risk to be very closely regulated and supervised.

From the previously mentioned points, it is very clear that the concept of an SFB is significantly different from that of an MFI. While most of the SFB licensees have been awarded the in-principle licenses in recognition of their business model of working in the inclusive finance space, their operations as banks will be fundamentally different, and a preparation to migrate to this environment was the issue that the players were grappling during the year.

In addition to the conceptual issues that involved the design of the organization, there were other conditions that were to be met before the RBI accorded a final license.

ISSUES IN TRANSITION

There are multiple concerns and issues in transitioning from the current form to a regulated entity. The top line issues that affect the SFBs are discussed in this section.

Branch Licensing

First, unlike in the NBFC, opening of branches have to be approved by the RBI to the extent that the SFBs have at least 25% of their branches in rural unbanked locations. Unlike in the case of PBs where the presence has been defined as touchpoints, in case of SFBs, the definition of a branch is that of a traditional brick and mortar branch, and once a location is declared as a branch it is bound to offer certain services. While there could be discussions on what should entail a branch in the era of digital services being provided on the palm through mobile banking, the policy has to evolve. The autonomy that the players had in strategizing their delivery models depending on the location will have to undergo a change with these entities moving into a regulated and supervised status.

While the RBI seems to have given some dispensation to Bandhan Bank to define its rural branches as doorstep service centers, there are concerns on how light a branch could be and what does a physical presence entail. This seems to be an issue with some of the players who are predominantly operating in urban areas. With more and more banks jostling for the same space, are the "unbanked" locations where one could do economic activity in dearth? The RBI is clear that there would be no forbearance on any of the aspects that were a part of the guidelines on which the licenses were issued. However, if there is a change in how it sees the emerging technology, the interoperable white label business correspondent network, and connect with the customers, it is possible that the RBI looks at that issue comprehensively. However, when the RBI looks into this issue, it is also considering the dichotomous request of wanting to do technology led banking in rural areas, while wanting traditional bank branches in urban areas—areas where technology could be deployed more effectively.

However, the branch licensing policy is a significant step ahead compared to the policy adopted with LABs, where the licensing was more stringent both in examining the case-to-case requirements as well as in applying the ratio that was applicable to the universal banks.

Priority Sector Lending Requirements

One significant issue where the SFBs are different from the universal banks pertains to the priority-sector lending norms. Unlike the universal banks, which need to have 40% of the ANBC in the priority sector, the target for SFBs is 75%. However, the sub-targets for agriculture and micro-enterprise loans are the same as applicable to the universal banks. While as of now there are no issues in achieving the targets because most of the entities are in the business that would be defined as priority sector, there was a question on whether this could be an issue going forward, particularly if some of the entities fall marginally short of the target—whether that shortfall could be achieved through purchase of securitized assets from other NBFCs. While the universal banks are allowed, as per the current guidelines, the SFBs will not be allowed to make up their shortfalls through such purchases. The logic for disallowing is clear—this is the differentiator in the SFBs as that is expected to be the core business.

However, there may be a favorable forbearance if the SFB has achieved 75% target overall but is unable to achieve some sub-targets which needs to be topped up. Similarly, there may be a forbearance if standard assets are bought from NBFCs (after having achieved the targets) to manage portfolio risks.

During the interim period of grandfathering, where the NBFC-MFIs have borrowed from another universal bank, only the bank would be eligible to claim the targets. The new SFBs will be able to claim the achievements on priority sector only on incremental lending.

Scheduling of Banks

A significant issue that is of concern for the SFBs is that they are not being accorded a scheduled status. While the universal banks get scheduled from the day the commence operations, the RBI has indicated that scheduling is not a right and the process will start after due examination of the operations. This affects the business of the banks in multiple ways and the SFBs will have to deal with those issues in the short run till they get the status of a scheduled bank.

Scheduling is important for the banks to access deposits from governments and public institutions; there are issues pertaining to availing of refinance facilities including from MUDRA and NABARD. However, this issue seems to be a routine aspect that the RBI will address in due course.

Basel Applicability and Capital Requirements

Overall, it is expected that the SFBs would be subjected to BASEL II norms for risk-weighting of assets. The capital adequacy requirements of the SFBs are higher, representing the riskiness of the assets. However, as there would be a price premium on these loan assets, it is expected that the returns would be good enough to service the increased capital requirement. The idea of making Basel norms applicable is to have the capital to be sensitive to risks.

Loan Products

As of now, most NBFC-MFIs are offering completely unsecured loans. Going forward as banks, while there is no specified limit on unsecured loans, it would be appropriate to have a mix of loans. The risk involved in lending is known. The new banks will have to have a framework where risk is measured, known risks are mitigated, there is knowledge on loans going bad, and they have to be managed. Each of the loan products have to factor in the risk premium in pricing. The major issue would be the obverse. Once the SFBs move to the micro-enterprises segment (some of the MFIs like Equitas are already there), they are mandated to give loans without collateral as they are covered under the Credit Guarantee Trust of Micro and Small Enterprises. The issue is whether the SFBs could take a token collateral for signaling the seriousness. However, the rules on this part of the portfolio seem to be clear in prohibiting the banks from obtaining collaterals. The operational aspects of the loan products will also have to align with the facilities and restrictions available to the banking system. That is one change that the transitioning organizations will have to grapple with.

Last-mile Connectivity

One issue that is important in the transition is about how the SFB touches the customers. The legacy issues point to the fact that NBFC-MFIs had a large number of credit officers who were paid much lesser than a typical bank employee, to do the plain vanilla function of collections at the meeting point. This had a significant cost advantage and brought in tremendous amount of efficiency in the operations. As these players transition to an SFB format, the question of how to do this last-mile connectivity with the small ticket microfinance clients in an inexpensive and efficient format remains. One option to do this is to have a business correspondent network, where all the current credit officers who do not make the cut to the mainstream banking activity could be transitioned. As of now, the norms do not permit the SFBs to promote subsidiaries to operate as BCs. While this is not permissible as of now, the indications were that the RBI may be willing to be considerate and accord a permission if the case were to be made.

Client Protection Issues in the New Dispensation

One of the major concerns to be discussed is the client protection framework. Given that most of the NBFC-MFIs will continue to operate significantly in the inclusion market, there is an expectation of a very large overlap with the MFI customers. Currently the post-Malegam guidelines are applicable only to NBFC-MFIs. These guidelines include that the clients should not be indebted beyond ₹100,000 from all sources at the time of making the loan, their household income levels should be less than ₹100,000 and ₹160,000 per annum in rural and urban areas respectively, and a maximum of two NBFC-MFIs can lend to one customer either directly or through a group. These norms will not be applicable to the new banks, while a large part of the customers may migrate to the bank. If we consider Bandhan which became a bank last year and the eight large MFIs that are becoming SFBs, we see that about 60% of what could have been considered as the MFI portfolio would have moved to the banking system. This has implications for how customers would be handled in SFBs and also how the MFIs process the data to understand indebtedness and sources of borrowing of their clients.

The data discussed in Chapter 10 on MFIs shows that there is significant growth in the MFI sector during the past few years. This has been achieved on a large base, without a concurrent growth in the number of offices and employees leading to the belief that there might be overleveraging. This is the situation in which client protection issues assume paramount importance. There have been reports of ghost lending, pipelining, and some defaults. There have been attempts to understand the heat points. MFIN has been receiving calls on its helpline that seem to indicate underlying problems. This needs to be managed carefully to avoid another AP-like situation.

The issue for consideration are broadly pertaining to reporting, monitoring, supervising, and if need be, taking action. Given that there is a dichotomy on the supervisory and regulatory framework, it is necessary to address the issues and either the players come to a negotiated dialogue or the regulator (the RBI) to step in. If we were to follow the spirit of the NBFC-MFI guidelines, basically, the customer protection points are coming from three concerns that were expressed during the AP crisis: multiple lenders leading to over indebtedness, coercive recovery practices, and usurious interest rates. The notification addresses these problems by defining who the customers of MFIs could be—by defining income levels; how much could they borrow—by defining overall indebtedness and number of lenders and the interest they are charged, by putting an overall interest rate cap, as well as a margin cap.

Now that the MFIs are migrating to become SFBs, they would be taking their legacy customers who are a part of the asset book with them. Which means both Bandhan Bank and the SFBs will continue to have the MFI clients, now defined as customers of the banking system. While the form of organization has changed, in spirit, the issues remain. Therefore, there is a need to re-look at the wording and applicability of the two-lender norm, to take it beyond two NBFC-MFIs to two formal-sector lending institutions.

In addition, there are issues pertaining to the reporting to credit bureaus and the data provided by the credit bureaus. While the RBI guidelines specify that irrespective of which credit bureau the NBFC-MFIs have a subscription, the credit data is to be uploaded to all the credit bureaus. Similarly, there is a need to move to a situation where the credit data of each individual borrower is captured in an integrated manner and provided when a query is raised. There are doubts on whether the data of the MFI clients are being provided only to the extent of the MFI-related loans or whether the person is being mapped across all sources of borrowing. A clarity on this issue is urgently needed. The Aditya Puri Committee (RBI 2014) has made some important recommendations with regard to the information sharing—not only with regard to the NBFC-MFI clients, but also with the clients of the financial system in general. This report was submitted in January 2014 and some highlights as applicable to NBFC-MFI customers and customers transiting to SFBs are captured in Box 11.2.

Box 11.2 Extract from Aditya Puri Committee Report on Credit Information Sharing

Adequate amount of quality information on counterparties is a critical component of financial infrastructure. Reducing the information asymmetry between lenders and borrowers will provide a fillip to growth of credit, especially among disadvantaged sections of society, and foster financial inclusion and inclusive growth. An efficient system of credit information sharing reduces cost of intermediation. It allows banks to effectively price, target, and monitor loans and thereby enhances competition in the credit market. It also reduces credit defaults benefitting consumers with reduction in average interest rates. The overall systemic impact would be better quality of credit portfolios freeing the capital for further credit growth and thus deepening of credit markets. Additionally, it promotes objective and transparent scrutiny/processing of credit proposals making the process less expensive. Aiding and enabling bank supervisors to monitor build-up of systemic risks including in sensitive and unregulated sectors is another positive outcome from credit information.

When enquiry is made with one CIC, a specified user will get only such information that has been provided to the CIC by its members, which may not include all credit institutions which have an exposure to the borrower. The committee recommends that all commercial banks, RRBs, LABs, and financial institutions, including HFCs and SFCs, may become members of all CICs. Cooperative banks and NBFCs with asset base of ₹100 crore and above may become members of all CICs. Others may be encouraged to become members of all CICs. CICs may make membership fees and annual fees as low as possible.

Data quality issues result in rejection of data at the CIC level. These arise mainly on account of lack of a widely accepted unique identifier. There is also no check and monitoring of poor quality of data resulting in repeated rejections. To get over this problem, data submitted by credit institutions should be populated with at least one of the commonly used identifier fields. The other measures include CICs sharing with banks the logic and validation processes involved, parameterizing the reasons for rejection and circulating among the credit institutions, making rejection reports simple and understandable, and stipulating a timeframe for rectification of rejections and for uploading of data by credit institutions.

Providing customers with a free copy of their CIRs would help create awareness about the need to have credit discipline, enable customers to correct their behavior and improve their score well before they plan to avail fresh credit of any kind, help identify identity theft at an early stage, help CICs correct and validate their database, and increase their business in the long run. The RBI may consider implementing the recommendation in due course.

When CIRs on the same borrower are accessed by more than one specified user simultaneously, say, within a period of one month, an alert may be provided by the CIC to all the specified users who have drawn the reports to avoid multiple financing for the same purpose/to avoid fraudulent transactions.

Source: RBI (2014).

ROLLOUT PLANS: UPDATE FROM BANDHAN BANK

The MFIs that are transforming into SFBs are making significant plans. These will be discussed in this part. However, it may be good to start with an update on the Bandhan story—though Bandhan is not transforming to an SFB, its learnings are equally applicable to SFBs as well.

THE JOURNEY OF BANDHAN BANK

In the last report, we had traced the story of conversion of Bandhan MFI into Bandhan Bank. Bandhan Bank started operations as a bank in August 2015 and by the time this report goes to the press, the bank would have had one year of operations. While this has not been the first instance across the world where an MFI has converted into a bank, the journey of Bandhan seems to be distinctly different.

There have been three high-profile instances where institutions that were initially in the microfinance space operated universal banks. The first instance was that of Bangladesh Rural Action Committee (BRAC), which had and continues to run a very successful microfinance program. In 2001, BRAC promoted and established BRAC Bank Limited. However, unlike the other microfinance experiments, BRAC did not fold in its microfinance activities into the bank. Instead, BRAC continued its microfinance activities, clearly identifying that the strategy toward microfinance needs to be different from banking for other categories of customers. BRAC conceptualized this aspect in Figure 11.1. As can be seen in the figure, the pinnacle of the triangle given in the figure represents the SME sector. The BRAC Bank, established as a new independent entity, (adequately ringfenced from BRAC) was designed to cater to the SME sector and segments beyond that and undertake mainstream commercial banking. Two other examples worth discussing here is that of BancoSol and Compartamos.

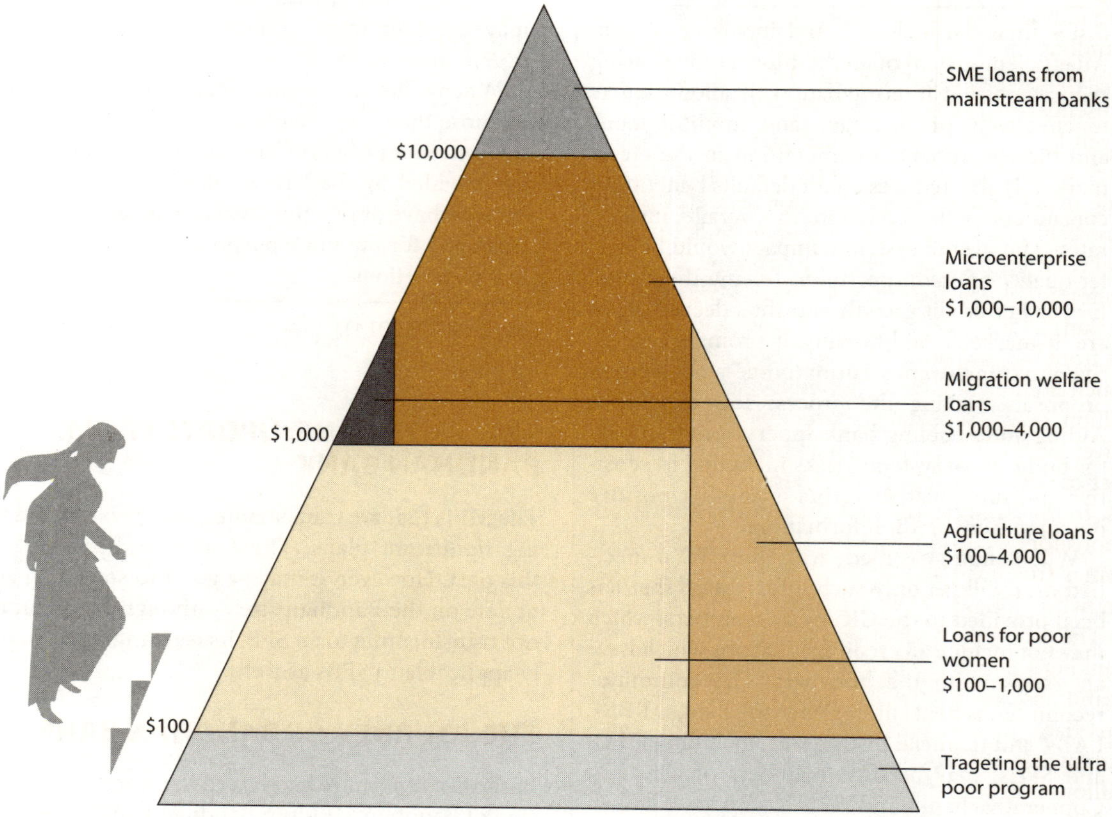

Figure 11.1 Slicing of Microfinance Market and Determining the Limits: BRAC

Source: BRAC Website. 2016, http://brac.net/microfinance-programme/item/855-overview, accessed on April 29, 2016.

The Bancosol experiment indicated a classic clash between the original mandate of serving the smaller clients and the commercial imperatives of the listed bank. The clash of ideologies between the original promoters and the later investors was resolved with the revival of the microfinance program of PRODEM.

In the case of Compartamos, much of the criticism was that the original NGO and its promoters themselves actively took the bank toward commercialization.

Bandhan Bank has till now escaped the criticism of moving away from its traditional clients and there might be a lesson in how Bandhan is maintaining its core strength for the other MFIs ready to convert as SFB.

In the past year, we had identified the initiatives taken by Bandhan in involving its client base in bringing in about ₹10 billion of deposits by asking its 10 million customers to bring in at least ₹1,000 per head as deposits. However, the limitation of collecting savings from the customers who are borrowing from Bandhan was evident—it could give a good starting point, but it would not really lead to growth on the liabilities side.

As of now, Bandhan continues to be a bank with a very significant part of its loan book in the inclusive finance space. Its portfolio in the year ending 2015 was about ₹100 billion, which has grown to ₹150 billion by financial year 2015–16. The book growth of clients that cannot be classified as inclusive finance is about ₹1.5 billion—a really miniscule proportion of 1% compared to the overall base. This means that as a strategy Bandhan is naturally expanding in the segment that knows how to serve and is very cautiously expanding to other sectors. Mr Chandra Shekhar Ghosh in an interview said,

> as long as there is adequate scope for deployment of the resources we raise in the traditional markets that we know, there is no need to look for other market segments. In any case I do not want to expose the deposits of smaller customers to large corporates. (Ghosh 2016)[3]

[3] Ghosh, Chandra Shekhar (2016), personal communication with the author, April 29, 2016.

In addition to direct lending to microfinance, Bandhan has also lent small amounts to other MFIs in areas where Bandhan does not have a strong presence—particularly in the South. The argument given by Ghosh is that microfinance is a business they understand best. Of the portfolio that is outside of the microfinance definition, half of it is in affordable housing, vehicle finance, and commercial vehicles, while the rest is deployed in the MSME sector, including bulk loans to other MFIs.

Bandhan Bank has also been able to raise deposits from the customers to the extent of ₹120 billion, much higher than the expected target of about ₹30 billion. While about a little over 20% of the deposits have come in as current and savings deposits, the rest of the deposits are in the form of fixed deposits. In the fixed deposits, about a third is from bulk depositors, while a large two-thirds of the deposits comes from retail depositors from their 600 urban branches opened across the country.

The legacy borrowings of Bandhan MFI from the banking system was about ₹90 billion which was grandfathered and folded into Bandhan Bank. Of this liability, Bandhan Bank has repaid the legacy borrowing of Bandhan MFI to the extent of ₹60 billion through the mobilization of fresh deposits (while also growing the loan book). In seven months of commercial operations, Bandhan Bank has been able to add one million new customers, mostly depositors at the branches. In one way, the transition of Bandhan into a bank as of now has a split—with the traditional branches doing most of the liabilities side of the business (deposits) and the door step branches basically managing the assets side of the business.

However, because of its banking license, Bandhan Bank has also been able to add three additional services to its customers going through the door step banking channel: a basic savings account, option to have a fixed deposit, and remittances. Raising deposits from the "inclusive" customers is more about putting the habit of savings rather than about having a target of raising deposits. One way in which this is being done is to encourage the borrowers to deposit the difference between the instalments due and the rounded amounts they get for loan repayments into the deposit accounts.

As of now, Bandhan Bank, by following its traditional model of inclusive finance, also has surplus achievements on its priority sector lending targets which can be traded as PSLCs. This could be another smaller source of income for the bank.

Bandhan Bank continues to operate significantly as a bank in the inclusive finance space and needs to be tracked as it evolves its loan book.

ROLLOUT PLANS: UPDATE FROM OTHER SFB LICENSEES

Ujjivan

The major issue for Ujjivan in the transition was to reduce foreign holdings to bring it in line with requirements for the final license. These were issues common to most of the MFIs but only two of the MFIs took to the markets to address the issue. The idea was that the existing company would go in for a public offering of shares, raise resources to ensure that there was adequate capital, and invest the proceeds downstream into a new company which would be a wholly owned subsidiary. The business of the current NBFI-MFI would be transferred to the new company which would apply for an SFB license. The holding company would then remain as an investment company with no other operations. Box 11.3 gives details of the transition plan. Figure 11.2 gives the transition path from a predominantly foreign-owned company to a domestic company, as required by the licensing norms.

Box 11.3 Transition of Ujjivan into SFB

Proposed Transition to the SFB Regime

- The transformation work in the business front is continuing in full force, and had commenced before the in-principle license was issued. Ernst & Young was appointed as the consultants for the overall project. On the technology front, key additions to the current infrastructure are in progress. We are in the process of implementing the Finacle core banking and treasury systems from Infosys, CRM solution from CRM-Next, mobility solutions from I-Exceed, comprehensive risk management system from SAS, upgrading the human resource module from RAMCO, and Oracle Accounting System, hardware from Oracle, CISCO, and so on and Wipro has been engaged as the system integrator.
- Extensive work is in progress on the human resources side where key management positions at the leadership level have largely been filled and the second level recruitment is in progress. Competence mapping of existing staff for various positions in the SFB has also been undertaken. Training programs are proposed to be held during the six months prior to the launch. IT training has already commenced. Along with this, we have started a 'mindset change' training

for existing staff from a loan-giving institution to that of an institution which will provide a full range of services including savings.

- We plan to consolidate our existing branches and convert them to full service SFB branches. We will open the required number of new unbanked rural branches (UBRB) over the year as per the SFB guideline requirement. Considerable research and planning has gone into the location of the UBRBs. We see this as a new business opportunity. These branches will be designed to meet the requirements and aspirations of our target customers. The physical infrastructure of all these branches will require considerable investment and time. We understand that the RBI is planning to come up with a comprehensive policy on new branches later this year. We hope this will give us leeway to pace our branch conversion to ensure that we can do this in a feasible and viable manner.
- In order to provide the customers multiple channels/access points, we will supplement the branches with alternate delivery vehicles such as ATMs, phone banking, banking correspondents, and also Internet banking. This is also being planned to be executed in a phased manner.
- On the product side, we have undertaken considerable research on the savings habits, likes, and dislikes of the target market customers. We are designing the products and services accordingly. In addition, we are working on remittances and third-party insurance products which will be launched in a phased manner. We are also enhancing our loan products for the SME sector.

Source: Ujjivan (2016), p. 11.

In terms of business, Ujjivan expects to continue with its core strength of microfinance loans and the other product it currently has and gradually grow other businesses.[4] The new products on offer would be personal loans and products linked to the liability side—an OD product on current and savings accounts. Unlike others in the microfinance space, Ujjivan is not very enthusiastic about offering vehicle finance and gold loans, at this time. However, there is intent to catch up on the MSME as well as the housing segment. While Ujjivan wants to convert half of its current branches into full-fledged branches and covert the rest into smaller micro-banking units (like the doorstep centers of Bandhan Bank),

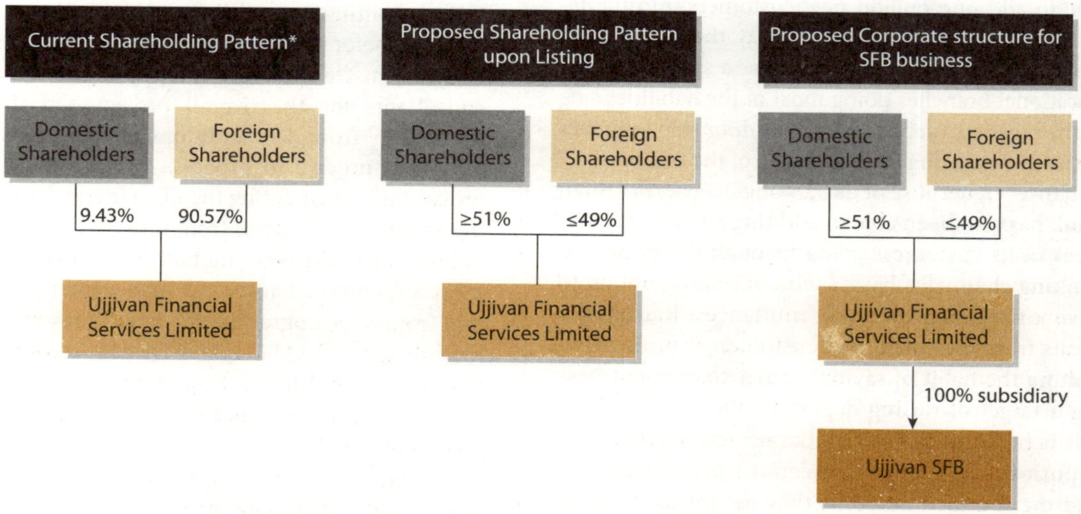

Figure 11.2 Transition to a Domestically Owned and Controlled Entity

Source: Ujjivan (2015), 116.
*Without considering the dilutive impact of outstanding employee stock options
Notes: i. ≥ means greater than or equal to.
ii. ≤ means less than or equal to.

[4] This portion of the write up is based on two research reports: *Ujjivan Financial Services: A Confluence of Positives by HDFC Securities*, June 27 2016 and *Systematix Institutional Equities*, July 18, 2016.

there seems to be a regulatory road block in doing this. There are issues on opening 25% branches in unbanked rural areas and the nature of a micro-banking unit versus the full-fledged branches needs to be sorted out. While the branches that generate assets is not so much a problem in terms of viability because of the pricing premium, if they were to concentrate on liability products disproportionately, that would turn out to be expensive.

On deposits, Ujjivan hopes to tap in to its existing customers and get new customer—largely focusing on term deposits. This follows an assumption that there are large amounts of resources lying around in the proximate areas where Ujjivan operates, and these resources are held by people who are unserved or underserved. There would be significant investments in technology that would possibly facilitate reaching customers through nonconventional digital channels.

On the human resources front, while the company plans to continue its own employees and only hire on the basis of need, it recognizes the need for retraining and re-orienting the employees toward banking. In this regard, Ujjivan has tied up with Manipal Academy for its training needs. Similarly, the technology architecture is to be re-engineered, which Ujjivan is managing through an outsourced integrator.

Equitas

Equitas started its operations as an NBFC-MFI, but as it grew it had three companies doing distinct businesses, and all these three companies were integrated through a common holding company which owned them as subsidiaries. While the core business that Equitas started with was microfinance, the other two companies were doing asset financing and housing finance. The asset financing company was significantly involved in vehicle finance, but was also doing financing small and micro-enterprises that went beyond the regulated limits that a microfinance company could do. This arrangement was done through an agreement between the microfinance company and an asset finance company where the microfinance company would refer its 'graduating' customers to the asset finance company for a fee, and the acquiring company would then do the due credit check and legal due diligence. The process of diversification of Equitas portfolio was done five years back, and by the time they applied for an SFB license, the microfinance business was only about 50% of the book.

Equitas as a group had 540 branches operating and another 40 branches would be added during the financial year 2015–16 and all these would eventually be converted as bank branches. Right from the beginning, Equitas was a very urban-based microfinance company, with only about 30% of its branches located in rural areas. This serves the transition process well, since the SFB licensing norms requires the bank to have 25% of its branches in rural/unbanked areas. As an SFB, Equitas intends to (and is required to) merge these three verticals and bring them under a single umbrella. This would give the SFB a ready and diversified portfolio. All the loans currently being made by the Equitas group are of ticket sizes less than ₹2.5 million, and all the loans made by the organization are classified as priority sector. Thus, Equitas readily complies with both the significant norms laid out for SFBs on the portfolio size and the proportion of portfolio being exposed to priority sector. Of the 580 branches, Equitas proposes to convert 400 branches to acquire liability products as well, while the remaining would be pure lending branches. The decision is based on the potential and ability to raise deposits.

The other challenge that Equitas—and all other converting entities have—is to replace bank borrowings in the NBFC with their own deposits in the bank. While the RBI has permitted grandfathering (holding the bank borrowings on books till they mature, while raising incremental public deposits), Equitas may not opt for this facility. With the issue of equity and augmentation of resources, it is possible for Equitas to replace the borrowing with its own sources of funds within a short time from the commencement of operations. That Equitas has a significant part of its microfinance operation in urban areas, and the other businesses are in urban locations, makes the task that much easier. However, Equitas estimates that its clients will fill up the liabilities side of the balance sheet by not more than 15–20%, while another 20–25% of deposits might come from proximate areas. They will have to get the rest of the resources from nonclient segments using different models to reach out to them since it is costly to do small value transactions.

In the pilots that Equitas is presently running in using to do the liability products, it is finding the channel challenging. It is expensive, given the small transaction size and the stickiness of the pricing and the reputation risk as the principal is significant, if it is on deposit products. So the channel has to be carefully calibrated to ensure that there is a good mix of both products and enough incentives for the channel to gain income on the assets, while offering liability agency on a thinner margin. This would evolve over a period of time.

The challenges for Equitas and other SFBs would be more about the nature of the portfolio that remains unsecured and the additional capital cover that it needs to provide in order to maintain the capital adequacy under the Basel norms. There are other general challenges that face the SFB and microfinance sector as a whole which will be discussed later.

Janalakshmi

Janalakshmi had applied to be a universal bank in the last round, but failed to obtain a license. Since the roadmap for SFBs also indicate the possibility of moving to be a universal bank in future, they would like to have their structure in a way that the transition becomes easier in future. However, due to the high foreign holding, Janalakshmi had to go through a two-tier structure for holding the operating entity—the Janalakshmi SFB.

Janalakshmi had focused on technology even as an SFB—first having a CBS for itself. The technology platform and the payments-led analytics are outsourced to IBM, the office operations is managed by Accenture. The customer acquisition and identification KYC module is with Janalakshmi themselves. While it is more expensive to outsource, this call was a strategic choice. Janalakshmi believes that in a large market, the most challenging issue is the execution story. The model is to ensure that both the employees and customers have a certain amount of stickiness and are with the company for a longer time. Even in terms of risks, Janalakshmi sees the risks mostly as operational and product rollout risk rather than credit and portfolio risk. Therefore, it believes that a very strong operational control framework would help in keeping the model more profitable.

As Janalakshmi moves to be a bank, its operating strategy will not undergo a significant change. The only challenge would be on two aspects—garnering deposits and opening UBRBs), given that their current business model is predominantly urban. While Janalakshmi hopes to be on target as far as UBRBs are concerned, on the resources side, they plan to use neighborhood kirana stores as business correspondents. For the model to be viable, there must be enough touchpoints to provide access, and at the same time adequate business for each one of them. This balance is something that Janalakshmi has learnt to achieve over a period of time. These stores will be a BC not only managing both the stock and flow of the business.

In addition to the existing products, Janalakshmi intends to move from microfinance to micro-enterprises and housing. In addition, it is looking at larger businesses where it could have an exposure of more than ₹2.5 million per customer. On the liabilities side, it intends to mop up deposits using the kirana-BC model in addition to raising bulk deposits.

The model of Janalakshmi will be technology led, but with a human touch at the last mile. Since a significant part of the business is outsourced to specialized agency, they intend to have a strong ombudsman system. The argument is that if they are purely Fintech-led bank, then there is no advantage, vis-à-vis the Fintech players—they need to have a human touch which gives the competitive edge. The question is how to design this element into the business model. In general, Janalakshmi seemed to have lesser back-end issues in transition and have ambitious plans to rollout as a bank. Possibly this is because the thinking about being a mainstream bank started much earlier than the others.

Utkarsh

Utkarsh is the smaller of the MFIs that have got an SFB license. Unlike the SFBs discussed elsewhere in this chapter, Utkarsh looks at transitioning into a bank in a very seamless manner as far as the business model is concerned. They intend to have only three business verticals—the microfinance business, the smaller of the MSMEs, and housing. As per their plans, even after five years of setting up the bank, the microfinance portfolio is expected to have the largest share of about 58% of their portfolio. Utkarsh also plans to continue offering third-party products like insurance. Utkarsh is working with two large consultants in the transition process—with KPMG for regulatory risk, compliance, audit, and project management while P.J. Nayak is helping them with their business strategy. On the other services, including technology, Utkarsh believes that the medium-sized service providers are providing more value for money than the larger ones. Utkarsh is going with Intellect—a product supplied by Polaris for their CBS.

Utkarsh is uniquely located and will have about 125 new branches, of which 25% will be converted from current MFI branches and the rest would be new. As of now 98%, of their clients are rural and they would like to build on this strength. Most of the branch expansion strategy will depend on how the regulatory forbearance given for satellite branches and service points by the RBI as the guidelines for SFBs evolves.

On the human resources front, Utkarsh believes that the public sector bank employees are very expensive at the lower level and they will have to find a new set of employees to hire for the bank. Even the current employees will have to be reoriented to move toward banking. However, retired bankers seem to be a good source for training and re-orientation programs. Managing employee expectation and litigation falling out as a result of mismatched expectation are the twin challenges in moving from an MFI to a bank. All employees will be on a single track of the bank without any differentiation of MFI and mainstream banking functions.

The other challenges that Utkarsh is facing are pertaining to getting leased accommodation for the offices, with rentals being a large problem that could put questions on the quick break-even of branches.

On the liabilities side, Utkarsh is clear that these resources have to come from the mainstream, and the current clients would not be able to contribute significantly on this product. The idea is to try and get business from RRBs and co-operative banks in the proximate area by offering better service and a premium. It is expected that they can raise ₹18 billion of deposits in about 18 months. As of now, paying a hundred basis points higher than the market is feasible as the pricing on MFI product allows to charge such a premium. However, at a stable state, the competition will have to be purely on the basis of flexibility and service.

Suryoday

Unlike the other players who have had significant structural changes in order to meet the domestic ownership requirements, Suryoday was able to convert the operating entity directly into a bank. While it raised an additional capital, it also locked in the shares of the existing domestic investors for a period of three years to meet the requirements of the RBI guidelines.

Suryoday will open with a net worth of ₹3.5 billion. Suryoday wants to remain small and grow slowly. The idea is to try and learn from the mistakes others do. Much thought has gone into the type and size of branches, and they have come to a conclusion that if there are not many walk in transactions there is no need to have branches which cost in the vicinity of ₹4–5 million. The idea is to use and leverage the current methodology and have simple brick and mortar structures that are minimalistic. The higher the size, the more difficult it will be to be nimble. Therefore Suryoday does not want to get into areas that are not in the comfort zone—like bulk deposits. In their estimate, liquidity risk could be much higher than anticipated and, therefore, it is important to reduce the risk of roll up of liability.

There is a lot to be learnt from the cooperative banks and much to be gained by getting employees from these banks if they are good. Alternatively, since this is a service industry, Suryoday thinks it is a good idea to draw HR from the hospitality industry as well. There is a certain element of customer stickiness to banks because of customer lethargy, but being nimble will help service the customers as well as draw customers from other players.

Suryoday wants to spend about ₹800 million over six years on IT solutions.

The major concerns that Suryoday has is how a couple of large SFBs might change the face of banking in India and its implication on Suryoday. In addition, there is an unknown risk of what happens if there is a failure that results in a contagion. Given that this is a new experiment, a negative fall-out might take a very long time to recover.

ESAF

ESAF does not seem to have a major issue on the raising the necessary capital as per the norms stipulated by RBI. The major challenge for ESAF would be handling of the transition of employees. The cooperative which has been associated closely with ESAF will operate as a BC for the bank. While the organization came from a purely developmental background, and banking is a different field, there is much learning to be done. ESAF sees that this will be the biggest challenge, with the initial euphoria of getting the license waning, there are questions about the role that the old timers could carve out for themselves in the new dispensation. The preference has been on getting internal applications first. For reorientation, the employees are undergoing training in a partnership arrangement with SBI learning center. This gives them banking orientation.

On the business front, the assets side would continue to be predominantly MFI business with new lines in housing, MSME and agriculture added. They intend to pursue a triple bottom line approach with a significant element of service bundled in. In addition there are significant number of inmigrants from the northeast and servicing them would be another opportunity that ESAF is looking at. On the liabilities side, the strategy is to leverage the advantage of being in Kerala and get significant amount non-resident deposits. The guidelines on the status of scheduling and the ability to take non-resident deposits would be important for ESAF as they grow their liabilities side. ESAF is confident that they would be able to get sufficient deposits if they price it right.

On the technology front, they have had multiple advisors, but they have chosen FIS as their partner. FIS is a preferred partner for four of the SFB aspirants.

RGVN

RGVN has a peculiar situation of being located in the most underbanked region of the country and, therefore, carries on itself a great burden to demonstrate that banking is possible in the terrain. It has survived as an MFI fairly successfully and wants to retain the regional flavor as it moves ahead as an SFB. The reason why northeast is embedded in the name is to ensure that the focus on the region remains. It is in an advantageous position as far as the requirements of 25% UBRBs are concerned. It already has 45% branches located in such locations. It currently has 154 microfinance branches which will be converted into regular branches as they go along.

RGVN hopes to continue its portfolio mix. Currently 40% of its outstandings are for agriculture and there are loan offerings for MSME and housing (home improvement) segments. The major challenge for the organization would be to change the mindset from a relatively less regulated NBFC to a bank. Training of the employees is turning out to be a major challenge. As the bank grows, initially they would prefer to focus on building an assets side, while the liabilities side will gradually grow as the bulk loans are wound down. They see Bandhan and Ujjivan as competitors in the region. However, since the name northeast is embedded, they expect that there will be much local support in placing deposits—both by the governments and individuals. They expect people to take pride in the local institution.

The fact that there is relatively less competition in the northeast will help it to grow slowly and steadily. They are willing to remain small and relevant and geographical focused for a long time. They will continue to be engaged with social investors rather than commercial investors for equity, because the operations need patient capital.

Fincare

The back end work of Fincare is significant because it involves the merger of two institutions which had a common investor into one and, therefore, the approvals needed to convert the company into one that fits the guidelines are significant. The organization intends to focus on the geographic focus of South and Western regions. As of now, they are having partnership with banks with more than 35% of the assets under management being originated on behalf of the banks.

The major concerns of Fincare are concerning how the overall ecosystem will pan out as they go forward. The unknown is how the liabilities side will pan out and if there would be any reputational risks of the sector itself. The real differentiator for SFBs would be to ensure that the asset quality is good. They believe that if the asset quality is taken care of, then the liabilities would flow in as people would have greater faith. They, for instance, think that the HDFC model, where the cost structure of liabilities is low, is worth emulating.

AU Financiers

AU Financiers is not an NBFC-MFI. It is an asset financing company which is transitioning into becoming an SFB. The issues that face AU are significantly different from the others both from the back-end capital structure and the front-end assets and liability management. Since AU is a family run organization, the most significant issue was to ringfence other businesses and divest from those businesses.

On the business model, they will have to diversify their product offering and gain domain expertise. While a significant part of the portfolio qualifies for the priority-sector lending category, they have no experience in agricultural lending. However, the tremendous capability of generating nonagricultural priority-sector assets will be the strength. Again, the liabilities side is expected to grow on the basis of a strong assets side. Luckily for AU, their own customers can contribute significantly to the liabilities side of the business.

The challenges for AU are to get diversity and professionalism in governance, ensure that the service levels are tracked, consolidate on the presence in the central and northern regions, and manage data at the customer level and leverage the customer data for more and more asset products. Overall, the intention of AU is to be a retail asset-led bank, with liabilities products priced aggressively and over a period of time stabilize at more moderate prices.

They are having a significant re-look at the internal processes and technology. Accenture has been hired to look at look at the technology platform, EY is looking at the product manuals and risk, and they are also looking at a large re-branding exercise. This has to be done on the run, while the current business should not slow down.

Overall AU faces similar challenges as MFIs but is a notch higher in its customer segment and its challenge would be to meet the statutory requirements of lending to the smaller people.

Capital Small Finance Bank

Capital has had the smoothest transition amongst all the licensees. The fact that they were already a bank ensured that there were no significant issues on the continuing operations. They had to ensure that the holding structure was in compliance with the guidelines and had to augment more capital in order to grow beyond the five districts in which they were operating as an SFB.

The most important challenge in modern banking has been of cross-selling, thereby giving the impression to the customers that these players will sell something that the customer does not want. The challenge is to sell third-party products in an ethical and customer responsive way. Since they were a niche bank and the name was quite well known, the transition has been smooth. Even as a LAB they had 81% of their portfolio in priority sector.

The strength of Capital has been that while at the policy level we are constantly looking for underbanked geographies, Capital has been responsive to underbanked customers. These customers are looking for a nonthreatening friendly place to transact. The core strength of Capital has been on giving great service, growing gradually, expanding contiguously, and keeping the employees in very high spirit and completely aligned with the objectives of the organization. They are an organization to watch.

CONCLUDING NOTES

These are exciting times to be in, with lots of action happening on the transformation from an MFI to an SFB. This is the biggest event after many of the MFIs which started as not-for-profits transformed into for-profit NBFCs. However, this transformation is significantly bridging the gap between the fringe and the mainstream and is to be celebrated. As it can be seen from the individual stories, each of them are adopting a different approach in structuring their organizations as well as in their business model and growth plans. In the next few years, we will be seeing a stabilized model of these organizations working and it will be an interesting aspect to track as the real risks and vulnerabilities and opportunities and profits show up in the segment.

REFERENCES

RBI. 2014. *Report of the Committee to Recommend Data Format for Furnishing of Credit Information to Credit Information Companies.* Mumbai: DBOD, RBI. Available at: https://rbidocs.rbi.org.in/rdocs/PublicationReport/Pdfs/APR220314FS.pdf (Accessed on October 9, 2016).

Ujjivan. 2015, December 31. *Draft Red Herring Prospectus.* Bengaluru: Ujjivan Financial Services Limited. Available at: http://www.sebi.gov.in/cms/sebi_data/attachdocs/1451908310679.pdf (Accessed on August 7, 2016).

———. 2016. *Annual Report 2015–16.* Bengaluru: Ujjivan Financial Services. Available at: http://ujjivan.com/pdf/Ujjivan_Annual_Report_2015-16.pdf (Accessed on August 10, 2016).

Payments Banks and the Challenges[1]

12

Chapter

INTRODUCTION

Last year, the report had listed 11 players as having received the in-principle license to set up PBs. The in-principle approvals for PBs were issued a few weeks before the announcements for SFBs were made. There were lesser applicants to set up these banks, and there was a sense of curiosity and apprehension about the nature of business of these banks. Talking at the 14th SEACEN Executive Committee Meeting in October 2015, Dr Reddy, former Governor RBI, expressed his views about the PBs:

> This is uncharted territory. We had a category known as Residuary Non-Bank Finance Companies (RNBFC), and two such entities out of six accounted for over 70% of total deposit-taking activities in the RNBFC category. They were permitted to take retail deposits across the country and expected to invest the money almost wholly in government securities. RBI viewed them with disfavour and encouraged them to quit and change their business model. But the payment banks are expected to be vastly different in some respects. (Reddy 2015)

Of the 11 who received in-principle approvals, three, namely Cholamandalam Distribution Services, Dilip Shanghvi (in association with Telenor and IDFC Bank), and Tech Mahindra, withdrew their applications and indicated that they would not be going ahead with their plans. Even though the guidelines for both SFBs and PBs were announced the same day, the list of the eligible licensees of PBs was released earlier. The people who got the licenses were the ones with deep pockets and vast experience in business. However, as this report goes to press, only one of the remaining eight (Airtel Money, now Airtel Payments Bank) had received a final license but was yet to commence operations. On the other hand, of the 10 SFBs that had got in-principle approval, 3 had converted this approval into a final license and two of them had already started operations by September 2016.

So, while there was much enthusiasm in the SFB space, there were some concerns in the PB space. The clarity on the business model, the regulatory architecture, and the benchmarks of performance were not clearly available for the PBs. In the light of this, it was but natural that they took a longer time to get their act together. Given the open nature of business, each of the players had varied strategic tie-ups and looked at their roll-out models differently. All of the players also had some concerns about how the regulatory space will pan out.

The guidelines for setting up PBs entail that they are in three broad business lines. Firstly, they can raise savings and current deposits from the customers up to ₹0.1 million. However, the PBs cannot deploy these deposits as credit; instead, they are required to deposit these amounts in safe securities—securities that qualify as statutory liquidity ratio requirements

[1] The author is firstly thankful to Mr P.K. Panda, Principal, College of Agricultural Banking, Pune and Chief General Manager, RBI, for organizing a one-day consultation on PBs which gave a perspective on the recent developments and helped in framing the chapter. Thanks are also due to Mr N.S. Vishwanathan, Deputy Governor, RBI, who spent a day with all the licensees to clear issues pertaining to regulation and to the licensees of PBs for attending the event. The author is also thankful to Ms Anuradha Eswaran, PGP student, class of 2016 at Indian Institute of Management, Bangalore, for her *Contemporary Concerns Study Report* and Ms Srishti Pandey, student of Masters in Public Policy, class of 2016 at the National Law School of India University, for her dissertation—both of which provided significant insights and inputs to this chapter.

and sovereign securities that are traded in the market. The revenue here is the arbitrage between the interest that the PBs pay on the deposits they hold and the interest yield from the investment activities. It is expected that these margins would be modest.

The PBs can be into remittance business and charge a fee on the remittance. This is where most of the players see some revenue coming from. There are two models of revenues here: the remittance on mere transfers, which could be government to individuals (subsidies and benefit transfers); wages; or person-to-person transfers, and payments made by individuals to merchant establishments, whether they are brick-and-mortar enterprises or e-commerce players. In the former, usually the remitter will have to pay a commission, and the amount of commission that the players can charge would be dictated by the market forces. The benchmarks available for such remittance commissions at this time are money order commissions from the postal department, commissions on demand drafts of the commercial banks, and commissions on electronic transfer from the banking system. As of now, some of the transfers in the banking system happen to be free, essentially because these transfers are cross-subsidized by the other facilities offered by the universal banks. They may also be free because the banks want to incentivize their customers to move to electronic forms of transfer from inherently expensive forms such as checks. Either way, the PBs are up against some competitive benchmarks in pricing.

The third source of revenue could be in selling third-party products to the existing customer base—this could be insurance, other financial products, tie up with banks for offering other savings and loan products, as well as mutual funds. This business line has possibilities, but the dos and don'ts of this business line will emerge over a period of time.

Therefore, it is clear that the PBs are actually up against an untested business model. Against this, the opportunities for these banks are immense. These opportunities come from synergies with existing business lines of the companies that have promoted the PBs. Four of the eight surviving licensees are telcos and there is significant synergy in customer on-boarding and leveraging the existing distribution network. The postal department has a network of post offices and postal agents who have been doing both the business of deposit collection and remittances through money orders, and there are possibilities of great synergy. Similarly, FINO PayTech has been a business correspondent to multiple banks and they have their networks in reaching out to a category of customers well laid out. Paytm is one of the most aggressive players in the prepaid wallet segment and has acquired millions of customers (including the banked customers) for its convenience product of mobile-to-mobile payments. As can be seen, each one of these players brings something unique to the table and, therefore, one can expect diverse business models rolling out. Each of the players looks at this space differently and would like to approach the market uniquely.

Box 12.1 Former RBI Governor Dr C. Rangarajan on Payments Banks

MSS: The other thing is that there are two–three new initiatives that the government has taken in the recent past. One is the SFBs and we have talked about it. The other set of institutions are PBs. I have not really fully understood how this would work at scale. Have you seen anything like this? What do you think?

Dr Rangarajan: The emphasis on credit as a significant element of financial inclusion has been pushed to the background. Our original idea of financial inclusion started with the desire and intention to provide credit to the vulnerable groups. I agree that financial inclusion encompasses facilities for savings, transfer of funds, and all that, and these aspects deserve attention. But much of the new initiatives are not credit oriented. Nevertheless, they have a role in the context of programs that have been launched recently, such as DBT schemes. This is not the whole of financial inclusion. Institutions like PBs focus only on one aspect, namely deposit and transfers. They have a partial role in relation to financial inclusion.

MSS: In fact, I have talked to a few people and I hear that they are yet to figure out the revenue model for the long run. There does not seem to be a clear verdict on the viability. Three players have surrendered their licenses.

Dr Rangarajan: There are pure fund transfer institutions like Western Union. Now we have combined it with savings. This combination is not very clear to me. I would have gone for pure payment systems in which the focus is on transfer of funds quickly and efficiently, something that could be a close parallel to Western Union.

MSS: In fact, there are institutions that operate prepaid wallets and possibly they could have been made two-way wallets.

Dr Rangarajan: I think that could have been a better model than combining it with the savings model. Then a question arises if you are paying interest for savings—what is the revenue? They could earn on remittances, what else? Are they allowed to invest in government papers?

MSS: Yes! 100% in government papers. Dr Reddy asked how PBs were different from residuary NBFCs like Sahara? Except that RNBFCs were initially allowed to keep 20% of their deposits in assets. Here, even that is not allowed.

Dr Rangarajan: That is not very convincing.

THE OPERATING ECOSYSTEM: BUSINESS

The three elements to the business ecosystem of PBs have different types of pressures and competitors. The first business ecosystem is about collection of deposits where the PBs are up against the traditional banking system—consisting of commercial banks, RRBs, cooperative banks, and the newly emerging SFBs. The mission mode in which the PMJDY has rolled out, and the possibility that the PMJDY account may be the default account for all DBT, is a challenge to the unique niche that PBs operate in.

While all these players, including the cooperative societies that are not regulated by the RBI, can collect both time and demand deposits, the PBs are constrained in collection-only demand deposits. On the other hand, the PBs are not allowed to build loan assets on the other side but are required to park these deposits in safe securities. In this sense, while they collect deposits like banks, they need to manage those resources like a mutual fund managing just a portfolio of sovereign securities. So, it needs the agility of a commercial bank and the ability of a mutual fund but with strong limitation on what can be done.

The only way out of this is to have strategic partnerships with universal banks—which most of the players have done—which gives the niche small ticket business to the new banks, while they transfer the residual larger business to the universal banks. The only way that this business, which has thin margins, can succeed is to bring out significant operational efficiency at the last mile for small ticket transactions. Here, the PBs are caught in a bit of a bind. It would be expensive to use owned infrastructure to bring in technology-enabled digitally supported transactions. It would be possible to have assisted human interface transactions but that is not going to be inexpensive either. It is possible to ride on the investments made by the existing players, but at this time the charges for use of those facilities are extremely expensive for the type and size of transactions that the PBs have, and it is impossible to transfer the costs to the customers, who alternatively get free services if they opt to be customers of the universal banks.

The universal banks are able to offer these facilities free because the benchmark for these transactions are even more expensive paper-based transactions that they have been historically offering. In any case, the larger banks have the ability to cross-subsidize these transactions from revenues from other streams.

The second business ecosystem is that of remittances. At present, the money order, the money transfer agencies such as MoneyGram and Western Union, and the electronic transfer services of banks and mobile wallets are operating in this space. Each one of these has a different model and some of them have both cash-in and cash-out facilities, while the wallets are closed on one end. The PBs will also have to reckon with technology-enabled, cashless business models as well as products that are emerging in the market. For instance, a big competitor that they would have to reckon with are banks on one hand who have sunk investments in technology for banking that can be leveraged for internet- or mobile-based transactions on a marginal cost basis. Similarly, the new players have to reckon with the people who have significantly invested in technology to provide an interface between a bank account and the last mile transaction, particularly the mobile wallets. Along with this, they have to reckon with the emerging technologies, such as the Unified Payment Interface—which takes the mobile-to-mobile payment that was operated through the Immediate Payment Services to the next user-friendly level. The niche that the PBs will have to draw out would be in assisted digital transactions or in acting as a low-cost last-mile agent for the bigger players. There are multiple issues here both in terms of how the business is structured and regarding the regulatory and the operating environment.

The big business that comes from DBT might just skirt the PBs, given that the state has opened PMJDY accounts on a mission mode. In one sense, PBs are coming in a bit late on the field and might have to make significant inroads to get that part of the pie.

For instance, unlike BCs who are agents of a bank, PBs themselves could be principals. They could appoint agents, and they could also be agents of another principal. These roles have to be defined in a manner that the PB's do not cannibalize their own business and hand it over to their principals. The art in this is to ensure that the last mile is low cost and unique and so specialized that even if the principals or the competitors understand the model, given the framework in which they are operating, they just cannot adapt the systems. Like, for instance, the banks find it impossible to adapt the microfinance model of Grameen replicators because it is so different from the wisdom and structure of the banking corporations. PBs will have to find such a niche. In finding that, they also need a benevolent regulatory environment that allows them to experiment and find their own operating model that is revenue positive.

However, there is immense potential in merchant-based payment systems, which companies like Paytm have taken a lead in. How deeply these applications would penetrate in the inclusive market is a challenge that the PBs will have to face up.

The third ecosystem is that of selling third-party products. This would require physical presence or tie-up with players in the logistics business. The third-party products that are electronically deliverable would be simple and easy to handle. The PBs need a database about their clients and should be able to model the data to understand the client–product match. This will be built over a period of time. The second strategy is to deliver the last-mile connectivity to the larger players who are offering financial products. A thin line between earning commissions for third-party products versus cannibalizing the products of the PBs needs to be navigated. However, if the third-party products are to be physically delivered, the PBs have a great opportunity but need to have the physical capability as well.

Competitors in the third-business ecosystem are largely direct selling agents of the commercial banks and BCs. There needs to be significant agility to manage this space.

THE OPERATING ECOSYSTEM: TECHNOLOGY

The concept of a PB is an idea whose time has come. This is because the technological ecosystem for the PB which works largely on the existing information technology architecture is already established. The universal banks have interoperable systems, the telcos have established their telecom towers, the satellite communication systems are working, the last-mile technology in the form of ATMs, and PoS devices are ubiquitously spread. Adding to all this is the identity project of UIDAI which has enrolled a billion people and is going strong, which gives a de-duplicated identity document electronically. Therefore, a new institution riding on these investments should be having it easy.

Elsewhere in Africa, M-Pesa has proven the remittances model; nearer in India, companies like Paytm are making transactions-on-the-run cashless; and institutions like NPCI are providing interconnectivity between devices, technologies, and institutions very seamlessly. Unlike the behemoths Visa and MasterCard, NPCI is promoted by the RBI and is incorporated as an entity that does not distribute profits (a Section 8 company) and, therefore, is not under quarterly pressure to show increasing and attractive returns to the investors.

This ecosystem should make it attractive for new businesses. However, if a reality check was done, that possibly is not indeed so. The new PBs will have to face up to the challenges posed by this ecosystem.

However, the PBs still have to face problems with the economics of technology. While these technological options listed above are available, there are gaps, and the PBs are standing at the point of these gaps. The gaps are at locations where the last-mile transaction has to happen on an assisted mode (and sometimes offline) and where even person-to-business transaction usually happens in cash rather than electronic mode. For the former, the solution is BCs, who are operating different types of devices depending on the business ecosystem they come from—could be a PoS device dedicated to the principal; it could be a PoS device that is interoperable across the banking system either through the backend NPCI or even by involving identity authentication bit through the AEPS.

In the person-to-merchant transactions, currently happening through cash, it is a mere switch to a cashless transaction at the operating level, which ideally should be simple, given that we have so much of interface software that makes it easy to operate. But in both these types of transactions, the PBs face a challenge of economics of technology. The sunk costs of these technologies are borne by multiple players—banks have their own ATMs, white label ATMs are set up by specialized companies, the backend bridge is provided by NPCI, the Aadhaar system is provided by the UIDAI, and the mobile companies have their own tower ecosystems. Each one of them is seeking to recover the sunk costs through charging a transaction fee. As of now, the transaction fee is set with a base fixed on a per transaction cost, which may vary with value at a higher level. If we are examining a model where a large number of transactions are bound to be small ticket transactions, the per transaction cost becomes unbearable. Institutions that already have an extant network usually earn from others using their network and they pay for using others' network, and this usually compensates with some residual costs. However, this is highly skewed against new players irrespective of whether they are a universal bank or a PB.

For a business model which is predicated on low margins, high volume, and low ticket transactions, this is a death knell. The operating models of the PBs have to crack the technology usage pricing in order to survive. This usage has to either provide a level playing field (allowing PBs to charge their clients for services) or reduce interchange charges. This clearly is a sticky point currently in the business model of the PBs, and it is hoped that some middle path will evolve as the market develops and people see the growth potential of the transactions of PBs.

THE OPERATING ECOSYSTEM: REGULATORY

There are some obligatory requirements that the PBs have to follow. Unlike the other players—telecom operators, the wallet players, or the direct selling agents—the PBs are ultimately designated as banks. Even if they are differentiated banks, the requirements that they have to meet as banks are obligatory. The question is whether some of these regulatory requirements could be met by leveraging the processes adopted by the partner agencies. A classic example in this is the requirement to establish the identity of the customer through the KYC norms. As of now, there are two norms required for establishing the KYC—one specified for Basic Savings Bank Deposit Accounts (BSBDA) and the other is for the full-fledged accounts. While eKYC could be used to enroll customers based on the Aadhaar platform, there could be other requirements that may require paper-based documentation. These requirements—of having to have recent photographs; having to have signature on forms for customers who do not have a Permanent Account Number (PAN) with the income tax department but may transact above a certain value—could add substantial costs to a model that operates on thin margins. These issues are beyond the licensees and the regulators. These are a part of the larger regulatory requirements that are outside the purview of the economic model of payments banks. However, there is also one caveat. Businesses cannot have an operating system solely based on eKYC because Aadhaar is not prescribed as the sole KYC document and, therefore, they should also have provisions for customers to offer paper-based KYC documents.

The question is that whether the PBs leveraging on the telecom network could use the KYC requirements fulfilled by the telecoms in an interoperable way while assuming all the liabilities of using a third-party verification. And, whether the PBs can share their KYC documents with a parent whose products they are selling—like the deposits of the universal banks, mutual funds, insurance products, or the pension products. The regulatory requirements are predicated on whether such data are sharable across two independent legal entities (even if the entities are from the same group), and if such data are sharable, then what are the customer protection clauses that need to be built that allow sharing of private information but do not become an intrusion on the privacy of the customer. Would an informed consent to share the details do, or should some extra consumer protection layers be put? How would the regulator enforce liability for a third-party verification? Would these KYC documents be interoperable between the institutions regulated by the RBI and Securities and Exchange Board of India?

Of course, there could be business opportunities in the regulatory requirements in enrolling the customers to get a PAN number or onboarding them on to other platforms for a fee, but the convergence and interoperability between various verticals need some attention and a regulatory framework.

The second issue is on the regulatory guidelines on interoperable transactions. For instance, the RBI requires that five transactions of a customer on ATMs of any bank should not be charged to the customer, while such transactions have to be paid for if they do not happen on host ATMs. If the PBs are migrating the inclusive customers to digital formats and providing them options to do electronic transactions, this requirement becomes onerous because all the PB transactions will be small ticket transactions and most likely would happen on the platforms of other banks. While the PBs themselves might have BCs on an assisted transaction mode, the interoperability charges on these might not be attractive to have a revenue line from the other players. In any case, even if these costs could be passed on to the customers, the customers themselves might not find it attractive to pay the interchange charges and move more toward cash-based exchanges—defeating the whole idea of digitally enabled transactions. This is a bit of a chicken-and-egg problem because unless the charges are attractive, the volumes would not pick up, and unless the volumes are picked up, the charges cannot be reduced. Since the PBs do not have extant investments in the payment infrastructure, the regulatory requirements of free transactions at the client end but to be paid for at the interchange level become a huge disadvantage for all the new players, particularly for the PBs.

INTEREST OF THE ECOSYSTEM

While there were much discussions about the business lines and viability of each of the business verticals discussed above, there was a great deal of interest in the model of this business and what it does to the customer database. For instance, the CICs wanted the PBs to be their members even though the PBs were prohibited for lending[2]. This request was made so that the CICs could track the data that emanate from the transactions to be subject to big data analytics to build probabilistic models for credit scoring.

Box 12.2 Former RBI Governor Dr Y.V. Reddy on Payments Banks

MSS: In the light of your discomfort with RNBCs, what do you think of the new guidelines and in-principle licenses accorded to the PBs? Recently, in a speech you said that PBs are like RNBCs, but since they are banks, they are better. Yes, the scope of the PBs are wider—in that they have scope for remittances and selling of third-party products, but the basic savings collection function, which is the FI part of the business, looks very similar to RNBCs—so, do you still think there is a cause for worry?

Dr Reddy: The RNBCs did not have revenue stream from transactions which PBs may have. Vulnerability of PBs is that they are in two separate businesses, and capital adequacy becomes little more problematic because of the combination of businesses. My own inclination would be to have a separate regulatory framework and deposit insurance window for PBs with stronger and instant relief for their customers.

MSS: When we look at the 11 in-principle licenses that were given for PBs, we find that 5 of them are telcos and 2 operate in the prepaid wallet space. So, where do you think these players would go?

Dr Reddy: Having this institutional choice is good. We should allow multiple models, and those who are good will thrive and other will innovate. There may be risks, but they are worth taking. We have to take advantage of technology. The institutional structures are important, and at this stage, we should allow institutional innovation. But, it also means that we are in multiple unfamiliar territories. We should be alert. We should insist on reporting and monitoring information and evolve a robust system as soon as possible.

MSS: So, do you think that this is better than RNBCs because it is better regulated?

Dr Reddy: No, all I am saying is that RNBCs are not entirely comparable to PBs. For RNBCs, mobilizing deposits is the main business; for PBs, peoples' transactions are the main business. The RBI cannot simply afford to take chances in regard to payment systems.

MSS: Yes, it is a totally new animal. Are you aware of anything similar anywhere else in the world?

Dr Reddy: No, actually the postal office was that.

PLANS OF INDIVIDUAL PLAYERS

While there are many issues that need to be addressed, each of the licensees is now gearing up to launch its respective bank. The following section gives an insight into how each of the banks is looking at the business.

Aditya Birla Payments Bank

Aditya Birla PB is looking at four distinct customer segments but also wants to leverage on its existing network. As of now, Idea has more than 170 million customers in 22 telecom circles with differing service penetration. Idea would like to use high penetration circles to acquire the PB customers. It is expected that Idea will roll out in 18 of the 22 circles in the next 2 years. One set of customers that Idea would be tapping into would be the existing telecom customers. Using data analytics of telecom relationship, a segment of these customers could be converted into wallet customers, and the base of the wallet customers is to be expanded. The regulatory issue is more to do with the increased KYC norms applicable to banks and whether the existing KYC database can be used interoperably. This issue has been flagged to the RBI and a view on this will be taken in due course. While the KYC norms are related to the

[2] http://www.moneycontrol.com/news/economy/credit-bureaus-want-rbi-to-make-payments-banks-its-members_7312921.html, accessed on August 24, 2016.

law that governs anti-money laundering, it is possible that as long as the stringent banking-related customer identity verification is done, the regulator may permit using the identity documents, with full consent of the customer and with the bank accepting full liability for the fallouts of any shortcomings in the process. The next set of customer acquisition would be targeting the non-Idea customers, which is going to be a greater challenge.

As the PB business progresses, there would be convergence with other group businesses, particularly in the financial services sector.

The plan is to roll out the business through multiple channels, largely by leveraging existing setups. Whenever a physical point is set up, a justification is needed to ensure that they have enough cross-sell business. This would largely be franchisee model-driven. The success of the entire business is based on how much of transactions can be technology-based, including enrolment of the customers. The basic differentiation in this space is going to be in customer experience as the product differentiation is going to be difficult. Therefore, offering a bouquet of all the intended services in an integrated manner is the strategy that is going to enhance the customer experience. A necessary element of this is a strong capability of analytics and high use of technology to reach out to the customer, while minimizing cash-in and cash-out transactions.

In summary, the bank intends to be a Pan-India operator, while the rollout will happen in a phased manner based on market opportunity and strengths of Idea in terms of customer base and distribution network; the KYC norms will be followed as per the RBI requirements; the intent is to have this as a paperless process so that accounts can be opened very quickly; the bank will leverage both Idea strengths in terms of customer base and distribution and group strengths in financial services and other businesses—which is unique; and it would have a strong focus on using technology, acquiring, engaging and servicing customers digitally, and ensuring profitability of the retail channel to keep them active.

However, the model is unproven and a lot depends on how the operational costs pan out. There is recognition that this business would be volume-driven with very thin margins and, therefore, all the focus would be on each element of the operational costs. For instance, if using the ATMs of other banks costs a certain transaction fee, the payments banks should look at either ensuring that the customers do not exercise the option of that channel very widely or negotiate a much better transaction price with the providers of the infrastructure. The secret of a potential success is in getting the operating model right and ensuring that the operating costs are completely under control.

Paytm Payments Bank

Paytm Payments Bank Ltd will start with an initial capital of ₹3 billion and is expected to become the second biggest revenue source for the parent firm after the core payments business in about two years. In the first year, the bank will look to grow its business in 12 cities in northeast and central India. Smaller markets such as parts of Bihar, Madhya Pradesh, and Uttar Pradesh will be high on the agenda. Paytm Payments Bank has set for itself the target of 200 million accounts across mobile wallets, current accounts, and savings accounts within 12 months of launch. It aims to touch half a billion accounts by 2020. Paytm already has close to 130 million wallets, so it expects a net addition of 70 million accounts in the first year.[3]

Paytm looks at itself as a tech company solving the financial inclusion problem. The way in which it looks at the issue is more from the customer experience perspective rather than as a bank providing financial services. Paytm wants to target not only the inclusive customers but also a wide spectrum of the customers both rural and urban. The idea is to leverage the technology to the fullest, but with the recognition that network and connectivity make it imperative to still use human interface.

Most of the onboarding would need human interface, but Paytm would like to use technology platforms that monitor the human interface on a real time basis. The data analytics is not only going to be used for targeting the customers with services but also as an internal control mechanism to ensure that the customer transactions are safe and secure. While some of this can be achieved by feature phone interface, most of the Paytm systems may need a smartphone. This is an area that most players need to consider on the technology choices at the last mile and whether these choices can leap frog into safe, secure, cash-free zones.

The PB plans to reinforce the image of customer-friendly company with a simplified experience and trust. The revenue model of Paytm is largely

[3] Verma, Shrutika. 2016, May 31. "Paytm's Payments Bank Targets Launch before November." *Mint*, http://www.livemint.com/Industry/MF4lMYfzcRCMuyJHZRB4SL/Paytms-payments-bank-targets-launch-before-November.html?utm_source=newsletter&utm_medium=email&utm_campaign=newsletter, accessed on May 31, 2016.

predicated on the fact that there would be much commerce driven through its interface which will pay for the services and that there would be significant third-party products that would be sold through its banking channel. In general, the approach of Paytm is not to charge the customers any fees (for transactions). Some strategic choices for cash management need to be exercised from outsourcing cash management, hiring cash management agencies, or working with white label ATMs.

Paytm is looking at five streams of revenue to start with—payments services whenever there is an interbank transfer (free within the Paytm ecosystem), insurance agency fees through partnership, credit referral services, savings services, and investment management services again via partnership.

The two-pronged strategy at customer acquisition would be to leverage current wallet customers who are growing organically and through its aggressive marketing push, but once the bank is in place, they would move focus on the unbanked population as well. However, Paytm would like to leverage its current consumer base and ecosystem to gain efficiency.

Vodafone Payments Bank

Vodafone comes with a ready learning from its M-Pesa experiment in Africa. Therefore, it is natural to expect that they possibly have the best answer on the business model. However, it appears that the operating model in India would be significantly different because of the regulatory and pricing architecture. In Africa, Vodafone's M-Pesa initiative is seen as a game changer. Vodafone will try and leverage its existing telecom customers in order to achieve the larger objective of inclusion of the unbanked customers.

One issue that Vodafone has to grapple with is in respect of foreign shareholding. As a result, the company is in talks with HDFC Bank as a strategic investor which will bring synergies between the PB and a universal bank. The Piramal Group is also negotiating investing in the venture. This will help Vodafone PB to offer a range of third-party financial products. Operationally, Vodafone expects to use its current physical network to gain footprint. The Vodafone PB will also provide the entire gamut of services, including savings, remittances, utility bill payments, M-commerce, and third-party products, including credit, microinsurance, and mutual funds. The idea is to have a presence on the entire plethora of services and compete on the quality of service instead of product offering because there the scope is limited. Having been in the wallets space, Vodafone would have some advantages over a few of its peers.

The common feature amongst the telco players is the interest in using the local *kirana* stores (mom and pop stores) and touchpoints, which even Vodafone would like to do in addition to leveraging the current touchpoints numbering 0.12 million. Ideally, the biggest target segment would be the youth, given the demographic profile of the country. Ultimately, the revenue model will work only if Vodafone is able to quickly acquire scale. The pricing would largely depend on the competition, both from the formal and informal channels. The biggest challenge would be the regulatory architecture on what permissions would be given on synergizing its current operations with the bank. Another challenge would be dealing with cash at the last mile.

FINO PayTech Payments Bank

If we were to look at all the licensees who received an in-principle license, FINO stands out as one organization that has been in the inclusive finance space but in a totally different capacity. While all the telcos and Paytm have existing clients who are subscribers of either the mobile telephony business or wallets, FINO has been in the business of being the link between the poor customers and the banks as a large BC. They have been providing comprehensive services as a bridge between the banks and the customers. In their new capacity as a PB, they are looking at continuing the service bouquet and expanding it to include deposits, DBTs, and remittances in addition to transaction intermediation.

The overall objective would be to ensure a sustainable model that generates revenue on its own as opposed to being an intermediary dependent on the fortunes of the parent. However, this needs some strong strategic tie-ups which FINO seems to have put in place. In terms of savings products beyond what PBs are permitted to do, FINO has ICICI bank as the anchor bank and it will be complimentary, help in parking deposit in excess of ₹0.1 million, offer products like fixed deposits and credit, and fill gaps of a financial supermarket. The model could veer toward a revenue share model rather than a fee-based model.

On the front end, it would be present as a significant player in the last mile, doing cash-in and cash-out for government schemes and payments. The urban unbanked will be served through *kirana* stores in an assisted model for transactions. Technology-enabled self-serving model could happen on a prepaid basis using mobile technology.

The most critical issue that FINO is currently facing is in bringing down foreign equity contribution and replacing it with Indian equity as per the conditions of the license. At the moment, the major shareholders of FINO PayTech include The Blackstone Group, ICICI Bank, IFC, HAV3 holding, and Intel Capital. The strategic tie-up with Bharat Petroleum Corporation Limited (BPCL) which acquired a 21% stake is an important step. This not only provides equity but also provides FINO a massive physical presence by leveraging the BPCL distribution network[4]. Such partnerships will be critical, given that the ecospace is significantly changing and competition may emanate from unknown sources like SFBs or it may be in the nature of a price war.

India Post Payments Bank

From amongst all the players, IPPB is one of the unique players. Not known to be technology savvy and neither being in the telecom or wallet space have not been deterrents. IPPB has a formidable network of post offices of India Post to leverage on. IPPB has been meticulously planning and has already set up a company, appointed board members, and hired consultants to work through this project.

While India Post offers different savings and insurance products (see Chapter 8), this will be a totally different business, partly cannibalizing its own money order product and partly poaching its own savings from the customers. However, it appears that the postal savings (which are collected and remitted to the state) and savings with IPPB (which will be managed as a treasury operation) will run in parallel. The idea is to use embedded network and knowledge of India Post and juxtapose it with technology and specialized banking. With the sovereign behind it, IPPB will be well capitalized and would have deep pockets that are accountable. Over 18,000 post office branches are on the CBS and the backend infrastructure of India Post can be very well leveraged. IPPB will also offer third-party financial products.

While the other players are talking about strategies to reach out to inclusive customers, IPPB's strength is in servicing the last mile and the inclusive customers. That is the advantage IPPB has over other players. India Post is expected to act as the corporate BC of IPPB. India Post will set up an average of at least one branch of its own per district but will use postmen and postal agents as a part of the ecosystem. IPPB sees itself as being a player which is creating a platform that is instrumental in bringing diverse clients to the table.

Airtel Payments Bank

Airtel Payments Bank is a subsidiary of Bharti Airtel. It has strategic investments from one of the most aggressive private sector banks—Kotak Mahindra Bank—and it has one of the best telecom penetration in the country. Airtel has a distribution channel spread across 1.5 million outlets, with network presence spreading across 87% of the country, covering about more than 0.4 million villages and more than 5,000 census towns. This network is available for leverage. Airtel already has customers on the wallets (known as Airtel Money), and these wallets are operational across 800 towns in India. All the Airtel Money customers will be migrated to the PB as it commences its business.

Airtel Payments Bank wants to provide innovative digital solutions to customers to fulfill their banking requirements by keeping the processes simpler, fast, and reliable. The differentiator even for the banked customers will be in the user experience. The bank will also try and bring in many more rural customers into its fold through its vast network.

Airtel Payments Bank being the first entity to get the final license from the RBI is in the process of its launching by streamlining their systems and strategies and will be commencing operations as a PB very soon.

Jio Payments Bank

Jio Payments Bank (JPB) has a strategic investment and partnership with State Bank of India (SBI). With one of India's largest corporate houses and the largest bank with deep branch penetration, this is the most formidable partnership in the PB space. Added to this is the telecom network that Reliance is rolling out through its new venture under the brand Jio. This will be one player to watch out.

In one of the interactions, Mr Mukesh Ambani, Chairman of Reliance, said that "The PB is integral to RIL's digital initiative in a rapidly converging world of telecom, Internet, commerce, media and financial services"[5]. The PB hopes to ride on the distribution of the telecom and retail initiatives and will also leverage on the strengths of SBI in the financial services sector. Ultimately, the idea is to

[4] http://www.business-standard.com/article/companies/bpcl-acquires-21-stake-in-fino-paytech-116072901432_1.html, accessed on August 27, 2016.

[5] http://www.business-standard.com/article/news-ians/payments-bank-license-to-promote-massive-digital-transactions-mukesh-ambani-115082101265_1.html, accessed on October 10, 2016.

be present in the frontier areas, where technology can bring in revolutionary changes in both access and provision of services. The strategy of this venture would be to target segments that could quickly move into cashless and paperless transactions, but being inclusive with retail, small enterprise, and marginalized customers.

The challenge for the operations would largely be in how the regulatory architecture (discussed above) will allow players to leverage on their extant strengths and improve the volumes in the low-margin high-volume business. The plan is to see how to upgrade the clients on to the cutting edge technology (through users of smart phones) and reach out the services to customers who are entering the market (as users of feature phones). The details of how this would roll out are not in the open yet.

NSDL Payments Bank

NSDL looks at PBs as completely differentiated banks. NSDL, with its experience in digitizing the investment space, is now planning to use its paperless strategy on to the transactions space as well and focuses on initiating the customers into the digital payments ecosystem. For this, the ecosystem has to evolve to recognize that PBs are different. While NSDL has been able to move the investment-based transactions into cashless, digital model, the challenge is whether it will be able to do that in the retail transactions and payments space.

When it rolls out, the bank will challenge the current system that incentivizes paper, plastic, and cash to digital. The details of how the touchpoints with the customers will pan out are not known. However, a look at the strategy of its parent would indicate that NSDL may use a lot of the ecosystem players to push traffic to the formidable backbone that NSDL payments would build. NSDL's role as a facilitator for Aadhaar, PAN, NPS, and National Skills Registry would come in handy to build the bank.

For this to happen and evolve, there must be freedom in pricing or flexibility in designing for providing superior services.

CONCLUDING NOTES

From the interactions and examining of the plans of the individual PBs, it is apparent that most of the players are looking at the business model being driven and transactions and revenues emanating out of the transactions. Taking the PBs' concept and integrating with the merchant systems is going to give the players a stable source of revenue. The fact that these banks can take deposits is seen more as a facilitating role than as a strategic business vertical. Unless the deposit limits and products are diversified, this vertical is not going to create much excitement amongst the players. There is a recognition that this is a highly competitive market, and the competition comes from other PBs, wallet providers, technology companies, and universal banks, each of them having their unique strengths and competing on a subsegment of their business, while this is a bread-and-butter business for the licensees.

REFERENCE

Reddy, Y. 2015. Financial Inclusion and Central Banking—Reflections and Issues. BIS. Geneva: Bank for International Settlements. Available at: http://www.bis.org/review/r151029a.pdf, accessed on May 24, 2016.

New Institutional Initiatives

13

Chapter

INTRODUCTION

While this year should be seen more as a year that consolidated on the initiatives taken in the past year–roll out and stabilization of Bandhan Bank, which continued to be a microfinance bank; granting in principle licenses to 11 PBs and 10 small finance banks—of which two are operational; there was more to come. The following initiatives are worth mentioning:

1. The RBI put up a note on regulating peer-to-peer lending platforms.
2. It opened up the possibility of the banking sector having a regime of on tap licensing, but putting out the draft guidelines.
3. The RBI indicated that it would put out the guidelines for interest free banking as well as wholesale and custodian banks.

The first two initiatives may have implications on the institutions in the inclusive financial space. The peer-to-peer lending regulation will bring the players into the legitimate regulatory framework and the on tap licensing will building aspirations. The microfinance institutions are aspiring to become SFBs at a future date and the SFBs going forward may actually aspire to become a full-fledged bank.

PEER-TO-PEER LENDING

The most exciting of the announcements may be the announcement of the possibility of licensing peer-to-peer lending. Using information technology platforms, this could be a significant step in providing platforms for disintermediation between the lender and the borrower, thereby giving both a better deal. In the past, cooperatives as mutuals provided this sort of a service where only users of the service could be members of a cooperative. However, while it was an activity within the community, the cooperative society actually provided the intermediation services by devolving the losses/profits on to the collective. However, the peer-to-peer lending platform goes one step further and connects up the lender and the borrower directly, thereby devolving the risk of default on to the peer lender that is absorbing it institutionally. The platform is expected to provide information intermediation between the lender and the borrower including some further information involving risk profiling, and rating of the individual borrower.

According to what is envisaged by the RBI:

> Peer to Peer lending involves the use of an online platform to bring lenders and borrowers together and help in mobilizing unsecured finance. The borrower can either be an individual or a business requiring a loan. The platform enables a preliminary assessment of the borrower's creditworthiness and collection of loan repayments. (RBI, 2016)

There could be debates on whether this sector is large enough to be regulated or whether the regulatory framework will drive more players to come into this space. However, the fact of the matter is that there are already many lending platforms that provide such services, and providing a regulatory framework is not only forward-looking, but it will also bring all the players on to a common regulatory and reporting standards, which would help to set up customer protection norms.

While organizations like Rang De, Micrograam, and Milaap have been around for several years and have created the ecosystem for the peer-to-peer lending to happen, it is still not happening completely in the spirit of a peer-to-peer lending. The subtle difference between peer-to-peer lending and the models is that the platform essentially operates more as a crowdsourcing model, with attempts being made to connect the borrower and the lender. The models do have a ground level partner NGO which manages the ground level disbursement and recovery of loans. The significant advantage of this is of course the cost of the loan which is significantly lower than alternative channels and that would turn out to be an advantage to the inclusive customer. However, with the digitization of the ecospace for inclusive banking happening in a big way, there is scope for true peer-to-peer transactions to happen. With the emergence of PBs, which are prohibited from undertaking lending activities, but digitally savvy, there might be a scope for collaborative arrangements between them and the peer-to-peer lenders.

The promise that this sector holds is evident from the newer players who are coming into the market and scaling. There are around 30 start-ups in the peer-to-peer lending platform, of which 20 were set up in the last year. For example, Faircent which started its operations in 2013 sold 9.84% of its equity to JM Financial.[1] The organization received ₹15.2 million from Singapore-based M&S Partners, and an undisclosed amount from Devesh Sachdev and Ashish Tiwari (of Fusion Microfinance). It also received an undisclosed amount from Aarin Capital, promoted by Mohandas and Ranjan Pai as capital infusion.[2]

LOCAL AREA BANKS

While there is a need to discuss new institutional initiatives, the RBI was also looking hard at the past initiatives that may not have worked. In an unusual admission, the RBI suggested that it may actually review the existence of LAB and it may take some action with the existing three LABs. One of them received a small finance bank license and has already commenced its operations. The RBI stated that "Consultations with the central government on broad options for the future set-up of LABs were underway during the year" (RBI 2016). If indeed the local area banks are closed down, that will be the end of what was the first experimentation of the private sector involvement in the agenda of financial inclusion, much ahead of the microfinance regulation. There could be discussions on whether LABs were an idea ahead of times, but the fact is that none of these except Capital LAB scaled and seemed to provide a credible alternative from the private sector to the RRBs.

Agenda for 2016–17

There are many initiatives that the RBI has announced that it would roll out in 2016–17 which need to be watched with interest. The Committee on Medium Term Path on Financial Inclusion had recommended multiple initiatives—some of which have already translated into draft guidelines. But, given the base documents of this committee and the approach paper on differentiated banking, there would be more draft guidelines for niche banks. In the radar of the RBI, at this point, seem to be wholesale banks and custodian banks. The RBI also put out draft guidelines for setting up NBFC Account Aggregator services to provide a consolidated view of the customers' financial holdings. This information, which could be potentially shared with third parties with the consent of the account holders, will also give scope for data analytics and counseling and planning of financial future for the customers. However, this might have limited impact on the inclusive customers who are struggling to open their first account with the formal financial system.

On the financial inclusion side, the RBI indicated that it would focus on three recommendations of the committee—creating a registry of BCs, formalizing a training and certification program for BCs, and training and accreditation of credit counselors who would operate in the financial literacy space.

MUDRA AND PMMY: REVIEW OF PROGRESS

One more significant initiative the GOI took last year was the setting up of MUDRA. This announcement was made in the budget speech of the finance minister, where it was envisaged that MUDRA would be set up with a corpus of ₹200 billion (Jaitley, 2015). While there has been significant action on this front, it is important to break up the achievements to understand the niche that MUDRA is serving and the impact it may have made.

MUDRA was launched as an NBFC on April 8, 2015. While the initial indication was that it would be launched as a bank, through an act of Parliament, it was eventually registered as a wholly owned subsidiary of SIDBI. It appears that the government is no longer considering the possibility of converting MUDRA into a statutory corporation. The launch of MUDRA should be seen from two

[1] VCCircle, Faircent raises funding from Aarin http://www.vccircle.com/news/technology/2016/05/10/jm-financial-picks-984-stake-p2p-lender-faircent (accessed on August 14, 2016).

[2] VCCircle, http://www.vccircle.com/news/technology/2015/10/12/faircent-raises-funding-aarin (accessed on August 14, 2016).

perspectives. The first is the setting up of a separate company MUDRA and the second is that of launching the PMMY.

PMMY was launched on April 8, 2015. The PMMY consisted of launching of three loan products pegged at ₹50,000 called the "Shishu" loan; loan product of amounts ranging above ₹50,000 up to ₹500,000 called "Kishor"; and loan product amounts ranging above ₹500,000 and up to ₹1 million called "Tarun". These three loan products were largely targeted at noncorporate small businesses and microenterprises—basically looking to fund the unfunded. The instrumentality through which these products would be rolled out were to use the vast network of bank branches as well as co-opt microfinance institutions, cooperatives, and other players who were in the business of financing, thereby expanding the institutional scope of the scheme.

From the above description it is clear that while there was a renewed focus and thrust on the segment and that there would be close monitoring, this was a segment that several agencies were in any way serving. Around the same time, the new priority sector lending norms released by the RBI had a renewed target (which did not exist before) given to banks that 7.5%[3] of their adjusted net bank credit was to be directed toward microenterprises.[4]

Launching the PMMY around the same time gave a greater focus to the lower segments of the microenterprises. In addition, the setting up of MUDRA as a refinance agency added to the availability of the resources should these smaller units need.

Box 13.1 Dr Reddy on MUDRA

MSS: What do you think of MUDRA Bank? This is something that was announced in the budget last time and it's now been established as a subsidiary of SIDBI, but the ultimate objective is to have a statute passed, get the MUDRA Bill passed.

Dr Reddy: What is the difference between MUDRA and SIDBI?

MSS: The difference between MUDRA and SIDBI will be that MUDRA can give loans up to ₹1 million. SIDBI is a small industries thing, so it has no limitation…

Dr Reddy: When originally the "small industry" was defined as units within a particular level of capital, SIDBI was supposed to cater to those "small" industries. Subsequently, the definition of small industries was changed. You could always achieve the focus on small or tiny industry by a policy decision. We can do that by indicating that a certain percentage of the financing should be reserved for units below the defined threshold size. As a concept, a design and a strategy, how is MUDRA different from SIDBI?

MSS: But as you know, this is a new institution. It has already been set up. Though, it is true that there was not much of a discussion or indication before the announcement was made.

Dr Reddy: So, really how different is it from SIDBI? Let me tell you a mystery to me, when I was in the government and RBI. SIDBI which finances small units was always making profits, while small industry segment had many sick units.

MSS: From the announcements we know that the ultimate intention, at least when they announced it, was to have it similar to National Housing Bank—that it will not only do refinance but also regulate the microfinance sector.

Dr Reddy: Plus direct lending, as I understand. Is that true?

MSS: Yes, plus direct lending. Dr Rajan said that RBI has made it very clear to the government that regulation is out of question, and it should only be RBI. But we don't know ultimately when the act comes and what would be the detail. So this is much more a design question, is it good to have an arbitrative agency regulating a sector?

Dr Reddy: Yes. So, in essence, a refinancing institution should have a concessional finance from the government. In refinancing, the primary financing unit assumes risks. In MUDRA, which is the primary financing unit that assumes risks in lending? What is the regulation that you are trying to make, of whom and for what? What is the objective of the regulation? So here if MUDRA bank is collecting deposits, then it is a deposit taking institution. Does it regulate itself in terms of depositor protection?

[3] RBI, "Priority Sector Lending Targets and Classification," https://rbi.org.in/scripts/NotificationUser.aspx?Id=9688&Mode=0#ANN (accessed on August 10, 2016).

[4] Microenterprises are defined as enterprises having an investment of less than ₹1 million in equipment for the service sector and ₹2.5 million for enterprises in the manufacturing sector.

MSS: No, the idea is they will also regulate MFIs and allow MFIs to take deposits.

Dr Reddy: Then we are talking of MFIs and regulation of MFIs. That is a matter on which there is no agreed view. What is the role of state governments in the work of MUDRA? Possibly, RBI should encourage, promote, and help the state level financial regulatory institutions and enable them to regulate. Jalan proposed this for UCBs in 2001. All these MFIs could be regulated at the state level. And we have to have a national deposit insurance which it is able to enforce. Something like that can work.

MSS: Is it because they have the intelligence and coordinating mechanism?

Dr Reddy: They have knowledge of local conditions. They have huge administrative machinery at the local level. Strengthening the capabilities of the state government for regulating MFIs is important. That can include chit fund, anything that involves deposit, small deposits, and which jurisdiction should be confined to the state. Some states will do a good job while some states will do bad, and those states that do good will learn over a period of time. We must create strengths or state level institutions for regulation of financial intermediaries with localized operations.

PMMY overlaps with the loans that MFIs were giving (up to ₹100,000) and has taken it further to a limit ₹1 million. This has now brought a renewed focus and data is being gathered in a granular fashion and monitored. However, it is clear that the role originally envisaged for the proposed MUDRA Bank is significantly altered in the new dispensation. The achievements of MUDRA and PMMY are separately analyzed in the following section.

MUDRA was set up with a capital of ₹7.5 billion and a refinance corpus of ₹50 billion (as against an envisaged amount of ₹200 billion specified in the budget speech). The functions of MUDRA were not only to extend refinance, but work more effectively in the ecosystem. The functions of MUDRA are captured in Figure 13.1.

In addition to the refinancing depicted in the picture above, MUDRA also does securitization of portfolios and would be adding further credit enhancement products in future.

As of March 2016, MUDRA had extended total loans on its own books to the extent of ₹32.87 billion. However, the achievement of MUDRA need not be seen only in terms of the credit enhancement that it has provided, but in the performance of the PMMY for which MUDRA is a monitoring and nodal agency.

The region-wise performance of PMMY is shown in Table 13.1. As against a disbursal of ₹32.87 billion directly from MUDRA as refinance, the scheme

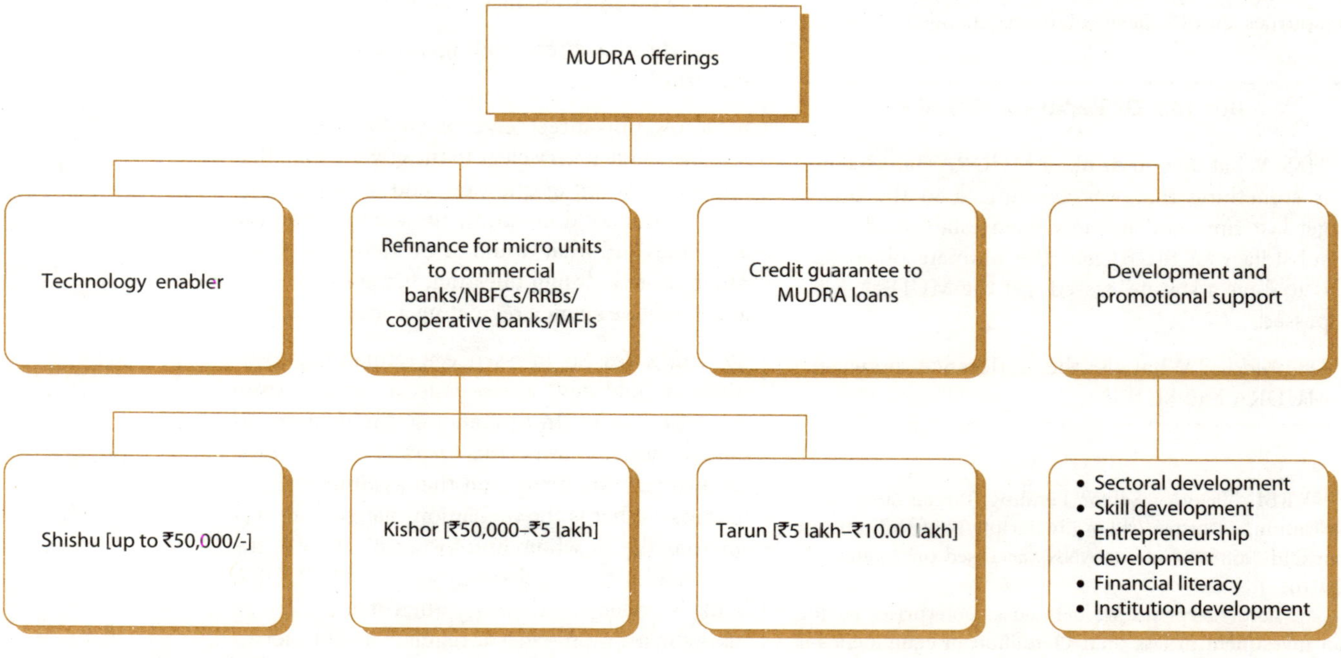

Figure 13.1 MUDRA Offerings

Source: MUDRA offerings, http://www.mudra.org.in/Offerings (accessed on August 10, 2016).

Table 13.1 PMMY—Region-wise Performance of Accounts Serviced and Amounts Disbursed

(₹ in Million)

	Shishu		Tarun		Kishor		Total	
Region	**A/cs**	**Amount**	**A/cs**	**Amount**	**A/cs**	**Amount**	**A/cs**	**Amount**
North	2,794,263	54,986	246,165	56,554	79,430	59,118	3,119,858	170,657
Northeast	497,926	10,096	50,206	9,879	7,989	5,766	556,121	25,741
East	7,929,210	135,461	345,386	63,135	53,128	36,960	8,327,724	235,556
Central	6,487,241	123,282	300,958	61,230	68,092	51,003	6,856,291	235,514
West	4,350,599	88,806	247,570	54,810	71,119	53,302	4,669,288	196,918
South	10,3418,07	207,645	879,176	165,125	130,659	92,390	11,351,642	465,161
Total	32,401,046	620,277	2,069,461	410,733	410,417	298,538	34,880,924	1,329,547

Source: MUDRA, Review of performance of PMMY, http://www.mudra.org.in/ (accessed on August 11, 2016).

itself had disbursed about ₹1.3 trillion both through the banking and other channels. The bank-wise and state-wise detail of disbursements under the PMMY is given in Appendices 13.2 and 13.3.

From Table 13.1, when we look at the regional spread we find that the southern region is leading both in terms of number of accounts that were serviced and the amounts disbursed. This is followed by east and central regions, while the western region lags behind. Northeastern region expectedly has a very small percentage of accounts and amounts disbursed. This trend of the east and the central region gaining some focus from the banking system on MUDRA is welcome, particularly because Gujarat and Maharashtra—representing the western region are usually expected to find more offtake of credit. This coupled with the growth of MFIs (as discussed in Chapter 10) seems to indicate a level of enterprise taking off in these regions which were traditionally underbanked.

While the growth on the books of MUDRA itself has been a modest amount of ₹32.87 billion, the overall growth to this segment from the banking sector as a whole was substantial. From a comparable figure of ₹330 billion in 2014–15,[5] the disbursement from the public sector banks itself was ₹561 billion. Other banks also contributed significantly taking the total disbursement by banks to ₹870 billion. The disbursement by institutions other than banks (largely MFIs) was around ₹459 billion. The performance review put up on the MUDRA website[6] indicates that about 36% of the accounts that were serviced belonged to new entrepreneurs, about 79% of the customers were women—which was not surprising given that the significant number of accounts in the Shishu category is originated by MFIs, about 60% of the accounts belonged to the weaker sections of the society, and about 12% of the accounts were originated from minority communities.

From the data, it is also clear that the banks have been largely focusing on Kishor and Tarun loans, while the MFIs had a large share in the Shishu loans (less than ₹50,000). Table 13.2 provides the details these accounts.

Overall, from the reports available till now, it appears that both MUDRA and the PMMY have enhanced the availability of credit to what was traditionally referred to as the "missing middle." While, MUDRA and the PMMY would have definitely played a credit enhancing role, it is also to be recognized that this portfolio already existed both on the books of the banks and MFIs and the initiative would have catalyzed the growth.

Table 13.2 Details of Accounts Opened and Disbursals by Institutional Form (as of March 31, 2016)

Details of A/cs (No.)	**Banks**		**MFIs**		**Total**
Shishu	8,704,579	27%	23,696,467	73%	32,401,046
Kishor	1,972,507	95%	96,954	5%	2,069,461
Tarun	409,411	100%	1,006	0%	410,417
Total	11,086,497	32%	23,794,427	68%	34,880,924
Details of amounts disbursed (₹ in million)	**Banks**		**MFI**		**Total**
Shishu	169,838	27%	450,439	73%	620,277
Kishor	402,916	98%	7,817	2%	410,733
Tarun	297,749	100%	789	0%	298,538
Total	870,503	65%	459,045	35%	1,329,548

Source: MUDRA, Review of performance of PMMY, http://www.mudra.org.in/ (accessed on August 11, 2016).

[5] Mudra, "Review of performance of PMMY," http://www.mudra.org.in/ (accessed on August 11, 2016).

[6] Mudra, "Review of performance of PMMY," http://www.mudra.org.in/ (accessed on August 11, 2016).

APPENDIX 13.1
Borrower Category-wise Performance of PMMY for 2015–16

(Accounts in '000s; Amounts in ₹ billion)

	Shishu				Kishor				Tarun				Total			
Category	A/cs	Sanctioned	Disbursed	Outstanding	A/cs	Sanctioned	Disbursed	Outstanding	A/cs	Sanctioned	Disbursed	Outstanding	A/cs	Sanctioned	Disbursed	Outstanding
General	14.68	290.72	285.23	218.78	1.46	317.71	302.86	268.59	0.34	263.69	249.49	215.25	16.48	872.12	837.58	702.62
SC	5.95	108.11	107.16	77.26	0.14	28.05	26.80	24.41	0.02	13.59	12.96	11.57	6.11	149.75	146.92	113.24
ST	1.61	30.22	29.83	22.52	0.06	12.49	11.79	10.50	0.01	6.07	5.80	5.18	1.68	48.78	47.42	38.19
OBC	10.16	199.89	198.06	149.55	0.40	72.28	69.27	62.64	0.04	31.67	30.30	26.70	10.61	303.84	297.63	238.88
Total	32.40	628.95	620.28	468.11	2.07	430.53	410.73	366.12	0.41	315.02	298.54	258.69	34.88	1,374.49	1,329.55	1,092.93
Of the above																
Women	27.10	690.39	506.40	369.69	0.47	90.68	86.75	74.69	0.05	40.77	38.75	33.43	27.63	821.84	631.90	477.81
New A/cs	11.08	214.26	209.42	159.25	1.19	242.65	229.92	202.92	0.20	159.59	149.74	127.91	12.47	616.50	589.08	490.08
Minority	3.83	69.40	68.41	48.11	0.22	45.28	43.09	38.96	0.03	25.49	24.10	21.01	4.09	140.18	135.60	108.08
PMJDY OD	2.42	4.46	2.71	1.61	0.00	0.02	0.02	0.02	0.00	0.00	0.00	0.00	2.42	4.48	2.74	1.63
MUDRA Card	0.46	6.01	5.56	4.96	0.05	4.23	4.06	3.15	0.01	4.53	4.29	3.44	0.52	14.77	13.91	11.55
Skill trained	1.87	25.35	25.19	14.54	0.03	5.93	5.27	4.65	0.01	5.13	4.68	4.11	1.91	36.41	35.14	23.30

Source: MUDRA, Review of performance of PMMY, http://www.mudra.org.in/ (accessed on August 11, 2016).

APPENDIX 13.2
Source-wise Performance of PMMY

(Number of Accounts Serviced and Amounts Disbursed in ₹ Billion)

	Shishu		Kishor		Tarun		Total	
Type of Institution	**A/cs**	**Amount**	**A/cs**	**Amount**	**A/cs**	**Amount**	**A/cs**	**Amount**
NBFC–MFIs	22,953,181	431.79	96,260	7.68	1,006	0.79	23,050,447	440.26
SBI and associates	925,650	13.76	259,973	68.51	114,966	87.73	1,300,589	170.00
Public sector banks	4,081,928	67.08	1,047,953	197.29	177,107	126.90	5,306,988	391.27
Private sector banks	2,667,337	59.39	299,495	69.87	100,854	71.00	3,067,686	200.26
Foreign banks	–	0.00	295	0.09	152	0.12	447	0.21
RRBs	1,029,664	29.61	364,791	67.15	16,332	12.00	1,410,787	108.76
Non NBFC–MFIS	743,286	18.65	694	0.14	–	0.00	743,980	18.78
Total	32,401,046	620.28	2,069,461	410.73	410,417	298.54	4,880,924	1,329.55

Source: MUDRA, Review of performance of PMMY, http://www.mudra.org.in/ (accessed on August 11, 2016).

APPENDIX 13.3
State-wise Performance of PMMY

(Number of Accounts Serviced and Amounts Disbursed in ₹ Billion)

	Shishu		Kishor		Tarun		Total	
State	**A/cs**	**Amount**	**A/cs**	**Amounts Disbursed**	**A/cs**	**Amounts Disbursed**	**A/cs**	**Amounts Disbursed**
Andaman & Nicobar	15,724	0.64	8,275	1.01	720	0.48	24,719	2.12
Andhra Pradesh	612,312	13.12	165,306	31.52	18,070	13.27	795,688	57.91
Arunachal	3,194	0.08	977	0.27	454	0.36	4,625	0.72
Assam	390,320	7.59	32,121	6.15	4,831	3.54	427,272	17.28
Bihar	2,310,112	41.13	129,001	22.28	12,326	9.24	2,451,439	72.66
Chandigarh	18,082	0.32	3,238	0.75	1,285	0.97	22,605	2.05
Chhattisgarh	605,051	11.79	28,559	5.12	6,101	4.65	639,711	21.56
Dadra	815	0.01	254	0.07	167	0.12	1,236	0.21
Daman	835	0.01	189	0.05	85	0.06	1,109	0.12
Delhi	341,933	6.93	36,077	10.03	16,378	11.62	394,388	28.58
Goa	36,247	0.89	7,441	1.56	1,783	1.30	45,471	3.76
Gujarat	975,320	21.72	85,245	18.52	25,842	18.87	1,086,407	59.10
Haryana	693,408	13.72	39,525	8.47	12,602	9.33	745,535	31.53
Himachal Pradesh	59,757	1.03	21,122	4.93	4,685	3.70	85,564	9.66
Jammu	19,057	0.62	34,388	7.38	4,529	3.52	57,974	11.52
Jharkhand	828,785	15.15	36,637	7.81	7,446	5.50	872,868	28.46
Karnataka	4,153,714	90.72	264,744	47.45	41,151	26.53	4,459,609	164.69
Kerala	707,492	14.14	107,975	21.94	14,944	11.19	830,411	47.27
Lakshadweep	551	0.01	170	0.03	19	.01	740	0.05
Madhya Pradesh	2,406,310	46.11	84,343	16.54	20,538	15.05	2,511,191	77.69
Maharashtra	3,337,382	66.16	154,441	34.62	43,242	32.94	3,535,065	133.72
Manipur	20,943	0.35	2,679	0.59	399	0.26	24,021	1.20

(Continued)

(Continued)

	Shishu		Kishor		Tarun		Total	
State	**A/cs**	**Amount**	**A/cs**	**Amounts Disbursed**	**A/cs**	**Amounts Disbursed**	**A/cs**	**Amounts Disbursed**
Meghalaya	15,451	0.40	3,051	0.74	649	0.48	19,151	1.62
Mizoram	5,473	0.19	1,993	0.35	306	0.23	7,772	0.78
Nagaland	3,247	0.10	1,418	0.36	469	0.29	5,134	0.77
Odisha	2,281,495	37.54	51,401	9.78	10,365	7.05	2,343,261	54.36
Puducherry	74,516	1.46	7,482	1.21	868	0.65	82,866	3.32
Punjab	594,025	12.31	43,347	9.95	16,601	12.58	653,973	34.84
Rajasthan	1,068,001	20.04	68,468	15.05	23,350	17.39	1,159,819	52.48
Sikkim	5,491	0.12	1,145	0.24	253	0.18	6,889	0.55
Tamil	4,506,237	82.32	234,824	42.82	40,506	29.83	4,781,567	154.97
Telangana	286,985	5.88	98,675	20.15	15,101	10.91	400,761	36.94
Tripura	59,298	1.37	7,967	1.41	881	0.59	68,146	3.37
Uttar Pradesh	3,149,078	58.49	160,502	33.25	35,802	27.06	3,345,382	118.81
Uttarakhand	326,802	6.89	27,554	6.32	5,651	4.24	360,007	17.45
West Bengal	2,487,603	40.87	118,927	22.02	22,018	14.51	2,628,548	77.40
Total	32,401,046	620.28	2,069,461	410.73	410,417	298.54	34,880,924	1,329.55

Source: MUDRA, Review of performance of PMMY, http://www.mudra.org.in/ (accessed on August 11, 2016).

REFERENCES

Jaitley, A. 2015. *Budget 2015–16*. New Delhi: Ministry of Finance, Government of India.

RBI. 2016. *Reserve Bank of India Annual Report, 2015–16*. Mumbai: RBI, https://rbidocs.rbi.org.in/rdocs/AnnualReport/PDFs/0RBIAR2016CD93589EC2C4467793892C79FD05555D.PDF (accessed on September 2, 2016).

Acknowledgments

1. ACCESS Development Services
   Vipin Sharma, CEO
   Radhika Agashe, Executive Director ACCESS Assist
   Lalitha Sridharan
   Anshu Singh
   Keerti Bhandary
   Sivani Shankar
2. Aditya Birla Payments Bank
   Mukul Sharma
   Sudhakar Ramasubramaniam
3. Airtel Payments Bank
   Shashi Arora
   Shanmugam Sundararaj
4. Aquarius India
   S.N. Subramanya
5. APMAS
   C.S. Reddy, CEO
6. AU Financiers
   Sanjay Agarwal, CEO
7. Bandhan Bank
   Chandra Shekhar Ghosh, CEO and MD
8. Capital Small Finance Bank
   Sarvjit Samra
9. CRIF Highmark
   Parijat Garg, Vice President, Business Development
10. EDA Rural Systems
    Frances Sinha, Director
11. Equitas Small Finance Bank
    Vasudevan P.N.
12. ESAF Microfinance
    Paul Thomas
13. Fincare
    Rajeev Yadav
    Prakash Sundaram
14. Fino Paytech
    Rishi Gupta
    Shailesh Pandey
15. Grameen Foundation
    Chandni Ohri, CEO
16. Janalakshmi Financial Services
    V.S. Radhakrishnan
    Rangarajan
17. Jio Payments Bank
    Srikrishnan H.
18. India Post
    Ramanujan M.S., Member Banking and HRD
    Madhumita Das, Deputy Director General, Postal Bank of India
19. Indian Institute of Management Ahmedabad
    Professor Chinmay Tumbe

20. Indian Institute of Management Udaipur
    Professor Janat Shah Director
    Professor N. Vishwanathan
21. IndusInd Bank
    Bonam Srinivas, Head Inclusive Banking Group
22. IFMR
    Amy Mowl
    Parul Agarwal, IFMR Lead
23. MCril
    Sanjay Sinha, Managing Director
24. Microfinance Institutions Network
    Ratna Viswanathan, CEO
25. MicroSave
    Manoj Sharma, Managing Director
26. Mudra
    Jiji Mammen, CEO
    Surendra Srivastava, CFO
27. National Bank for Agriculture and Rural Development
    G.R. Chintala, CGM, MCID
    Dr U.S. Saha, GCM, IDD
    Subrata Gupta, CGM, DFIBT
    A.G. Das. GM, IDD
28. National Federation of State Cooperative Banks
    Brahma Subrahmanyam, CEO
29. National Payments Corporation of India
    M. Balachandran, Chairman
    A.P. Hota. Managing Director and CEO
    Anubhav Sharma, Associate Vice President—Product Development
    G.M. Giridhar, Vice President and Head—NACH and CTS Operations
30. NSDL Payments Bank
    Prashant Vagal
    Aneesh Khanna
31. Omidyar Network
    Ameya Upadhyay
32. Paytm Payments Bank
    Shinjini Kumar
    Vipin Surelia
33. RangDe
    Ramakrishna N.K.
34. Reserve Bank of India
    N.S. Vishwanathan, Deputy Governor
    Pramod Panda, Chief General Manager and Principal CAB
    S.S. Barik, Chief General Manager Incharge
    Anita Bhattacharyya, General Manager
    N. Ramasubramaniam, Assistant General Manager
    Pallavi Chavan. Assistant Adviser, DEPR
35. RGVN North East
    Rupali Kalita
36. Sa-dhan
    P. Satish, Executive Director
    Somesh Dayal, Associate Director
    Harihara Mohapatra, Associate Director

37. Suryoday Microfinance
    Basker Babu
    Narayana Rao
38. Ujjivan Financial Services
    Samit Ghosh
39. UK Aid
    Ragini Choudhary
40. Utkarsh Microfinance
    Govind Singh
41. Vodafone Payments Bank
    Suresh Sethi
    Samir Garud
42. Sector Experts
    S. Ananth
    Ajay Tankha
    D. Krishna, Former CEO National Federation for Cooperative Urban Banks
    Brij Mohan, Former Executive Director SIDBI
    Y.C. Nanda, Former Chairman NABARD
    Alok Pandey, formerly with DFS and Additional DG All India Radio
    N. Srinivasan
    Girija Srinivasan

Technical Partner

CRIF HIGH MARK

Together to the next level

CRIF High Mark is India's leading credit bureau with the largest credit bureau database of individuals in the country. It is the only full-service credit bureau covering all borrower segments—MSME/Commercial, Retail and Microfinance. CRIF High Mark started India's first Microfinance Bureau in 2011, which has transformed into being the world's largest microfinance database. This pioneering work to support microfinance industry has been recognized at Manthan Awards 2014 and SKOCH Financial Inclusion Award 2012. CRIF, which owns majority in CRIF High Mark, is a leading FinTech from Continental Europe which specializes in credit information, business information, analytics, scoring, decision, and credit management solutions. It has operations in over 50 countries across four continents. CRIF in India now also offers Business Information Report, Analytics and Scoring services, and Credit Management and Decision solutions in India.

For more information, please visit: www.crifhighmark.com; www.creditsolutions.crif.com

About the Author

M.S. Sriram is a faculty at the Centre for Public Policy, Indian Institute of Management Bangalore (IIMB), Bengaluru. He is also a Distinguished Fellow at the Institute for Development of Research in Banking Technology—set up by the RBI. In the past, he was the ICICI Bank Lalita D Gupte Chair Professor of Microfinance and Chairperson of the Finance and Accounting Area at IIM Ahmedabad; on the faculty of Institute of Rural Management, Anand and was the Vice President (Finance and Information) at BASIX. He has also taught at IIM Udaipur, Solvay Brussels School of Business and Economics, Brussels, and the Azim Premji University, Bengaluru.

Sriram is the coauthor of three books—*Beyond Microcredit* published by SAGE-Vistaar and two books on flow of credit to small and marginal farmers. He also authored the Inclusive Finance India Report 2015.

Sriram has served on several committees set up by the GoI, RBI, and NABARD. He served on the External Advisory Committee of the RBI for granting licenses to small finance banks. He also writes regularly in the financial press. He is currently on the board of NDDB Dairy Services, Centre for Budget and Policy Studies, and is a Trustee of Pratham Books and Dastkar Andhra.